D1491993

The Italian Journal
of Samuel Rogers

by the same author

*

ENGLAND AND THE ITALIAN RENAISSANCE

1. Samuel Rogers in 1821, *aet.* 58

The Italian Journal of
SAMUEL ROGERS

edited
*with an account of Rogers' life
and of travel in Italy in 1814–1821*

by

J. R. HALE
Fellow of Jesus College, Oxford

FABER AND FABER
24 Russell Square
London

First published in mcmlvi
by Faber and Faber Limited
24 Russell Square London W.C.1
Printed in Great Britain by
R. MacLehose and Company Limited
The University Press Glasgow

To
R. M. H.

Preface

Rogers's earliest biographer, P. W. Clayden, described how the poet's first acquaintance with Italy had begun on a tour in 1814 and ended soon after the news of Napoleon's escape from Elba reached him at Naples. During this period 'nothing escaped his notice, and almost everything he observed was elaborately described and criticised in a diary written day by day, in evident and careful preparation for some future work. This diary is far too long to be reproduced here. It would fill a volume, and if published would constitute a guide book to the natural beauties and the artistic treasures of a great part of Italy. It contains much of the material out of which his poem of "Italy" was afterwards wrought.'[1]

These are intriguing words, but the diary he referred to was long lost to sight. Since its rediscovery it can be seen that Clayden's description was substantially correct. As a guide book it accurately reflects the taste of the last wave of travellers who retained the outlook, and who shared the social background, of the tourists of the eighteenth century, (the years between 1814 and 1821, the date of Rogers's second visit to Italy, forming, as it were, the Indian Summer of the Grand Tour). It also contains, as Clayden pointed out, the raw material for the work that contains much of Rogers's most individual poetry.

It has, in addition, the interest of providing an extensive record of his first thoughts. Hitherto Rogers has been largely known from the accounts of others, from edited table-talk, and from his own carefully polished letters. A poet who was offered the Laureateship; a dominant figure in society from the turn of the century; one of the most carefully, if conventionally, cultivated men of his generations—for his personality fascinated and exasperated observers of the London literary scene for over fifty years—Rogers is well worth knowing better. I should like to feel that this glimpse of him as a traveller might correct the temptation to see him always at the breakfast table.

[1] *Rogers and his Contemporaries*, 2 v., London, 1889 i, pp. 158–9.

9

Preface

Not long after his death, when auctioneer's labels were stuck on his lovingly collected furniture and pictures, John Mitford, the ex-editor of the *Gentleman's Magazine*, spoke to the poet's man-servant, Edmund Paine, and was told some of the circumstances of his last illness. For some weeks before his death 'he had at periodical [?] times, a strong state of *Excitement*, which generally came on from 3 to 4, in which he fancied he was Travelling, that the Chairs were Alps, and he spoke in French, & ask'd why he was stopping, & not moving on.'[2] This book deals with the traveller's first crossing of the Alps and what he saw beyond them. I have tried in the Introduction to show what sort of man he was and the conditions of travel at the time: in the notes to the text the sort of people he met: and through the plates the actual appearance of some of the scenes he visited.

[2] British Museum, Adds MSS. 32567 (Commonplace Book), f. 364.

10

Acknowledgements

M y greatest debt is to Professor Egon Sharpe Pearson for allowing me to print the Journal, and to borrow this and whatever else I needed from the documents concerning Rogers in his possession.[1] I cannot list the many people, both here and in Italy, who helped me with points of detail—it would, indeed, look ostentatious if I were to try, but I must record my special sense of obligation to Mr. Ian Jack, who in reading the proofs corrected some errors of fact and very many of style. I should also like to thank the staffs—so patient, accurate and helpful—of the various institutions where I worked at this book: the British Museum, the British School and the Keats-Shelley Museum in Rome, the Taylorian Institution in Oxford, and, above all, the Bodleian Library. My wife shared in much of the drudgery involved in preparing this edition, but her help has been of so pervading a nature that it is best acknowledged baldly but comprehensively in a dedication.

For permission to reproduce photographs of works in their possession I am grateful to Lady Martin; to Mr. J. B. Ward-Perkins, who allowed me to use some of the Hakewell drawings in the British School at Rome; the authorities of the Museo Topografico in Florence; the Keeper of the Department of Prints and Drawings at the British Museum; Messers Schroll of Vienna (publishers of Egger's *Römische Veduten*), Hoepli of Milan (publishers of Bertarelli and Monti: *Tre Secoli de Vita Milanese*), and Alinari of Florence (plates 12 and 17).

I owe the English text of the letter to Foscolo on pp. 109–10 to Professor E. R. P. Vincent. It is printed in Italian in his *Ugo Foscolo esule fra gli Inglesi*, Firenze, 1954, p. 233.

[1] Among them the Commonplace Book quoted on pp. 49, 274; the notebooks quoted on pp. 55, 120, 121; the presentation poem by Schiantarelli quoted on p. 166; and the other versions of the Journal referred to in the 'Note on the Text.'

Contents

INTRODUCTION

I. Rogers: The Years of Fame   19

II. Winning a Reputation: From Samuel Rogers, Clerk, to Rogers-the-Poet   35

III. Rogers Leaves for the Continent   51

IV. English Travellers in Italy, 1814–1821
     i. Numbers   56
     ii. Motives for going   62
     iii. Getting there: coaches and passports   74
     iv. The itinerary   81
     v. Board and lodging   87
     vi. The English attitude   93

V. Rogers as a Tourist   100

VI. The Italian Journal and the Poem *Italy*   107
     Notes to the Introduction   116

THE ITALIAN JOURNAL

Note on the Text   131

The Italian Journal   133

Appendix 1: Passages omitted from the Text   301

Appendix 2: Books used by Rogers   305

Appendix 3: The Evolution of 'Meillerie'   307

Index   313

Illustrations

———————————————

1. Samuel Rogers in 1821, *aet. 58* *frontispiece*
   Oil painting by Sir George Hayter, in the possession of Lady Martin.

2. Tourists fleeing before Napoleon *facing page* 58
   Caricature, The Fox & the Goose; or Boney broke loose!
   by Cruikshank.

3. French excavation: the temple of Jupiter Tonans in
   1809 and 1813 59
   From Le Comte de Tournon, Études statistiques sur Rome et la partie occidentale des états Romaines, 2v., Paris, 1831, vol. 2.

4. Travellers resting by a diligence 80
   Drawn by J. W. M. Turner on his trip to Italy in 1819. From Sketchbook CLXXIII, in the British Museum.

5. A page from Rogers' journal 81
   See page 160.

6. Piazza del Duomo, Milan, *c.* 1808 96
   From A. Bertarelli and A. Monti, Tre secoli di Vita Milanese . . ., Milano, 1927.

7. The grand canal, Venice, showing the Rialto 97
   From the drawing made in 1817 by James Hakewell, now at the British School in Rome.

8. A tourist at Tasso's cell, Ferrara 176
   From J. Isabey, Voyage en Italie en 1822 [Paris, 1823].

9. The Arno and ponte S. Trinita from a point near
   Schneider's hotel 177
   From the oil painting by G. Gherardi in the Museo Topografico di Firenze.

10. The cathedral, Florence 192
    Another painting by the same artist from the same collection.

11. The arcades of the Uffizi 193
    An engraving by Cosimo Rossi from the same collection.

12. 'Is not this the best in Florence?' The Martyrdom of
    St. Catherine, by Bugiardini 208

15

Illustrations

13. The entrance to Rome from the north: Porta del
    Popolo   *facing page* 209
    From Nuova raccolta di cento principali vedute antiche e
    moderne dell' alma città di Roma e delle sue vicinanze dis-
    poste secondo il metodo dell' itinerario di Roma, *Roma*,
    1818.

14. A side view of the Coliseum   224
    From H. Abbott, Antiquities of Rome, 1820.

15. Tourist being shown the baths of Livia   225
    From I monumenti piu celebri di Roma antica con l'aggi-
    unta delle quattro principali basiliche di Roma moderna.
    Illustrati da A. Nibby ed incisi da Pietro Ruga, e Pietro
    Parboni, *Roma*, 1818.

16. The Stations of the Cross in the arena of the Coli-
    seum   228
    Drawing by Franz Caucig, reproduced from H. Egger,
    Römische Veduten, *bd. 1, Wien*, 1931.

17. Daniele da Volterra: the taking down from the Cross   229
    Fresco in the church of the Trinità de' Monti.

18. Blessing the horses of Rome   236
    From Un an à Rome et dans ses environs . . . publié par
    Thomas, *Paris*, 1823. *The original is in colour.*

19. The Carnival: pelting bystanders with starch   237
    From the same book. Also coloured in the original.

20. Naples and Vesuvius from above Virgil's Tomb   256
    *From the drawing by James Hakewell at the British School
    in Rome. Done in 1816.*

21. Tourists in the street of tombs at Pompeii   257
    From Le antichità di Pompei . . . incise dall' architetto L.
    Rossini, *Roma* [1831].

22. Paestum   272
    From J. Isabey, Voyage en Italie en 1822 [Paris, 1823].

23. Tivoli   273
    *From the drawing by James Hakewell at the British School
    in Rome.*

In text

Panorama of Rome from the tower of the Capitol. *page* 210
    *From An explanation of the View of Rome taken from the
    Capitol. Now Exhibiting at H. A. Barker and J. Burford's
    Panorama, near the new church, in the Strand, 1817.*

16

Introduction

I
Rogers : The Years of Fame

───────◆◆◆───────

There is no satisfying *Life* of Samuel Rogers, and no recent life at all. Yet the material is abundant. He does not tease by appearing abruptly in the records of his time only to vanish after a brief blaze; he was no comet, but a fixed star of some magnitude, and to look among the vast literary constellations that crowded the heavens from the last decade of the eighteenth to the middle of the nineteenth century is to see him, a cold but constant point of light. He knew nearly all his great contemporaries, but while our shelves are loaded with modern lives of these men there is none devoted exclusively to the man who was known by them all. Most of the *Journals*, the *Memoirs*, the *Lives* that concern his day contain some reference to him, but these have not been collected; Rogers' name seems to appear more naturally in an index than upon a title page.

'For more than half a century', wrote a friend in the *Edinburgh Review* in 1856, the year after Rogers' death, 'a small house in a quiet nook of London has been the recognized abode of taste, and the envied resort of wit, beauty, learning, and genius. There, surrounded by the choicest treasures of art, and in a light reflected from Guidos and Titians, have sat and mingled in familiar converse the most eminent poets, painters, actors, artists, critics, travellers, historians, warriors, orators, and statesmen of two generations. Under that roof celebrities of all sorts, matured or budding, and however contrasted in genius or pursuit, met as on the table land where (according to D'Alembert) Archimedes and Homer may stand on a perfect footing of equality.' The biographical sketch that opens in this manner could be that of a restaurateur of international fame, or the steward of some pleasantly exclusive club: the institution to be dealt with first and then the man; and the nature of Rogers' personality has become obscured partly because his house did become a sort of exclusive club, and because he himself had become by middle life a sort of institution. He lived so long; long enough to have known Charles James Fox and Gladstone, Robertson and Macaulay, Crabbe and Tennyson, long enough to have seen women taken to Tyburn and to have inspected, from a wheel chair, the Great Exhibition, to have heard the pronunciation of London change from 'Lonnon', contèmplate to còntemplate, and—it almost made him sick—balcòny to bàlcony. The boy who had only been prevented by a last-minute shyness from knocking on Dr. Johnson's door became the friend of Dickens and an early champion of Tennyson. Of his older contemporaries, Sheridan, Talleyrand, Grattan, Horne Tooke, the Duke of Wellington, he had much to tell, and he told it well. His reputation as a poet, as an exquisitely cultivated *amateur*, as the most knowledgeable of gossips-about-town, added to his attraction as a host. It became the done thing for persons of distinction or promise to have taken a meal of Rogers; it was a sign that one had officially arrived. And because he had become a legend during his lifetime his visitors knew what they would find before they arrived—either a corpse-like figure with a bitter tongue, or a frail old gentleman of formal but benevolent demeanour—and tended to select whatever occurrence would support their preconception. For nearly half his life Rogers was judged more as legend than as an individual, praised or blamed for what he represented in public imagination rather than for what he was.

Much of the evidence is therefore suspect; and there is another obstacle for a biographer to overcome: Rogers lived an artificial life artificially. Whatever he did he did with care, often with preparation. The haphazard, the irrational, the sudden— these were banished always from his conversation and as far as possible from his life. In the printed records he appears chillingly self-conscious. His conversation leads deliberately to some carefully rehearsed anecdote. His letters are often the result of previous drafts or passages modified from his journals. The modern biographer peers baffled at this polished surface: nowhere is the endearing flaw, the obvious weakness that is so much more easily comprehended than excellence, and so much easier to explain. To a generation that prefers works of art that are not too highly finished, that retain some traces of the creative process, the life of Rogers makes little appeal. In the gallery of early Victorian worthies he appears as the Academic Portrait *par excellence*, meticulous and finicking. In poetry he believed that posterity would reject what was offered it carelessly, spontaneously, not realizing that what posterity values in a man's life as well as in his works, is urgency of intention, not the gloss of a perfect finish.

Another difficulty is that he appears in the baleful light cast by a series of memorably virulent attacks. He stands there spitefully caricatured by pens that told few actual lies, but set down all in malice. He was the sort of man whose faults lend themselves so inevitably to caricature that the extent of the distortion involved becomes increasingly hard to remember.

The first hint of what was to come was given by Lady Caroline Lamb's novel *Glenarvon*, which was published anonymously in 1816. She had been spurned by Byron, and it was an attack upon him and upon his friends. Rogers appears as the simpering, sneering, malicious court-poet of the Duchess of Madagascar (Lady Holland). On his first appearance he is described as 'this yellow hyena', and we last see him baffled by the heroine's ingenuous question as to whether she could expect kindness from the Duchess: 'The Poet's naturally pale complexion', says the author, 'turned to a bluish green at this enquiry.'

The next attack came from Byron himself. He had once been the intimate friend of Rogers and the champion of his methods as a poet, but in the vengeful and suspicious mood in which he left England after the scandals that followed his unhappy marriage, Rogers—who had first introduced him to Lady Byron —was swept to the centre of the stage which his imagination had filled with jeering and malicious gossip-mongers. There he transfixed him while he called down—probably in the spring of 1818—this memorable curse:

QUESTION & ANSWER

QUESTION

Nose and Chin that make a knocker,
Wrinkles that would puzzle Cocker;
Mouth that marks the envious Scorner,
With a Scorpion in each corner
Curling up his tail to sting you,

In the place that most may wring you;
Eyes of lead-like hue and gummy,
Carcase stolen from some mummy,
Bowels—(but they were forgotten
Save the Liver, and that's rotten),
Skin all sallow, flesh all sodden,
Form the Devil would frighten G—d in.
Is't a Corpse stuck up for show,
Galvanized at times to go?
With the Scripture has't connection,
New proof of the Resurrection?
Vampire, Ghost, or Goul, what is it?
I would walk ten miles to miss it.

ANSWER

Many passengers arrest one,
To demand the same free question.
Shorter's my reply and franker,—
That's the Bard, and Beau, and Banker:
Yet, if you could bring about
Just to turn him inside out,
Satan's self would seem less sooty,
And his present aspect—Beauty.
Mark that (as he masks the bilious)
Air so softly supercilious,
Chastened bow, and mock humility,
Almost sickened to Servility:
Hear his tone (which is to talking
That which creeping is to walking—
Now on all fours, now on tiptoe):
Hear the tales he lends his lip to—
Little hints of heavy scandals—
Every friend by turns he handles:
All that women or that men do
Glides forth in an innuendo—
Clothed in odds and ends of humour,
Herald of each paltry rumour—
From divorces down to dresses,
Woman's frailties, Man's excesses:
All that life presents of evil

Make for him a constant revel.
You're his foe—for that he fears you,
And in absence blasts and sears you;
You're his friend—for that he hates you,
First obliges, and then baits you,
Darting on the opportunity
When to do it with impunity:
Your are neither—then he'll flatter,
Till he finds some trait for satire;
Hunts your weak point out, then shows it,
Where it injures, to expose it
In the mode that's most insidious,
Adding every trait that's hideous—
From the bile, whose blackening river
Rushes through his Stygian liver.

Then he thinks himself a lover—
Why? I really can't discover,
In his mind, age, face, or figure;
Viper broth might give him vigour:
Let him keep the cauldron steady,
He the venom has already.

For his faults—he has but one;
'Tis but Envy, when all's done:
He but pays the pain he suffers,
Clipping, like a pair of Snuffers,
Light that ought to burn the brighter
For this temporary blighter.
He's the Cancer of his Species,
And will eat himself to pieces,—
Plague personified and Famine,—
Devil, whose delight is damning.
For his merits—don't you know 'em?
Once he wrote a pretty Poem.

The manuscript was sent to John Murray in 1820 with instructions to show it only to a favoured few, but in 1833 *Fraser's Magazine* got hold of it—'by the kindness of a fair friend, whose name must be a secret'—and the verses at once became widely known. They were not included in Byron's works, but in 1847 Thomas Medwin revived them in his *Life* of Shelley. Rogers was looked at afresh through the clever couplets, and sometimes, it was thought, the cap fitted. Reflecting on Rogers' attitude towards Wordsworth, Crabb Robinson believed it 'to go far towards justifying Lord Byron's attack:

> *Hunts your weak point out, then shows it,*
> *Where it injures, to expose it.'*

and again, 'I cannot help thinking also that the inference is justly drawn:

> *'Tis but envy when all's done.'*

The same author substantiates Medwin's story that when Rogers came to visit Byron at Pisa in 1821, his host contrived that he should seat himself unwittingly upon a copy of these verses. And hardly less edifying was another episode described by Medwin as occurring on the same visit. Knowing that Rogers was about to call, Byron loosed his English bulldog Tiger in the room where he was playing billiards. Rogers arrived, was shown in, but Byron feigned to be absorbed in the game. 'In the mean time Tiger rushed furiously at the stranger, who backed to a corner of the room shivering and breathless with terror. Byron, without casting a look towards the poor bard at bay, contented himself with drawling out, at intervals—"T - i - ger; Ti - i - ger," but in such an accent as rather to encourage than check the baiter, who continued a furious concert of menaces at "Death in life, or departed Mr. Rogers". Byron at length pretended to discover the cause of the affray: to kick Tiger aside, and press his "dear friend" in his arms, was only the affair of an instant.' Nothing became Rogers better than his own comments on the reunion with Byron in Italy. He speaks of it in the section 'Bologna' in the 1824 edition of the first part of *Italy*, and goes on to say

> *Yes,* BYRON, *thou art gone,*
> *Gone like a star that through the firmament*
> *Shot and was lost, in its eccentric course*
> *Dazzling, perplexing. Yet thy heart, methinks,*
> *Was generous, noble—noble in its scorn*

Rogers: The Years of Fame

Of all things low or little; nothing there
Sordid or servile. If imagined wrongs
Pursued thee, urging thee sometimes to do
Things long regretted, oft, as many know,
None more than I, thy gratitude would build
On slight foundations.

Throughout the 20's, the violently anti-Whig newspaper *John Bull* made a butt of Rogers, who, with his Holland House connections, was a fair mark. One of the barbs discharged at him was the description in the issue of January 16, 1826, of an imaginary lawsuit brought by Rogers against a drunken hackney-coach driver.

'Sir RICHARD BIRNIE desired the complainant, whose name was ROGERS, to come forward—after the lapse of some minutes, a small, weezen-looking person stepped up to the table, and proceeded to detail his grievances in an undertone.'

'The poor little body' was desired to state his case. He had called the cabman who would not come. ' "Why Sir," he said, "D—n me, if I carry subjects—so you had better go back to your grave, for into my coach you don't get, and nobody shall put you in."—Jarvy smiled—the *audience* looked at the complainant, and laughed immoderately.'

The attack was sustained by *Fraser's Magazine* in 1830 with the publication of a caricature of Rogers by Maclise over the caption ' "De mortuis nil nisi bonum!" There is Sam Rogers, a mortal likeness—painted to the very death!' Accompanying the portrait was a character sketch of the poet, of which these are some characteristic lines:

'He has a pretty house, with pretty gewgaws in it—he gives tolerable dinners, and says very spiteful things; he is an ugly man, and his face is dead, and his jokes flat. His poetry is poor, and his banking-house rich, his verses, which he purloined, will be forgotten, his jests (which others made for him) may be remembered.' William Maginn, the probable author of this squib, expressed the opinion elsewhere that Rogers' reputation as a poet was based on the dinners with which he bribed his critics, and there is no doubt that Rogers' wealth and the brilliance of the society he moved in provoked the jealousy of those who did not know, or did not choose to remember, that he had been acknowledged as a poet before he was accepted as a crony by the great.

The circles he frequented were indeed among the highest. As the oracle of Holland House he had a room named after him and his favourite resting place in the park was known as Rogers' Seat. He breakfasted several times with the Princesses at Buckingham House, and was embarrassed on one occasion when Queen Caroline invited herself to dine at only a few hours' notice. Macaulay wrote to his sister of an invitation to breakfast 'If you knew how Rogers is thought of you would think it as great a compliment as could be paid to a Duke'.

He was renowned as an arbiter of taste, and his house at 22 St. James's Place was thought to exemplify how the thoughtfully acquired collections of a lifetime might be disposed. He bought the house in 1803 and altered it to his own plans. He wanted a bachelor establishment designed for study and for frequent entertaining on a small scale, and for the display of his works of art so that they should appear the natural furniture of a man of taste, without the deadening smack of gallery or museum. It looked out on the Green Park through large low windows. The drawing room was hung with crimson silk. Its mantelpiece and the ornaments of the ceiling were designed by Flaxman. The sideboard and a cabinet in the dining room had been carved by the young Chantrey, a cabinet designed and painted by Stothard, and the rest of the furniture was made in the Greek taste from the best patterns. A marble hand kept his letters in place, a marble foot held the door open. Round the staircase was a frieze copied from the Elgin marbles. His paintings, vases, bronzes, marbles, books and coins were all worthy of comment, but their most perceptive admirers did not praise individual items without praising the *ensemble*.

'His house', wrote Dr. Waagen the great art expert, 'exhibits the accumulations of a long life in works of art of a most varied and refined description, so that the visitor is at a loss whether most to admire the diversity or the purity of his taste. Pictures of the most different schools, alternately attract the eye, every object being placed with so just a feeling for the space assigned it, that the rooms are richly and picturesquely ornamented, without in any way being overladen. Among all these objects none are insignificant, while many are of the highest class of beauty.' Among the paintings were four now in the National Gallery, Titian's great '*Noli mi tangere*', Bassano's 'The Good Samaritan', Guido's '*Ecce Homo*', and the Giorgione study of San Liberale for the Castelfranco altarpiece. There were others by Raphael and Rubens, and two famous works by Reynolds, 'Puck' and 'The Strawberry Girl'. Yet it was an indication of the thoughtful arrangement which lent an importance to simple things that among the things Macaulay singled out for special mention was a mahogany table on which stood an antique vase.

This was the setting—to some it seemed almost a shrine—for his breakfast parties and his dinners. The collections were obviously valuable—they turned out on his death to be worth over forty-four thousand pounds—but Rogers was made a trustee of the National Gallery, and a Commissioner for the encouragement of the Fine Arts in the building of the new Houses of Parliament, not because of their value, but because of the taste and knowledge with which they had been formed.

For the greater part of his life Rogers was not only famous as a figure in society, and collector of works of art, but also as a poet. His first long poem, *The Pleasures of Memory*, sold over twenty-two thousand copies in fourteen years, and within a few years of its first publication in 1792, he was firmly established as 'the poet Rogers', and as such wrote an epilogue for Mrs. Siddons to speak on her benefit night in 1795. *The Pleasures of Memory* alone was published at least six times in America before his death. It was translated into French in 1825. His *Human Life* was translated into Italian in 1820, the year after its appearance in England. The extraordinary success of the poem *Italy* will be considered later. His career as a poet was crowned by the offer, on the death of Wordsworth, of the Laureateship. But he was then eighty-seven and wrote to Prince Albert 'I felt as if it left me no alternative, but when I came to myself and reflected that nothing remained of me but my shadow—a shadow so soon to depart—my heart gave way'. The honour went to Tennyson instead.

Rogers' standing in the social and intellectual worlds of London is easy to demonstrate. His character, for the reasons already suggested, is less easy to describe. A popular estimate of it in his old age is given in Lady Blessington's novel

27

Rogers: The Years of Fame

Strathern, published in 1845. The author knew Rogers personally, but still better by repute, and her portrait incorporates a long tradition of Rogers-interpretation. Her readers would not have been troubled by a flicker of uncertainty as to whom the full-length portrait of 'Rhymer, the poet' was meant to portray; most of them would have granted the likeness to be a good one, or at least to correspond with what they had always heard about him.

It is a story of high life, of fashionable society in London and Rome, its pleasures, intrigues and romances. Through the pink and white and gold of youthful patricians and gay salons moves the jaundice and black of the baleful poet. As the story develops he is used whenever an illusion is to be blasted by a mean word, or a character mocked at with particular venom.

The first quality established is Rhymer's sensitiveness about his commoner's rank. 'Would you believe it,' he asks his young friend Lord Wyndermere, on whom he calls at the beginning of the novel, 'when he—the Duke of Aberfield—writes to me, he commences with "My good Sir"—yes, positively. My good sir—ay, and ends in the same style.' Lord Wyndermere tries to soothe his wounded *amour propre* by saying that the Duke wrote to him as 'My good Lord' but Rhymer insists on seeing a letter and notices 'with bitterness' that it is addressed to 'My dear Lord'. Rogers was, of course, a commoner. His grandfather was a glass manufacturer turned banker. For the first forty years of his life Rogers mixed in the respectable dissenting society of his own family's circle of friends and had a certain literary acquaintance. Of his early days at Holland House the story was told that piqued by seeing his friend Ward (Lord Dudley) so much at ease: 'Aye there they go', he said, '—they're all cousins!' Rogers was ambitious for two things: fame as a poet, and the friendship of the great, and as he lacked the fire and originality usually needed for the former, and the passport by birth to the latter, the attainment of these aims was attended by painful doubts and embarrassment. He awaited the reception of his poems with keen anxiety—Rogers 'looks pale and thin, and has every appearance of having been lately confined', wrote Sydney Smith before the appearance of *Human Life*—and his promptness in snapping up introductions to famous men was noted with some distaste. Unfortunately the gap between wanting to know

28

celebrities for their unique qualities of mind and mere tuft-hunting is small, as is that between an admiration for aristocrats and snobbery: it is tempting to believe the worst. Indeed, *Strathern* ends with a direct accusation of snobbery laid against Rogers. We close the tale with the hero and heroine happily united, 'and when their splendid mansion is opened to give some brilliant *fête*, it is allowed, by all those who attend it, with one solitary exception, that the parties at Strathern House surpass all others. The exception is Mr. Rhymer, who prefers the fêtes of some two or three dukes of his acquaintance.'

It was not snobbery for which Rogers was most widely blamed, however, but malice; a malice quiet, accurate and deflating. In the course of his early conversation with Lord Wyndermere Rhymer is made to say ' "I am an old man, though not nearly so old as some of my kind friends would wish to make me out, and I know by experience that the good-natured are trifled with and laughed at, while the fastidious and serene are feared and respected."

' "*Your* experience has, I should think, not been much exercised in the good-natured line," said Lord Wyndermere, laughing. "Or was it, after having tried its inefficacy, as a means of acquiring popularity in society, that you had recourse to—"

' "*Ill-nature*, you would say," returned Mr. Rhymer. "Well, be it so; call me morose, cynic, what you will, but defend me from being confounded with the grinning herd who flock from house to house, be praising all and everything, pleased with every body, and most with self. *A-propos* of being pleased, as you have wished for my opinion of your new house, may I tell you candidly that I don't like it." '

In volume two he is made to appear in a still more sordid light, and the passage is an unpleasing reflection of the darker side of his reputation. Rhymer sees the hero, Strathern, supremely happy at a ball, and falls to intimating that his love, the beauteous Louisa Sydney, is consumptive.

' "All the family are consumptive", continued he to Lady Melcombe, in a somewhat lower tone, but still loud enough to be heard by Strathern. "What a life of misery awaits the man who weds this beautiful but sickly flower!"

'Strathern turned from him with terror to look into the face of his beloved. . . .

' "I have spoilt his evening's amusement, however", thought Rhymer. "He was so wondrously happy, so insultingly happy! I hate to see people happy. But it's easy enough to interrupt their enjoyment, and that's some comfort." '

This ugly scene echoes a passage in one of Moore's letters to Byron. 'After seeing my little girl,' the Irish poet wrote, 'who is now as blooming a creature as can be, instead of saying anything kind about her as I expected, he asked me whether she was healthy, as her flesh felt very soft; and then said with an ominous look, that it was a pity I had not a third child, as to hang by but two threads was fearful.' The bachelor Rogers cannot be expected to have understood the susceptibilities of fathers, but, even with this in mind, it is doubtful if the story is literally true. Rogers was fond of children. Moore, in 1822, was anxious to say what would be pleasing to Byron, and his own feelings for Rogers were complicated; he was grateful and in part genuinely fond, while tempted to join the opposition and add his own tales of Rogers' sharpness to the common stock. But the story, for all its dubiousness, is interesting as a component of the anti-Rogers tradition, upon which Lady Blessington drew to fill in the gaps in her own observation.

The ballroom scene, being a dramatized version of a falsified event, is itself doubly false. But to deny that Rogers was in fact malicious would be absurd. He had an eye for weak spots and a tongue to describe them. An error, an eccentricity, an absurdity, a social blunder were not likely to pass without quiet pointed comment. A caricature of him showing his head on the body of a wasp was considered highly appropriate. 'Some surprise is excited by your staying so long at Amphill,' wrote Sydney Smith to Lady Holland in October, 1818, 'but Rogers I find has been sent for as a sort of condiment or pickle. . . .' Lady Granville gives a good example of the condimental power of Rogers as a guest. 'Think of Lady Cowper', she wrote to a friend, 'overhearing a conversation between Rogers and Luttrel, herself the theme. She had converted her dressing-room into a bedroom for the former. Rogers was saved by the weakness of his lungs, Luttrel by the honesty of his friendship. She never heard Rogers' attacks, but that they were such she knows by the replies, all on the defensive. "Upon my honour, I cannot judge her so harshly, she is so unaffected, so good-tempered." "Oh, come, come, women will have their beaux." "Well, I really don't know, but I have loved her from a child." '

A man with little power of sustained invention, and little aptitude for abstract speculation, who nevertheless passes a great part of his life in conversation must needs deal in personalities; such tattle is hardly memorable unless it is loaded with epigram; the number of epigrams designed to praise anybody can be numbered on the fingers of a hand. Effective, too, is the surprise, the astounding piece of information that staggers and appals. No-one was better informed than Rogers, no-one could gain more effect from an off-hand reference to the illegitimate children of a peer or sodomy in high places. He astounded Scott with a series of stories about Sheridan, one of which concerned his committing a rape on his sister-in-law on the day of her husband's funeral. 'Others', he noted, 'were worse.'

Rogers planted his scandals and his barbs as a dram-taker lifts his glass—compulsively. The habit—part instinctive, part nurtured perhaps in the days when his voice, not only weak but obscure, was straining for attention—was a chronic one. Rogers accepted the charge himself. 'I have a very weak voice,' he explained, 'if I did not say ill-natured things no-one would hear what I said.' An inveterate gossip, he was too clever not to gossip about himself. His malice did not necessarily spring from a considered desire to wound. 'His tongue is viperish to be sure,' admitted Lady Holland, 'but many times it is darted without intended mischief.' He was unable to resist a glib gibe at a friend if occasion offered, but it was not a symbol of an approaching breach of that friendship. After dining with him in his last years Crabb Robinson noted that 'he was, as usual, acrimonious and affectionate at the same time towards the same person'. It was a freak that puzzled some of those who knew him best. Those who watched him plant his deadly little thorns for the first time—and how many of Rogers' casual visitors described that first meeting as though they had grasped the Whole Man! —tended to think him a sick misanthropist seeking to poison and punish the world he envied.

How far was this from the truth is proved by the many acts of kindness with which he can be credited—private, unpublicized benevolences. Strathern himself finds this to say for him: 'If I may be allowed to parody the observation applied to Charles II,

I should say that Rhymer is known never to have *said* a kind thing, and never to have *done* an unkind one. He has come to the assistance of many a man of genius in those vicissitudes to which individuals of that class more than any other are liable, when they depend on literature for support. Towards artists, his good word to would-be patrons, possessed of more gold than taste, has never been wanting, yet, such is his peculiarity, that, while ready to *serve*, he is seldom willing to avoid offending, and evidently finds a pleasure in saying disagreeable things.' And he concludes, 'Nevertheless on the whole, perhaps the system of Rhymer, if system it be, is preferable to that of the generality of persons, who make it a point to *say* civil things, and leave undone kind ones.'

Among the men of genius Rogers helped were Sheridan, Campbell, Wordsworth and Moore, Chantrey, John Gibson the sculptor, and Lawrence—to name only the most famous. He helped his friends not only with money but advice on how to make the most out of their works; he reconciled their quarrels and introduced them to people who might be of more use than he could be. In the records of meetings with Rogers there is frequently a note of surprise expressed that he was not so black as he had been painted. After one breakfast Crabb Robinson made the somewhat patronizing entry in his diary 'He evinced a benevolence of disposition which I had not given him credit for. There was very little of that severity of remark for which he is reproached—candour and good sense marked all he said.' Dr. Charles Mackay confessed himself a convert. 'Before I had ever seen him, I had formed an image in my mind in accordance with the spiteful epigrams that Lord Byron and others had written against him, and was agreeably disappointed with the reality of his personal presence and the kindly suavity of his manners.' A visitor from America who came, unprejudiced, with an introduction to Rogers, puts the extreme case for the defence. 'Breakfast was extremely agreeable. The vast amount of Mr. Rogers' recollections, extending back through the best society for sixty years; his exquisite taste, expressed alike in his conversation, his books, his furniture, and his pictures; his excellent common-sense and sound judgement; and his sincere, gentle kindness, coming quietly, as it does, from the venerableness of his age, render him one of the most delightful men a stranger can see in London.' A note appended to this account is a dismal tribute to the anti-Rogers tradition. 'From what I have heard since, I suppose Rogers is not always so kind and charitable as I found him both today and whenever I saw him afterwards.'

Strathern suggested that the lack of charity sprang from a physiological cause. 'May not Rhymer's sarcastic *bon-mots* and insidious compliments', he asked his friend, 'be accounted for by this constitutional *malaise*, which, continually preying on him, engenders the bitterness which finds so little indulgence, even from those who are aware of his good qualities? Look at the countenance of those known to be sarcastic, and you will observe the yellow tinge, dull eye, and scornful lip which indicate derangement of the biliary system.' Rogers had been a delicate boy, vivacious but weak, and had needed long holidays at Margate and Brighton to strengthen him. He had the longevity of those whose pendulum-swing from health to illness is so slight as hardly to jar the system. But all his life he was thin and pale, and for half that life it was a fashionable game to refer to him as if he were already dead. His associates referred to him as 'the deceased poet', 'the spectre', 'the late Mr. Rogers' and invented stories a good deal less amusing than one told of a visit made by the poet and some friends to one of the Roman catacombs: Rogers emerged last and as he stood in the entrance Lord Dudley shook his hand. 'Goodbye, Rogers', he said. What was a game to London society was sometimes—as with the stories of his savagery—taken seriously by his provincial or foreign visitors, who were relieved to find instead of a terrifying being—

> *. . . a corpse stuck up for show,*
> *Galvanised at times to go—*

a man who, though no beauty, with his large bald head, pale blue eyes, thin cheeks and prominent chin, was able to compose these unpromising features into expressions of dignity, kindliness and charm. In his last years he used cosmetics, as did other elderly gentlemen of the old school. His groom massaged his chest and back every morning. He scrutinized every street before crossing it and cosseted each small ailment as he had all his life. But if throughout his life he was something of an old maid he remained a remarkably lively one. Until the accident that crippled him he would not allow himself to use an easy chair or sofa, dined out regularly in his eighties and even took a trip to Paris. What galvanized him to keep going was a constant interest in people, old friends and new faces. It was not of a corpse that Lady Eastlake exclaimed that it 'wrung our hearts' to hear of his accident in 1849, and a letter from Brougham in the following year shows the affectionate esteem in which he was held. Out of the season, he wrote, 'You will find your confinement irksome for want of visitors. So this idea came into my mind: there is no difficulty in having yourself transported to the railway station and taking the whole of a carriage in which your bed is to be put. You get there in eight hours; you have an apartment on the ground floor, close to a garden; and for the next two months there will be a succession of your friends here, besides ourselves. Do think of this.' Yet the malign tradition continued, and his death in 1855 was taken as an excuse to disinter some of its nastiest features—as for instance by Harriet Martineau in an obituary notice for the *Daily News*.

Much of the antipathy felt to Rogers was doubtless due to the anomalous position he seemed to hold in society and in the world of letters. At a time when Browning and Tennyson were in full vigour it seemed odd to offer the Laureateship to a spare, didactic poet of the school of Goldsmith, who had written only a few frail lines since 1834. To many, Rogers was merely a name on the back of a pretty book kept on a boudoir table for the sake of the illustrations. His progress in society from comparative obscurity to a world glittering with coronets—this too was watched with jealous distrust. A banker on Parnassus! and straying through the most exclusive groves! How did this come about?

II

Winning a Reputation:
From Samuel Rogers, Clerk,
to Rogers-the-Poet

━━━━━━━━━━━━━━◆━━━━━━━━━━━━━━

It is difficult to remember that Rogers, who died in 1855, was already forty when he moved into St. James's Place. His life is most fully documented after this move in 1803, and it is provoking that there is little evidence that concerns his early years. He left no autobiography, no formal memoirs; some travel diaries, some engagement books, his letters, his MS Commonplace Book and his poems, these form the bulk of the evidence in Rogers' own hand, and they date from his maturity. In the British Museum, however, there is an unpublished auto-biographical fragment, in part versified for *Italy*—and therefore written before 1830—which shows the ageing poet reflecting on his early days.

'God Almighty denied me many things at my birth—but he gave me what I value beyond them all—a passionate love for Music, painting, sculpture, poetry, for the beautiful in nature, a setting sun, a lake among the mountains, an ingenuous counten-ance and a generous action.—I was born—not in a great town—nor yet where the curfew-bell was unheard at night-fall—on a summer evening—my parents not noble yet not ungentle [*above the line* not ennobled by the breath of kings]—eminent as were my ancestors in the best days of England for fervour of religion, high-mindedness, souls above this world—nor would I exchange them with the noblest in Europe—From my earliest years I was melancholy even to sadness—yet I had dreams that made amends for all. Nor was I excelling in sports, or quick in my class at learning. Yet from the first I learned to do some-thing that might give me a name.

Rogers: *Winning a Reputation*

'I had a mother who said to her children I care not so much whether you are happy—may I never live to see that you are not good—[*at end in another ink* I had a father who breathed the romantic spirit of honor—] My constant wish has been to live with those who were eminent—I was always inclined to the society of those older than myself—who had left the conflict— whose bustle was over—the young whose minds were full of youth, breathing the essence [?] of the early flowers in spring- time—a young man, who is not young, was a coxcomb—always my aversion—the greatest resource and consolation of my life has been my turn for verses—a crowd, a bustle cannot prevent me—in an instant I am at work—'

The spot which was no great town, but within sound of a great town's curfew, was Newington Green, just outside London. His parents were Thomas Rogers, who set up as a banker with the money derived from his father's glass-manu- factory, and Mary Radford, whose father, a dissenter, was in trade in London. The Presbyterian Meeting House at Newing- ton Green, safely outside the Five Mile Limit, was the centre of the family's religious life, and among Rogers' ancestors eminent for 'fervour of religion' was Philip Henry, expelled from his living in 1662 under the terms of the Act of Uniformity.

Of his childhood Rogers told two stories, one about the tender- heartedness that prompted him to let imprisoned gnats and flies out at the window, the other which must be left in his own words, as it is the most endearing tale about him that exists. 'When I was about thirteen,' he recalled, 'my father and mother gave a great children's ball, at which many grown-up folk were also present. I was dancing a minuet with a pretty little girl; and at the moment when I ought to have put on my hat and given both hands to my partner, I threw the hat among the young ladies who were sitting on the benches, and so pro- duced great surprise and confusion in the room. This strange feat was occasioned by my suddenly recollecting a story of some gallant youth who had signalised himself in the same way.'

When he was seventeen the *Gentleman's Magazine* published the first of a series of short essays, and when he was twenty-two appeared his first volume of poetry, *An Ode to Superstition, with some other Poems*. It did little to bring him fame because it was published anonymously, but a heartening reception quickened

the ambition he spoke of in the Fragment. His other ambition—
to live among those who were eminent—depended for its fulfil-
ment partly on his position at the Bank. As a clerk he had not the
time, the money or the independence to visit largely or to
entertain, and he was only the third son. Fortunately his eldest
brother, Daniel, had no taste for business and early decided on
the placid life of a country squire. The next brother, Thomas,
died in 1788, five years after his father, and Rogers was thus
head of the firm when he was twenty-five. And when his
younger brother Henry became a partner in 1795, Rogers was
able to leave more and more to him, and gradually to detach
himself from the day-to-day running of the concern.

As his independence grew, so did his circle of acquaintance.
His family was not entirely without literary and artistic connections. A cousin of his father's, Richard Payne Wright, was
well-known as a writer on Art and a collector of Greek antiques;
while a cousin of his mother's, William Coxe, was a historian
and the author of a standard guidebook to Switzerland, a
detailed, learned and accurate work. A man of great influence in
Dissenting circles at the time was Dr. Richard Price, a regular
preacher at Newington Green. Both he and another prominent
nonconformist, Andrew Kippis, introduced the young poet to
their literary friends in London. Both men were Fellows of the
Royal Society, both were copious writers, Kippis being a frequent contributor to the *Gentleman's Magazine* and the *Monthly
Review*. Rogers always followed up the introductions they secured him. Significantly, by way of a Preface for a printed
edition of his recollections of some great contemporaries, he
used a passage from Clarendon's *Memoirs of his own life* which
ended 'He never knew one man, of what condition soever,
arrive at any degree of reputation in the world, who delighted
in the company of those who were not superior to himself.'

In 1789 he made a journey on horseback to Scotland, and
thanks to introductions from Kippis, was able to meet Robertson, the historian, Henry Mackenzie, author of *The Man of
Feeling*, and Adam Smith: he met the Piozzis, too, who were
staying at the same hotel in Edinburgh. By 1791 he had come to
know another writer, Dr. John Moore, famous then as author
of the widely-read novel *Zeluco*, and still remembered as a
traveller. Not merely of interest but of crucial importance were

two other acquaintances made at the same period: Richard Sharp and Sutton Sharpe. The former was a learned and cultivated man who mixed freely in London literary and fashionable circles where he was known as 'Conversation Sharp'. He was later to become an M.P. Sutton Sharpe was responsible for the greater part of Rogers' artistic education; he introduced him to Opie, Shee, Stothard, Bewick and Flaxman among other painters he knew. Some of them were later to illustrate his poems.

To see more of his new friends, and to return their hospitality, Rogers moved to London soon after his father's death, first to Paper Buildings in the Temple, then to lodgings in Prince's Street, Hanover Square, and finally to St. James's Place, where his dinners no longer had to depend on the treacherous memories of outside caterers. Clayden suggests that the move from suburb to metropolis involved a 'mental struggle'. It is true that the poet declared in *An Epistle to a Friend* (published in 1798) that

> *Still must my partial pencil love to dwell*
> *On the home-prospects of my hermit-cell,*

and it is true that the lover of setting suns and mountain lakes could remind himself that

> *When April-verdure springs in Grosvenor-square,*
> *And the furred Beauty comes to winter there,*
> *She bids old Nature mar the plan no more;*
> *Yet still the seasons circle as before.*

But Conversation Sharp and Sheridan would be incongruous guests in a hermitage; an ambitious young writer and would-be man about town owes more to the Season than the seasons; and the toping Porson would hardly be content 'with brimming pitcher from the shadowy glade'. Rogers loved Nature sincerely, but Society came first in his affections. Nature was above all a setting for man; the imitator of *Alexander's Feast*, the author of *Human Life*, the lover of Claude and Poussin was hardly likely to think otherwise. To a high priest of the pathetic fallacy, even a pyramid could be indignant.

It was during the competitive period of his residence in London, when he was seeking recognition as a poet and conversationalist, that some of the criticisms of his character gained ground. He was accused of envying the success of his fellow poets. Sydney Smith once claimed to have got a dinner out of him merely by abusing Campbell. And he was accused, too, of abandoning old friends in order to catch hold of more important ones, and of giving up opinions if they ceased to be fashionable. His popularity, nevertheless, as guest and host, constantly increased. He flattered older men, leaders of the society he cherished, by the attention he gave them, and this came easily, for he preferred their company to that of his contemporaries. He did not compromise the usefulness of his bachelor state by getting married; in spite of feeling a timid fascination for them, his relations with young women were conducted—or at least related —with a sort of arch embarrassment. ' *Badinage* apart,' he wrote to Richard Sharp from Margate in 1795, 'I have been making experiments on my own heart in this great laboratory by the sea-side. I dropped it into the crucible, and when I looked for it again, it was—shall I say not there? No, but it was not so sound as I left it.' He flirted at times with the idea of marriage, and made at least one actual proposal, but it is difficult to believe that he would really have preferred a wife to an efficient housekeeper. The Edinburgh Reviewer of *Human Life* who referred to 'our uxorious poet' was pulling his leg.

Not that women were excluded from his table. Among the breakfasts recorded by Mackay, one was attended by Macaulay, Lady Blessington and—a very frequent guest—Mrs. Norton. At another was Miss Cushman, the celebrated female Romeo, a part which she played opposite her sister's Juliet. The guests at two of the others he mentions were in the one case Prince— later Emperor—Louis Napoleon, Whately, the archbishop of Dublin and Lord William Pitt Lennox; in the other, Sydney Smith, Daniel O'Connell, the great Irish agitator, Sir Augustus d'Este, a grandson of George III, and the novelist Harrison Ainsworth. Rogers preferred entertaining at breakfast—at 10 a.m.—when the mind was clear and concentration was not sacrificed to complicated victuals. He gave dinners, but it was said that they were a probation for his breakfasts. The purpose of his meals was to secure the right conditions for good talk. He asked only a few guests—from three to five for breakfast, a few more for dinner—and chose them in order to provoke an easy and even flow of conversation: not more than one professed wit, not more than one Lion at a time. He himself was not a monopolizer of the talk and nothing mortified him more than to see someone else attempt to be. Rogers remained all his life a Whig, and the talk was sometimes political, but more frequently it was about personalities, or about literature and art. If a quotation were to be verified, Rogers rang for his butler to fetch the book, if it were a question of taste, he liked to lead the company to one of his paintings, or to settle a point by opening a portfolio of drawings. Time passed unfretfully in the pleasant room with its chaste uncrowded furniture; the breakfasts commonly lasted until twelve and often till one. If there was a complaint levelled against him as a host, it was that at dinner the lights were arranged so as to show off the pictures more flatteringly than the diners.

The mood of the period in entertaining is described in Lady Shelley's Memoirs. 'It was not, in those days, customary to have more than three or four women at dinner-parties, where there were eight or ten men, and dinners were not, as now, a jumble of pairs like the animals entering the Ark. Dinners were then arranged with care and thought, so as to secure the most agreeable conversation. This lent a particular charm to those select gatherings. Tommy Moore, Luttrel, Rogers, and Sydney Smith were the regular "diners out". They were invited especially to give the *ton*, and to lead the conversation, whose brilliancy had often been prepared with as much care as a fine lady bestows upon her Court dress. The conversation was seldom impromptu —like the talk of my lively, and most agreeable husband—yet everyone accepted its charm, without scrutinising too closely the manner of its "get-up".'

Rogers prepared his own talk, at least the anecdotes he expected to tell, and this practice, added to a low, slow considered manner of speaking, made his conversation remarkably well formed; it could have been published with only a little correction. Many of the regular 'diners out' glanced at their lines before stepping into their parts. Rogers considered that his friend Sir James Mackintosh had jeopardized his career by preparing so elaborately for what he was going to say not in the House, nor from the Bench, but over the fish. The practice, a natural one in a somewhat closed society, where even those in business had plenty of leisure, could be a source of embarrassment. Richard Sharp came by accident on one occasion on some notes drafted by his partner, Samuel Boddington, for his conversation that evening. Sharp memorized them, and when the time came, steered the talk obligingly towards Boddington's *mots*, and then forestalled him by telling every one himself.

It was not simply because he was a wealthy man and could afford to give meals that had to be returned that Rogers was found so frequently at fashionable tables. He was not a brilliant talker and was not particularly witty; he had neither the sense of fun of a Sydney Smith, nor the ebullient spontaneity of a Macaulay; his humour was of a dry sarcastic kind. His manner of speaking, too, was dry and carefully pointed. He had a fine ear for the effective pause. There was a favourite anecdote about his court dress, which was probably unique in having been borrowed by two Poets Laureate, Wordsworth and Tennyson. He was asked once 'Do you happen to know whether Mr. Wordsworth went to the levee or not?' 'Well—I ought to know, for he (pause) went in my clothes and in my carriage.' And a snatch of conversation recorded in 1820 by Mrs. Trench, mother of the Archbishop of Dublin, suggests something of the uneasy chill that grew on his listeners as the little sentences stepped about their prey.

'So, Mr. Wilmot, you are going to the Duchess of ——'s?

Mr. Wilmot.—Yes, immediately.

Rogers.—How *fat* you'll grow.

Mr. W.—*Fat*, how so?

R.—You will sleep so much. They go to bed so early.

Mr. W.—No, I never go to bed early.

R.—You will, indeed.

Mr. W.—No, I always read in my room.

R.—You will not. *Measure your candle.*

(*Exit Mr. Wilmot.*)

Rogers (to the remaining circle).—That Mr. Wilmot is a sensible man. I don't say so from my own knowledge; not the least. He wrote a book, too. That, you'll say, was nothing. And printed it. I don't say that from my knowledge, either, for I never read it, never met anybody that had.'

Though it was as a sardonic commentator on the social scene that he was best known, it was not as a humorist that he was most valued. It was rather for a knack of saying what was interesting and to the point in a peculiarly precise, lapidary way, of drawing on his knowledge to select not the most striking or exotic illustration but the one that was most helpful to the discussion at large; his conversation was not a series of tactical triumphs but—at its best—the exercise of a calmly masterful strategy. As time passed he was increasingly appreciated for the anecdotes he could tell of the famous and unusual persons he had known. He told them simply, with no attempt to make each version more dramatic than the last; the carefully lucid language was itself a medium flattering to the illustrious shades who could be seen so clearly through it. Sometimes, indeed, his anecdotes were so unemphatic as to appear flat. Robinson sourly noted his retailing 'a *mot* of Charles Lamb to Barry Cornwall: "Samson made many a worse remark and many a better!" ' Rogers could play the wit, and was often expected to do so by his visitors, but he did not then show himself at his best. The material he chose was too personal, too felt, it ran the danger of sliding towards malice, or of being expressed in allusions only fully comprehensible to a clique. It was partly for this exclusiveness that he was lampooned by *John Bull* as the wag of the Whigs. Through the 20's there was something like a Samuel Rogers department in the paper, where three or four times a year a bad pun or a weak joke was fathered on him. The following, which appeared on April 15, 1822 under the heading 'Facetiae of the Whigs', is the only one to contain a true note of parody:

BON-MOT

Sam Rogers, the poet, the pleasantest creature on earth to look at and live with, was on the point of drinking a glass of cherry-water, at a certain great house not a hundred miles from Albemarle-street, one evening early in the present month, when the Dowager Duchess of Richmond came into the room. 'Here comes the Duchess of Richmond', whispered Luttrel to Rogers; upon which Rogers, with a quickness that set the by-standers in a roar, said—'*So she does!!*'

It is quite impossible to describe the convulsive effect produced by this extremely happy turn; those who know Mr. Rogers will know that he often says things equally as ready.

Rogers: *Winning a Reputation*

The position in society that Rogers had won, so secure that he was worth pillorying, was due not only to the pleasure of his company but also to his reputation as a poet; he wrote, as well as talked himself there. Ten years after the appearance of *The Pleasures of Memory* even Coleridge, who neither liked nor respected Rogers, admitted that it was known to every school-girl. To Byron, it was 'a very beautiful poem, harmonious, finished and chaste', and in conversation with Shelley he affirmed strongly: 'I say the "Pleasures of Memory" *will* live.' Lord Holland wrote an inscription in a summerhouse in the grounds of Holland House:

> *Here Rogers sat, and here for ever dwell*
> *With me those Pleasures that he sings so well,*

and years later, in 1818, when Rogers had published *An Epistle to a Friend*, and the less generally approved *Columbus* and *Jacqueline*, and had completed most of *Human Life*, Henry Luttrel wandered to the spot.

> *Let me in*, he wrote, *and be seated. I'll try if thus placed*
> *I can catch but one spark of his feeling and taste,*
> *Can steal a sweet note from his musical strain,*
> *Or a ray of his genius to kindle my brain.*
> *Well now I am fairly installed in the bower,*
> *How lovely the scene! how propitious the hour!*
> *The breeze is perfumed by the hawthorn it stirs;*
> *All is beauty around me—but nothing occurs;*
> *Not a thought, I protest, though I'm here and alone,*
> *Not a line can I hit on that Rogers would own ...*
> *So I rise, since the Muses continue to frown,*
> *No more of a poet than when I sat down;*
> *While Rogers, on whom they look kindly, can strike*
> *Their lyre at all times, in all places alike.*

These men, as cronies, were partial. It is more interesting to pursue the opinion of Byron. Temperamentally, the two men could hardly have been more different, yet Byron expressed an admiration for Rogers' works almost as perverse as his occasional antipathy to his person. They first met in the autumn of 1811, and Byron told Moore that he was proud, undeserving as he was, to have been praised by such a man. Byron had previously saluted the elder poet in a flattering couplet in *English Bards and Scotch Reviewers:*

> *And then, melodious Rogers! rise at last,*
> *Recall the pleasing memories of the past.*

and he continued to salute him in work after work, and even developed for him the pet name of Ruggiero. Byron's *Lara* was published together with *Jacqueline,* and the *Giaour,* the plan of which had been suggested by Rogers, was dedicated to him. 'You are one of the few persons with whom I have lived in what is called intimacy', he wrote five years after his first meeting and two before the composition of *Question and Answer.* To Byron he remained 'our *poetical papa*', 'the last Argonaut of classic English poetry, and the Nestor of our inferior race of living poets.' And in the famous pyramid sketched in 1813, he placed Rogers as second only to Scott:

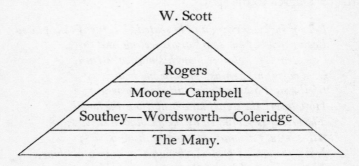

W. Scott

Rogers

Moore—Campbell

Southey—Wordsworth—Coleridge

The Many.

though he added that this order represented the popular view rather than any decided opinion of his own. Writing to Murray in 1817 he went further and emphasized that he, together with Scott, Moore, Campbell, Southey and Wordsworth were 'all in the wrong, one as much as another; that we are upon a wrong revolutionary poetical system, or systems, not worth a damn in itself, and from which none but Rogers and Crabbe are free; and that the present and next generations will finally be of this opinion'.

This opinion is perverse, not because it was personal and eccentric—indeed, it fairly represented much popular taste—but because it was concerned less with the quality of Rogers' poems than the system according to which he wrote them. Byron was not saying that Rogers wrote greater poems than the rest of them but that from the point of view of the future he was setting a safer course. Rogers' nag was the enduring steed; under Pope, Goldsmith, Crabbe, it could gallop, canter and trot, under Rogers it ambled, but it ambled along the highroad. Poets of any period could scramble into the saddle and be sure that they were going in the right direction. But Byron and the others had chosen to risk a horse with wings, to whom the mountain peaks were not inaccessible, a bolting Pegasus. It is true, he wrote to Moore from Venice in 1818, that 'we keep the *saddle*, because we broke the rascal and can ride. But though easy to mount, he is the devil to guide, and the next fellows must go back to the riding-school and the manège, and learn to ride the "great horse" '. Nothing is more gratifying than to do the wrong thing with resounding success, and Byron, in praising Rogers, was also obliquely congratulating himself; but his belief in the superiority of Pope to any poet writing in his own day was sincere, and it explains his affectionate regard for the *Pleasures* of Campbell and Rogers.

The fact that Rogers followed the poetic fashions of his youth with no drastic changes for the whole of his career as a poet endeared him to those who liked the tradition of Goldsmith, Crabbe, and William Crowe, author of *Lewesdon Hill,* and protected him from competing with the Titans of his age. It did not protect him from criticism, it is true. Hazlitt scolded him with gusto. 'He is a very lady-like poet,' he began in one of the *Lectures on the English Poets*, 'he is an elegant but feeble writer. He wraps up obvious thoughts in a glittering cover of fine words; is full of enigmas with no meaning to them; is studiously inverted, and scrupulously far-fetched, and his verses are poetry, chiefly because no particle, line, or syllable of them reads like prose.' His poetry, the author went on to say, quickening his stride, 'is a tortuous, tottering, wriggling, fidgetty translation of every thing from the vulgar tongue, into all the tantalizing, teasing, tripping, lisping *mimminee-pimminee* of the highest brilliancy and fashion of poetical diction.' In Leigh Hunt's *Feast of the Poets* only Campbell, Southey, Scott and Moore were invited in by Apollo to dine; Rogers, together with Spencer and

Montgomery, were asked to come back to tea. Justifying this exclusion from dinner, he has a note explaining that 'the fault of Mr. Rogers is direct imitation of not the best models, written in a style at once vague and elaborate'. But on the whole Rogers was spared the Periodical lash because he did not aim too high; he was patronized but never flayed.

In some quarters Rogers was sniffed at as an amateur, 'the banker poet'. When he was writing the *Pleasures of Memory*, certainly, he was working at the bank from 10 a.m. to 5 p.m., and he claimed that he preferred it so; literature was best pursued as an exquisite pastime. This did not mean that he took his work casually. He lavished on it the minutest care, revising and hesitating until the last possible moment. His friends were pestered with queries about tiny points of expression, were urged to choose between almost identical phrases. Even when the work was set up at the printers he would secure a further postponement by having a few copies privately distributed for further comment before publication. He was never more discomposed than when in the throes of a poetic accouchement. Moore saw him in the 'very agonies of parturition' before the appearance of *Human Life* and Sydney Smith suggested that it would be charitable to lay straw in the street in front of his door to dull the sound of passing traffic even when he was working on a couplet. In his commonplace book Rogers noted the time he had taken to finish each of his works. He was occupied two years with the seven stanzas of the *Ode*; the two hundred-odd lines of *An Epistle to a Friend* required six. The only poem he wrote in a hurry was *Jacqueline*, which he finished in one. The commonplace book also contains the form of a letter sent by Rogers to aspirant poets who wrote to him for advice. 'Let him lay aside his composition for some months and then look at it with fresh eyes—and let him in the interval read attentively some of the Great Masters (Milton and Dryden for instance) and then read what he has written. His good sense and feeling will thus enable him to come to a much better judgement concerning himself than any criticisms of mine. I may be wrong, but such was my practice, and I would recommend it to others.'

Such care produced a high finish, enamelled and brilliant. Byron, playing with the *concetto* of Apollo presenting suitable cups for different bards to drink from, suggested a wooden bowl would be fitting for Wordsworth, a scooped pumpkin for Crabbe, for himself a skull, chased with gold, and for Rogers, an antique vase, formed of agate. Yet, paradoxically, though individual phrases are jewel-like, the general sense of Rogers' poetry is by no means crystalline. His meaning is frequently obscure; and this in spite of constant revision, and his belief that simple words were the best, that the feelings of the heart could best be uttered in the language of the nursery.

The flaw lay in the weakness of his imagination. What Rogers felt strongly about, other people took for granted—the pleasures of childhood, and their fleeting nature, the charm of the relations between husband and wife and child—and he wrote about them so feelingly that his themes were greeted with pleased recognition. It was magazine stuff, but written by a man of taste and with a high degree of finish. When he embarked on a less commonplace theme, as in *Columbus,* he could not sustain it, it broke up into Fragments, and remained unfinished. Like most sentimental men he was easily moved by the obvious: his fault as a poet was that he mistook these easy tears for the tremors of creative insight. He recognized neither how pedestrian his muse was, nor how obscure. His revision was thorough, but it was restricted to the polishing of details. He revised not sense, but expression. He neglected the sentence for the sake of the phrase, the phrase for the word. The result was that as the parts came to gleam more brightly they ceased to make up a whole, and the effect was not tautness but discontinuity.

This tendency is least damaging in *Italy,* where the use of blank verse deprived him of rhymes to fiddle with. In this poem, too, he was describing in unforced language things he had seen or read, and there is a relaxed but disciplined music in many passages that enabled them to give a lasting pleasure. In this poem, too, he was most himself. The work of the men who influenced him, Milton, Dryden, Goldsmith, and Wordsworth among them, had been absorbed; the enjoyment of *Italy* does not depend upon the pleasures of Memory. Ruskin, on his first meeting with Rogers, made the *gaffe* of complimenting him on the illustrations while making it clear that he had not read the verse, and posterity has seized on the half-truth in the saying that *Italy* 'would have been dished if it had not been for the plates'. But in fact Rogers became a famous poet because his poems were liked. His first work to contain illustrations was the fifth edition of the *Pleasures of Memory*. Nor can his success be explained, as Macaulay implied, by saying that he bought it. It is true that all his poems, except *Jacqueline*, were brought out at his own expense, and that *Italy*, after the initial failure, was given a second chance because he could afford to spend thousands on adorning it, but his name was made before he was rich, his investments in himself paid because the goods found a ready market—and not only among the circle of his friends, for pirated editions, and an edition in parts with double columns, small print and scanty illustrations continued to sell alongside the *editions de luxe*. No matter how tricked out, Robert Merry's *The Pains of Memory* (1796) could never have competed with Rogers' *Pleasures;* no more could Chaloner's *Rome*, Sotheby's *Italy*, or Reade's *Italy* compare with the *Italy* of Rogers.

His initial success was doubtless aided by the lack of competition, and its continuance by the public's continuing taste for the delicate manipulation of foil and epée in the plain while the Romantic armament detonated in the mountains. When Rogers published the *Pleasures of Memory* the fame of Cowper was already dying; Crabbe and Erasmus Darwin had a limited audience, Blake almost none, and Burns was little known in the south; Moore was at school, Coleridge at Cambridge, Scott was unheard of and Wordsworth broke almost inaudibly into print in the following year. There was no poet, let alone a Movement, to drown the thin new voice.

Discoursing as it did of homely everyday things, the charms of memory, the changing scenes and stages of human life, the voice retained an audience: the drawing room and the schoolroom had nothing to fear from it, for had not the poet written of himself in the *Epistle*

> *In the clear mirror of his moral page*
> *We trace the manners of a purer age.*
> *His soul, with thirst of genuine glory fraught,*
> *Scorned the false lustre of licentious thought?*

And before this, as early as 1793, Rogers had penned the lines which he prefixed to all the collected editions of his poems:

> *Yet should this Verse, my leisure's best resource,*
> *When through the world it steals its secret course,*

Revive but once a generous wish supprest,
Chase but one sigh or charm a care to rest;
In one good deed a fleeting hour employ,
Or flush one faded cheek with honest joy;
Blest were my lines, tho' limited their sphere,
Tho' short their date, as his who traced them here.

Beckoning no-one from the high road of common, shared experience into psychological crossways of ominous aspect, always the gentleman in his avoidance of excess and his constant awareness of divine providence, Rogers was the name that occurred most naturally to a young man in search of a keepsake for his sweetheart, or a paterfamilias for his wife and daughters. But it must not be forgotten that in Rogers' hands the type of verse associated with the *Keepsake*, the *Album*, or the *Poetic Banquet*, was brought to a quite unusual level of serious purpose and elegant finish.

In a volume by Rogers it was not only the verse that was appreciated. It was fashionable at the time to include notes explaining the allusions and commenting on special points of interest in the text. Rogers followed this fashion, and more effectively than anyone else. Only Hobhouse's notes to the fourth canto of *Childe Harold* can compare for style and interest to those of Rogers, especially the notes for *Italy*. He lavished great care on them, revising and re-casting them as thoroughly as ever he puzzled at his verse. On one he spent a whole month. He took prose seriously. 'Poets the best Prose writers', he noted in the commonplace book. 'Shakespeare, Cowley, Milton, Dryden, Pope, Gray and Addison. Burke and Rousseau began with Poetry, as did also Voltaire.' The novels he believed would give foreigners the best notion of English genius were *Robinson Crusoe* and *Gulliver's Travels;* he aimed himself at the clarity and economy of style of Swift and Defoe. He intermixed prose essays with the verse sequences of *Italy*, and of one of them Mackintosh said that Hume could not have improved the thoughts nor Addison amended the language. More complimentary still, had he known of it, was Moore's jotting, apropos the essay 'On Assassination': 'Feel it would do one good to study such writing, if not as a model, yet as a chastener and simplifyer of style, it being the very reverse of ambition or ornament.' No biographer of Rogers can afford to ignore the notes to *Italy*. They reveal much about the quality of his mind and its resources, and are comparable with the *Table-Talk* in suggesting his charm as a companion.

It was this two-fold appeal that explained Rogers' literary standing. It was not only because of his wealth, or the fashionable company to be found at St. James's Place, that Ruskin set off to his first meeting with the old man as to 'a sacred Eleusinian initiation and Delphic pilgrimage', or that Peel asked if he might have a portrait to join those of Byron, Southey, Wordsworth and Scott in his gallery of eminent men at Drayton Manor. It was to Rogers the author that works as different as *Lalla Rookh* and *Master Humphrey's Clock* were dedicated. It is not always easy to remember, after generations of glancing references to Rogers-the-Poet, that the man who is being referred to is Rogers, the poet.

III

Rogers Leaves for the Continent

In May, 1814, Napoleon abdicated and retired to Elba. With hostilities at an end travellers could once more cross the Channel. Rogers at once began to make plans for a journey to Italy. He had already been twice to the continent, to Revolutionary Paris in 1791 and to Consular Paris during the Peace of Amiens in 1802, but he had gone no further. And now, like many Englishmen of his tastes and means, he was anxious to make up for the long delay in making his Grand Tour. He was fifty-one years old, and at the height of his reputation and powers. No-one was in a better position to make the most of such a journey.

He went as one of England's most famous poets, sure of being received in society wherever he went. His wealth, and the friendship of such notables as the Hollands, who were in Italy at the same time, meant that he received the hospitality traditionally offered to the *Milor*. He had read widely in Italian history and literature, and, in a halting fashion, spoke the language. Although no longer in a mood to join in peasant dances, or take a turn at driving the post horses as he had in France in 1791, he was still fit and vigorous. 'How quick that old gentleman runs upstairs', exclaimed one of Sydney Smith's maids the year after his return, and the fatigues of sightseeing did not dim his interest in what he saw and heard for a single day. He knew what to look for in galleries and churches. He was determined not to have eyes only for the relics of antiquity, but to remember that Italy had had two lives, two golden ages—in the Classical Period, and at the Revival of Learning.

His education had been a bald one, but in the long holidays he was forced to take for his health's sake, he worked at filling its gaps. One long winter in particular—at Exmouth in 1799—he spent reading the classical authors he had only skipped through, or heard of, at school. And his interest in Italian painting grew during the war years. In *The Pleasures of Memory* the only works of art the poet had to look back on were family portraits. Six years later, in the *Epistle to a Friend* he spoke enthusiastically of Greek sculpture and Italian painting. His own collections were not yet begun. He was still content with copies and engravings.

What tho' no marble breathes, no canvass glows, the frugal author exclaims,

> *From every point a ray of genius flows!*
> *Be mine to bless the more mechanic skill,*
> *That stamps, renews, and multiplies at will*

and thanks to which

> *Thy gallery, Florence, gilds my humble walls;*
> *And my low roof the Vatican recalls!*

Many of the works Rogers was to see in Italy were already familiar to him in reproduction. His first contact with some of the great originals, and the most important step in his artistic education, was the time passed in Paris in 1802, a great part of which he spent in the Louvre. In that museum was brought together, at the command of Napoleon, the most astounding collection of great paintings ever to be seen under one roof. By treaty and private bargain, many of Italy's most famous pictures and sculptures had been shipped to Paris: from 1802 to 1815 the visitor to the Louvre could see in a day what would cost him weeks of travelling in 1816. The bronze horses from St. Mark's in Venice were there, the Medici Venus from Florence, the great Caraccis from Bologna, Raphael's Transfiguration and the Apollo Belvedere from Rome. Rogers wrote a poem on the famous Torso from the Vatican, and studied the paintings with care.

The decade that followed was a formative one for his taste. It was in the year before he left for Italy that his house was described in a well-known passage from Byron's journal. 'If you enter his house—his drawing-room—his library—you of yourself say, this is not the dwelling of a common mind. There is not a gem, a coin, a book thrown aside on his chimney-piece, his sofa, his table, that does not bespeak an almost fastidious ele-

gance in the possessor.' There was little in the Italian art
esteemed in his day that Rogers had not trained himself to
enjoy. Byron goes on to guess that Rogers' delicacy of taste
must have cost him many jarrings in his contact with life. But it
is a mistake to think of him as squeamish and delicate. His
journal, indeed, is notably free from the English tourists' ready
screams of dismay at dirt and delay, and petulant disapproval of
foreign manners. Sydney Smith had ignited many squibs at the
expense of Rogers' failings, but he wrote of him to Lady Holland
at Rome in February 1815, in the following terms: 'I think you
very fortunate in having Rogers at Rome. Show me a more
kindly and friendly man; 2, one from good manners, knowledge
fun taste and observation more agreeable; 3, a man of more
strict political integrity, and of better character in private life. If
I were to chuse any Englishman in *foreign parts* whom I should
chuse to blunder upon, it should be Rogers.' The emphasis is
a little baneful, but the compliment is nevertheless a comprehensive one.

There appeared no cause to leave for Italy in a hurry. The
roads of France were still scored by the wheels of cannon, a
number of bridges were broken down, and inns were some time
in preparing for a renewed tourist trade. In London, moreover,
there were celebrations to greet the arrival of the allied
sovereigns. Rogers decided to wait for the usual season, late
summer, before setting out on his tour.

He took with him his eldest unmarried sister, Sarah, nine
years his junior, who shared his tastes and for whom he felt a
close affection. As a travelling companion they had Sir James
Mackintosh. Rogers had known him for many years and admired him as a writer and as a talker. But the arrangement was
not a fortunate one. Rogers was never lucky in the friends he
travelled with. Boddington had been something of an embarrassment previously in France. He had insisted on standing
up in churches where everyone else was kneeling, and when
a Friar came up on one occasion and begged for alms, his
answer was a brusque 'Allez travailler!' Byron, in 1821, infuriated Rogers by getting up so late that they missed many of
the sights on the road, and particularly annoyed him by not rising
one day till after lunch so that they had to enter Florence in the
dark. And Rogers could not quite hit it off with Mackintosh.

Rogers leaves for the Continent

The landmarks Rogers was most interested in were literary ones. Mackintosh was more concerned with local government, civic improvements and the like. All went well in France, but in Switzerland a series of petty differences occurred that will be recognizable by anyone who has travelled with a not entirely sympathetic friend. At Lausanne Rogers and Sarah took the last volume of Gibbon's *Decline and Fall* to read its concluding passages on the very spot where they were written. This, Rogers said, 'was not to Mackintosh's taste, he meanwhile was trotting about, and making inquiries concerning the salaries of professors, etc.' They fell out over the beauties of Swiss scenery. To Mackintosh who wrote in his diary at St. Gingoulph 'Till this morning, I never thoroughly believed that any scenes could surpass those of Scotland and the Lakes; but they are nothing', it was infinitely provoking to hear Rogers whispering some days later that lake Lucerne was not 'superior to Windermere'. And Rogers, loyal to his ideas of Italy, may have been impatient with his companion's laudation of the Swiss character and his deep feeling for the country as a whole.

It was the little incidents that boded worse than a difference of taste. At Geneva, Rogers could not find his *sac-de-nuit* so he bought a new one. To his mortification, on getting into the carriage, he saw that Mackintosh had it, and had stuffed it with books. When they went out in a steamer on Lake Geneva Mackintosh very coolly got Rogers' courier to hold the umbrella over his own head, and took no notice of the unprotected heads of Rogers and Sarah. And matters were bound to come to a head with a man who, like Mackintosh, helped himself at the *table d'hôte* to the breast and wings of a chicken and then pushed the rest of the carcass over to his travelling companions. In the event an open rift was saved by the arrival of Mackintosh's daughter from Baghdad. He left the Rogers at Zug in order to meet her at Basel, and Samuel and Sarah completed their travels alone.

The scene at their departure from Brighton was later described by Rogers' nephew, William Sharpe. 'In the middle of August my Uncle Samuel Rogers and my Aunt Sarah Rogers spent a day and night with us on the eve of starting for a tour of the Continent—a journey which so many people took at that moment when the peace had opened to Englishmen and to

54

peaceful travellers in general, those countries from which they had been excluded by the War for twenty years with the exception of the short peace of Amiens in 1803. I saw my Uncle and Aunt with their travelling companion Sir James Mackintosh embark at Brighton late on the evening of (about) 15th or 16th August. They were carried in the arms of the Sailors, thro' the Breakers to a small boat which took them to the sailing packet, lying a short distance off, ready to convey them to Dieppe.'

The packet was the *Nautilus,* and it landed them at Dieppe after thirty hours on a rolling sea.

IV

English Travellers in Italy
1814–1821

────────◁◇▷────────

I. NUMBERS

In England, one of the more frustrating aspects of the Napoleonic wars was the ban on foreign travel. The English were the continent's greatest travellers. Among the wealthy, the Grand Tour was still a living tradition; both the classical curriculum at school, and the training of manners at home, confidently looked to it to complete their work; while the artist fretted to be back in the mellow light of the Campagna, the budding author to add his impressions to a market already overstocked, but usually able to absorb yet one more book of Italian travels.

Italy was not completely out of bounds before the turn of the century. Mariana Starke wrote a guide book as a result of her residence there in 1797 and 1798, and wrote reassuringly in 1800 that the dangers were very slight. Indeed, 'I am strongly inclined to believe, that English Families travelling for health may, at this moment, reside in any City of Italy with as little risk of inconvenience attributable to war, as they could before the invasion of BONAPARTE.' But for the ordinary tourist the Peace of Amiens was the first chance to get abroad after the beginning of the war. Many went no further than Paris, seduced by the opportunity to see the prodigy, Bonaparte, and by the Louvre, which already housed some of the greatest masterpieces of Italian art. But enough went to Italy for the King of Naples, Joseph Bonaparte, to talk of an English colony there, and 'it happens, indeed, most fortunately,' as one traveller recorded, 'that among this crowd of British travellers there is not one individual of doubtful character: many of them are persons of the highest rank, and all of the greatest respectability.' Two of them, Joseph Forsyth and John Chetwode Eustace, were to write records of their journey that speedily came to rank as classics, and helped to whet the appetites of their tantalised readers during the last years of isolation.

When war broke out again the travellers rushed for home. Not all of them got there. Forsyth was arrested at Turin in May 1803 when on his way to Switzerland and was imprisoned in France. An attempt to escape was punished with a forced march of six hundred miles and from this and other hardships his health was so impaired that he only lived for a year after his release in 1814. His book was written in a vain attempt to call the attention of Napoleon, as patron of the arts, to his plight.

After 1803 only American citizens could travel freely, and the English, who tended to look upon Italy as part of their birthright, had to rely upon Yankee descriptions of her. A notable exception was Coleridge, who was in Rome early in 1806, where he met one such author and two other distinguished Americans, Washington Irving and the painter Washington Allston. But he had been brought from Malta to Naples in a naval vessel, and as a result of tightened French regulations, had to leave hurriedly in May, getting clear of Rome only just in time to escape arrest.

The sense of relief that came in 1814 was immense, when, in the words of a guide book, 'the gates of IMPERIAL ROME are again opened to the traveller.' The reaction of Lady Shelley may be quoted as a typical one. 'Every wish of my early years', she recorded, 'had centred in a tour of the continent; and ever since my marriage I felt that the comforts of my happy home might, for a time, be both pleasantly and profitably exchanged for a rambling life, which would enlarge my mind, and make me a pleasanter companion by the fireside of old age. The change in the political world in 1814, at last promised to gratify my wishes in that respect; and we determined to devote two years to travelling over France, Germany, and Italy.' But their departure was delayed by the illness of a relative, and when they were ready to leave in the following March, the news of Napoleon's escape from Elba forced their plans to be postponed for a second time. Hundreds were more fortunate, and left in time to bask in the sun and enjoy the sights of Italy before being chased home by the Corsican Ogre's return.

By September 1814 they were flowing richly through Switzerland. In Geneva, Lady Charlotte Bury noted with pleasure, 'there is a picked society of intelligent and superior persons resident in or travelling through the country', and another traveller, while pleased to see that in hotel registers the names of his fellow-countrymen outnumbered those of other nationalities by two to one, was irked by the effect on prices of their needless prodigality. An influx of English had been noted at Florence as early as May, but a dinner in Naples in June to which all the English had been bidden was attended by less than twenty. The pace quickened as autumn drew on, for this was conventionally the time to appear in Italy. In November, Rogers' friend Millingen, who lived in Rome, wrote to a friend in Florence 'The English arrive every day in crowds, and as a result lodgings have become very expensive. If they continue to come in these numbers many of them will be forced to camp in the Piazza d'Espagna for want of other quarters. And it's said to be the same in Milan, Florence and Naples.' The *Annual Register* for 1814, preoccupied with high prices and new competition from foreign goods, watched all this very sourly. 'The opening of the long-cherished interior of Europe has produced a vast exportation of English tourists, who, whatever returns they may bring of amusement or instruction, will certainly not improve the balance of trade.' The writer was perhaps one of the few who could afford a wintry grin when the news came that Napoleon had landed near Cannes on March 1st, 1815.

Rogers was at Naples when the news arrived. There were many conjectures: the Queen—Napoleon's sister—was reported to have fainted. Mosbourg, the finance minister, summed up the feeling in Naples in a phrase: 'Un peu d'espoir, et beaucoup de desespoir.' Even when Murat declared for his ex-Emperor and mobilized an army to advance against the Austrians, Rogers did not at once plan to return. All over Europe the English were wondering what would happen, half dubious of the success of the madcap march for Paris, half hopeful that the whole affair would be settled domestically in France. When the Neapolitan army was on the point of marching north Rogers could still listen to a band comfortingly playing 'God save the King' outside the windows of his hotel.

It was not an omen that could be trusted. English tourists

2. Tourists fleeing before Napoleon

3. French excavation: the temple of Jupiter Tonans in 1809 and 1813

began to withdraw from the continent with a mounting sense of urgency. 1803 could come again, the fate of the miserable Forsyth could be repeated. Rogers moved up to Rome. While he was there the Neapolitan troops entered Papal territory and the Pope fled north. Rogers followed. 'The English, like startled hares, are all running upon Genoa,' noted a member of the British garrison there. 'The Pope has left Rome, the Princess of Wales has left Naples, and *hurry-scurry* is the word.' At Florence there were wild rumours and the rumble of refugees passing through in the night under his hotel windows. His friends were not sympathetic. 'I think that a little gentle squeeze from Buonaparte would do Rogers no harm,' Lady Donegal wrote to Moore, 'for he certainly was too partial to him.' And Lord John Russell, who was in Florence at the time, noted in his diary on April 2nd a report that 'the Neapolitans had entered Bologna— great alarm among the English. Rogers off in a hurry, all the horrors of captivity in his face.' When the poet reached Bologna he found the Neapolitans indeed in occupation, but he was protected by Mosbourg, who was with the army. The morning after his arrival he saw wounded in the streets and prisoners being led in from an engagement of the previous night. In spite of Lord John's gibe, he spent the day actively seeing the sights. On the way to Mantua the following morning there were signs of carnage: 'Soldiers on the road, New graves. Fresh earth. Straw spread. Fragments of cloth. Men raking the ground smooth. A house full of bullet-holes.' After Modena he left the area occupied by the Neapolitans and entered Austrian-held territory, but again, at Mantua, no one thought to disturb him as he made a round of the churches. Safely through Austria he was given no option for his route north from Innsbruck by the frontier authorities, and was kept clear of troop movements until Cologne, where he saw the bridge of boats thrown across the Rhine to help the allied army cross into France. At the opera in Amsterdam he heard 'God save the King' again together with national airs of the other allies. There were troops on the road to Antwerp, and work was proceeding on the town's fortifications. Wellington was in Brussels, which was 'full of Gaiety and Warlike Preparations'. The road to Ostend was crowded with English cavalry, and the last entry in the journal, on May 6th, is 'Saw the horses slung from three transports. Cannon balls landed on the shore. Wind NNW'. Waterloo was not fought until the following month, and by that time the continent was almost as desolate of visitors as it had been early in the previous year. The few English who remained in Italy found one cause at least to be grateful. Colonel Finch confided to his journal his relief that thanks to the shortage of foreigners, lodgings in Rome were once again easy to come by.

The lull was only a brief one. As soon as the news of Waterloo was received the tourist trade jumped back into its full stride. There was a tendency, in the first months, for the English to be booed and hissed as they crossed France, but within two years shops and inns were hanging out signs in French and English, bills of fare were produced in both languages, and establishments were quick to point out that there was someone who spoke English on the premises. In Paris there was ill-feeling at first on account of the stripping from the Louvre of foreign works of art, a process grudgingly undertaken largely on the initiative of Wellington. Feelings even among the English were mixed, as the loads of canvas and marble filed back over the Alps and the Rhine. It had all been very wrong, of course, but it had been immensely convenient. Rogers was back in Paris in October, and, Italophile as he was, the spectacle of the great gallery, full only of picture frames and pedestals, was a grievous sight. But to the tourist in Italy, no longer fobbed off with plaster casts and copies, or with Canova's Venus in the place of the Venus de' Medici, the return of the originals was a matter for congratulation.

The number of travellers grew to such an extent that Byron wrote petulantly to Moore from Venice in March, 1817, 'I have not the least idea where I am going, nor what I am to do. I wished to have gone to Rome; but at present it is pestilent with English,—a parcel of staring boobies, who go about gaping and wishing to be at once cheap and magnificent. A man is a fool who travels now in France or Italy, till this tribe of wretches is swept home again. In two or three years the first rush will be over, and the Continent will be roomy and agreeable.' The rush did decline a little after the first two seasons that followed Waterloo, but in the winter of 1818 it was calculated that there were still over two thousand English there at once—one seventeenth of the total population of the city. No-one was forced to camp in the Piazza di Spagna, but the huge travelling carriages, which were too large to get into most Roman stables, were parked there, and the citizens could gauge the number of visitors by inspecting the tarpaulin-covered hulks drawn up at the Babuino end of the Piazza. When Rogers returned to Rome in 1821 he was amazed at the changes he found. His lodgings, for instance, which before the English invasion had been sparely furnished, were now fitted up with carpets and ormolu, and English money had not only led to an increase in the number of performances at the opera, but an improvement in their quality.

It must be remembered that there was a fairly definite seasonal pattern for travel in Italy. The custom was to spend Christmas at Rome, then leave for the milder air of Naples before returning to Rome for Holy Week. The pattern for the north was less rigid and depended on the route by which Italy was entered. If from Switzerland, then Milan and Florence were visited on the way to Rome and Venice on the way back, if from Germany and Austria, then vice versa. This tendency to move in herds—which made each migration a nightmare for couriers trying to find horses for their clients' carriages—meant that probably not more than one third of the English in Italy were roaming about independently, and that a figure of two thousand for Rome meant that there were about three thousand present in the whole peninsula.

Florence was almost as much visited as Rome though less time was spent there. November was the most crowded month. Arriving on the 3rd, in 1819, Lady Lyttelton announced with her usual vivacity that 'we found this town up to the brim with English, and with difficulty found a place to put our heads in. However, we did at last at Shreydorff's [Schneider's, the principal hotel] insinuate ourselves into the still warm dirt of a family who had gone away two hours before.' To cater for visitors there was a reading room that took *The Times* and the *Chronicle*. Reading sauce and Woodstock gloves and the latest novels were available in the shops, and as long as the tourist did nothing out of the ordinary, English was the only language he needed. On the Cascine races were organized on the English model with English horses, and so great was the English taste for reproducing home recreations abroad that a pack of hounds was maintained at Rome, and the author of one of the most pleasant of all Italian travel books described how he saw in Naples 'a regular double-wicket cricket match going on;—Eton against the world;—and the world was beaten in one innings!'

Two years after Byron's prophecy that the rush would die down, his correspondent, Moore, broke passionately into song in the course of a tour of his own:

> *And is there then no earthly place,*
> *Where we can rest, in dream Elysian,*
> *Without some curst, round English face,*
> *Popping up near, to break the vision?*
> *'Mid northern lakes, 'mid southern views,*
> *Unholy cits we're doom'd to meet;*
> *Nor highest Alps nor Apennines*
> *Are sacred from Threadneedle-street!*

At home there were dark hints that the tourists were spending abroad the fortunes secured by the blood and sacrifice of their fellows during the years of war, and were thus acting like traitors. There was even a recrudescence of the centuries-old fear that so much traffic with the Scarlet Woman could spell doom to the traveller's faith. But though the type of traveller changed, as we shall see, and the state of mind in which a tour was embarked on was modified, nothing stopped the flow. And English still outnumbered visitors from other countries. To Italians the word *viaggatore* had become a synonym for *Inglese*. And among those who stayed at home, the appetite for reading the accounts of other people's travels in Italy reached a peak in the twenties, as the post-Waterloo wave registered itself in print. For ten years from 1819 an average of seven travel books on Italy appeared every year.

II. MOTIVES FOR GOING

It would be depressing if the motives that lead people to travel could be entirely explained and categorized. Some whim, or at least some combination of circumstances baffling to the investigator, must determine a fair number of cases—perhaps less then than now, because the time involved was greater, and necessary impedimenta more burdensome, but, even so, a comprehensive explanation would not be a scientific one. Nor are

motives that seem close to modern ones always easy to inter-
pret. Then, as now, the southern sun was greeted with joy.
Rogers' rival Sotheby claimed that he was not likely to forget

> *The transport of that moment, when, at first*
> *Freed from tempestuous Simplon's gloom profound,*
> *And earth in ice-chain bound,*
> *From hail-stones and the frozen gale I burst,*
> *And view'd the purple cluster wreath'd*
> *Round green Dorredo's brow,*
> *And felt, from opening paradise below,*
> *Airs that of Eden breathed.*

But the pleasure of finding a warmer climate, to which this is a
strained and conventional tribute, was not quite our pleasure. It
was not nearly so personal. It did not mean sun bathing and
light clothes: neither was envisaged. The sense that the southern climate bestowed physical refreshment, sensuous enjoyment, is almost never present; the sun and the clear blue sky
are valued rather because in such an atmosphere objects look
especially beautiful. The idea that there was anything lusty and
recuperative about Italy had little appeal to the majority of
visitors; they were sufficiently healthy and wealthy and worldly
not to court another way of life. To explain the first voluntarily
sunburned English female cheek would involve a profound socio-
anthropological study.

In a prose essay on 'Foreign Travel' in *Italy*, Rogers assumed that the overriding motive was pleasure; novel impressions crowding in upon senses quickened by a certain irrespon-
sibility and adventurousness, but he suggested a few categories.
'Ours is a nation of travellers', he pointed out, and added in a
footnote, 'as indeed it always was, contributing those of every
degree, from a *milord* with his suite to him whose only attendant
is his shadow—None want an excuse. If rich, they go to enjoy;
if poor, to retrench; if sick, to recover; if studious, to learn; if
learned, to relax from their studies.'

Many, indeed, come to escape from the high cost of living at
home. A precarious income at home would provide a house and
servants in Florence with a carriage and a box at the opera.
Health, too, was a motive that brought invalids to Pisa and—
outside the malarial hot months—to Rome, as it brought Keats.

Far more important from the point of view of numbers, however, was the lure of fashion. There was no rival to the fashion-
ableness of Italy in the winter. 'The English everywhere,' wrote
an American in 1818, 'and in all great collections, formed a sub-
stantial part of society in Rome during the whole winter. . . . I
went to the Duchess of Devonshire's *conversazioni*, as to a great
exchange, to see who is in Rome, and to meet what is called the
world.' The members of that world did very much the same
thing in very much the same manner. A morning's sightseeing
after a late breakfast, dinner in the afternoon with some English
family or at the *table d'hôte* of the hotel, a reception in the evening at one of the great Roman families who kept open house for
the visiting English of substance. And after the move to Naples
the same pattern reasserted itself. An excursion until about
three, dinner with English friends, then the opera or one of the
casual assemblies typical of Italian society, where the English
visitor was one of so many that he was announced not by name
but simply as a 'Cavaliere Inglese', as was Rogers at the
Princess Massima's in Rome.

An interest in art was expected of the rich, and was usually
found there, even if it was only informed among the studious. In
1814 and 1815 there was the disadvantage, already mentioned,
that many of the most famous works were absent in Paris and
replaced by casts or substitutes. But most of the travellers had
seen them on their way through Paris, and the gaps were perhaps not very much more infuriating than those labelled 'in
restauro' or 'alla mostra di —' today; in any case, though there
was much comment there was little complaint. For the collector,
the years after the war years had an especial interest. Thanks
to the financial straits in which many Italian families and
religious houses found themselves, large numbers of works were
on the market. 'Why do collectors buy in England', asked
Finch, who had seen early Florentine panels adorning his tailor's
shop, 'doubtful works from dubious dealers, whereas here their
genuineness is indisputable, as many of them were painted for
the families to which they belong, whose degenerated descen-
dants are very ready to part with them for handsome sums.'
Rogers saw fragments from the Borghese collection for sale in
the street. And newly-discovered works were coming to light all
the time. 'What an inexhaustible mine is Rome!' he comments

on seeing 'a bushel of bronze collected yesterday from the farms & cottages hard by. A bull, a sheep, a dolphin, a key, the bracelet of a gladiator, an adder's head with silver eyes, many human figures, &c &c.'

Perhaps the outstanding interest for scholarly visitors was the changed aspect of ancient Rome. Thanks to the strenuous excavations of the French between 1810 and 1814, the city, formerly sunk in debris to the shoulders, was now cleared to the waist. In 1802 Forsyth had complained that the proportions of certain classical buildings were difficult to grasp in their half buried state, and faced with the ruinous and neglected condition of the Coliseum, he had prophesied that a generation not very remote would have to be content with pictures of it. But in fact, the postwar generation saw more of the original Rome than their ancestors had ever seen. The Coliseum, especially, was cleaned and strengthened. It was freed from the great mound of earth and refuse that had piled up against its north side, the arena was dug out, the corridors and vomitories were scoured and opened. Post-war guide books continued to include engravings of the Forum based on Piranesi, but they no longer reproduced what the eye saw. The Temples of Jupiter Tonans and Jupiter Stator, of Concord and of Peace, and of Antoninus and Faustina were dug out to their bases, and parts of the Sacred Way itself were revealed between cliffs of earth and debris some thirty feet high. Later buildings that surrounded the Arch of Titus and the Pillar of Phocas were demolished. Outside the Forum the changes were fewer, but the round temple of Vesta had been freed from the walls joining its columns together.

Excavations continued under the aegis of the Pope, and one of the favourite recreations of travellers was to watch the galley slaves toiling in pits in the Forum. A number of them were employed by the Duchess of Devonshire, whose antiquarian ventures were looked upon with mixed feelings by the English community. The scene was one of some confusion, for beside the Pope's straightforward excavations—the exposing of the Arch of Septimus, for instance—and the fervent amateurism of the Duchess, the Forum, then known far more popularly as the Campo Vaccino, was living up to its name as a cattle market, and the galley slaves toiling in their chains were watched by a motley crowd including not only their armed overseers and foreign tourists, but cow herds and goat boys. A move in 1817 to stop its use by local farmers was greeted by one tourist with passionate approval. 'Thank Heaven! the stain is removed,' she exclaimed. 'The Roman Forum has been rescued from this infamous degradation.' But in the following year Matthews noted in his journal: 'I was arrested in my way through the Campo Vaccino this morning by an extraordinary sight. There was a large herd of about a hundred pigs, and I arrived just as three men were commencing the work of death. Each had a stiletto in his hand, and they dispatched the whole herd in a few minutes.' The aspect of the place was still strongly dashed with the picturesque; the half uncovered ruins appealed more strongly to the historical sense of visitors than the bleached skeleton lying rigid between the Capitol and the Coliseum today; instead of explanation, which is the province of the learned, there was speculation, which was open to everyone. The Coliseum still made a complex imaginative appeal. About its arena the stations of the Cross still attempted to consecrate the place of cruel sports and martyrs; there was a chapel, and a hermit to show the visitor round. The walls, though renovated, still kept, in a thousand crannies, flowers and shrubs—a botanist counted two hundred and sixty-one different types of plant in 1815—and when Severn climbed up on a ledge to fetch a wallflower for the dying Keats, he noted that 'the eye was doubly charmed with the grandeur of antiquity and the freshness of nature exulting over it'.

The French had made improvements in other parts of Italy. At Tivoli a path had been made down to the Grotto of Neptune, with an inscription saying that it was done in the service of lovers of the arts. The amphitheatre at Verona was cleaned, and in this city, as at Milan, public walks were opened and remained popular places of resort in the evenings. But most dramatic of the changes outside Rome were those at Pompeii. Forsyth had been depressed there, as he was at Rome, by the likelihood that beauties would perish. The guides who showed visitors the wall paintings rubbed the dust off to make them visible, removing no doubt a thumbful of paint in the process, as the librarians of Athos do to this day in demonstrating the richness of their illuminated manuscripts. But after 1806, not only was excavation planned on a large scale, but measures were taken to remove especially vulnerable works and to protect others.

Among other sites, the street of tombs, which so much moved Rogers, was uncovered, and for the first time a comprehensive idea could be formed of the working lives of its inhabitants. In Pompeii as in Rome the tourist of 1814 found more to stimulate his imagination than his predecessors had found. But enough of the town was still buried in lava to remind him that civilization was at the mercy of nature, just as the trees and goats of the Forum reminded him that it was at the mercy of time.

The preoccupation with ancient art far outweighed the interest felt for living artists; but a visit might be paid to the studio of Camuccini, the capital's most fashionable painter, and the work of one man did rival the antique, and furnished an exception: Canova was the most admired, the most famous sculptor in Europe, and in 1814 he was to be seen working in Rome. His studio was on the itinerary of every *cicerone* and guide book, and there the great man could be seen, amid a crowd of assistants and blocks of marble in every stage of preparation, his worsted stockings about his ankles and with a mason's paper cap on his head. Unaffected and welcoming for all his fame, he told Rogers of his early loves and showed him how he kissed his bed every night before getting into it. The Danish sculptor, Thorwaldson, less well known, but already his rival, was also to be seen at work, and it was fashionable to visit his studio in order to compare the work of the two men.

Rogers had met Canova before, in Paris, in 1802, when he was working on a statue of Bonaparte; in 1814 he was made conservator of the Vatican marbles by the Pope whom Napoleon had kidnapped and kept a prisoner. Napoleon, indeed, was looked upon with mixed feelings in Italy. His exactions had been a burden and a humiliation but his defeat had been widely regretted, and the English who had allowed Italy's old and even less considerate masters' return, were greeted at times with hostility. This was least true in Rome. The Pope had gone so far as to ask his officials to drop law suits against them whenever possible. The greatest resentment was felt in Milan, where the English were disliked for allowing the resumption of Austrian rule.

The tourist, for his part, had taken little interest in Italian politics since the decay of Venice in the seventeenth century and was not going to be interested again until the Risorgimento. Men like Byron and Wordsworth who felt strongly about the stifling of freedom in Italy were rare. Yet in 1814 it would be fair to say that political interest ranked as a motive for coming to Italy. Not an interest in constitutions—in what would happen when the Napoleonic iron lung was removed—but an interest in personalities. For in Italy illustrious ex-enemies could be seen holding court or living in comfortable exile, as, for example, the Bonapartes, entertaining the English visitors with ices and music as though the head of the family had not kept Europe in a state of war for over a decade and cost England thousands of lives. Lucien Bonaparte was already known from his residence— following his capture at sea when *en route* for America—in the home counties, but there were other brothers and sisters of the Emperor to be seen; Louis and Pauline in Rome, where Cardinal Fesch, Napoleon's uncle, and his mother also resided, Elise at Naples, wife to king Joachim Murat, lately the Emperor's crack cavalry general. Pauline excited the most interest, though it was mingled with some disapproval. She had posed for a nude statue by Canova, and although she had explained, in palliation of this eccentricity, that there had been a good fire in the room, some of the English chose not to visit Palazzo Borghese when she was in residence. Rogers does not mention her, but Louis and the Cardinal occur in his pages, and he saw much of Lucien, whom he liked, and his family. 'Murat and his Queen were extremely civil to me', he later said of his days in Naples. 'The Queen once talked to me about the *Pleasures of Memory*. I often met Murat when he was on horseback, and he would invariably call out to me, rising in his stirrups, "Hé bien, Monsieur, êtes-vous inspiré aujourdhui?" ' This provoking salute perhaps explains why the king appears in Rogers' journal in such a vivid and satirical light. He is portrayed dancing 'with the balancing air of a Rope dancer—or of a dancing master teaching ease to his scholars', and at court 'richly dressed in a Kemble-habit, such as kings seen on the stage are wont to wear'. But the English were not easily impressed by foreign potentates, and most would have approved the patronizing tone of Rogers' description of his audience with the Pope, and have thought it very proper that 'the sort of hysteric laugh half subdued with which he spoke generally to us, as we were named to him, discovered a modesty and anxiety to please, which were very engaging'.

Tourists arriving in Milan full of admiration for the genius who had planned and executed the superb pass of the Simplon were intrigued by the attempts of the authorities to purge away any reminder of him. Napoleon had constructed a great oval amphitheatre for land and water games; it was joined to a parade ground with a triumphal arch on its northern side, the Porta di Sempione, at the end of the road leading up to the pass. The buildings were conserved, but changes in detail were made. For instance, one of the bas-reliefs designed for the arch showed the Austrians capitulating after Marengo; henceforward they were to be the vanquished French. As all the figures were portrayed in classical armour, the substitution of Napoleon for the unfortunate Mack could be made without the loss of much verisimilitude. A similar problem was solved when a head of Napoleon on the cornice of the Amphitheatre received the addition of a beard, a hood and a wrinkle and became Neptune; Josephine, in a less likely transformation, was given a helmet and became the virgin goddess Minerva. A parallel change was made at the Quirinal. It had been decorated for Napoleon with mythological scenes. Among the changes made when the Pope returned was the painting-out of the bows and arrows in the hands of the little cupids who hovered about the ceilings, and the substitution of the papal keys and mitre.

Not only was the interest taken in the political state of Italy of a superficial nature, but, in comparison with the attitude of eighteenth-century travellers, there was little interest in the customs and habits of the Italians. It was taken for granted that, by and large, the Italians were degenerate, but there was not the same interested speculation as to why they were. The laxity of manners and the grossness of superstition that had been the object of tolerant analysis by many earlier travellers were increasingly condemned on sight. In part this was due to the growing number of middle-class travellers, less easy-going, less worldly-wise than their predecessors, travelling in a different manner and with different aims from the majority of Grand Tourists before the war.

For, as was suggested in the Preface, the years after the war saw the gradual outnumbering of Grand Tourists by travellers who might, though anachronistically, be called Cook's tourists. The visitor to Italy who possessed high birth, wealth, leisure and a knowledge of the country's history and arts was becoming increasingly rare; the middle-class visitor, with a modest purse, restricted time, and either little prior knowledge, or an intense but specialized one, was increasingly common.

The first guide books to appear after Waterloo spoke in the accents of the previous century; they assumed that the traveller would have servants and time at his disposal, they spoke of the grand tour, and in travel books of the same years the word Tour is spelled with a capital. With regard to wealth, however, the effect of the war was felt at once. In December, 1814, Millingen wrote from Rome to say that artists were complaining that the English no longer patronized them, and so were the shop-keepers. 'It seems', he wrote, 'that economy is now *à la mode* in England.' Stendhal introduced into *La Chartreuse de Parme* an English scholar who 'never asked for the smallest trifle without first looking up its price in a guide book, whether it was a turkey, an apple, or a glass of milk'. And with some visitors leisure was as short as money; the tendency was to 'do' sights as quickly as possible. Rogers commented tartly on two English-men at Naples who went to Pæstum and back in a single day; though there had always been travellers who had been bored by churches and art galleries, it is only from the early 1820's that it became a standing joke that the Englishman saw as little of the cities of Italy as the post horses that clattered him through them.

In part this was because many visitors had not had the standard gentleman's education which helped the tourist to find interesting classical associations in Italy—even if it did not ensure a just appreciation of anything of later date. The new travellers found Italy more 'foreign' than the old, and remained more isolated. It was this that Washington Irving had in mind when he wrote—basing it on his own Italian experiences—such a story as the 'Adventures of the Popkins Family'. He describes there a typical English family carriage. 'It is an epitome of England; a little morsel of the old Island rolling about the world. Everything about it compact, snug, finished, and fitting. The wheels turning on patent axles without rattling', and he talks of 'the ruddy faces gaping from the windows' and 'the dickeys loaded with well-dressed servants beef-fed and bluff; looking down from their heights with contempt on all the world around; profoundly ignorant of the country and the people, and devoutly certain that everything not English must be wrong'.

The ignorance of master as well as servant, and the increasing pretension and folly of the ill-educated traveller which reaches its fullest literary expression in Lever's *The Fudge Family Abroad*, was first worked out and developed in novels in the '20's.

A combination of scorn for the Italians, and lack of intelligent interest in the Italian scene, led to an increase in offhand and disrespectful behaviour on the tourist's part. If a story of Stendhal's is to be trusted, the authorities of the Naples museum were forced to shut it before dinner—i.e. 2 p.m.—instead of at four, when the English became so rowdy in their cups that they threatened to damage the statues. In 1820 the Pope had to appeal against the casual use made of St. Peter's as a fashionable promenade, and in 1827 there were complaints that English tourists took sandwiches into churches with them, and scattered ham and chicken bones on the pavement of the Sistine chapel during Lent.

This sort of behaviour could not be expected from one who, like Robert Finch, looked on Rome with the deepest reverence and devotion. In his journal in May, 1815, he declared that 'it seems a kind of foretaste of that pleasure we shall find in another world (if we are found worthy) from an amalgamation of the purest, sublimest, and most just ideas, convey'd to us thro' different channels in this alloy'd scene of virtue and vice, happiness and misery. As then our knowledge will be perfected, so are our classical notions corrected in visiting these interesting scenes'. Finch speaks as a clergyman and a prig, but the tone conveys something of the seriousness of purpose that was one of the best features of the Grand Tour; a desire to learn, and to test knowledge by experience on the spot. It was the mood that led Rogers to try to fit his recollection of the ancient historians to the scenes through which he moved, and that caused Hobhouse to take an interleaved copy of Gibbon's *Nomina Gentesque Italiae* with him on his tour of Italy in 1817.

In the Preliminary Discourse to his work on Italy, Eustace gives his idea as to how the traveller should prepare himself. He should speak Italian before he goes so that time is not wasted in learning it. He should be versed in Italian history. He should know something of medals, and their value to the chronologist. He should have a general knowledge of the principles of architecture, sculpture and painting. The only faculty he should not

train is musical appreciation. Italian music was insidious, effemi-
nate, and beckoned to the most dangerous passions. A taste for
music could lead to dishonourable connections. A young man's
eye should be ready, his tongue fluent, his memory alert, but his
ear should be starved lest it betray the other faculties to cor-
ruption. Eustace, it should be noted, had a vested interest in
giving good advice, as he had travelled in Italy as a tutor, but he
must have realized that this last advice was likely to go un-
heeded. Rogers is no exception in the eagerness with which he
does the fashionable thing and goes to the theatre on arriving
at a new city; English travellers had an inexhaustible appetite
for opera and ballet—those mixed performances which gratified
every taste for sound, spectacle and licence, and which could
indeed lead, as in the case of Fabrizio del Dongo, to such
deplorable acquaintanceships.

Eustace's advice in other respects was closely followed by
great numbers of prospective tourists. Thus prepared, they
approached Italy with emotion, and it was with feelings of awe
and delight that they saw, from the hill south of Baccano, the
cross and dome of St. Peter's. 'Rome was just ready to break
upon my straining sight', recorded one of them. 'I found myself
strangely affected. I grew uneasy and impatient. It seemed even
as if an important epoch in my life were approaching; and I had
a kind of confused and indescribable expectation, which I never
experienced before, and which, perhaps, no earthly object could
ever again excite.' And another wrote of the same place. 'I was
now about to enter that city, the reading of whose history had
beguiled many an hour, and whose greatest citizens, in succession, I had resolved to take as my model. What various feelings
animated me!' One of the most delightful tourists of this period
was Samuel Butler, headmaster of Shrewsbury. An outstanding
and sensitive classical scholar, he had crossed the Simplon in a
fever of expectancy, pining to 'sleep, if my feelings will allow
me, for the first time on Italian ground'. How much greater was
his expectancy when within a score of miles of Rome! At the
famous spot from which St. Peter's could be seen he was filled
with the most painful sensations. He longed to leap from the
carriage and run up the bank by the roadside that would afford
him that incomparable view. Yet he feared the malaria. Its
noxious vapours could kill. He drove on miserably with the

windows tight closed. Dusk fell as they crossed the plain and he could only tell that they were entering the Eternal City by the sudden drumming of the wheels on a different surface. When they stopped it was too dark to do anything but go to bed. But early next morning he climbed the tower on the Capitol, and there the long-hoped-for moment came. 'I could not contemplate from this spot which commands all the monuments of Antient Rome without feeling very strong sensations. In short I could not refrain from an actual gush of tears.'

But such intense feeling was becoming rarer. Intending travellers were assured that Italy could be enjoyed without a classical education. An English lady, confronted with the bust of Cicero— labelled with the Italian form Cicerone—was heard to say that she supposed he was the guide who showed the ancient Romans the way about the capital. The author who recorded this remark, overheard another woman ask for Raphael's 'Transmigration', and certainly the standard of artistic knowledge was declining with that of the classics. This, again, was nothing revolutionary. Rossi, in his play *Il Calzolajo Inglese in Roma*, written late in the eighteenth century, had introduced an English character who, on being asked what he thought of the Coliseum, replied that it was fine, very fine, and would be something really remarkable when it was finished. Psctth, however, was only a shoemaker posing as a Milord, and another version of the story puts it in the mouth of an Italian—the English constantly reproached the natives for ignorance and neglect of their own monuments. Tourists had been bored in galleries before, and had hacked their initials in prominent places, as Rogers, Byron and Hobhouse did on Tasso's cell in Ferrara; Mrs. Eaton was painting a recognizable type in Saunders McMuckleman, the Scots clergyman who, when first confronted with the Venus de Medici, exclaimed 'Gude Lord, why she's stark naked!' But the author of *Continental Adventures* was also the author of a work purporting to be a guide to Italy, and Rome in particular, whose standard of inaccuracy would not have been tolerated a generation previously, let alone allowed to persist into a fifth edition. Before the gates of the Florentine baptistery she brightly explains that 'they were executed by Laurentius Ghiberto, a Florentine, who flourished in the—I am sorry I cannot remember positively what century, but I believe the fourteenth'. Of the oldest gates,

she says that they are 'the work of a native of Pisa, whose name
I have forgotten'. But it would be unfair to make of Butler's
tears a symbol of the Grand Tour that was now passing, or of
Mrs. Eaton's blithe ignorance a symbol of the new tourism, and
thereby imply that one was good and the other bad. The very
tradition of learning that was part of the Grand Tour could
produce a narrow sympathy for the past alone, while the jaunty
independence of the nineteenth-century tourist could lead eventually to an interest in every phase of Italy's history, and a less
stereotyped interest in her arts.

III. GETTING THERE: COACHES AND PASSPORTS

As soon as peace was established in 1814 the channel services
were reopened. There were regular services from Dover to
Calais at a guinea a head, from Brighton to Dieppe and Southampton to Le Havre at two guineas. Packets left for French and
Dutch ports, too, from Margate, Portsmouth and Harwich. The
shortest route was not necessarily the quickest. Though Samuel
Butler reached Calais from Dover in under three hours it was
common for the trip to take twelve. The route Brighton—Dieppe
was supposed to take on an average eight to ten hours, but
Rogers was at sea for thirty and others took even longer. This
was a popular route. A packet left every afternoon after the
arrival of the London coach, but as there was no harbour,
passengers had to be taken on board in a rowing boat, which had
to be paid for, and it was not possible, as at Dover, to load
carriages. Travellers taking their own coaches, therefore, sailed
for the most part from London or Dover. The vehicles were
either taken to pieces and stowed away, or, if the weather was
not too bad, secured on deck. The young Harriett Campbell,
describing in her journal the passage from Dover, wrote 'as we
sailed out the motion became dreadful. The sailors even said so
and I quickly put away all writing implements and shutting
myself up in the carriage resigned myself to all the horrors of my
fate.' By the early 'twenties it was possible to go from London
or Brighton by steam packet. There was some excitement in
travelling by these novelties—Leigh Hunt described one as
'trembling all the way under us, as if its turning body partook of

the fervour of our desire', and some gain in speed—London to Calais in thirteen hours—but also some uncertainty, for in 1824 the Brighton packet blew up.

It was possible to go to Italy direct by sea, but the voyage was a long one, averaging five to six weeks compared with two to four by land, and was not necessarily cheaper than going by land. The cheapest form of coach travel was to go by diligence: the fare from Paris to Turin, for instance, was five pounds, and seats could be reserved. These vast, and by English standards unwieldy vehicles, with seats on top and on the driver's box, and with an enormous basket hung on the back for luggage, seldom went at more than five miles an hour, and were advertised to take as long as fifty-four hours from Calais to Paris, an average of four. The manner in which they were driven, however, with five or six or even seven horses harnessed with rope traces so long that they were allowed to range all over the road, created an atmosphere of danger in which the coach seemed to be going faster than it was. Diligences could cover up to eighty miles in a day, and were run according to fairly reliable timetables. Unfortunately they only traversed the most frequented routes, and in Italy they were few, and, south of Lombardy and the Veneto, none at all. Thus to travel freely, above all in Switzerland and Italy, another method had to be followed.

It was possible, of course, to hire smaller coaches for a sum that included changes of horses. A cabriolet that held four persons cost five guineas between Calais and Paris, for instance, and nineteen from Paris to Lyons. Or the coach alone could be hired, and horses paid for independently. For a journey from Paris to Geneva as little as eight guineas might be asked, but here again, this service was only available on the busiest routes, where the owner of the coaches could be sure of finding a traveller who would hire them for the return journey. The most convenient scheme for the independent traveller was for him to have a carriage of his own. Horses were available at post stations along every road of any size and could be hired for each stage at a regular published tariff. Prices, and the regulations governing the number of horses to be employed, differed from country to country, but the basis of the system was international.

Especially was it pleasant for a family to take their own carriage with its familiar compartments and cubby-holes, and possibly the 'travelling *chaise-percée*, made to fit the well of a carriage' which Miss Starke advised every family to take with them. Two disadvantages were the cost of getting it across the channel—six guineas from Dover—and the import duty of a third of its value payable on entry into France, only two-thirds of which was returnable when the vehicle left the country. It was more common to buy a carriage on arriving in France. The larger inns at the channel ports had a selection of different types which they bought back from returning travellers; a second-hand one could also be bought in Paris. Some preferred to go by diligence to Switzerland and buy a carriage there. They could be obtained very cheaply. Finch bought an old Saxon calèche in Paris for twelve pounds ten, but the gaps in his journal are a telling argument against such a bargain. 'A sad chasm has occurred in my diurnal narrative,' he wrote at Turin, 'owing to a very large and troublesome boil at the end of the spine, brought on by my rubbing against the back of our most in-commodious vehicle.' He was already in great pain on reaching Lyons, and 'I could not stand during the remainder of our route, but was oblig'd to be lifted in and out of the carriage during the remainder of the journey'.

At every few miles on every main road in Europe were post stations where fresh horses were available, though at the peak of the season there were liable to be delays, and there was some competition in overtaking other carriages in order to be sure of horses at the next station—especially the processions that carried the staff and belongings of persons of note. The expenses of travelling post were theoretically calculable in advance from works like the French *État général des postes*, which was revised every year. But in fact, however much guide books tried to work out a foolproof method which the travellers could stick to, there was always the likelihood—and especially in Italy—of local bickering. 'Even with a Tarif', wrote one exasperated traveller, 'it is almost impossible to escape imposition when travelling in Italy; and the constant battling and grumbling of the postilions rob one of half the pleasure which would be enjoyed in passing through this delightful country.' Another uncertain factor was the state of the roads. When they were particularly bad, extra horses had to be hired, and oxen had to be added in Italy to cross the higher reaches of the Apennines. Their drivers waited with them at the beginning of the ascent and the animals were then harnessed in front of the horses by a rope fastened to the end of the shaft.

Travelling post involved a speed akin to that of the diligences, between four and six miles an hour, and it was usual to go from fifty to seventy miles in a day. In Italy another means of travelling existed which was considerably faster and could result over a long journey in an average of seven miles an hour. This was to accompany the official courier with the mails. He had first claim on horses at every post station and travelled all night. The cost was slightly higher than by other modes of public transport, and the service was naturally restricted to a few important routes. The courier only had accommodation for two or three passengers.

The most popular method of travelling in Italy for the tourist who wanted to combine cheapness with freedom, was to go by *vettura*. This involved coming to an arrangement with the owner of a suitable vehicle for a fee which included transport, food and accommodation. The journey was performed with the same horses or mules all the way and thus posting expenses were saved. It was convenient, too, to be saved the conventional chaffering at inns. Travelling in this style need not cost more than fifteen shillings a day, and the only important drawback was its slowness. To save the animals, the rate of progress averaged three miles an hour, and a usual daily stint was thirty-five miles. This involved getting up around dawn, for the driver liked to rest during the mid-day heat, and the plodding pace induced a tendency to doze, and thus to miss objects of interest along the way, which some travellers resented. Finch—who had sold his Saxon bargain—had another complaint. 'The drivers very frequently stop their horses to make them stale,' he wrote of a journey from Carrara to Pisa, 'which is a very long and tedious business, as they will invite the horse to do this by crying ush, ush, for 10 minutes together; and if he is not compliant, they are absolutely indignant.' One of the pleasures of this mode of transport, for the traveller who was not in a hurry, was the opportunity for walking—the more energetic used the *vettura* as hardly more than a moving hold-all. It was a very personal way of travelling. An agreement was entered into fixing the price, the meals the driver was responsible for providing and what they should consist of, the number of days the journey was to take, and—if it were to be a long one—the days of rest and sightseeing that were to be allowed. This was the point, too, at which it could be stipulated that the carriage was not to start too dauntingly early in the morning. The vehicles were of no fixed type, either as to number of wheels or roominess. Some were drawn by a mule, some by a horse, or horses, or by a mule and a horse. Travellers tended either to love or loathe both vehicle and driver by the end of the journey—a journey which, posting, might have taken half the time. A *vettura* took five or six days from Florence to Rome instead of three; three to four from Rome to Naples instead of two.

The long hours spent in the coach gave the travellers of this era ample time to note the scenery and enjoy it. In France Rogers and Sarah 'gathered apples and pears from the barouche-box as we passed', and there was more awareness of the life of the countryside than has been common since, especially in Italy, where the slow movement through the country roads helped to correct the feeling that Italy consisted of city states where the interest was confined within the walls.

There was time also for the traveller to read and prepare himself for what he was going to see at his next destination. In spite of the crabbed attitude of customs officials, it was usual to take a number of books; the popular works on Italy of Eustace and Forsyth, or the older accounts by Addison or Lalande; the works of classical authors, poets and historians, perhaps a phrase book and an up-to-date guide. The connoisseur might take, as Rogers did, a copy of Vasari's lives of the painters, and most took a selection of novels. Hariett Campbell found Miss Edgeworth's new novel *Harrington* so enthralling that while reading it she only spared a glance 'over the surrounding undulated plains waving richness'. 'I think the first day is generally worst,' she wrote at the beginning of her trip to Italy, 'as after a short time one gets accustomed to the rumbling of the carriage. Indeed I often think that very rumbling is a composing sound at least when it is [not] too violent. The noise is sufficient to exclude all others and it is too monotonous to disturb thought.'

But for the thoughtful traveller perhaps the greatest advantage of this slow pace was the sense of expectancy it generated, and which, for a man like Rogers who had looked forward for many years to his first sight of Verona, Venice, Florence, made arrival at these places moments of such keen pleasure that they amply compensated for the jolting, the dust and the delays.

The most provoking delays in travelling were caused by passport and customs regulations. These were especially vexatious in Italy, and especially resented by the English tourist, who was unused to them. 'It is very tormenting to an Englishman', wrote Miss Waldie warmly, 'accustomed to roam at will about his own country without anyone challenging his motives, to have his passport eternally demanded in every varying tone of insolence, and to find himself so frequently taken for an itinerant dealer in contraband goods.'

Passports were not always needed for France, though they were an advantage as a guarantee of the traveller's bona fides in case of trouble with the police or disputes with an inn-keeper. But they had to be procured before leaving for the south. They were obtainable at the British Embassy in Paris, and had to be *visé* by the Ministry of the Interior and the Prefecture. A journey to Milan demanded, in addition, the signatures of the Austrian ambassador and the Swiss and Sardinian ministers. The signatures had to be obtained in person and the whole operation was only by the happiest of accidents performed in a day. Failure to obtain an Austrian signature before approaching the Milanese frontier meant being refused admission, and the infuriated tourist was forced to return over the Simplon to find the Austrian minister in Switzerland. In travelling from the Simplon to Florence via Bologna the traveller was first stopped at Isella where there was a passport check and a customs examination. At Belgirate passports were checked again and marked for the King of Sardinia's dominions which had briefly to be crossed before entering Austrian territory. At Sesto the Austrian customs got to work and on the outskirts of Milan passports were impounded in exchange for a residence permit which had to be handed over in person before the passport could be reclaimed. Then permission had to be obtained to leave Austrian ground. At Piacenza the customs officers of Maria Louisa opened all baggage and examined passports. If baggage was not to be examined in every customs post on the way to Bologna—and they occurred at nearly every posting station—it had to be sealed, for a fee. Thereafter there were examinations on leaving Bologna, on reaching Tuscany at Pietra Mala, and on entering

Florence itself. Innkeepers in Austrian territory had to fill out a form for each visitor giving his name, condition, age, religion, birthplace, passport particulars, purpose of visit, and saying where he came from, with how many others he was travelling, and where he was going to, in what sort of conveyance. All this was no more than exasperating for the tourist, but for the native this was the Italy of the *Chartreuse de Parme*, where a flaw in one's papers could lead to imprisonment or death. Nor was it better in the south. There were dozens of points between Naples and the frontier of the Papal States where carriages could be halted and searched, and before the tourist could leave the city, up to six signatures had to be secured and paid for.

It is in the uninhibited pages of Robert Finch, that admirable *touriste moyen sensuel*, that the most outspoken reaction to officialdom can be found. His first tilt at their impassive Fabianism took place at Messina, in November, 1814. Finch wanted to leave for Naples. He had a passage booked. All he needed was a passport. He applied at the Police Office at 9 a.m. and was told nothing could be done till noon. 'Such is the method of transacting business amongst Barbarians', he noted. At noon he came ashore again and found the Police Office closed. He was told to return at five. 'I proceeded to M. Walsh [the British Consul], who inform'd me that the hour meant must be 3 p.m. as the office shuts at 5. Then even, said he, you may not obtain your passport, but have to wait until tomorrow.' Finch was so upset by this news that he cancelled his passage to Naples and went to Genoa instead. The following April found him wanting to leave Florence for Rome and trapped, once more, by formalities. One morning a verbal message came from the Commissary of Police asking him to call. Finch went round, and found the official out. 'I left for him the following epistle,' he recorded that evening, not without some satisfaction, 'couch'd in terms perhaps not very agreeable to him. "Monsieur . . . permettez moi de vous dire qu'un Anglois, et surtout un Anglois distingué et d'une naissance illustre ne se soumettra jamais au caprice ou à l'insolence d'aucun gouvernment sur la terre. Je suis cité devant vous par un order *verbal*, je le répète, comme un de la canaille, et je vous assure qu'en condescendant à vous remettre une reponse écrite, je fais un compliment au Gouvernment du Grand Duc." ' The letter went

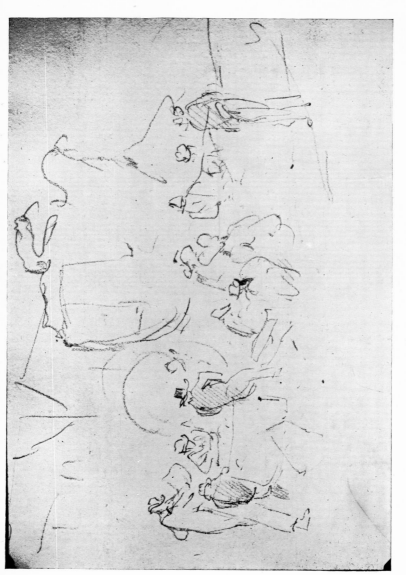

4. Travellers resting by a diligence

Ascended for 4 hours, & at a small stone house had a delicious breakfast of strong coffee, cream, eggs &c. The man, who attended upon us, in a courteous & gentle accent, said he at the top a deep silence — no murmuring, no whistling passed the winter alone, with only of winds — ~~their~~ ~~accustomed~~ foliage — a single attendant. At almost no extensive view — no distant gleam, of inhabit every mile was a strong stone country — a chaos of rock & snowy peaks building inscribed Refuge &c rising, (one behind another — the sky of a or N. Passed the Hospice, a convent blue almost black — no foliage to blow thro', in which are only two monks, for the relief of Travellers. It stands in a little valley & was once of signal use.

Ran down to Semplon, a little town or village, & there changed horses, taking 3 instead of five. Fell suddenly into a deep valley, & now opened or rather

5. A page from Rogers' journal
See page 160

on to say that he would return at three o'clock. But on applying for his passport next day at the British Embassy he met with delays that were no less vexatious, and an apparent disinclination on the part of the secretary there to worry the local authorities on his behalf. This was too much. 'Good God', he stormed, 'What a wretchedly administer'd government is that of England, where such boys and blockheads compose the Corps Diplomatique! Instead of protecting the subjects of Great Britain, instead of assuming a lofty tone with a foreign nation, and backing the complaint of a British subject . . .'—the tone is a familiar one. The aggrieved outcry against a not very efficient state, worried about its own concerns on the eve of what promised to be another European war, and puzzled by an Englishman who wanted to go south at a time when all the others were jostling to go north—this is the seamy side of the Anglo-Italian tradition: damn your war, I want to see your ruins. It rings more immediately in modern ears than the rattle and jar of the carriage wheels that were soon bearing Finch, pompous and culture-hungry, to Rome.

IV. THE ITINERARY

The majority of visitors to Italy went for a stay of some months, and avoided the summer. It was usual to leave in September and to return to England in the early summer of the following year. The London season did not call imperatively during the winter months, that of Rome increasingly did.

Italy was also considered to be dangerous in the hot months, and there was some truth in this. Talking of the effects of the *mal aria* Forsyth warned that 'last autumn four thousand persons died victim to it in the Roman hospitals. It is a battle renewed every spring, and lost every fall.' The danger was especially great in the vicinity of Rome. 'The land there', wrote Miss Starke, taking up the warning, 'is ill-cultivated, and worse drained, so that fogs and igneous vapours prevail during night; it likewise abounds with sulphur, arsenic, and vitriol.' It was thought dangerous to remain in Rome from the third week of July, and if residence then was absolutely necessary, the visitor should remain as much as possible indoors, or safely within his carriage. Other advice included the warning to travellers forced to spend a night in the open that they should avoid the dense shade of trees, or, on the other hand, the direct rays of the moon. The fears of tourists were, no doubt, exaggerated; Samuel Butler would probably have been quite safe with his carriage windows open, but the authorities themselves emphasized that there was real danger from the beginning of the hot season to the first rains of autumn. 'Tertiary and pernicious fevers attack almost all those who are so imprudent as to pass even a single night exposed to their malign influences.'

The main modification of the conventional itineraries of the Grand Tour within Italy was effected by the building of the Simplon Pass. After 1814 this replaced the Mt. Cenis as the most popular route by which to enter Italy. The guide books extolled the ease and swiftness with which it could be crossed. The scenery was known to be of an impressive grandeur, while the pass had the glamour of having been conceived by Napoleon. This led more travellers to stay in Milan, and the town was, in any case, more attractive to visitors owing to the improvement of its amenities by the French. As the Mt. Cenis was used less, fewer tourists went to Turin, though the small circuit—Simplon—Lake Como—Milan—Turin—Mt. Cenis was popular with those who had little time to spend in Italy. Venice had been declining in popularity throughout the preceding century, and though it was still visited as a marvellous curiosity, few English stayed there for more than a few days. Florence, Rome and Naples were the cities which detained them most. Society in Venice was felt to be less brilliant than elsewhere, and the atmosphere of decay which hung about her buildings and her constitution alike—for at last Venice had lost her long-vaunted freedom—was found depressing. The visitor was less intrigued by the glorious than by the sinister aspect of the city's past. Rogers' morbid preoccupation with the machinery of state justice and its instruments, the *pozzi* and the *piombi*, where the captive lingered damply below the level of the canal, or stifled under the leads of the ducal palace, was characteristic. But his partiality for the atmosphere of the romantic gothic novel and his pleasure in the literary associations of Venice led him to take rather more pleasure in the place than was usual.

Rogers' own outward itinerary was a usual one. Milan— Verona—Padua—Venice—Bologna—Florence—Rome — Naples. The news of Napoleon's landing affected his return journey, though to leave, as he did, by the Brenner was a common practice after entering by the Simplon. Some tourists preferred to reserve Venice for the return journey. In order to secure accommodation in Rome, and taste a few of the pleasures of the Season before the festivities of Christmas, the tourist generally quitted Florence in late October or November for Rome. The journey made a strong impression, partly from the squalor of the inns, partly from the striking change on entering Papal territory south of Radicofani, the country appearing deserted, scarcely cultivated and poverty-stricken. Many a moral was struck off to this theme. The grim plains, with their few dwellings and occasional stunted trees, the oppressive silence and the exhibition of robbers' legs and arms hanging from gibbets by the roadside, these contrasts with the richness of classical times, together with the danger of malaria, produced a powerful effect on the traveller's imagination.

> *Groves, temples, palaces,* wrote Rogers,
> *Swept from the sight; and nothing visible,*
> *Amid the sulphurous vapours that exhale*
> *As from a land accurst, save here and there*
> *An empty tomb, a fragment like the limb*
> *Of some dismembered giant.*

This desolation helped to underline the excitement felt at first beholding Rome; though a few travellers, like Finch, thought the view of St. Peter's inferior to that of St. Paul's.

'Naples', wrote Lady Morgan in a sympathetic passage, 'is the ordinary termination of a stranger's pilgrimage to Italy. The memory—overloaded by the numerous remembrances committed to its keeping—the mind exhausted by the reiterated calls made on its perceptions—novelty exhausted, curiosity blunted, all dispose even the most ardent traveller to a repose, whose indulgence has become both morally and physically necessary. More churches to visit, more palaces to see, more monuments to study, would become a duty, and cease to be an amusement; and it is a relief, rather than a disappointment, to learn that Naples contains few of any of those objects worthy to arrest that attention on which Florence and Rome have already so deeply drawn.' But though the city itself was less demanding, there were many classical excursions to be made. At least one visit would have to be made to Herculaneum and Pompeii, and no-one of spirit would willingly have forgone the ascent of Vesuvius.

After the eruption of 1794, which overwhelmed the village of Torre del Greco, the volcano for some years was thought to be exhausted. In 1814, however, it erupted again through a new crater, and until the next major eruption of 1822 was constantly in some sort of activity. When Rogers climbed the volcano it was throwing up lumps of blazing matter, and watching the crater was a dangerous and an awe-inspiring business. The climb was well organized. The tourist went on horseback up the first stretch, then was hauled by guides up the steep cindery slopes above—either by a sash round the waist or by hanging on to a sort of harness round the guides' shoulders. Near the summit was a hut where a hermit lived who could supply some simple food and drink, and there was a book for visitors to sign. The ascent was not without its hazards. The gases issuing from crevices near the crater had the effect of turning ladies' hair embarrassingly straight, and there were a number of casualties from falling debris.

Naples was as far south as most tourists got. Some made an excursion to the temples of Pæstum, as Rogers did, but hardly any carried on into Calabria. Nor was Sicily much visited. The accommodation was primitive, transport poor; the common conveyance was a sort of litter balanced between two mules. Prices were high and the society of Palermo and Messina had little to attract the English. At parties, Finch noted, the ladies 'not only cram to excess, but likewise fill their pockets and their ridicules'.

Rogers wrote of the kingdom of Naples that it was

> *a land*
> *Where laws are trampled on and lawless men*
> *Walk in the sun,*

and not only there but in many parts of Italy there was danger to be anticipated from bandits. It is hardly possible to talk of itineraries without mentioning them. They kept visitors out of some regions and forced them in other places to change their routes. Everywhere they had the effect of discouraging exploration, and preserving the stereotyped patterns suggested by the main roads, where not only lodgings but some degree of protection was available. In 1814 the tales of violence that filtered up from Italy persuaded some tourists to stay north of the Alps. Pistols were considered normal equipment. Rogers was not attacked, but everywhere there were reminders of less fortunate travellers. Entering Tuscany he was escorted by cavalry in long white cloaks and white helmets, past the spot where the mail had been robbed the week before. Towards Rome the *vetturini* bunched together for protection at nightfall. South of Rome he took more guards and again on the way back to Florence.

The great preserve of brigandage was the south. It was on happenings south of Rome that Irving based his stories of 'The Italian Banditti' in his *Tales of a Traveller* (1824). But their activities were not confined to the south. The mail and private travellers were robbed in Austrian dominions and in Tuscany. Finch, at Siena, complains that 'it is extremely disagreeable to be annoy'd by the constant expectation of meeting with Brigands and to travel with a vigilant eye, and one's pistols constantly cocked'. The road between Rome and Florence was so infested with brigands at one period in 1817 that travellers took the Adriatic road north instead.

Even the pleasure trip from Rome to Tivoli was not without its darker side. 'In different places by the side of the road', recorded a tourist, 'are exposed the detached limbs of malefactors, suspended on posts, a practice which has not produced the effect of preventing robberies on the road near Tivoli.' And Moore, after retailing stories of ears being cut off by the robbers in those parts, asked 'who can enjoy such a party of pleasure as we had today, armed as we were with pistols, daggers, sword-canes, etc., etc?' At times tourists were almost besieged in Rome, unable to make expeditions to Casinate, Subiaco, or Poli. Those who persisted were given two pieces of advice: it was best to leave as soon as the news of a murder was received, as the police might have been startled into momentary efficiency, and it was better not to offer the slightest resistance to the bandits, once in their hands. Nor was rumour the only evidence of the existence of bandits. In 1818 a large band of them was to be seen in the Castel S. Angelo. They had taken advantage of the rewards offered to give themselves up, and so weak was the government that the cash had apparently been converted into a specially light prison sentence. While the men chatted to visitors, their wives and daughters earned a living by posing to artists in the city.

In 1802 conditions on the roads from Rome to Naples were so bad that it was difficult to obtain postillions, and many of them were ex-convicts, who were forbidden to crack their whips or blow their horns lest this should be a signal to possible accomplices. The French improved matters, but they were far from cured when tourists once more arrived. Troops were stationed at short intervals along the way, and carriages were sometimes made to take soldiers on the box. Crimes did not cease. In January 1817 a traveller noted that as a result of the posting of guards, the road could be regarded as perfectly free from danger. And indeed, he met with no excitement on the way to Naples. *En route* for Pæstum, however, he was 'suddenly appalled at finding on the road, in a lonely wood, a recently murdered corpse'. And shortly after, on the main road, another traveller came upon a similar scene. 'We were on our way north from Naples,' wrote Henry Sass, 'when we beheld a sight shocking to humanity, and disgraceful to the government in whose territory it occurred. Strewed in our path, and stretched in the arms of death, lay a traveller, the victim of assassination. His horse, likewise, lay dead at his side.'

Fear of bandits was only one factor that kept travellers to the high roads connecting Milan, Venice, Florence, Rome and Naples. The by-ways had to wait not only for physical improvements—better roads, better inns, railways—but a broadening of taste, in particular a deeper interest in the middle ages. Towns like Verona and Viterbo were visited because they were on main roads, but little interest was shown in the latter save as a posting station, and Verona was remarkable for the Roman amphitheatre and the literary associations of Romeo and Juliet rather than for the possession of churches like S. Zeno. The popularity of Ravenna, Perugia, Assisi, Orvieto, San Gimignano and other towns that depended for their main appeal on medieval monuments had to wait until the traveller's taste was ready to seek them out. For the average informed tourist this depended—among less tangible factors—on the writings of men like Lord Lindsay, Ruskin, Augustus Hare and John Addington Symonds, and was a process that was only fully worked out towards the end of the century.

For the years after 1814, however, the standard routes gave deep satisfaction. 'A journey in Italy', wrote an American, Matthias Bruen, 'may be compared not unaptly with the course of human life. The plains of Lombardy, and the vale of Arno, are rich, and smooth, and beautiful as youth; we come to Rome for the sights, and experience, and reflections, which suit manhood; we return after the bustle of life to the comforts congenial to age and which are provided in sunshine, and air, and the bounties of nature, as we find them at Naples; and we at last behold Pæstum, as the soberest evening scene, which shuts up our wearisome pilgrimage, and ends our toil.'

V. BOARD AND LODGING

A tribute to the high proportion of English visitors was the number of inns and hotels which tried to make them feel at home. At Brig, the last stage before the Simplon was tackled, an *Hôtel d'Angleterre* was built to deal with the increased traffic since Waterloo, and similar names beckoned in every important town in Italy. At Milan there was the *Gran Brettagna*, and Geneva had a hotel of the same name. At Verona there was the *Torre di Londra*, at Vicenza the *Regina di Inghilterra*, and Venice had a *Regina di Inghilterra*, as well as a *Caffè di Londra*. In Naples there was another *Gran Brettagna*, and a *Villa di Londra* and the *Isole Britanniche*. Rome was full of familiar signs: *Villa di Londra, Pensione di Londra, Albergo di Londra, Albergo allo Isole Britanniche, Albergo di Inghilterra*, and in Piazza di Spagna the *Caffè Inglese* was more popular with the English even than the *Caffè Greco*, though tea was available here and a room was reserved for Englishmen. Other big hotels, like *Schneider's* in Florence, were known to cater especially for the wealthy English traveller. There was even a rest station near the summit of Etna known as the *Casa degli Inglesi*.

There was a sharp contrast between the comfort obtainable in big towns, and on the roads that led to them. Rogers remarked of France that 'there is still wanting a middle class to command into an inn the comforts and elegancies of life'. The poor traveller fended for himself and slept where he could, the aristocrat journeyed from one château to another and had no need of an inn. It was the same in Italy. Even on the main roads there was nothing to compare with the steady, year-long traffic that made inns a good business proposition in England. A traveller might go from Florence to Rome in six days and meet, as Hazlitt did, fewer than ten carriages. There was a constant burden of complaint about the inns on this route. Milk and butter were almost unobtainable, candles were a luxury, the rooms without fires. The regular processions of tourists were too seasonal to make much difference. Rogers reported on his second trip in 1821 that the inns were no better, 'not a jot'.

If a stay of some length in a town was intended, it was customary to go straight to a hotel, and then, with this as a base, to look for lodgings. The area of search in Rome centred on the Piazza di Spagna, which was practically a British preserve. The *Inglesi* in its cant name *Ghetto degli Inglesi* meant foreigners rather than English, but in fact all other nationalities were greatly outnumbered. The approach from the north led straight to it—through the Piazza del Popolo and down the via Babuino. Henry Matthews, describing his entrance into Rome, wrote 'We were soon in the Piazza di Spagna—the focus of fashion, and the general resort of the English. Some travellers have compared it to Grosvenor-square;—but the Piazza di Spagna is little more than an irregular open space, a little less nasty than the other piazzas in Rome, because the habits of the people are in some measure restrained by the presence of the English.' The other squares were nasty because there were not enough English there to undermine the lower orders' practice of relieving themselves in public places. When seeing the sights, Finch observed, 'a snuff box, or a scented handkerchief, is no inconvenient passport, as one's nose is unremittingly assailed by a most overpowering essence of combin'd stinks.' The Piazza di Spagna was unpaved, and its surface was uneven. Early in the morning flocks of goats were led round it, stopping from door to door. Cows were also available, if their milk was preferred.

This lack of sophistication did not make the Piazza less fashionable or popular. Number 26, which now houses the Keats-Shelley Museum, was only one of many houses which had a regular complement of English lodgers. No. 26 had the special advantage, however, of being run by a niece of Vasi, whose guide books were very widely used. He sold them, together with prints of Rome, at a shop just off the Piazza up the via

Babuino, and recommended his niece to purchasers who were looking for rooms. Of the travellers mentioned in these pages, both Mayne and Finch stayed there. When Keats came to the house he found an Englishman living above and an Irishman on the floor below.

Mayne paid seven pounds six shillings a month for the six rooms at No. 26, and this included a servant's wages. The price was reasonable for comfortable lodgings in a fashionable district. Matthews and his companion, three years later, paid fifteen pounds a month between them for their rooms at Rome, which consisted of two sitting rooms, three bedrooms, a kitchen and a room for the servant. In Naples their lodgings were cheaper, eight pounds between them, and Matthews thought this a representative price. In Florence a small family could rent a comfortable furnished apartment for seven pounds a month, and could find accommodation of a sort for as little as from two to four—including silver and linen, and the washing of the linen. Lodgings in Venice were even cheaper because there was less demand for them. What Coxe's guide book of 1815 described as a 'genteel appartment and dinner' cost from four to five shillings a day. He calculated that a single man could live in comfort, with a servant and a gondola, for one hundred and fifty pounds a year.

Yearly rents differed greatly, of course. Finch had a friend who paid thirty pounds a year for a house in Genoa, and Leigh Hunt, in 1822, paid under twenty pounds a year for a house with forty rooms, marble staircases and 'a marble terrace over the portico'. This was at Albano, just outside Genoa, where prices were exceptionally low. 'The living here is extremely cheap', he wrote exultantly. 'What do you think of the finest grapes, exactly a halfpenny a pound? What of eleven of the finest peaches for three half-pence? Thirty or forty apricots are to be had for three farthings;—they are three halfpence a gallon. Half-pint glass tumblers, that would cost in England one shilling and sixpence a piece, one a penny halfpenny. Twelve eggs are fourpence halfpenny; beef and veal, both excellent, threepence and fourpence a pound; sixteen fresh figs are three farthings; three quarts of oil two shillings and ninepence; and a quart of the best native wine, extremely pleasant and wholesome, about threepence halfpenny.'

Prices in Florence were higher, but it was possible to live there in luxury for the price of a merely comfortable existence in England. The Campbells came in 1817 to retrench, and Harriett noted down their expenses. 'The house though in itself dirty and ill furnished is large and commodious and the hire of it moderate. It comes to about two hundred a year. A carriage and horses 25 Sechinis a month which is about 13 guineas and a half, and a box at the Opera going three times a week which mamma hires with the Miss Berries who are just come from Genoa cost all together 14 guineas for 3 months. Now these are cheap luxuries when compared to what they cost in England and it is certainly a great pleasure to be able to indulge in them. There is a cook who comes here every day to make our dinner etc., etc., he furnishes every thing in order to avoid the trouble of having all the different tradespeople to fight with. He asks 16 franks a day to feed the whole family. This comes to about 18 pence English a head and certainly nothing could be cheaper. This is the manner in which all the English manage their eating as being the most economical and the least troublesome. The lacquais de place who sleeps in the house but normally feeds at home gets 4 Paoli a day which in English money is 1 shilling and 10 pence.'

Hotel charges were cheap by English standards. Prices were higher in small towns, where visitors were unusual. 'The Land-lord of the paltry Inn at Novara demanded four francs (3/4d) for my bed, but I paid him only two', wrote Finch in March 1815. 'At these paltry towns one is more likely to be impos'd upon than in the great cities.' A certain amount of bargaining was expected at all except the largest hotels. Rooms were cheaper than meals, the average price at the equivalent of a modern two star hotel in a large city being two shillings for a single room. Matthews, who travelled without stinting himself, paid six shillings a day at Venice for an excellent room, and a good breakfast and dinner. At Milan it cost him seven and six. The most expensive hotel he stayed at was Schneider's in Florence. Here, bed, breakfast and dinner cost ten shillings. 'For this, you have a good room, an excellent dinner of two courses, with a desert, and as much of the wine of the country as you like. . . . Mould candles are also thrown into the bargain;— if you burn wax candles you pay for them, and an extra charge is made for fire. The dinner alone (in England) would cost more than the whole daily expenditure.' At the *Hotel of the Four Nations*, in the same city, the cost was under four shillings a day.

Food in Florence was cheaper than in other large cities. A good meal at a traiteur, i.e. a restaurant, cost about two shillings, including wine. Elsewhere an average price for a satisfactory dinner ranged from three to five shillings. Prices in Naples and Venice were slightly higher than elsewhere. The architect Joseph Woods, however, noted that in Naples if you were content to order a fixed dinner, and not *à la carte*, 'you may have an excellent one for six carlines [2/–], or, if you wish to be luxurious, for ten [3/4d], when you will have eight dishes, besides various little things to excite the appetite, fruit and wine of a better quality than that commonly drunk.' The prices of wines varied. In Rome, for instance, while Orvieto cost elevenpence a bottle, Velletri was sevenpence for two quarts.

Imported goods were expensive—English windsor soap cost one and three a piece—but if the traveller was prepared to buy Italian products he could do very well indeed. The best shoes were made for five shillings a pair, for instance, and the finest gloves cost tenpence. Theatres were reasonable. A box at La Scala was five and tenpence, a seat at the San Carlo two and sixpence, or four shillings on a gala night. Lesser houses charged a shilling or less. The hire of a coach for a day was between five and ten shillings. James Galiffe gives the prices of some excursions he took from Naples. To go to Portici cost a pound, and a trip to Pompeii cost the same, including tips and the hire of the carriage. An excursion to the Grotto del Cane cost seven and sixpence, and this included 'the experiment of the dog' which involved holding a dog in the gases exhaling from the Grotto until it became unconscious. A tourist in Italy who lived in comfort, ate well, had a servant, employed a guide and was actively engaged in sightseeing, might find himself spending something like a guinea a day. The best and commonest way of obtaining money for these expenses was by means of travellers' cheques—circular exchange notes, payable at sight—which could be obtained before leaving England from Harries, Farquhar, and Co. of St. James' Street, or from Hammersley and Co., Pall-Mall, or, if a long stay in one particular place was anticipated, letters of credit were useful, as these amounted to an

introduction, while an account at the Duke of Bracciano's bank
was a passport to the best society in Rome.

English tourists were stubbornly believed to be extremely
rich, and prices were adapted accordingly. They were expected
to pay considerably more than Italians for the same things. The
fervour with which Mayne had fought against overcharging
right across France and Switzerland had abated by the time he
arrived in Italy. Resigned to the inevitable through sheer
exhaustion, he noted that 'at Velletri our entertainment was in
all respects as good as we could have desired; but we Englishmen, were charged ten pauls (5/–), while our Italian friends paid
but seven. We thought this difference so reasonable (it usually
being the double or treble) that we paid it without a murmur.'

The main business of the tourist, sight-seeing, was catered
for fairly well. The Uffizi was open every day except Sundays
and holy days, though on Saturdays it shut early, at eleven-
thirty. A disadvantage was the constant vigilance of the attendants. Visitors were not allowed to wander as they pleased, but
each room as it was entered was locked, and then they had to
move on in a group to the next room, while the last was locked
behind them. But the attendants were courteous and were not
allowed to take tips. Forsyth had complained bitterly of the tips
extorted at Rome. 'Entrance-fees are a serious expense to the
curious at Rome. You pay for admission to the Pope, to the
cardinals, and to all the other antiquities[!]. Your first and your
last call on a private friend cost you a testone [a reference to the
custom of tipping domestics when making the first and last of a
series of calls on their master].' Small churches were generally
closed, and it was advisable to send to the sacristan a day in
advance, but the larger ones were open. Finch was not so easily
satisfied. 'I paid a very early visit to the Cathedral,' he wrote in
Milan, 'but it is in vain to attempt to work tranquilly and
leisurely in it, since they are always celebrating masses, or
chaunting psalms.' A stern judgment from a tourist in holy
orders! He had trouble with secular edifices, too. Palaces and
Villas that contained collections, or individual works of art of
some fame, were usually opened to visitors who had written
beforehand to ask permission; in Isola Bella the family of Prince
Borromeo carried on their billiards and their piano playing
while visitors were led through the rooms. However, when the

Duke di Sora is addressed by Finch asking permission to look over the Villa Ludovisi, 'he returns answer that he never receives letters from persons who are unknown to him. This is a very curious anecdote, and the ignorance and brutality of a Roman noble in the eighteenth [sic] century is scarcely creditable. I fancy I should have receiv'd no such reply from Cicero, Hortensius, or Atticus.'

The Vatican and the collections of the Capitol were open to the public on Thursdays and Sundays only, but small parties could be shown round on application at any time. A particular attraction was a torchlight tour of the Vatican sculptures. Bundles of candles were moved about among them, so that here the Egyptian sphinxes seemed to move mysteriously in the shadows, here Apollo appeared on the point of striding forward from the sun. For galleries and ruins alike there were plenty of guides available, the most expensive of whom preferred to call themselves antiquarians. And to supplement or to supplant them a wealth of guide books was available, for all Italy and for individual cities, though the great majority of these were in Italian or French. Vasi, who published an English edition of his Roman guide, was the oracle of the British tourist, and morning by morning, with a sketching pad, a note book and a Vasi, the visitor climbed into his carriage and rattled off to fill in the seven hour gap between breakfast and the first solid meal of the day.

VI. THE ENGLISH ATTITUDE TO ITALY

The taste represented by the guide books was intensely conservative. Nearly all of them were written generations previously and merely vamped up to supply the sudden demand after 1814. They enshrined the opinions of the mid-eighteenth century, and drew attention to the works most valued then. Apart from Michelangelo and the late Raphael, the heroes of the guide books were Titian, Guido, Domenichino, Guercino and the Caracci. And on the whole these were the heroes of the tourists who read them. 'Whenever I think of paintings,' wrote Galiffe, 'the name of *Guido Reni* is the first that occurs to me.' Taste had been static for so long that there was little interest in re-valuing the work of an artist, whether famous or obscure, just as the traveller had little interest in 'discovering' neglected monuments, or out-of-the-way towns. The works of the most famous masters were familiar in reproduction, and to the traveller who had prepared carefully for what he was going to see, the greatest pleasure lay not in coming upon the unexpected, but in a measured reaction to the familiar. Preparation, in fact, led to a ready acceptance of the old views. Lack of it, coupled with confidence in one's own taste, could lead to surprised, perhaps defiant revaluations. Faced by Michelangelo's Virgin and Child in the Uffizi, Mrs. Jameson declared that 'if all the connoisseurs in the world, with Vasari at their head, were to harangue for an hour together on the merits of this picture, I might submit in silence, for I am no connoisseur; but that it is a disagreeable and hateful picture, is an opinion which fire could not melt out of me.' She could not like 'a Virgin, whose brick-dust coloured face, harsh unfeminine features, and muscular arms, give me the idea of a washer woman'. Hazlitt, with a streak of Smollett's cussedness, and a journalist's shrewd investment in the unconventional, said of the same artist's David that it was 'as though a large mass of solid marble fell upon one's head, to crush one's faith in great names. It looks like an awkward overgrown actor at one of our minor theatres, without his clothes; the head is too big for the body, and it has a helpless expression of distress.' Such examples of independence are rare. The great majority of tourists found their time fully occupied in verifying impressions of the works they had learned to consider great during the long years of exile from Italy.

The greater part of the pleasure of the whole tour, in fact, consisted not in discovery, but in recognition. So much had been written about Italy, its landscape, its towns, its monuments, and so much of it was known from the works of painters like Claude, Panini and Salvator Rosa, that the country was familiar even to those who had not yet visited it. The actual place sometimes disappointed. The ruins of Rome were less spacious, and less strewn with picturesque objects than the engravers suggested. Actual works sometimes had little more pleasure to give. Of the Medicean Venus Moore complained that 'the form was so familiar to my eye, that I cannot say I was much struck with it. I mean I was not critic enough to discover the difference between the original and the copies, so as to give any new elevation to my mind at the sight of it. . . . Titian's Venuses, perhaps for the same reason, did not much inspire me; they had become hackneyed to me by copies; I knew every bit of them by heart.'

Careful preparation for the tour helped to dull the eye in another way: by emphasizing the memory. In a note to *Italy* Rogers wrote that 'it has been observed that in Italy the memory sees more than the eye'. Every stone, every road had its historical association. A scene could not be fully appreciated unless the memory peopled it with illustrious shades. Buildings only gave adequate satisfaction if the voices of their ancient inhabitants could still be heard. Matthews comforted himself for missing Pæstum with the reflection that 'however fine the ruins may be, there is no story of the olden time to make them particularly interesting'. From such a viewpoint nothing was seen for its own sake; the burden of appreciation fell more heavily on the memory than upon the eye; between the actual object and the watcher hung a gauze of association, painted with figures and words. The obstinacy with which associations lingered about Italian scenes caused an American visitor to break out indignantly: 'Surely, I have frequently exclaimed to myself, these woods, hills and streams, which I now behold with feelings that overpower me, yield in beauty and sublimity, to our transatlantick scenery. From what cause, then, do they derive their extraordinary influence over the imagination?—From their connexion with some of the most eventful periods of time.'

In the same way that an Italian scene could not be taken for granted by those who peopled it with associations, it was not looked at for its own sake by those who expected a good view to concede something to the intellectual canons of the Picturesque. The generation of Gilpin and Uvedale Price—both friends of Rogers—had an eye for the correct in landscape as well as in painting; they were tempted to see and to appreciate Nature in terms of art. This attitude was guyed by Lord Normanby in his novel *Matilda*, which deals with the adventures of English families abroad. The Rev. Mr. Tynte, the great connoisseur, is described in these terms by one of the female characters: 'With him art is not second nature, but nature second art. The finest view would be to him uninteresting, unless it would make a good composition. I question whether he could not see, even you [the heroine] without admiration, unless fortunately you reminded him of some famous Guido, or well-known Titian.'

Such landscape fanciers had their own jargon. Nature's tactless waste of her own materials could be corrected if the spectator placed himself whence the best *coup d'œil* could be obtained. Hills of a certain painterly quality were no longer hills, but *collines*. Countryside was not merely sombre, it was *triste*, not merely graceful but *riant*. When one of the families in *Matilda* see the Alps for the first time, their courier says 'See one grand view, *Serr*; those are des montagnes très affreuses—de mountains ver much frightened; and là-bas, un pays très-riant—a countrie which is ver laughable.' To Finch, landscape fell clearly into one category or another, with recognized transitional stages. The Jura 'exhibited striking examples of the soft picturesque'; after the 'horrific defile' of the Echelles de Savoy the country contained 'a great deal of romantic and less terrific scenery'. Waterfalls were not always praiseworthy, but along the Mt. Cenis 'cataracts every where tumble in the most elegant forms'. Samuel Butler, in the same manner, reprimanded the Jura, because their summits 'were not sufficiently broken to be picturesque'. In the Alps, however, things were better arranged. There were places where it was 'impossible to look up without feeling a mixed sensation of the terrific and sublime', and having hoped fervently for a storm to catch him among the mountain tops, because it would suit them, he was forced to greet the one that struck him there with rapture, even though it involved hailstones the size of walnuts.

The picturesque view of nature suited the tourist of the time with his somewhat bookish approach to the countries he travelled through. Even the most urban temperament could apply with pleasure to the countryside a series of values learned from paintings. The delight of remembering what had happened in a certain historic building was paralleled by the pleasure of recognizing in nature the tones of a Poussin, the sort of clearing that would have appealed to Claude, or a meadow occupied by peasant roisterers of the kind Teniers might have painted. Travellers did not yet go to Italy to experience an emotional upheaval, nor to let the imagination run riot. They went for the pleasure of reconstructing the past, of recognizing in nature what they were familiar with in art, of tracing the movements of fictitious characters—the heroes of Mrs. Radcliffe or Madame de Staël's *Corinne*; the footsteps of Julie and St. Preux were

6. Piazza del Duomo, Milan, *c.* 1808

7. The grand canal, Venice, showing the Rialto

followed with scrupulous devotion about the shores of Lake Léman—to the educated tourist all was association, historical, artistic, literary. A change was coming—at the opening of Mrs. Eaton's novel *Continental Adventures* (1826) the heroine, Caroline, 'threw down her book—one of the innumerable new "Travels in Italy", and embarked enthusiastically on a parody of "O Caledonia! stern and wild!"

> *"O Italy! serene and mild!*
> *Meet nurse for a romantic child!"* '

—but the years that followed Waterloo still belonged to the classical age of Italian travel, not the Romantic.

Just as the amateur of the picturesque demanded a certain ordered disorder in nature, he required a harmonious irregularity to prevail among groups of buildings. Finch wrote of the environs of the cathedral at Pisa 'the view would be much more picturesque, were not three of these buildings in a direct line, which makes them appear stiff and displeasing to the eye'. For individual buildings, however, the severest harmony must prevail, here no discords, however calculated, could charm. The Rev. William Berrian, looking at these three buildings, the cathedral, the leaning tower and the baptistry, condemned the first as 'a corrupted style of Grecian architecture, with a few scattered traces of the Gothic'; the second for being divided into so many parts that it was not grand but 'merely beautiful'; and the third for containing a 'mixture of style and profusion of ornaments' that 'must offend the eye even of the common observer'. Time after time buildings are castigated for violating the rules. These rules were based on classical architecture as it was reinterpreted and commented upon by Palladio and his followers, to which were added rules deduced from the Gothic of the north. These rules made monsters of the less familiar Gothic buildings of the south, the cathedrals of Siena and Florence, for example. One author said of the first that it was in a style 'which they have the impudence to call Gothic', and of the second that it was a monument of false and meretricious taste. 'Neither Greek nor Gothic', Finch said of it; 'awkward, squat, clumsy'. The baptistry too was 'altogether incorrect'. And the caprciiousness of Luccan architecture, and of St. Mark's and the Ducal Palace at Venice, brought down the most scathing of judgements. They simply could not be assimilated to any accepted rules.

It was left to sentiment to enlarge the boundaries of taste set by knowledge. It was a process that accelerated throughout the nineteenth century. 'It is in vain', wrote Lady Morgan, 'that the fastidiousness of virtu and the rigour of criticism have discovered innumerable faults in the DUCAL PALACE of Venice. To the painter and the poet, to the imagination that gloats upon the romantic era of the middle ages, that wanders from the fields of Palestine and the Roncesvalles to the feats of the Dandoli and the Falieri, this is the edifice, *par excellence*.' And certainly, as interest in Italy's medieval past grew, it became easier to appreciate the monuments of that time. And to a state of mind that was becoming more widely shared, no such stores of medieval knowledge were needed. In the third volume of Lady Charlotte Bury's novel *Conduct is Fate* (1822) Bertha and Jane fly incognito and in dire distress to Milan. Haunted by the dreadful and highly complicated events of the previous two volumes, they enter the cathedral and try to find comfort and peace of mind. 'After all,' says Jane, 'what signifies telling me that this beautiful structure is not according to any of the rules of architecture? Why contend that there is no beauty, no grace, save in one species of building? If what is called Gothic, or of the middle ages, or what you please, possesses majesty, and mystery, and intricacy, and interest—they may talk as long as they like about bad taste and dark ages; but such buildings will ever be the haunt of those who love to feel and fancy.'

For the fathers and brothers of such young women the middle ages had little appeal. For them Italy was a classic land, and, from the coming of Raphael to Rome, a land of artists. It was her classic past that underlay their education, the books in their libraries, the tags and analogies which lit up their oratory. The canvases on their walls dated for the most part from the last two hundred years. The average tourist knew something about the Medici, the Renaissance Popes, one or two of the medieval doges, but these figures were detached from any background; they were the vivid illustrations in a largely unread book. Nor did recognition of the role played by Dante, Petrarch and Boccaccio in the revival of letters lead to sympathetic consideration of the other arts of their time. As a result the tourist's daily round concentrated upon every signal from antiquity, and on collections of sculpture and paintings. The great medieval churches were visited for their monuments, their modern pictures, and, as in the case of the Roman basilicas, for their place in a great hierarchy of pilgrim fanes. But in marked contrast to the late nineteenth-century tourist, the visitor to St. John Lateran or St. Paul without the walls paid little attention, if any, to their mosaics or cloisters: nor did his guide books suggest that he should.

In part this indifference to Italy's medieval past was bound up with lack of sympathy for her religion. And this lack of sympathy, joined to a contempt for the political ineptitude of Italy, for her divided and degenerated state, helped to maintain a certain contempt for the Italians themselves, and a lack of real interest in them. By the sixties the great increase in English converts to Catholicism, an outburst of writing about every period of Italy's history since classical times, and her emergence as a unified country—all these were factors that led to quickened sympathies and renewed admiration. At the same time came a wider taste for the domestic details of the southern way of life and larger numbers of English families went to settle there. These aids to understanding were either absent or only partially felt in the years after the Napoleonic wars. Visitors then were still few enough, and, most of them, of sufficiently high birth, to be entertained by noble Italian families. But they found it difficult to think of the Italians as equals. When Finch met a woman, the Duchess of Caserta, whose presence and wit were out of the ordinary—his comment was 'I pity such a woman for not being an English woman'. Italy remained a museum with a few illustrious families among the exhibits.

V

Rogers as a Tourist

———————◆≈◉≈◆———————

R ich, leisured, and well-connected, Rogers had much in
common with the majority of travellers who were able
to take advantage of the reopening of the continent. He
could stay where he wished, meet almost anyone he chose, and
looked forward to staying away at least until the following
summer. He followed the usual routes. A few days in Paris to
revive old Consulate memories; the road from Fontainebleau to
Dijon, and from Dijon into a country increasingly evocative to
the connoisseur: 'Descent into Doll magnificent—an extensive
plain skirted by mountains—a Claude—a Poussin—the first
distance yet seen in this country, and first rate'; a stay in Geneva
at the fashionable hotel; a dawdle through the Rousseau country
and the country of William Tell; the Simplon, that superb
novelty, then Milan, Venice, Florence, Rome for Christmas,
Naples—all this was part of a familiar pattern. The inspection
of ruins, a service in St. Peter's to listen to the choir, an
assembly in the evening with music and cards and ices—all this
was part of a common routine. And familiar too was the haze of
association and analogy, through which he saw that despised
race, the Italians, and their magnificent, saddened country.

> O Italy, how beautiful thou art!
> Yet I could weep—for thou art lying, alas,
> Low in the dust; and we admire thee now
> As we admire the beautiful in death.

The very apostrophe to fallen Italy was conventional, for
Filicaja's famous sonnet was paraphrased by many tourists to
express their own regret at the consequences of that fatal gift of
beauty.

Rogers certainly prepared himself with more than usual care
for his journey, and he was aware that commonly too exclusive

100

an attention was paid to the relics of antique Italy. 'All our travellers from Addison downward', he wrote in a note to the first part of *Italy*, 'have diligently explored the monuments of her former existence; while those of her latter have, comparatively speaking, escaped observation. If I cannot supply the deficiency, I will not follow their example.' In his journal he exclaimed 'Italy has had two lives! Can it be said of any other Country?' And the sentiment was echoed in the poem:

> *Twice hast thou lived already;*
> *Twice shone among the nations of the world.*

But the second age appeared in the poem as hardly more than a confusion of great names, romantic stories and uncertain chronology. *Italy* may have added a few more illustrations to the book of Italian history in medieval and early modern times, but the text remained, for most, an unattractive one. Rogers was more at home with the classical past, an age of which he knew not only the literature but also the history. Nothing more recent stirred his imagination as much as Pompeii. 'As we looked down into the vintner's shop', he noted in his journal, '& on the jars inclosed in the counter cased with various bits of Marble, I thought I saw the man serving his customers—& as the shadows of evening came on, & standing alone, I looked up the street of tombs towards the city-gate, the strange silence & deserted air of the place almost overcame me.' And even when working on *Italy*, reading far more Italian history than he had known in 1814, he remained primarily interested in the ancient world; in romantic stories set in the present, like the tale of Montorio and the Adventure with the bandits; and in a few similarly romantic stories, set it is true in the middle ages, but already familiar to his readers. Byron's *Foscari* was published in 1821, and the outlines of the story had been set out in the *View of Society in Italy* by Rogers' friend Dr. Moore, referred to in a note to the *Pleasures of Memory*. The miserable story of Bianca Capello was well known, as was the tale of the young Ginevra who hid in a chest with a spring lock and never reappeared. In Venice he recalls the opulence of her commerce and tells the story from Sanuto of the brides who were captured at the altar by corsairs. In Florence he remembers Petrarch, Boccaccio, Pulci, Machiavelli, and Galileo, and the judicial slaughter by

Cosimo I of his murderer-son Don Garzia, told 'by an honest chronicler'. But these names, coupled with a few earlier ones gleaned from Dante, do not tell the reader much that travellers with a taste for affecting anecdote did not habitually retail. *Italy* did not redress the balance between Italy's first life and her second.

He knew what it was going to be like, as the coach toiled up among the Alps, as he looked down from the Apennines towards Florence, as the road wound among the orange groves of the Kingdom of Naples. He had read about it in English travellers and Italian poets; the painters of both countries had told him what to expect. As the experiences came, he checked them off: —'a night among the Alps'; an 'extensive view of a Tuscan valley'; and as the warm sun fell on the lemons and cypresses of the south—'we now feel ourselves in Italy!'

The literary associations came hard on one another's heels. It was natural to think of Petrarch at Arquà, of Tasso and Ariosto at Ferrara, of Boccaccio at Florence and Milton at Vallombrosa and at Rome; almost more piquant were the associations that were less directly biographical, to read *La Nouvelle Héloïse* on the Isle St. Pierre, and to think of Udolpho and Otranto in passing a ruined castle and church. Everywhere were associations with great men. How much a traveller's pleasure depended on them! He regretted that in England the French and Swiss custom of labelling the homes of famous men was not followed. In Italy 'we now tread on classic ground: every hill and valley, every bit of pavement in every town "by sacred poets venerable made!" ' He wrote enthusiastically to Richard Sharp from Venice 'Oh, if you knew what it was to look upon a lake which Virgil has mentioned, and Catullus has sailed upon, to see a house in which Petrarch has lived, and to stand upon Titian's grave as I have done, you would instantly pack up and join me.' Sometimes the associations were more important than the scene itself. Of a day's sightseeing in the country about Rome he noted: 'It was a brilliant day, the scene interesting beyond all others, yet melancholy rather than beautiful, and grand rather from association than reality.' Nor was it only the wilderness that depended on association to lend it charm. 'How rich in association is Tivoli', he wrote. 'Horace and Catullus, Claude and Poussin have given it a lustre not its own, yet in itself it is a gem of the first order.'

These artists and many others were often in his mind's eye. Near Cortona 'the innumerable groves of olives and the mountain-ridges beyond them, line beyond waving line, gave what Claude has so well given. The olive-tint reminded me of G. Poussin.' On a desolate road near Tierni they saw by a ruined castle three mysterious 'Salvator-like figures', a cripple in the church at Sion was 'a figure for Rembrandt': in Switzerland there were window panes like those in an Ostade. In Milan he noticed 'the balcony to every window from which a female figure is almost always looking as in P. Veronese and Tintoret'. Among the worshippers in Santa Maria Maggiore were some 'every habit and figure and implement (the Greek bishops how imposing in their long beards) such as Raphael saw and gave us!' and in the chapel on Monte Cavallo 'the Pope knelt, leaning on the same stool as in the miracle at Bolsenna'. Over the bay of Naples played 'a blue light I had never seen before but in a Claude'.

He was always on the lookout for a good pictorial effect, a happy arrangement of mountain, houses and cypresses, or a group of peasants, a girl leaning from a window. Crossing the Brenner on the way home he made a remark that reveals much about his attitude to landscape; there was 'a spire always in sight, and almost always where it should be, where you would wish to find it'. There was a tendency to look at objects not for their own sake but for resemblances they suggested to art. And because Rogers had not the strong visual imagination of an artist he saw not so much what could be a fresh and individual composition, as something that had already been painted. And his imagination lent itself to the vignette rather than to a wide canvas. One of the scenes he recorded in the journal, a little girl at a well, drinking out of her mother's hands, became an actual vignette in *Italy*.

The light from whatever Rogers saw was in this way doubly refracted. It first passed through the lens of association, and took from it some literary, or historical colour. It then passed through the lens of pictorial reminiscence and took a little more. What Rogers saw was already a picture of itself. His failure to see things directly is reflected in the references in the journal to their being like a dream, dream-like. And when he described a scene in verse, a certain partiality for trite and conventional words and images introduced a third hindrance to direct expression. But the charm of Rogers' work was its accomplished appeal to the familiar; he did not try to impose a new vision, or to break the barriers that led to some new area of feeling.

His feelings about life were as unvital as his feelings for things, and sentimentality in his handling of one was a parallel to conventionality in his handling of the other. Rogers was moved by the graves of children in Switzerland, with here and there a broken porringer upon them. He was struck by an inscription, which he copied down: 'Je prie pour vous—Vous, priez pour moi.' In common with many of his Protestant countrymen, he was part fascinated part repelled by the apparatus of Catholicism. 'Who could not fall in love during the celebration of high mass?' he asked in a disconnected entry in the journal; and noted some early examples: Petrarch and Laura, Boccaccio and Mary of Aragon. Women at confession exercised a strong fascination; in his imagination they were always young and beautiful, the priest bigoted and sly. In Milan cathedral he noted 'the kneeling attitude of a young woman, her face hidden, the affected or real mystery or delicacy of the Priest, his ear turned towards her, his face to us, but half hidden'. Catholic funerals, in which the face lay uncovered on the bier as the procession wound through the streets, were horridly attractive, too. In 1821, on his second visit to Rome, he wrote disappointedly that 'I have not met a funeral' but added in partial compensation that he had seen one passing at a distance. Naturally, it 'was said to be that of a most beautiful young woman by those who saw it'.

The ceremony that shocked and intrigued Protestants most, however, was a nun's taking the veil. Coxe's guide book praised the French for suppressing 'convents, and other houses devoted to the incarceration of heaven's best and fairest gifts'. It went on to give a description of the ceremony, by now a somewhat rare one, and concluded with Rogers' lines from the *Pleasures of Memory*, part two, about 'The beauteous maid, who bids the world adieu', and who cannot forget the happy memories of her early life until old age, for

> *Not till the rushing winds forget to rave*
> *Is Heaven's sweet smile reflected on the wave.*

Rogers as a Tourist

There was great competition to be present at such a scene, and many references to 'the lovely victim', the 'fatal words' with which she made the 'dreadful sacrifice' of youth and womanhood, the 'fatal shears' that cropped her young hair as a symbol of her denial of the world. Feeling among the spectators could run high. Lemaistre described a ceremony to which he had obtained, as was customary, a ticket of admission from one of the front seats which 'were reserved exclusively for foreigners'. 'The English assembled on this occasion, feeling both pity for the object of sacrifice, and indignation against those who were the authors of it, were at one instant overcome with grief, and the next animated with an enthusiastic wish to rush forward and by force to rescue the victim of superstition from the hands of bigoted relatives.' The longest connected passage in Rogers' journal is devoted to describing the ceremony of taking the veil —and how eloquent is the hiss of the reprise in the description of her reappearance as a nun, crowned with gold '(how like a victim for sacrifice!), her receiving the kiss from each of the Nuns, each and all calling her *the Sposa*—the Sposa!' The episode was made into a verse tale for *Italy*, and paints the dreadful contrast between the morning, when

> She arose at home,
> To be the show, the idol of the day;
> Her vesture gorgeous, and her starry head—
> No rocket, bursting in the midnight-sky,
> So dazzling

and the evening:

> On thee now
> A curtain, blacker than the night, is dropped
> For ever! In thy gentle bosom sleep
> Feelings, affections, destined now to die,
> To wither like the blossom in the bud,
> Those of a wife, a mother; leaving there
> A cheerless void, a chill as of the grave,
> A languor and a lethargy of soul,
> Death-like, and gathering more and more, till Death
> Comes to release thee.

The feeling was that the people who could prompt, and suffer,

105

such an act as this were not to be admired, and though Rogers
came to respect individual Italians, like Foscolo in London, and
the Archbishop of Tarentum in Naples, he shared his contemporaries' indifference to the race. He attended the fashionable
gatherings of Rome, but made no friends among the Italians
who entertained him; such entertainment was, in fact, of so
formal and conventional a nature that it seldom led to close
acquaintance. His favourite home was that of a Frenchman,
Lucien Bonaparte, but the people he saw most of in Rome and
elsewhere, were English. It was not for the Italians that he came
to Italy. But no other element was lacking in his enthusiasm to
see the country that stood for much that was best in history,
literature and art. He had thought of the journey so often that it
was difficult to believe that it had actually taken place. 'Am I in
Italy? have I said to myself a thousand times. Am I crossing the
Alps? Am I on the Lago Maggiore, am I in Milan? Do I at last
see the Last Supper of Leonardo da Vinci, and the works of
Bramante?' And again, 'to me it seems like a dream that I am to
be at Verona today, the town of Romeo & Juliet;—& to-
morrow at Padua & the next day at Venice. Yesterday my
thoughts were wandering, when they were suddenly called back
by the sight of a direction-post "To Verona, To Mantua!"'

Yet for all this wonder, all this expectancy satisfied, Rogers
did not altogether regret his premature return, partly, perhaps,
because what he came to see were things rather than people,
monuments rather than a way of life. He was rather relieved to
be in Austria, to accept the attentive mothering bustle of the
inns there, in contrast to the reserved courtesy of the Italians,
who left the traveller to himself. It was pleasant to see again the
familiar green slopes and dark forests of the north, to observe
the respect of the country folk, to see—in place of the indifferent
Italian—the peasant pulling off his hat, the children coming
forward to kiss the traveller's hand. There was something con-
soling about the neatness of the inns. Increasingly he was reminded of home. Boats on a river reminded him of Kew or
Barnes, a landlord's pretty daughter of Richardson's Pamela.
German cooking was more to his taste than Italian, and in
Holland he found 'the houses small and unassuming, but with an
air of comfort how grateful to the eye of an Englishman'. The
Grand Tourist was not sorry to be home.

VI

The Journal and the Poem

————————◦◦◦◦————————

T here is nothing to suggest that in 1814 Rogers was plan-
ning a large-scale poem about Italy. The journal contains
some careful observation and a certain amount of moraliz-
ing, and both were to be useful in *Italy* later on, but he had only
just begun work on *Human Life*, and until 1819 he was largely
occupied with evolving that. The poet told Mitford that he first
wrote out *Human Life* in prose, and there is some evidence in the
journal that for 'Meillerie', and for 'Pæstum', he was beginning
to shape the prose springboard from which the verses of *Italy*
could eventually take off. At the end of one of the notebooks are
pencil jottings about Pæstum which appear to have been made
on the spot, and which were used when he wrote up the journal
later on, perhaps on his return to Naples. These jottings are in-
corporated into the journal entry without much change; when
there is one, it is characteristically away from close observation
and towards something more 'beautiful'. The jotting: 'the kites
are sailing over it [the site], & the oxen, released from the
plow, are grazing near it—nothing is heard but them as they
bite & blow—' becomes 'the hawk is sailing over them [the
temples] . . . & no noise is heard but . . . the grazing of the
silvery-grey ox just released from the plow—'. For the evolution of 'Meillerie', see Appendix 3.

Rogers may well have thought that the journal as a whole
might at some time come in useful, but the careful record of his
Italian days can be amply explained by the use he made of it as a
commonplace book: from it he copied whole paragraphs of his
letters home; he told stories from it, and read extracts from it to
his friends on his return. Richard Sharp read some of these
letters to his friends while he was away, thus passing on to them
some of the text of the journal, and Moore wrote to Rogers on
his return 'My desire to see you for *yourself alone*, is still more

whetted by all I hear of the exquisite gleanings you have made on your tour. The Donegals say you have seen so much, seen everything so well, and describe it all so picturesquely, that there is nothing like the treat of how you talk of your travels— how I long for that!'

By the autumn of 1821 he had written enough verses on Italian themes to consider printing them. He sent the manuscript to the Longmans. While it was still in their hands he set off on a second Italian tour. Sarah again accompanied him as far as Switzerland; she left him in October and came home to see the poem through the press, and to incorporate the corrections which she received in letter after letter from Italy. On the way out, Rogers had stopped in Paris to see Moore, and had read him the story of Foscari, which Moore admired, and by a strange coincidence when he received a few weeks later a manuscript from the Longmans with a request that he should look it over and see if it were worth publishing anonymously, it turned out to be Rogers' *Italy*.

Even before Longmans had given their opinion Rogers began thinking of improvements and sending them home. On October 15th he wrote to Sarah from Venice 'Pray, when you go to St. James's Place, search in the drawer of the table that stands in the middle of my bedroom, and I think you will find a thin blue copy-book in a blue cover, as blue as the inside of a band-box. It contains "The Brides of Venice". If you find it, print it in its place. If not, it must be left out altogether, as I have forgot it, and have in vain tried to recall it. Among the chapters is one entitled "A Retrospect". Pray entitle it "The Alps" instead. I have ventured to send some lines on Mont Blanc for a *note*. If you don't think them tolerable, don't let them be printed.' From Florence, in November, he sent a number of corrections, as to matters of fact, the whereabouts of portraits of the Medici, the tomb of Masaccio, and so forth. From Florence he went on to Rome, and early in the following year Mrs. Jameson saw him at the Villa Albani.

'We found Rogers in the gardens: the old poet was sunning himself—walking up and down a beautiful marble portico, lined with works of art, with his note-book in his hand. I am told he is now writing a poem of which Italy is the subject; and here with all the Campagna di Roma spread out before him—above him, the sunshine and the cloudless skies—and all around him, the remains of antiquity in a thousand elegant or venerable or fanciful forms: he could not have chosen a more genial spot for inspiration. Though we disturbed his poetical reveries rather abruptly, he met us with his usual amicable courtesy, and conversed most delightfully. I never knew him more pleasant, and never saw him so animated.' For Rogers, however, the inspiration came from the remembrance of old impressions rather than from the impact of new ones. He was a little saddened by his failure to respond with the same eagerness that he had shown in 1814, but was comforted by thinking that this—if in part a comment on the coldness of age—was partly a tribute to the depth of his former feeling for the place.

A small edition printed at the end of the previous year was published in 1822 by Longmans, with the title *Italy, a Poem. Part the First.* It was anonymous, and to cover his tracks Rogers gave the impression that he had entered Italy by the Great St. Bernard, instead of by the Simplon. It attracted very little public notice, though one reviewer attributed it to Southey. On his return to England Rogers appeared to know nothing of it. 'Rogers made his entrée at breakfast', wrote Lady Holland in May, 'giving a most agreeable *prose* account of Italy: that in verse I carefully avoided to touch upon.' When challenged, Rogers neither denied nor owned the poem. Some thought Lord Holland had written it and Rogers was unable to resist admitting that he thought *that* was probably a mistake. Moreover the lines on Pæstum, eventually included in the second Part of *Italy*, had already appeared with *Human Life* in 1819, and were included in a new edition of his *Poems* in 1822. The blank verse form and the general treatment of the subject were precisely similar to the North Italian sections in *Italy, Part the First*, and it is impossible to believe that Rogers did not see that their common authorship must be obvious. Increasingly, in fact, it was felt to be his. Wordsworth wrote outright in September, 'I detected you in a small collection of Poems entitled Italy which we all read with much pleasure.'

Rogers, meanwhile, continued to correct and add. He took advantage of the presence of the Italian poet, Ugo Foscolo, in London, to ask him some minute queries relating to the Venetian section, and 'Coll 'Alto'. 'Pray may I venture to trouble you with two questions? I think you said that the back-door at Venice, which opens into the street, is called La porta della strada—Near Bassano there is a house haunted by a ghost, called the *White Lady*. What would she be called there—La Signora Bianca? Is not Murato a technical word for the punishment of inclosing a man in a wall? Pray forgive me the trouble I am giving you.' Another edition appeared in 1823, published this time by John Murray, and this time bearing the author's name. It contained three additional sections—'Coll 'Alto'. 'The Gondola' and 'The Campagna of Florence', some trifling alterations in other parts, enlarged notes and a preface. 'Whatever may be its success', Rogers said of the poem, it had led the author 'in many an after-dream through a beautiful country; and may not perhaps be uninteresting to those who have learnt to live in Past Times as well as Present, and whose minds are familiar with the Events and the People that have rendered Italy so illustrious'. Another edition in 1824 also carried Rogers' name.

This public acknowledgement did little to help the poem. It remained virtually unreviewed, the copies mostly remained unsold. This was something new for Rogers, but there was an occasional note of comfort. Wordsworth wrote in 1825 to repeat his liking for the poem, which he often read. And in 1828 Rogers brought out the second part, also published by Murray, and also bearing the author's name. But no more notice was taken of part two than of part one, and as soon as this was clear, Rogers bought up all the remaining copies of either—some two thousand—and destroyed them.

He had not, however, lost faith in the work and had already decided to bring out an embellished edition. Neither the 1st nor 2nd parts had been illustrated, and the success of the numerous *Annuals* and other drawing-room gift works showed that public taste was veering strongly towards pictures. Even before the appearance of part two, Wordsworth wrote 'How goes on your Poem? The Paper spoke of a new edition being intended with numerous engravings, which, if executed under your presiding taste, cannot but be invaluable', and in 1830 the new edition was ready. It was scrupulously designed to impress by the most careful attention to typography, ornament and illustration. Works by Turner and Stothard and Prout among others were commissioned and engraved by the finest craftsmen available,

under the constant supervision of Rogers himself. He got on so
well with his artists that in at least two cases he was allowed
to put figures by Stothard into landscapes by Turner. He spared
neither time nor expense to make it perfect. The cost of the
edition was, indeed, staggering. Including a year's interest, it
came to seven thousand seven hundred and fifty-five pounds four
shillings and ten pence. But the result of the time spent was a
masterly taste and unity, and of the money, technical perfection.
No other work illustrated with steel engravings could compare
with it, though modern taste may prefer the simple line blocks
of his earlier works, and some of the later editions of them. Text
and illustration perfectly complemented one another, the placing
of both on the page was a lofty rebuke to the pretty volumes
lying on a thousand sofa tables. 'I used to say', wrote Macaulay
to the author, 'that if your "Italy" were dug up in some Pompeii or Herculaneum two thousand years hence, it would give to
posterity a higher idea of the state of the arts amongst us than
anything else which lay in an equally small compass.' And it was
not merely praised, it was bought. Nearly four thousand copies
at one pound five (boards) or thirty shillings (silk) were sold
before the end of the first year. By May, 1832, nearly seven
thousand had gone and only seven hundred odd remained to sell
before the work began to show a profit.

There is no need to dwell on the fame of *Italy*. In a short time
it had become, like Rogers himself, an institution; known to all
and read by at least a few. For two generations it remained the
ideal present for those about to leave for Italy or who had just
come back. It appeared in edition after edition, simple and
elaborate. Nor was it valued for the plates alone. Ruskin, as is
well known, claimed that he owed to his first sight of Turner's
plates the whole subsequent course of his life; but the numerous
references to the poem scattered through his work show that he
cared for the verse as well. When tired and indifferent with
Venice, he told Rogers, an infallible way of recovering the right
tone of thought was to read these lines:

> *There is a glorious City in the Sea.*
> *The Sea is in the broad, the narrow streets,*
> *Ebbing and flowing; and the salt sea-weed*
> *Clings to the marble of her palaces.*

No track of men, no footsteps to and fro,
Lead to her gates. The path lies o'er the Sea,
Invisible; and from the land we went,
As to a floating city—steering in,
And gliding up her streets as in a dream,
So smoothly, silently—by many a dome,
Mosque-like, and many a stately portico,
The statues ranged along an azure sky;
By many a pile in more than Eastern pride,
Of old the residence of merchant-kings;
The fronts of some, though Time had shattered them,
Still glowing with the richest hues of art,
As though the wealth within them had run o'er.

These are the opening lines of 'Venice'. They recall the smooth and easy pace of the gondolas that fascinated Rogers so much. The speed and lightness of the metre recalls what Lamb said of it: ''Tis so far from the stiffness of blank verse—it gallops like a traveller, as it should do.' The phraseology recalls the traveller himself. 'As you row up the Great Canal', he wrote in his journal on October 20th, 'many a half ruined Painting, Giorgione's perhaps, broken not faded, surprises you with its rich colours wrought up with gold, the colours alive, the images scattered and gone.' And next day, he wrote of S. Marco 'The mosaic paintings on the outside in the concave spaces over the doors of the great church certainly very ornamental, the splendour overflowing from within.'

This is only one of the many instances in which he used the imagery of the journal over again. Some of the most striking phrases do not reappear, being inflexibly prosaic, the comment on the pilgrims climbing the Scala Santa, for instance: 'the noise as they mount together is like that of horses in a stable', but others seem to ask for resurrection—the description of Vallombrosa in decay as 'a place for owls to hoot in', the reference to 'orange-trees and lemon-trees full of fruit, such as a child would draw, who thought he could never put in fruit enough'. These are very much in the Rogers manner. They have the kind of charm that much of *Human Life* possesses. But yet others were put to good use, and some of the most successful parts of *Italy* are indebted to the poet's prose impressions on the spot.

Another passage that Ruskin admired was the description of Michelangelo's Lorenzo monument in the Medici Chapel, a description that according to the Edinburgh Reviewer of Harford's *Life of Michael Angelo* in October 1857 was known to every lover of Art:

> *That is the Duke Lorenzo; mark him well,*
> *He meditates, his head upon his hand.*
> *What from beneath his helm-like bonnet scowls?*
> *Is it a face, or but an eyeless skull?*
> *'Tis lost in shade; yet, like the basilisk,*
> *It fascinates, and is intolerable.*
> *His mien is noble, most majestical!*

This combines two passages from the journal. In one, Rogers said of Lorenzo: 'He sits, a little inclining from you, his chin resting upon his left hand, his elbow on the arm of his chair. His look is calm and thoughtful, yet it seems to say a something that makes you shrink from it, a something beyond words. Like that of a Basilisk, it fascinates—& is intolerable!' In the other: 'The visage of Lorenzo under the shade of that scowling & helmet-like bonnet is scarcely visible. You can just discern the likeness of human features; but whether alive or dead, whether a face or a scull, that of a mortal man or a Spirit from heaven or hell, you cannot say. His figure is gigantic & noble, not such as to shock belief, or remind you that it is but a statue. It is the most real & unreal thing in stone that ever came from the chissel.'

A third example will suffice to show the dependence of the poem on the journal. This studio working-up of sketches made in the field was not, of course, peculiar to Rogers, but was a common practice. Byron is only one other instance of a poet who used his own prose, not merely jottings conceived from the first as poetry. Pæstum, perhaps, made a greater impression on Rogers than any other scene he visited in Italy, and 'Pæstum' became one of the most popular sections of *Italy*. The prose sentences which follow are re-arranged to follow the order of the verses, which begin abruptly with a reference to the site's three ruined temples.

They stand between the mountains and the sea;
Awful memorials, but of whom we know not!
The seaman, passing, gazes from the deck. . . .
How many centuries did the sun go round
From Mount Alburnus to the Tyrrhene Sea,
While . . . they remained
As in the darkness of a sepulchre,
Waiting the appointed time! All, all within
Proclaims that Nature had resumed her right. . . .
No cornice, triglyph, or worn abacus,
But with thick ivy hung or branching fern;
Their iron-brown o'erspread with brightest verdure!

    From my youth upward have I longed to tread
This classic ground—And am I here at last?
Wandering at will through the long porticos,
And catching, as through some majestic grove,
Now the blue ocean, and now, chaos-like,
Mountains and mountain-gulfs, and, half-way up,
Towns like the living rock from which they grew?
    The air is sweet with violets, running wild
Mid broken friezes and fallen capitals—
                  Nothing stirs
Save the shrill-voiced cicala flitting round. . . .
Or the green lizard rustling through the grass,
And up the fluted shaft with short quick spring,
To vanish in the chinks that Time has made.
    In such an hour as this, the sun's broad disk
Seen at his setting, and a flood of light
Filling the courts of these old sanctuaries. . . .
In such an hour he came, who saw and told,
Led by the mighty Genius of the Place.

'—the temples in a plain on three sides shut in by the mountains—on the fourth open to the sea. . . . Now the fisherman of Salerno as he passes, sees them standing on the desert plain. . . . How many suns have risen from behind the mountains, & set in the Tyrrhene sea, throwing these gigantic shadows aslant the green briary floor! . . . the plain strewn with fragments—corn here & there—the columns of the richest & warmest tint—like metallic rust that relieves the bright verdure with which

Nature has touched them above. . . . To muse by moonlight in the temples of Pestum, to gaze on the shadowy mountains thro' those gigantic columns, & the dark blue sea . . . the little towns —Capaccio old & new—that hang upon the mountains like an eagle's eyrie look down always upon them . . . fluted fragments of columns—& mouldings of cornices among briars strew the middle space between the temple & the basilica . . . innumerable violets in blow among the fragments—the air sweet with violets . . . the columns & cornices of the richest tints & climbed by the green lizards that flee into a thousand chinks & crannies at your approach. . . . Is it true that they remained buried for ages in the night of woods, till a young painter or a shepherd fell in with them? Was it on such an evening as this, after a sleep of 2000 yrs, the sun's disk just shining thro' them . . . ?'

Rogers did not look upon *Italy* as finished until the edition of 1834. By that time he was seventy. But if it had received an old man's care, it was not an old man's book. It is the liveliest as well as the longest of his works, and though finished over a decade after his second visit to Italy, retains the enthusiasm of first impressions. Behind the great wide-margined pages with their minutely beautiful engravings lie four small note books, crammed with descriptions of the Italy of twenty years before.

NOTES TO INTRODUCTION

page *line*

19   1   The latest book on Rogers is R. Ellis Roberts, *Samuel Rogers and his circle*, London, 1910. The two works by P. W. Clayden, *The Early Life of Samuel Rogers*, London, 1887, and *Rogers and his contemporaries*, 2v, London, 1889, comprise the only full description of his life. While full of interesting detail, and maintaining a fairly impartial attitude to Rogers, they are complications of miscellaneous facts in chronological order rather than a coherent biography. The latter work is referred to in these notes as *Contemporaries*.

   27   Abraham Hayward, July, p. 73.

21   28   Byron, *Letters and Journals*, ed. R. E. Prothero, 6v, London, 1896–1901, iii, p. 96.

24   11   *Henry Crabb Robinson on books and their writers*, ed. Edith J. Morley, 1938, ii, p. 547.

   16   Thomas Medwin, *Angler in Wales*, 2v, London, 1834, i, p. 26. Of the sofa incident, which occurs in the same author's *The life of Percy Bysshe Shelley*, 2v, London, 1847, ii, p. 190, Clayden remarks that it was 'a piece of rollicking fun' not to be taken 'even by dulness itself, for earnest'. *Contemporaries*, i, p. 337.

25   34   *Dublin University Magazine*, Jan., 1844, p. 89.

26   11   G. O. Trevelyan, *The Life and Letters of Lord Macaulay*. ed. 1908, p. 162.

27   1   *Treasures of Art in Great Britain*, 3v, London, 1854, ii, p. 74.

   10   *Op. cit.*, p. 163.

   11   'I *do* thank you from my heart', wrote Mrs. Jameson in 1850, 'for all the delight and improvement I have had in your society and from the beautiful and glorious and precious things assembled round you, and which make of your house a temple and a sanctuary.' *Contemporaries*, ii, p. 373.

   14   *Sale Catalogue*

Antiquities	£4,334.	17.	6
Pictures	30,180.	16.	0
Drawings, etc.	6,291.	19.	6
Engravings	1,559.	12.	6
Books	1,415.	5.	0
Coins	600.	7.	0

   30   See below, p. 108ff.

28   30   *Journal of Washington Irving (1823–1824)*, ed. S. T. Williams, Harvard, 1931, p. 82. The story comes possibly from Lord John Russell.

Notes to the Introduction

page	line	
28	38	*The Letters of Sydney Smith*, ed. Nowell C. Smith, 2v, Oxford, 1953, i, p. 317.
30	11	Byron, *Letters*, ed. G. E. Prothero, vol. 5, 1901, a letter from Moore, July 8, 1822.
	28	*Letters of Harriet Countess Granville 1810–1845*, ed. Hon. F. Leveson Gower, 2v, London, 1894, i, p. 133.
	31	*Op. cit.*, i, p. 302.
31	2	*Op. cit.*, letter to Lady Morpeth, i, p. 256.
	12	For such gossip see J. Mitford, *Recollections*, B. M. Adds. MSS 32, 567, *passim*.
	15	Prothero in a footnote on p. 69 to vol. ii, of Byron's *Letters and Journals*, 1898, quoting from a MS of Scott's on the poet's *Detached Thoughts* (Ravenna, 1821).
	22	*Contemporaries*, ii, p. 125.
	26	*Elizabeth, Lady Holland to her Son, 1821–1845*, ed. the Earl of Ilchester, London, 1946, p. 32.
	30	*Op. cit.*, ii, p. 728.
32	26	*Op. cit.*, ii, p. 467.
	31	*Through the long day*, Edinburgh, 1887, p. 201.
33	4	George Ticknor, *Life, Letters and Journals*, Boston, 1876, p. 410.
	17	Alluding to the notorious body-snatchers, Burke and Hare, Sydney Smith wrote to Richard Sharp in 1829 'Take care you are not killed for dissection. If I see a fat man and a thin man together I feel sure that it is a surgeon and his suffocator, and I run for it. There are men out after Rogers to my certain knowledge.' *Op. cit.*, i, p. 488.
	19	Some examples:

1819. 'Fuseli . . . expressing himself of Roger's face, said: 'I met Rogers to-day, and he offered me his hand, but I declined it. I was not prepared to make one in death's dance.' 'A happy painter's image' commented Crabb Robinson. *Op. cit.*, i, p. 227.

1821. Byron, in a letter to Douglas Kinnaird from Pisa: 'At Bologna I met with Rogers, and we crossed the Apennines together. . . . I took him to visit our old friend the sexton, at the Certosa . . . who looked at him very *hard*, and seemed well disposed to keep him back in his skull-room.' *Letters*, ed. Prothero, vol. V, 1901, pp. 481–2.

1824. Washington Irving: 'Moore says—I have often thought, when I have had a little too much of Rogers and been where I could not get rid of him—"who shall deliver me from this Death".' *Op. cit.*, p. 209.

1830. Lady Granville: 'Mr. Luttrell was asked whom he had met at the Hollands. "The quick and the dead, Lord Clanwilliam and Mr. Rogers."' *Op. cit.*, ii, p. 60. The same story is told of Foscolo and Rogers.

Notes to the Introduction

1843. Lady Morgan, speaking of an assembly at which Rogers shook her hand: 'We looked like an illustration of *Death and the Lady*, and I had a mind to ask Landseer, who stood near me, to take it for his next subject.' *Lady Morgan's Memoirs*, London, 1862, ii, p. 474.

34   15   Lady Eastlake, *Journals and correspondence*, ed. C. E. Smith, London, 1895, i, p. 250. The Brougham letter is printed in *Contemporaries*, ii, p. 368.

          18   Reprinted in her *Biographical Sketches*, London, 1869. *v.* e.g. p. 373.

35   10   MSS 26,053. f. 19, 20.

36   35   *Table Talk*, ed. Dyce, 1856, p. 3.

37   19   In the Bodleian there is a superb large paper Extra Illustrated version of the edition of 1794, of the sort Rogers would have relished. He himself used the less pleasing, but more practical guide book by Ebel on his first journey to Switzerland in 1814.

          40   *A view of society and manners in France, Switzerland, and Germany*, 1779, and *A view of society and manners in Italy.* .., 1781.

38   35   The indignant pyramid occurs in the 4th stanza of the *Ode to Superstition*. It is a pity that the useful table 'Amount of Pathetic Fallacy in the works of twenty-four Poets' in Josephine Miles' *Pathetic Fallacy in the nineteenth century*, U. of California, 1942, takes no account of Rogers.

39   19   P. W. Clayden, *Early Life of Samuel Rogers*, London, 1887, p. 299.

40   17   *The diary of Frances Lady Shelley*, 2v, London, 1912, i, p. 39.

41   38   The story of the court dress is told by Lady Eastlake in the *Quarterly Review*, Oct., 1888, p. 507. The other is in *The Remains of the late Mrs. Richard Trench*, ed. the Dean of Westminster, London, 1862, pp. 426–7.

42   40   A few more examples will show the extent to which Rogers had become the paper's Joe Miller.

May 26, 1823. 'Speaking of Mr. Rogers . . . we cannot refrain from repeating a remarkably pleasant *bon-mot* which we happened to hear two days since; we had been calling upon Wilkie the painter, and strolling towards the turnpike, we perceived the wit emerging from a Hammersmith stage at the gate of Holland House—he appeared mortified and worried at being late [Lady Holland was a notoriously intolerant hostess], and said to the coachman, "Why, bless my heart, you have been more than an hour bringing me here; what do you call your coach"?

"The Regulator, Sir", said the man.

"The Regulator!—ah", replied Rogers, "it is very properly called the *Regulator*—for all the other stage coaches *go by it!*"

Nov. 26, 1827. (At the end of the Lord Mayor's day festivities, transparencies and oil lamps fell on the heads of the dignitaries present). 'Somebody in describing to Mr. Rogers the accident at Guildhall, said, that the appearance from the other hustings of the lamps falling on the Lord Mayor's head was quite awful—"No doubt", said Rogers, "the *coup d'oil* must have been tremendous".'

Mar. 10, 1828. TO JOHN BULL.

My dear B.—Many thanks for your frequent kind notice of me—answer this—

"Why is a percussion gun like Death?"

"Because it is a *det-o-nator*—(debt o' nature)."

Yours, always, till life,

S.R.

St. James' Place, March 5, 1828.'

43	9	If Thomas Medwin is to be trusted. *Conversations of Lord Byron*, 2v, Paris, 1824, ii, p. 8.
	31	The Earl of Ilchester, *Chronicles of Holland House 1820–1900*, London, 1937, p. 494.
44	6	e.g. *Beppo*, stanza 76.

Hints from Horace, Pollio = Rogers.

Don Juan, Dedication, stanza 7.

In a note to *The Bride of Abydos* he refers to the *Pleasures of Memory* as 'a poem so well known as to render a reference almost superfluous; but to whose pages all will be delighted to recur'. His poem 'Absent or present, still to thee . . .' is addressed to Rogers.

	24	'You are one of the few persons . . .': Byron, *Letters and Journals*, ed. Prothero, iii, p. 375.

'Our poetical papa': *ib.* iv, p. 89.

'The last Argonaut': *Letter . . . on the Rev. W. L. Bowles's Strictures on the Life and Writings of Pope*, 1821.

Pyramid: Prothero, ii, p. 344.

'all in the wrong . . .': *ib.* iv, p. 169.

	26	Crabb Robinson wrote of a party at Monkhouse's on April 4th, 1823. 'Our party consisted of Wordsworth, Coleridge, and Lamb, Moore and Rogers, five poets of very unequal worth and most disproportionate popularity whom the public probably would arrange in the very inverse order, except that it would place Moore above Rogers.' *Op. cit.*, i, p. 292.
45	16	Moore, Prothero, *op. cit.*, iv, p. 197.
46	6	Characteristic was the *Edinburgh Review*'s notice of *Human Life*, March, 1819, p. 325. 'These are very sweet verses. They do not indeed stir the spirit like the strong lines of

page	line	

page   *line*

Byron, nor make our hearts dance within us, like the inspiring strains of Scott; but they come over us with a bewitching softness that, in certain moods, is still more delightful—and soothe the troubled spirits with a refreshing sense of truth, purity and elegance.' This was written by Jeffrey.

47   **3**   *A Journal of the conversations of Lord Byron with the Countess of Blessington*, London, 1893 ed., p. 321.

       8   *Some Particulars of the Life of Samuel Rogers*, by his nephew, Samuel Sharpe, prefixed to Rogers' *Poems*, 1867, p. lviii.

48   **3**   And *cf.* L. L. Schücking, *The Sociology of Literary Taste*, Eng. trans. London, 1944, pp. 47–8. 'It is not always easy to ascertain after the event how far certain stages on the path to Parnassus have been paid for, so to speak, with false coins. . . . Samuel Rogers . . . was a rich man with great influence in social and literary life, popular and, on the other hand, feared for his sharp tongue; these conditions were not without importance in determining his literary standing during his life. His works have not earned lasting fame. But this is poor consolation for those whom he threw into the shade while he lived.'

      15   In omnibus editions Rogers' *Pleasures* helped to sell Merry's *Pains*, and Campbell's *Hope*, too, especially in the United States. The other works mentioned are J. Chaloner, *Rome, a Poem*, London 1821; William Sotheby, *Italy, and other poems*, London, 1828, incorporating much matter from his *Farewell to Italy, and Occasional Poems*, London, 1818; John Edmund Reade, *Italy: a poem, in six parts; with historical and classical notes*, London, 1838.

      30   He would surely have been pleased to know that in 1859 a special edition of the *Pleasures of Memory* was printed by the Senate of Calcutta University as a Subject for Examination in the English Language.

49   **25**   *v.* MS note in Dyce's copy of the 1845 ed. of Rogers' *Poems*, at end of vol. 2. *N.b.* Clayden, in *Contemporaries*, ii, p. 6, f.n., says, incorrectly, that it is Dyce's copy of *Italy* that contains MS notes. The majority of these are actually in his copy of the 1834 ed. of the *Poems*. Cf. note to p. 111, l. 3.

50   **11**   British Museum, MS 40548, pp. 38, 39.

51   **20**   MS notebook, Jan. 22. 'Rode a post in company with B [Samuel Boddington] in Jackboots, and performed it in a canter, but found them very uneasy from the inward direction of the feet. Was obliged to be helped on and off.'

53   **1**   Prothero, *op. cit.*, ii, p. 331.

      16   *Op. cit.*, i, p. 252.

      40   Mitford, *mss cit.*, 32, 566, f. 104, 106.

54   **11**   *Table-Talk*, as is also the story, below, of the *sac-de-nuit*; p. 196.

Notes to the Introduction

page	line	
54	15	*Memoirs of the life of the right honourable Sir James Mackintosh, Esq.*, edited by his son, 2v, London, 1836, ii, p. 289.
	30	Both stories recorded by J. Mitford, B.M. Adds MSS 32567, f. 22.
55	8	MS Notebook, (anon), vol. i, p. 52–3.
56	18	*Travels in Italy*, London, 2v.
57	2	J. G. Lemaistre, *Travels after the peace of Amiens through parts of France, Switzerland, Italy, and Germany*, 3v, London, 1806, i, p. 420.

5 Joseph Forsyth, *Remarks on antiquities, arts and letters during an excursion in Italy in the years 1802 and 1803*, London, 1813. J. C. Eustace, *A tour through Italy . . . with an account of the present state of its cities and towns; and occasional observations on the recent spoliations of the French*, London, 2v, 1813.

18 Robert Semple, author of *Observations on a Journey through Spain and Italy to Naples; and thence to Smyrna and Constantinople*, London, 2v, 1807.

25 *Hints to Travellers in Italy*, London, 1815, by R.C.H. Sir Richard Colt Hoare was a worthy and learned man who deserves every inch he has been given in the D.N.B., but this guide book is a worthless imposition, designed to brag of his own out-of-date knowledge rather than to assist the modern traveller. Most of its matter is pompous, pedantic and supererogatory. He is not even sure if there is a road over the Simplon.

34 *Op. cit.*, i, p. 86.

38 The passport figures are unreliable. This is in part because the records are incomplete, but also because not all travellers held passports, while some passports covered whole parties and others were issued in this country to foreigners. The available figures show that in July, August and September—the usual exodus months for making the Tour—1814, the figures rose from 78 to 158, 185 and 102. Between April, 1814 and March, 1815, while the continent remained open, 885 passports were issued at London, of which some five per cent were granted to couriers. The actual figure of travellers in that period was possibly in the neighbourhood of 1500–2000. But it would not be profitable even to guess how many of these actually went as far as Italy.

40 The experiences of some of them can be read in: T. Baring, *A tour through Italy, Sicily, Istria, Carniola, the Tyrol and Austria, in 1814*, London, 1817 (2nd ed.).
The journal of John Mayne during a tour on the continent upon its reopening after the fall of Napoleon, 1814. Edited by his grandson John Mayne Colles, London, 1909.
The unpublished journals of Robert Finch in the Bodleian.

58 26 'Lady Charlotte Bury': *The Diary of a Lady-in-Waiting*, ed. A. Francis Stewart, London, 1908, i, p. 270. 'Another

Notes to the Introduction

page   line

traveller': Hon. Richard Boyle Bernard, *A tour through some parts of France, Switzerland, Savoy, Germany and Belgium, during the summer and autumn of 1814*, London, 1815, pp. 29, 125–6.

'The English arrive': L-G. Pelissier, *Le portefeuille de la comtesse d'Albany (1806–1824)*, Paris, 1902, p. 218. This is from a letter to the Countess, whom Rogers visited on October 31st, his first day in Florence. The character of her *salon* is discussed in Carlo Pellegrini, *La Contessa d'Albany e il salotto del Lungarno*, Napoli, 1951.

59   8 Col. Montgomery Maxwell, *My Adventures*, 2v., London, 1845, ii, p. 62.

17 Lady Donegal's letter is in *Memoirs, journal and correspondence of Thomas Moore*, ed. Lord John Russell, London, 1853–6, ii, p. 73.

Lord John Russell's diary quoted in Spencer Walpole, *The Life of Lord John Russell*, 2v, London, 1889.

60   38 Theodore Lyman, *The political state of Italy*, Boston, 1820, p. 361.

62   3 Henry Matthews, *The diary of an invalid...*, London, 1820, p.171.

14 *Rhymes on the Road*, 1823 ed., p. 99.

64   4 George Ticknor, *op. cit.*, i, p. 180.

65   34 Lady Lyttelton, *Correspondence of Sarah Spencer Lady Lyttelton 1787–1870*, ed. The Hon. Mrs. Hugh Wyndham, London, 1912, p. 217, made a caustic note on Nov. 5, 1819. 'That witch of Endor, the Duchess of Devon, has been doing mischief of another kind to that she has been doing all her life, by pretending to dig for the good of the public in the Forum. She, of course, has found nothing, but has brought up a quantity of dirt and old horrors, and will not be at the expense of carrying it away and filling it in, so that she has defaced every place where she has poked. She is the laughing-stock of Rome with her pretensions to Mæcænas-ship.'

66   10 'Thank Heaven!': Jane Waldie, *Sketches descriptive of Italy, in the years 1816, 1817 ...*, 4v, London, 1820, ii, p. 175.

Matthews, *op. cit.*, p. 139.

25 William Sharp, *The Life and letters of Joseph Severn*, London, 1892, p. 82.

The botanist was Antonio Sebastiani. *c.f.* Richard Deakin, *Flora of the Colosseum of Rome; or, illustrations and descriptions of four hundred and twenty plants growing spontaneously upon the ruins of the Colosseum of Rome*, London, 1873. In his Preface he says that 'the collection of the plants and the species noted has been made some years; but, since that time, many of the plants have been destroyed, from the alterations and restorations that have been made in the ruins; a circumstance that cannot but be lamented. To prevent a further falling of any portion is most desirable; but to carry the restorations, and the brushing and cleaning, to the extent to which it has been subjected, instead of leaving it in its wild and solemn grandeur, is to destroy the impression and salutary lesson which so magnificent a ruin is calculated to make upon the mind.'

68   28   *Table-Talk*, p. 274.

34   Compare Maxwell's remarks about Murat, *op. cit.*, i, pp. 270 and 297. 'His majesty, I must say, when I first saw him, brought to my mind Molière's play of the *Médecin malgré lui*; for he looked for all the world like a fine athletic fellow, who had been picked up in the streets, had a fine coat put on his back, and been turned loose to act the gentleman and the King, 'His majesty, I was informed, had on the dress of high admiral of France, although to my mind it was more like that of a stage-player than any other, and evidently taken from the times of *Henri Quatre*.'

69   1   The Simplon was thought well worth seeing for its own sake, as a modern Wonder. A. Yosi, in *Switzerland . . . to which is added a short guide to travellers*, 2v., 1815, devotes an enthusiastic chapter to a description of the pass, which concludes: 'Such are the sublime and pleasing scenes which the traveller beholds upon the road over the Simplon, scenes which must impress his mind with the most exalted sentiments, and teach him, how sceptical soever he formerly may have been, "to look through nature up to nature's God."'

71   4   e.g. The most direct progenitor of the *Fudge Family* is Felix M'Donough's anonymous *The Hermit Abroad*, 2v, London, 1823. Other novels dealing with tourist life are: Lady Charlotte Bury, *Conduct is Fate*, Edinburgh, 1822; Charlotte Eaton, *Continental Adventures*, 3v, London, 1826; Sir Constantine Henry Phipps, Marquis of Normanby, *Matilda*, 2v, London, 1825. The French title of this work is *Mathilde, ou les Anglais en Italie*.

16   Stendhal's story is in *Rome, Naples, and Florence in 1817*, London, 1818, p. 131. That of the chicken bones is in *The Private Diary of Richard Duke of Buckingham and Chandos*, 3v, London, 1862, i, p. 316.

33   This is in the British Museum, MS 36,481, and bears his annotations.

73   9   'Rome was just ready': William Berrian. *Travels in France and Italy, in 1817 and 1818*, N.Y., 1821, p. 106. 'I was now about to enter': Henry Sass, *A Journey to Rome and Naples performed in 1817*, London, 1818, pp. 96–7. Samuel Butler made two journeys to Italy, one in 1819, the other in 1822. The first quotation is from the former, the second from the latter. Both journals are in the British Museum, MS 34,598.

Notes to the Introduction

page	line	
73	15	Jane Waldie, *op. cit.*, iii, pp. 353–4.
74	2	Mrs. C. A. Eaton, *Rome in the nineteenth century* . . . 3v, Edinburgh, 1820. 5th ed. London, 1852, i, p. 16.
	33	*A Journey to Florence in 1817*, edited by G. R. de Beer, London, 1951, p. 22.
75	1	*The autobiography of Leigh Hunt* . . . edited by Roger Ingpen, 2v, London, 1905, ii, p. 192.
76	37	H. W. Williams, *Travels in Italy, Greece, and the Ionian Islands*, 2v, Edinburgh, 1820, p. 71.
77	35	For a picture of the charms of travelling with a *vetturino*, see Augustus Hare, *The Story of my Life*, 3v, London, 1896, ii, pp. 46–7. This mode of travelling had in no way changed by 1857, the year of which he wrote.
80	6	Only Lady Morgan spoke of it as more than a personal inconvenience. All these hindrances, she wrote, 'forcibly illustrate the efficacy of a policy, that insulates the inhabitants of each petty state, and impedes the communication of thought and concentration of interests, which, by effecting the liberation of Italy, would raise it to the dignity of a nation'. *Italy*, 2v, London, 1821, i, p. 70.
82	9	*Annuario politico statistico topografico e commerciale del dipartimento di Roma per l'anno 1814*, Roma, 1814, p. 163. The advice about the moon is given in the various editions (from 1775) of *Le Véritable guide des voyageurs en Italie*, a widely used work printed with French and Italian texts on opposite pages.
	38	This is not to say, of course, that individuals, like Byron, did not take great pleasure in Venice. But Eustace was only one of the many who, 'tired of the confinement of Venice . . . left . . . without much regret.' And in W. A. Cadell, *A journey in Carniola, Italy, and France, in the years 1817, 1818*, 2v, Edinburgh, 1820, i, p. 73: 'Few of the English who visit Italy for amusement or curiosity pass any considerable time at Venice.'
83	26	With some this opinion persisted after entering the city. Hazlitt thought so, and that the Vatican did not compare with Napoleon's Louvre. What is more, 'the Stanzas of Raphael are faded, or no better than the prints; and the mind of Michael Angelo's figures, of which no traces are to be found in the copies, is equally absent from the walls of the Sistine Chapel.' (Hardly surprising, this). His conclusion: 'This is not the Rome I expected to see. No one from being in it would know he was in the place that had been twice mistress of the world,' was shared by increasing numbers of visitors who were neither prepared to accept second-hand opinions nor educated in a way that allowed the imagination to fill out what the eye saw to be fragmentary and degraded. *v.* his *Notes of a journey*

through *France and Italy* in *Collected Works*, vol. 9, London, 1903, p. 232. The *Notes* first appeared in the *Morning Chronicle* in 1824 and 1825.

83   39   *Op. cit.*, ii, p. 335.

85   31   'Recorded a tourist': Cadell, *op. cit.*, i, p. 448–9. Moore: *op. cit.*, iii, p. 71.

For a good account of banditry in this part of the country, see Maria Graham, *Three months passed in the mountains east of Rome, during the year 1819*, London, 1820. Sir Charles Eastlake, later Director of the National Gallery, was staying with her and sketched some of the local desperados.

86   11   H. W. Williams.

87   11   *Essays, descriptive and moral: on scenes in Italy, Switzerland and France*, Edinburgh, 1823, p. 14.

88   30   Forsyth, *op. cit.*, p. 134, had made this complaint most magisterially. 'Whichever road you take, your attention will be divided between magnificence and filth. . . . The objects which detain you longest, such as Trajan's column, the Fountain of Trevi, etc., are inaccessible from ordure. Ancient Rome contained one hundred and forty-four public necessaries, besides the *Sellæ Patroclinæ*. The modern city draws part of its infection from the want of such convenience.'

89   19   Henry Coxe, *A Picture of Italy; being a guide to the antiquities and curiosities of that classical and interesting country . . .* , London, 1815.

90   22   The following tables give the values for this time of the commonest coins mentioned by travellers:

France	1 louis	—£1
	1 {franc / livre	—10d.
Venice	1 franc	—10d.
	1 lira	— 5d.
Florence	1 sequin	—10/–
	1 scudo	— 5/–
	1 lira	—8d.–9d.
	1 paul	—5d.–6d.
Rome	1 sequin	—10/–
	1 crown	—4/2d.
	1 paul	—5d.–6d.
	1 bajocco	—just over ½d.
Naples	1 ducat	—3/9d.
	1 carlin	—4d.

91   3   *The Correspondence of Leigh Hunt*. Edited by his eldest son. 2 v, London, 1862, i, p. 193.

Notes to the Introduction

page	line	
91	9	*Letters of an architect, from France, Italy and Greece*, 2v, London, 1828, ii, p. 189.

| | 16 | Finch copied out the bill of fare at a *traiteur's* in Genoa in January 1815. Travellers might be interested in comparing it with the prices of a modern one. The soldo was worth one halfpenny, and there were twelve denari in a soldo. The dishes thus vary from *Zuppa all' Erbe* at about 3d. to *Anitra al Olivo* at 9½d. |

	Soldi.	D.
Riso Arrosto	8	3½
Zuppa all' Erbe	6	2½
Manzo Bollito	10	4½
Cappone ¼	18	8
Alettoni Farsite	12	5
Frittura di Sticchi	10	4½
Tomaselle	12	5½
Uccelletti (4)	14	6¼
Tordo Arrosto	12	6
Anitra al Olivo	18	8
Cappone Magro	12	5½
Granatine di Riso	10	4½
Pasticini a Boccone	12	5½
Gigotto in Salza	10	4½
Fegato Vitella	12	5½
Latte alla Spagnuola	10	4½
Cotellette di Montone	8	3½
Pollanca Arrosto (¼)	16	7½
Friccando	12	5½
Patate	6	2½
Arrangoste	16	7½
Cotelletti	10	4½
Alettoni fritti	14	6½
Cavofiori	6	2½
Broccoli	6	2½

page	line	
92	13	The tourist was expected, too, to be an insatiable purchaser of *objets d'art*. 'From the moment of our arrival' Mayne writes of Rome, 'we have had booksellers, painters, antiquarians, and vendors of curiosities sending up their cards and exhibiting their wonders to us. This morning a huge dish walked in for our inspection, painted by no less a man than Raffaello himself and, as the owner assured us, *"très antique"*.'
94	16	*Diary of an Ennuyée*, new ed. 1826, pp. 107–8.
95	24	James Sloan, *Rambles in Italy: in the years 1816–17. By an American*, Baltimore, 1818, p. 14.
100	28	'Italia, Italia, O tu cui feo la sorte!' etc. Byron's version is in *Childe Harold*, canto 4, stanzas 42 and 43.
102	32	*Contemporaries*, i, p. 172.

Notes to the Introduction

page	line	
104	4	cf. the comparison of Byron with Rogers in Ruskin's *Praeterita*, 1886 ed., i, pp. 270–1. 'Byron—though he could not teach me to love mountains or sea more than I did in childhood, first animated them for me with the sense of real human nobleness and grief. He taught me the meaning of Chillon and of Meillerie, and bade me seek first in Venice—the ruined homes of Foscari and Falier. And observe, the force with which he struck depended again on there being unquestionable reality of person in his stories, as of principle in his thoughts. Romance, enough and to spare, I had learnt from Scott—but his Lady of the Lake was as openly fictitious as his White Maid of Avenel: while Rogers was a mere dilettante who felt no difference between landing where Tell leaped ashore, or standing where "St. Preux has stood". . . . But Byron told me of, and reanimated for me, the real people whose feet had worn the marble I trod on.'
	28	Ibid, i, p. 328. One of the sections in *Italy* is called 'A Funeral'.
105	4	*Op. cit.*, ii, p. 66. For another account see Miss C. A. Waldie (later Mrs. Eaton), *Rome in the nineteenth century*, 5th ed. (1st ed. 1820), London, 1852, ii, pp. 216 ff. And *c.f.* 'Le "Notes on Italy" di A. W. Power' ed. Vittorio Gabrieli in *English Miscellany 3*, Rome, 1952, p. 275, where he says of a similar 'painful' ceremony that 'the Church, a small one, was quite filled with strangers, particularly the English Beau Monde'. This was in about 1828.
106	22	These two passages become in *Italy*:

> *Am I in Italy? Is this the Mincius?*
> *Are those the distant turrets of Verona?*
> *And shall I sup where Juliet at the Masque*
> *Saw her loved Montague, and now sleeps by him?*
> *Such questions hourly do I ask myself;*
> *And not a stone, in a cross-way, inscribed*
> *'To Mantua'—'To Ferrara'—but excites*
> *Surprise, and doubt, and self-congratulation.*

page	line	
107	5	There are no obvious reflections of the journal in the text of *Human Life*, and only two in the notes: a reference to falling in love in church, and to the ice-bound vessel of Capt. James.
	6	B. M. Adds MSS, 32, 567, f. 125.
108	5	*Memoirs*, etc. *ed. cit*, viii, p. 204. For a letter (misdated) written by Rogers to Moore containing literal quotations from the journal, see *ib*, viii, pp. 185–7.
	30	*Contemporaries*, i, p. 317.
109	7	*Op. cit.*, p. 212.
	23	*Elizabeth Lady Holland to her son 1821–1845*. Edited by the Earl of Ilchester, London, 1946, pp. 11–12.

Notes to the Introduction

page   *line*

109   36   *The Letters of William and Dorothy Wordsworth* arranged and edited by Ernest de Selincourt, Oxford. *The Later Years*, 1939, i, p. 89.

110   7   n.d. but postmark 18 Jan. 1823. *v.* Acknowledgements.

       17   London, Murray, The Fourth Edition. I can find no other editions than the previous ones of (Longmans) 1822, and (Murray) 1823. The 1834 edition of *Italy* was held by Rogers to be the first complete one. It was built up as follows:

Additions to Part One (1822):

1823 Coll'Alto; The Gondola; The Campagna of Florence.
1824 The Brothers; Bologna.
1830 Meillerie; Marcolini.

Also, many of the 1822 sections were changed in subsequent editions, either by additions, sometimes lengthy, or by minor alterations, e.g. in 'Venice' the 1st line of the 2nd paragraph from
      Thither I came, in the great passage-boat, (1822)
becomes
      Thither I came, and in a wondrous Ark, (1823).

Additions to Part Two (1828):

1830 Marco Griffoni.
1834 Montorio.

       27   v. *Contemporaries*, ii, p. 2. 'He was not disposed to question the taste of the public. . . . So he made a bonfire, as he described it, of the unsold copies, and set himself to the task of making it better.'
v. also Mitford, *Recollections*, B.M. Adds MSS 32,567, f. 18. 'Rogers said he bought up and destroyed two thousand copies of his first ed. of Italy.'

111   3   Note in Dyce's 1834 *Poems*, in the Victoria and Albert Museum. The vignettes concerned are those on pp. 151 and 248 of *Italy*, 1830.

       18   *Contemporaries*, ii, p. 88.

       35   Ruskin, Library Edition, xi, p. xxvi.

112   18   *The letters of Charles and Mary Lamb*, edited by E. V. Lucas, 3 v. London, 1935, ii, p. 53.

115   21   There was a large paper edition published in 1834.

The Italian Journal

Note on the Text

The journal is contained in four notebooks, measuring 16 × 10·5, 18·5 × 12, 19 × 12·5 and 20·5 × 13 cm., bound in boards, and each labelled in Rogers' hand *Journal of Tour in Italy (1 Part) 20 Aug to 15 Oct. 1814*; do. *(Part 2) Oct. 17, 1814, to 28 Dec.ʳ 1814*; do. *(Part 3) 29 Dec.ʳ 1814 to 21 March 1815*; do.—*Part 4.—22 March to 4 May 1815.*

Rogers himself copied out a revised version of part of No. 1, from August 20th, 1814 to Sept. 26th 1814. The only internal evidence that helps to date this is a reference to Napoleon on St. Helena. The revision involves a few alterations of fact, e.g. at the end of the entry for Sept 13, 1814: 'Walked with Dumont to Lady Holland, & returned thro' the gates with him & M. & Sismondi.' (Journal) 'Found Mᵐᵉ de Stael at Lʸ Hollands. Returned thro' the gates with Dumont & Mackintosh.' (Rogers' revision) and some dressing-up of some entries, e.g. his first view of the Alps, Sept. 7th, 1814:

'Went on & at a turn of the road had a full view of the Glaciers over a wood of firs. The snows of a dazzling brightness contrasted with the dark foliage filled us with surprize & pleasure, much as we expected to see them; yet the surprize was lessened, when I looked again, & I confess I felt little besides that exhileration I have so often felt in a bright winter's day.' (Journal.)

'Went on, & at a turn of the road had a full view of the Glaciers over a dark wood of firs; the snows of a dazzling brightness & giving me the exhileration I have often felt in an English shrubbery at Xmas; but it was mingled with other feelings; we now saw what we had so long wished to see; it was one of the days in our lives which we were sure to remember with pleasure; all was congratulation!' (Rogers' revision.)

Clayden used this revised version in *Rogers and his Contemporaries* before going on to the original notebooks but altered the punctuation and left out words, phrases and entries for entire days without any indication.

Note on the Text

There is a 'Fair Copy' (so endorsed) of the whole journal which uses Rogers' own fair copy as far as it goes and then reverts to the notebooks. It is in several hands, and contains numerous errors. It is at no point a trustworthy guide to the original text.

The text printed here follows the original notebooks throughout, as the portion revised by Rogers is only a small part of the whole, and nothing suggests that this was a final revision. To prevent the text from losing any of its character as an authentic travel diary, written up from day to day, it has been printed as it stands, with all its inconsistences of spelling and punctuation. Amendments have only been made where confusion seemed likely; these are in square brackets. The only changes made in Rogers' punctuation are those necessary to incorporate the frequent interlining—interpolated second thoughts, sometimes in pencil—that tangles the original text. Dashes have been used as best in keeping with these broken and often disconnected jottings.

The only other editorial changes are the italicizing of dates and these omissions:

(i) Lists of objects which include little or no personal comment, and

(ii) References to books when these do not occur in the course of a sentence, but stand alone. Both of these are fully given in Appendix 1 and 2.

(iii) Jottings on the end papers, and final sheets of the notebooks where these consist of no more than historical notes copied from books, names of individuals (when these occur in the text), and rough notes of the day's impressions when these are subsequently written up in the journal. When such notes are used as a basis for verse, they are mentioned: *v.* Introduction, chapter 6, and Appendix 3.

The journal is written in ink, though pencil is sometimes used for corrections and additions. There are a number of small drawings scattered through the text, of which an example can be seen in Plate 5. They do not pretend to do more than prompt the memory.

Journal of Tour in Italy

Aug. 20, 1814. Set sail at dusk from the beach at Brighton in a crouded boat. A luminous sea. In Loch Long[1] the foam was like liquid light. Here there was but little foam; & sparks of fire, like so many little stars were every where dancing in the dark sea under the boat. Met with the packet, & after many attempts, got on board. A long calm & short rolling sea. Hailed by a French Pilot-boat when within 6 leagues of Dieppe. voices of the Pilots in the night. Landed on the Quay at day-break & slept at De la Roux's[2] after a voyage of 30 hours.

Aug. 22. Set off after breakfast. Dieppe a pretty town. Open corn & clover fields. Chateaux & Maisons de Plaisance. Harvest people dining in groups near the way-side. A shepherd following his flock & knitting, his staff slung behind him. A hazel gallery along a hill-side, with loop-holes cut thro' it. Valley of Malaunay. Descent into Rouen. The Seine. The Boulevardes. The Cathedral! A young man, standing against the wall in the street, within a semicircle of 12 lighted candle-ends, playing on his violin Gluck's overture to Iphigenia, his wife collecting pence from the crowd—a small basket in the centre. A milliner's girls playing at cards. Went to the Theatre. Opera of Oedipus at Colonna—Music by Sacchini. Handsome theatre. Audience not very brilliant. Over the curtain, is inscribed the name of Corneille, a native of Rouen.

Aug 23. Many masses & a funeral in the Cathedral. Passing from the Market-place thro' a narrow lane the rue de la Pie I saw over

---

[1]. In 1812 Rogers went for a tour in Scotland. One result of this was a poem on Loch Long, 'Written in the Highlands of Scotland', dated September 2, 1812.

Clayden (*Contemporaries*, i, 109–10) prints a letter to Richard Sharp dated from Glenfinnart, Sept. 28, 1812, in which Rogers describes a boat trip 'down Loch Long to Glenfinnart, a singular voyage, as I met with a grampus, a shoal of herrings, and (after dark) a luminous sea, no unusual phenomenon on this lake'.

[2] Proprietor of the Hotel *du Roi d'Angleterre*.

a small foot-gateway by an ironmonger's shop-window, this Inscription

Ici

Est né 9 Juin 1606

Pierre Corneille

Saw in a small square near the market-place the fountain of the Pucelle D'Orleans on the spot where she was burnt. The road continues along the Seine—woods, villages, chalk-hills—church-spires, roofs of houses & chimney-tops seen from above—among trees—orchards—gathered apples & pears from the barouche-box as we passed. Houses of Marshalls Victor & Souchat.[1] Vineyards. Slept at a pretty inn at Mont. Lightning. Curran[2] & Webb.[3]

Aug 24. Forest of St Germains Villas & vineyards. Terrace of St Germains—Water-works at Marly. Mal-maison. Very pretty gallery, full of marbles pictures & Etruscan Vases. Cupid & Psyche, Hebe, Mercury & Terpsichore by Canova. The Seine still our companion. Grand Avenue from Neuilly to Paris—Place of Louis XV. Tuilleries—Louvre. Torso. Laocoon, Apollo, Venus, & the Horses from Venice. The Column of the Grand Army. Dined at the Hotel de Wagram with S[arah] & M[ackintosh][4] & went to the Theatre Feydeau—& walked in the Palais Royal...

Aug 29. Fete de St Louis, held on this day. Column of the Grand Army. Regimentals, boots, hats, swords, muskets, cannon, & banners thrown in confusion together on the base of it. Men in conflict with men, lance to lance & horse to horse winding in a spiral to the top of it, & so contrived as that the figures all the way shall bear the same proportion to the eye of the spectator

---

[1] Claude Victor, maréchal de France, duc de Bellune, 1766–1841. Souchat = Louis Gabriel Suchet, duc d'Albufera, 1770–1826.

[2] John Philpot Curran, the Irish Judge, 1750–1817.

[3] Curran's travelling companion, of whom he wrote before leaving 'I have fixed to set out for Paris on Tuesday with Mr. W. He is a clever man, pleasant, informed, up to everything, can discount the bad spirits of a friend [Curran was travelling to relieve a chronic melancholia], and has undertaken all trouble'. When Rogers met them they were on their way from Paris to Dieppe. W. H. Curran, *The Life of the Right Honourable John Philpot Curran*, 2v, London, 1819, ii, pp. 337 and 374.

[4] Sir James Mackintosh, 1765–1832, historian and philosopher. See Introduction, p. 53.

below. Napoleon to be seen continually in the lower part. Mont
Martre. View of the City & its environs from the church towers,
the march of the armies, & the field of battle before the capitula-
tion. St Denis. Dined at Beauvilliers. Thuilleries Gardens. Saw
the Fireworks from the terrace. A volcanic eruption of rockets
filling the sky!!

Aug. 30. Saw at Mass the King Dss. d'Angouleme, Monsieur &
the Duke D'Angouleme.[1] (Paris is the City of the Great King,
London of the Great People. Paris strikes the vulgar part of us
infinitely the most, but to a thinking mind London is incomparably the most delightful subject for contemplation.) The ceiling
of the room opening into the Chapel painted with the battle of
Austerlitz by Girard, the picture from which the print is taken.
Drove in a cabriolet thro' the champs elysees & the bois du
Boulogne to St Cloud. Was conducted thro' it by Buonaparte's
confidential servant; who had slept for months by his bed-side &
had followed him from Mal-maison. Never changed his servants. A new face was death to him. Slept so lightly, a mouse
stirring would wake him. Slept little, seldom above 3 or 4 hours,
never heard him talk in his sleep. Slept a little in the day, sometimes, not often. Walked quick, with his hands joined behind him
& his head inclined downwards. Spoke little, in the fewest words
possible, & brusquely—brusquement. Mimicked his talk & his
walk. Always at work—always writing. The room he worked
in, a library—Saw the works of Corneille there &c. He was
walking there in that alley before 4 oClock in the morning sometimes. Took coffee when he rose & at ten or eleven breakfasted
in that avenue, or covered walk, with the Empress on cold meat
—a la fourchette. He sat with his face to the windows, she looking down the avenue. A screen placed behind him sometimes,
when windy weather. Eat little. At dinner some bouillé, some
poulard. that was all; his snuff-box by his side. Much snuff—
threw it about—much coffee. played a good deal at chess—&
often with the ladies.

At dinner sat half-way down a long table vis-a-vis the empress.
Dined frequently tête a tête with her. Saw the table—very small
indeed—They lived on the best terms together—She was very

[1] Marie-Thérèse-Charlotte, 1778–1851, daughter of Louis XVI;
Charles Philippe, Comte d'Artois, later Charles X; Louis-Antoine de
Bourbon, b. 1775, duc d'Angoulême, his eldest son.

fond of playing on the piano-forte & of embroidering & painting flowers, & of playing at billiards with her ladies. Walked over the gardens & thro' the orange-trees from Versailles—& in the orange-house from which he expelled the legislative Assembly —& in the Theatre. Our conductor had been there thirteen years, but said the other knew more of Buonaparte. That he did not like observation, & that they were obliged to hide themselves when they saw him. Showed us how he himself ran behind the trunk of a tree at the sight of him, & mimicked him in his hurrying away the servants. That the Empress gave up to him in everything. That he was un homme dure. Went often on horse-back to see Josephine at Mal-maison, but his visits were unknown to Maria Louisa. That the two ladies never saw each other.

A magnificent view of Paris, the Pantheon, St Sulpice &c from the court-yard. No smoke, & bright sun-shine. The view unbroken by trees. At a distance it looks too much like a great rough stone quarry. A marriage-procession on foot as we left St Cloud. Many parties riding in the Bois de Boulogne on our return. In the evening went along the boulevards to the Theatre de la Gaieté & saw Le Chien de Montargis[1] As we came out, a man in the lobby held up the play in one hand for sale, & fondled the hero of it a rough curled spaniel with the other. Oh le charmant— c'est il qui l'a fait! Full moon—caffées & guinguettes every where full of company & glittering with lights thro' the trees. *Sept*. 1*st* Dejeuner at Very's.[2] Set off at 3 for Geneva. Retrospective view of Paris—Donjon de Vincennes—Bicatre.—passed by moonlight thro' the forest of Fontainbleau & supped in a room, where the King of Prussia had dined; as we were told by an Inscription—Walked before the Chateau.

Sept 2. If walls could speak, those of Fontainbleau—how much would they tell us? The gallery of Francis I, painted in fresco by Primaticcio (the chamber in which Leonardo da Vinci

---

[1] *Mélodrame* by R. C. G. Pixéricourt (1733–1844) first performed at the *Gaité* in Paris, 18th June 1814. It tells the story of the faithful dog, Dragon, who pursues and brings to book his master's murderer. Much of the play's success was due to the dog. The critic of the *Petites Affiches* concluded that 'c'est un acteur naturel, sensible, intelligent, et surtout modeste, qui me paraît digne d'être encouragé dans ses débuts'.

[2] A restaurant overlooking the gardens of the Tuileries; it was very popular with English visitors.

breathed his last is in the village. He was interred in the church there—) the gallery of Diana the scene of his gallanteries; the gallery of the Cerfs stained with the blood of Monaldeschi, the rooms inhabited successively by the Kings of France, their wives & their mistresses; by Henry the 4th, by Louis XIV; by Marie Antoinette, by Marie Louise, every one of which have left their footsteps, the rooms fitted up as a chapel or oratory in which for 14 months the Pope[1] performed his daily devotions, stirring out but twice, the church in which Napoleon signed his abdication the courtyard in which he took leave of his guards, standing in the midst of them, & embracing his marshals & his eagles, his carriage already at the gate to convey him away for ever—These now silent & empty serve only to remind us of the fleeting nature of things. Strait avenues. Post-house full of bullets. Cossack horses. Fields of battle. broken bridges. River Yonne. Cathedral at Sens. Tomb of an Archbp. sculptured in small bas relief by Primaticcio. Vineyards—Chateaux—Yonne—Joigny—River—boats—town along the shore under the hill, chateau & church. Walked on the bridge by moon-light & by day-break.
3ᵈ Sep Retrospective view of Joigny. Triumphal Arches in honor of Mˡˡᵉ· D'Angouleme—Avenues. Auxerre river—cathedral—convent. Avalons—looked from the public walk into a little valley full of cottages, bridges &—like a valley in the Peak of Derbyshire—College & garden.[2]
4ᵗʰ. Went on to Dijon among vineyards & hemp-fields & corn—a bleak open country, like Oxford-shire, the wind blowing. Le Bize est frais, Monsieur. Wore my great coat, & at the post houses sat before the fire—
Pretty approach to Dijon—rocky & woody hills, a crucifix here & there on the crags. Came in after dark.
5ᵗʰ. Park laid out by Le Notre—a square of forest-like wood, pierced with avenues, terminating in a circle in the centre, where the citizens dance. Ramparts—bourgeois reading in his alcove on the walls.—Museum—Dukes of Burgundy—breakfasted in a salon at the coffee-house. Maison Bossuet, a book-seller's. Saw

[1] Pius VII, during his detention by Napoleon.

[2] Fair Copy (S.R.) has a passage interlined by S.R. at a different time from Fair Copy (S.R.) itself: 'One of the Professors saluted me as the first Poet of the age; & in return (could I do less) I sent him back to render homage to our fellow traveller as the "most upright Judge", the most eloquent senator, & the future historian of Great Britain.'

his study & chapel, a cross still in the ceiling. Bought a Phedrus. Descent into Doll magnificent—an extensive plain skirted by mountains—a Claud—a Poussin—the first distance yet seen in this country, & first rate. Crossed the Soane on his way to Lyons. Public walk at Doll.A grand avenue led us into a new Country— Mountains in sight, & above all a snow mountain—not like a cloud or vapour—but full of lights & shadows & like itself. Second hay harvest—Women with large broad hats. Supped & slept at Poligny. Frankness and hospitality of the mountain-character. Supped on Greves,[1] small birds less than snipes, that fatten in the vineyards.

6th Septr. Magnificent ascent by a small church & convent. Vines up to the hill-tops—forests of firs. Moron—ruins of a castle on a summit in wood—sweeping fir-forests—gulphs & precipices— mountain-passes & tracks of torrents—children kneeling & crossing themselves in a begging attitude by the way-side long before you come up—The sunny features under the broad um-brella straw-hats the red or blue handkerchief, which when slung from the neck behind had a good effect—the blue or yellow petticoat & white apron. Breakfasted at Champignon. A fair. A mountain village—Water-mills—bridges—& craggy hills— houses tumbled about—Now in Jura—Fir-forests—Houses of Wood-cutters—Winding up & down continually Beauty & Grandeur—Dark & still character of the firs—almost all seem-ingly Spruce—& presenting the most elegant shrubberies as they open into the vallies—country cheerful & populous— women at work in the fields—& making nails in the houses— walked over rocks & thro a village—a christening in the church —Romantic descent into Moray—came in on foot—Church & houses reminded me of Cromford.—The french inn is little improved. In France there are still but two classes of Society. The first travel from chateau to chateau. The last shift as they can. There is still wanting a middle class to command into an inn the comforts & elegancies of life.—

Sept. 7. Walked a post & a half to the Rousses—A continual ascent—a church far up among the Mountains—Saw a milk girl climbing & singing a short stanza ending always in 'la guerre'— a lively air—She was coming from the valley with a long step, her pail under her arm—Breakfasted on Trout at the Rousses in

[1] i.e. *grives*, cf. the proverb 'faute de grives on mange des merles'.

a room in which Josephine had dined. The church. Confessionals. The church-yard looks up a bleak mountain-valley, with small patches of barley—& oats—& over a small lake or tarn—the valley shut up at the end by two peaks.—The church is so situated on the edge of the mountain, that the gutter which looks west sends its waters to the Rhone & the Mediterranean & that which looks east to the Rhine & the North Sea.—Behind the Rousses rises the Ridge or mountain, called Doll the highest point of the Jura which commands a great part of Swisserland.— Somewhere 3 or 4 leagues off in this wild region of the Jura stands the Chateau de Joux. There Toussaint[1] breathed out his heroic spirit. He died in less than 3mos after he came there. (Little did B. imagine that a few years afterwards his fate should be so similar. Formidable alike in themselves, & the constancy of their adherents they were conveyed across an ocean to linger —but there the parable ends—the first perished on his arrival— how we know not!) The left mountain-screen from the church- yard is in Swisserland, & much of it, pastured by cows, belongs to Mme. de Stael. Went on & at a turn of the road had a full view of the Glaciers over a wood of firs. The snows of a dazzling brightness contrasted with the dark foliage filled us with sur- prize & pleasure, much as we expected to see them; yet the surprize was lessened, when I looked again, & I confess I felt little besides that exhileration I have so often felt in a bright winter's day. Came to [?Gex] &, descending, the lake of Geneva, the vallais, from Geneva to Vevey, & the mountains, the alps of Savoy, Mont Blanc, above all, burst upon us. Passed a house of Louis Bonaparte, in which he was now living, & among orchards went on to Nyon—along the lake-side & slept at Copet. Found Simondi,[2] Sleigel[3] & Vernon[4] there.

[1] Toussaint L'Ouverture. The most famous opponent of slavery in Haiti. Named Commander-in-chief on behalf of the French, he used his power to make the island independent of France, calling himself 'the Buonaparte of St. Domingo'. He was taken prisoner by treachery and died at Joux, April 27th, 1803.

[2] J. G. L. de Sismondi, 1773–1842, author of *Histoire des Républiques Italiennes du Moyen Âge*, etc.

[3] August Wilhelm von Schlegel, 1767–1845, translator of Shakespeare. He dedicated his *Réflexions sur l'Étude des Langues Asiatiques* to Sir James Mackintosh.

[4] George Granville Vernon, 1785–1861, eldest son of the Archbishop of York.

Sept 8. Sercheron.[1] Maria Louisa.[2] Geneva. Public walks. A Prayer & Psalm in the Cathedral. A small round light closet near a Gateway from which Calvin preached, the streets rising rapidly in front of it. Ferney. His[3] bed-chamber—12 feet by 15—over his bed picture of Le Kain, besides those of himself, Frederic, Katherine—& Mme Du Chatelet. The last a most pleasing portrait. Portraits in crayons of a boy & girl, his sempstress, & supplier of wood for his fire. A delightful situation.

Sept. 9. Blue waters of the Rhone.[4] Bonneville. The bridge. View from it of a beautiful road, overarched with trees, skirted with Swiss Cottages & terminated by a church.

Septr 10. Cluse—its narrow street—vale beyond it wooded & shut in by Mountains. A Martin.—Set off on Mules—Lovely

---

[1] i.e. Sécheron, a suburb of Geneva, on the Lake, where was Dejean's *Hotel de l'Angleterre*, a favourite residence of English travellers. When Byron stayed there in May, 1816, he put his age down as 100. Lady Charlotte Bury writes of it in *The Diary of a Lady in Waiting*, i, 266: 'This hotel is all cleanliness and comfort,—the beautiful lake and its appendages in sight of the windows. I get up every now and then from my table to look at Mont Blanc. . . .'

[2] Rogers wrote this same day to Richard Sharp 'By the way, Marie Louise [the ex-Empress, second wife of Napoleon] is now at Secheron, and we met her at the garden gate as she passed through it this morning. She is tall and fair, and not plain, but certainly not handsome, and too erect to be graceful. She was going to angle in the lake.' *Contemporaries*, i, p. 165.

[3] i.e. Voltaire. He bought the property of Ferney in 1758 and lived there more or less constantly until his death—which ocurred on a visit to Paris—in 1778. It was one of the great Geneva sights.

[4] It might be helpful to give in advance a brief account of Rogers' movements in Switzerland.

1. After arriving in Geneva on Sept. 8th, he left next day for a trip to Chamonix, going south via Bonneville and along the valley of the Arve, and returning by the same route to Geneva on Sept. 13th.

2. A tour to the Forest Cantons. He left Geneva on Sept. 14th and went along the south side of Lake Léman and back along the north side as far as Lausanne, striking north there for Bern, where he arrived on the 17th. From Bern he went to Lucerne, and from there made excursions to Altdorf and Schwyz. He left Lucerne on the 23rd for the Lake of Bienne, where he spent a night on the Isle St. Pierre before returning to Geneva via the west side of Lake Neuchatel and Lausanne. He got back on the 28th.

3. He left next day for Italy, travelling once more along the south shore of Lake Léman, and then taking the usual road to the Simplon via Martigny and Brig.

valley. Swiss Cottages—An eagle on the wing, wheeling round
& round, now soaring & now descending. Arve. Pont Palissier!!!
A Mountain Pass, called Les Montées down which Arve ran,
thro' magnificent Firs, the Chateau de St Michel, giving its
name to the valley—a round tower in ruins on a lofty rock at the
entrance & Mont Blanc rising & shutting us in, in front. A cross
with an affiche from the good Bp of Chambray & Geneva
promising an indulgence of 40 days to those who would say a
prayer for the souls in purgatory. Church of Les Ouches where
the sun does not shine for 3 months—Village above on Mont
Bréven from which the people descend to Mass. The Glaciers
des Bossons, Mer de Glace. Chamouny.

Sep. 11. Sunday Montanvert. A girl watching her cows & reading her prayer book on the mountain. Wild flowers. Campag-
nola. Rhododendron. Clover. Spruce Firs. Larches—burnt by the
Peasants—Cabin. Went down to the sea of ice as far as a huge
block of Granite (in such mountain-waves & such abysses, that
the head almost turns at the sight of them) & thought of Capt[n]
Thomas James, & his company who went out to sport on the ice,
leaving the ship motionless as in a dry dock—the ship under all
its sails, & not one man in the ship—[1]

Descending Montanvert, had splendid visions of the Glaciers
thro' the evening mists. A Gentleman carried up & down in a
chair. Snow fell—met girls with milk & cherries, a rose & a
bouquet of wild strawberries. Group round the fire—met the
mules. An Albino—Chamougni. Model of it. The milk of 60
cows at once to make Gruyere cheese.

Sept 12. The Glaciers des Bossons. Blocks of Ice, innumerable,
not unlike Stonehenge—some of a steel-blue—Walked by it

---

[1] *The strange and dangerovs voyage of Captain Thomas Iames, in his
intended discouery of the Northwest Passage into the South Sea. . . .* Lon. 1633,
pp. 19, 20.

'The 28. and 29. [July 1631] we were so fast inclosed in the Ice, that not
withstanding, we put aboard all the sayle that was at yards; and that it
blew a very hard gale of winds; the Ship stirred no more than if she had
beene in a dry Docke. Hereupon we went all boldly out vpon the Ice, to
sport and recreate our selves, letting her stand still, vnder all her Sayles.
. . . wee dranke a health to his Maiestie on the Ice; not one man in the
Ship; and shee still vnder all her sayles.'

It has been suggested that Coleridge's *Ancient Mariner* owes something
to this work.

thro' cornfields & orchards full of summer & autumn. Met fruit & milk in Boissons. An eagle on the wing in the lower regions of Mont Blanc. A fair at Les Ouches. A girl with her lambs in a string. Descent by the Arve!—Delicious day in a heavenly country. A little girl fetched us grapes out of the vineyards. St Martin. Terrace. Salanche. A child at the church-door, half a day old waiting there for baptism. Inscribed on a cross over a grave. 'Je prie pour vous—Vous priez pour moi.'

13. Came on thro Cluse & its beautiful valley, full of groves & villages & breakfasted at Bonneville, on quails, grives, trout & coffee. The roads of Savoy strait & beautifully overarched by the fruit-trees on each side; & presenting the most enchanting vistas, when peasants or peasant-children were seen at a distance under them. From the bridge at Bonneville seen under a morning sun the charm alas, was gone. Came to Geneva & rowed & sailed on the lake, coasting the country houses round, each with its little grove or garden, Mont Blanc in great grandeur—& the Jura in deep shadow,—saluted by a gentleman rowing home to his country house. Walked with Dumont[1] to Lady Holland, & returned thro' the gates with him & M[ackintosh]. & Sismondi.

14. Walked to the Rue Rousseau & read on a stone tablet

Ici est né
Jean Jacques Rousseau
Le XXVII Juin MDCCXII

Was there told that he came there 15 days after he was born & was conducted to Nº 151. Place des Boucheries, a house with a terrace or gallery, looking sideways on the lake—There, we were told, he was born. Passed a house near it with this inscription

Ici est né
Charles Bonnet[2]
Le XIII Mars. 1720.

No such things with us. None on Dryden's House in Gerard St.

---

[1] Pierre Étienne Louis Dumont, 1759–1829. Came to London in 1785 and got to know Lord Holland. Became the disciple and editor of Jeremy Bentham. Returned to Geneva 1814.

[2] Naturalist and philosopher. He died in 1793.

None on Johnson's in Ball Court or Milton's in Jewin Street.
Set off along the southeast side lake—blue as a sapphire—Slept
at Thonon—As we approached it a romantic glen on the right,
hung round with wood & guarded by an old castle now in ruins
—Our Landlord, Quarter Master of a French Regiment of
Cavalry, had been at Moscow. Je n'ai que tué un Cossack—A
delicious walk towards Repail, the retreat of a Duke of Savoy.
Faire repail afterwards signified to lead a happy life & not to
have seen Repail to have seen nothing. Boats full of market
people coming in from Lausanne—A glorious sun-set. In the
town the viaticum & a number of lighted candles at a door.

15. Chesnut groves along the lake—the morning mists on the
Mountains. Meillerie—its grey rocks, like enormous battlements, a thousand fairy glades running here & there up among
them—St Preux[1]—Clarens in sight, & Dent de Jamant. Breakfasted at St Gingo—Ferried across the Rhone at the head of the
Lake at the Castle de la Ruche. Mountains topt with snow—hay
every where carrying in the meadows the road traversing them
as thro' a park—Beautiful villages in the Pays de Vaud—An old
castle, Chateau de Chillon, with its pointed towers, once used as
a State prison by the Government of Berne; now with a small
garrison surrounded by water. Clarens. Climbed up thro a vineyard to the Maison Rousseau now a heap of stones, supposed to
be the scite of Julia's[2] house—the lake heavenly—the rocks of
Mellerie in deep shadow. Chateau de Chatelard. Church of
Montreux. A house in which Rousseau is said to have lived with
M[me] De Warens by the roadside between Clarens & La Tour.
Vevay. Ludlow's[3] house on the edge of the lake—Read the
Inscription (Omne solum forti patria est Quia Patris. A.D.
1684.) on the front of it & also that on his tomb in the Church by
the light of a lantern. The Public Walks! Glorious sun-set.

16th. The Public Walks. Bowdler[4]—Continued along the lake
among vineyards above & below us; stone walls every where
running in parallel lines to prevent the earth from falling.
Villages & Chateaux; & cheerfulness. Lausanne; descending to

[1] The hero of *La Nouvelle Héloïse*.

[2] The Julie of *Julie, ou la Nouvelle Héloïse*.

[3] Edmund Ludlow, *c.* 1617–92, the Regicide. Impeached in 1660, he
fled to Switzerland. He died at Vevey.

[4] Thomas, the Bowdleriser of Shakespeare and Gibbon, 1754–1825. He
was in Geneva to settle the affairs of a friend who had died abroad.

The Italian Journal

the Lake. Gibbon's house in a street; his broad terrace, fenced with a low box hedge behind it, commanding the lake & mountains. His summer-house lower down. a small apartment, 9 feet square, & painted white, within & without. The walk or berceau leading from it, 47 yards long, 4 yds wide—now fenced with espaliers on the lake-side, a wall on the other. The acacias are gone. The view fine, but far less so than those from Vevay & Clarens, tho' not very different. Read part of his memoirs & some of his letters there, found in a French translation at a bookseller's. The house now belongs to a M.   to whose wife it came from Deyverdun. A pretty nursery maid here in her broad hat. Mme de Montolieu[1] lives here in the winter, & now lives a league off. Now old; but still writing. A long ascent from Lausanne, the lake behind us, & a long ridge of mountains, topt with snow long visible on the right. A soft, & woody country, meadows full of crocusses purple, & white; the flail sounding in every barn. Descent into Moudon.

17th. A soft & pleasant country, passing thro' several villages & by chateaux with round towers & terraces. Men & women with flowers in their hats. Payerne. Fountains ornamented with men in armour in bronze—such as are seen in the prints of Albert Durer. Queen Bertha's saddle—Plantas hist 32.[2] The lake of Morat among the hills. Morat. Breakfasted at a pleasant Auberge looking on the lake. A table d'hote in the room. Crossed the lake, being rowed over by a father & his two sons, & ascended a hill planted with vines & saw the lakes of Neuchatel & Bienne winding below; the isle of St Pierre not visible. Returned & went on & from a height saw the Alps, as from their bases stretching along the horizon, wrapt in snow, & of the most rugged & fantastic shapes. Well might Haller[3] observe 'No wheel ever crossed the Alps.' They looked like the barrier of another world & seemed to say to the curiosity of Man 'Hitherto shalt thou go & no further.'

[1] Mme. J. F. Montolieu, b. & d. Lausanne, 1761–1839. She published another book—*Anastase et Nephtalie*—the following year.
[2] The reference is to Vol. 1 of J. Planta, *The History of the Helvetic Confederacy*, 2v, London, 1800. The saddle belonging to the 10th-century queen was preserved at Payerne, he says in a footnote.
[3] Albrecht von Haller, 1708–77. Swiss anatomist and physiologist. Travelled widely in search of plants and wrote in 1729 a poem, *Die Alpen* (pub. in *Gedichte*, 1732) showing an unusually early appreciation of Alpine scenery.

The women now appeared every where with vast butterfly-wings of black crape & wire—a fashion as old as Albert Durer—driving goats or cows. The cottages vast & very picturesque with their broad sheltering eaves & numerous galleries. The long leaves of the Indian Wheat suspended under the roofs, still fresh & green had a very pretty effect. The window-panes, like those in an Ostade, of an Oyster-shell fashion. A beautiful valley opening at each end to the Mountains. A covered bridge of great breadth & extent & guarded by many gates over a river conducted into the canton of Bern. A star-light night. Bern. Language almost entirely german.

18. A misty morning. Very neat. The footways flagged & running under the houses, & opening thro' arches into the Street. The Fountains every where & like those at Payerne—Armed Knights, their hands on the head of a boy, or a small bear climbing their swords, Shepherds piping, & Ladies pouring water into urns. The great church. No monument to Haller, who is interred there. The house he lived in—is in the Rue des Gentilshommes. The stag, & his young ones. The two bears in the castle ditch. A dead fir in the centre, up which one had climbed.—Walks behind the great church very delightful. The Aar runs under them, & the surrounding hills covered with woods & country-houses, the Glaciers appearing beyond them. The hanging gardens & terraces behind the Rue des Gentils-homes & immediately over the river very rich & various, orange-trees & trellisses & vases of flowers & maisons d'eté of various shapes being interspersed among them. The road now ascended among woods, principally of fir, & ran thro' a rich, uneven & beautiful country, wood & meadow, chateau & farm-houses tumbled about, the glaciers continuing on our right. It was Sunday, & the people in their best array were at every door & window as we passed, & driving along in one horse-carts & chaises. Few people seen on horse-back here or in France. Dined at Bois la Duc 20^m from Bern. A large neat Inn. A Room below full of men & women drinking the small wine of Iverdyn. A croud such as Teniers has often painted. Walked in the Church-yard. A small weeping willow on a grave, & many pinks. A magnificent view of the Alps afterwards for some time, illumi-nated by the evening sun, their outlines & lights & shadows & cavities & projections soft & silvery & only less unsubstantial to

the eye than summer clouds. Passed thro' many beautiful woods, the road excellent. No poverty, no beggers in the Canton of Berne—Slept at Morgenthal or Morning dale. Not a stone or a tile any where out of its place, not a thatch but in its first neatness. Came in by moonlight. A boy singing gaily under the window at this moment.

19. The country still woody. Passed a castellated city on our left. Breakfasted at Zofinghen, a neat little town in the canton of Argovie, & there saw in a meadow, two vast limes close to each other & cut into chambers above chambers & green galleries—like Caligula's nest (see Gibbon c 31. 248 note)[1]—well-floored to which you ascend by a ladder. Were told they were 500 yrs old, & that upwards of 50 couple have waltzed at a time within them. Leaving the town, a castle on a woody rock appeared most picturesquely & a cross on a crag announced our arrival in the canton of Lucerne. A churchyard by the road-side full of graves—croslets—& of structures of wood or tin, gilt & painted, inclining more or less to the form of a cross; at the foot of most was a stone fount or jar of red clay pottery, full of holy water & a sprig of box or fir, or a stick with a tassel at the end, with which a relation or friend, kneeling, & saying her masses as she bids her beads with one hand, sprinkles the pinks that grow on the grave or heap of earth that extends from it. Saw a woman so employed. In another part saw the graves of the children, over which were only sticks crossed; & here & there a broken porringer upon them. Upon some of the former were pictures & inscriptions. In our way to Sursee the Alps, all snow, bounded our horizon, extending along a vast plain from east to west, in my wildest dreams nothing ever surpassed them. They shone in the sun, & seemed impassable; nor was their extent less striking than their altitude. Every thing indeed has has fallen perhaps a little short of my expectations, but the Alps alone. They have exceeded them, & whenever they appear, they affect me as much as if I was seeing them for the first time. At Sursee dined at the Table D'hote with a good looking young man, whose fingers were dyed with *blue*, & passing thro' the street were beckoned up

[1] In this note, Gibbon records that Pliny mentioned some plane trees 'of an enormous size; one in the Imperial Villa at Velitræ, which Caligula called his nest, as the branches were capable of holding a large table, the proper attendants and the emperor himself'.

into a house, where, after a repast, some people of the lower order were waltzing—to two or three fiddles. Walked on to the head of the lake of Sempach & gathered 14 different flowers. The lake accompanied us for 6 or 7 miles, on the other side at the other end the little town of that name—Passed by a covered bridge over the River Emmen. A foot bridge, 500 feet in length, covered in, & full of paintings—Lucerne a very neat town. Concerts & Ball there that Ev^g, superintended by a Bookseller. Concert began at 9. Ball lasted till 6.

20. Saw the model of the lake & mountains, executed by Genl. Peyffer.[1] Embarked at 11, leaving the market full & busy on the shore. Apples, pears, & a few grapes & peaches. A handsome girl in her flat straw hat & many-coloured ribbons. Three oars. Met a passage-boat, full of market-people. The town with its walls & numerous watch-towers, its bridges, cathedral & white country houses scattered up & down, where the lake opened to right & left, the right view but half illuminated, mountainous & very solemn. Stanstadt a town in the distance, in a deep recess of the lake among the mountains, dark & standing out in the water. A little chapel or oratory on a rock, dedicated to St Nicholas. Rowed on between two cantons & landed on one of them, that of Unterwalden, also on the little republic of Gersau—Its territory steep as a wall, woody, & hung with cottages. Its capital a village, not a town. Children presented us with apples, smiling & running away. Looked in upon a table d'hote. Overtook here the passage boat to Brunen—Passed the chapel of Child Murther among the woods, & on the opposite mountain saw another with a gilt spire dedicated to St Mary of the sunny hill. Landed & drank of the three springs at Grutli. Landed also on the other side at the chapel of William Tell, full of rude & gay paintings. Here, the Mountains folding over & shutting in the scene, with

---

[1] This celebrated model of the topography of Lucerne and the adjacent Cantons could be seen by the tourist for a small fee. Completed by 1785, 'the composition is principally a mastic of charcoal, lime, clay, a little pitch with a thin coat of wax; and is so hard that it can be trod upon without receiving the least damage. The whole is painted with different colours, representing the objects as they exist in nature . . . The plan is indeed so minutely exact, that it comprises not only all the mountains, lakes, rivers, towns, villages, and forests; but every cottage, every torrent, every bridge, every road, and even every path is distinctly and accurately represented.' William Coxe, *Travels in Switzerland*, 1789, i, 254.

their snowy summits, & night coming on, first appeared the Convent of Ursuline Nuns & then the churches of Fluellen & Altorf. Walked from F. to A. among the dark Mountains— Never was a more imposing scene, or one so full of splendid recollections. On that green eminence met three persons distinguished by their patriotism, their virtue, their humanity in a barbarous age; & they accomplished what even at this day exists. There Tell leaped from the boat, & here he shot, if we may believe the tradition, the apple from the head of his boy. A tower, adorned with many rude paintings, commemorates the spot in Altorf, & a fountain is decorated with his statue & that of his boy holding the apple. Four ambassadors had arrived there, two from Schwyz, two from Unterwalden, to persuade the people of Uri, to confederate with them & not with the other cantons.[1] They were full-drest in black, with cocked hats & swords & buckles in their shoes. We found them at dusk on the steps of our Auberge, & before 7 in the morning I met them again. Cry of the watchman.

21, The council had met yesterday & are now again assembling but are thought to be unfavourable. Just now we met the Landmannan in a full suit of black, a very gentlemanlike good looking man, walking between two officers in cloaks blue & yellow, to the senate house thus inscribed (a small handsome structure)   M D C   S P Z U   C C V I

From the Capuchin Monastery there is a good view of the vale. saw the church, the refectory—under the dinner-table a long trough full of saw-dust—the cloisters & one of the cells. The Friar, aged 87, said with a melancholy smile & shrug, 'petite,' when I entered it. Visited also a convent of Capucine Nuns—a Friar at the grate in conversation with three sleek-looking nuns. In a field a league off the people assemble. Met three young men & a little boy on the baggage horse on their way up Mont St Gothard. They had come in our boat from Gersau. Set off to return & met a boat full of cattle for the fair at Lugano! How near then did we feel to Italy! Passed under the right shore by the chapel of Tell, & by a little painting in a black frame, not above a foot square affixed in a very retired nook to the rock—

---

[1] Between the fall of Napoleon and the Federal Pact of August, 1815, a number of cantons were concerned to change the constitution outlined by Bonaparte.

probably some votive offering. A small harbour constructed of stone for boats in distress. Brunen. View from the door of the Cerf Inn!! perhaps the finest of all. A house breaks the view into two, one of which is a view towards Grutli & Tell's chapel, sublimity itself, a lake shut in by folding mountains—the other a view across a lake to a little cheerful town [Treib] under a mountain.—Two boys came forward with a cross bow & discharged an arrow at a target that hung out on the door of the house that divided the view. In a sort of chaise drawn by one horse went on to Schwytz, thro orchards & meadows, & among neat country houses. An excellent Inn. Went to the House of M. Reding an Ex Landamm. In the court-yard my hand was taken by a very pretty little girl, smiling & dropping a curtsey, who immediately afterwards took my sister's, leading her thro' the Hall & up a handsome staircase into a good apartment where at their coffee (after dinner—it was 2 oClock) sat M. & Me Reding their eldest girl a fine young woman, an old lady perhaps the Grandmother, the General who had served in Spain his brother now Governor of Majorca, &—   a Member of the Great Council of Berne. Great Courtesy & unaffected good manners. He was in the minority on the question of seceding from the confederacy. Went on thro' a rich & very beautiful valley among hanging woods & inclosures to the little lake of Lowertz & winded round it under a perpendicular rock. Met three young men on their way home to Schwitz, Students at Zurich. A high woody island—a chapel & the ruins of a tower upon it. Story of the girl, & her ghost persuing a man in armour. Terrible calamity 2 Sep. 1806! Valley full of fragments of the Mountain! Disappearance of Goldau. Descent to Arth. Walked thro' cherry orchards by a foot-path among cottages & farm-houses of the richest tints. A narrow valley—on the left the rocks or rather stages of rock, hung with woods receding & advancing, far beyond those of Matlock or Dunkald—Arth. Called at the House of Dr Zay, or rather his son, above 500 years Old. Very curiously wrought & furnished. A by-staircase or ladder from his chamber to his parlour below. Saw there the old Pike.—His wife. His courtesy! Would see us into the boat without his hat.—No french officer here, when they invaded it could by any bribe get here a spy or a mistress. The names of those who fell are all in the parish register.—Coasted the right side of the lake, being rowed by two men & a woman. hanging woods, vineyards, farmhouses, water-mills & Chapels. Not a house but in its natural colour of the fir. & many hung with vines. A lovelier chain of hills never seen by a lake-side. Met many boats, one with only a woman on board. The Rigi on the opposite side, with a cross on its summit, near which is a chapel dedicated to our Lady of the Snows. Dusk. Moonlight. Zug. Table d'hote. A Colonel, a Professor, an Attendant on a German Princess—the master & mistress, & their daughter, a pretty little child, 10 years old, waited upon us. Victims at Lowertz—[1]

22. Rain. After breakfast the little girl sung us some songs, among which was the Tyrolese. Parted with Mackintosh,[2] who set off for Basil to meet his daughter, the Resident's Wife at Bagdad. Embarked again on the lake of Zug. National songs of the Boatmen—One sung by the people of Schwyz, when they fought the french. One, very old & a favourite in the small cantons, the burden of which contained the words Schwyz & Faderland. They sung it twice & the air, tho' now & then rapid, was grand, simple, & affecting. The Tyrolese song seems a favourite one on the lakes. We heard it again that evening on the lake of Lucerne. Landed at Immensis a small village with its chapel as gay within as the rest, & ascending by a path among orchards & woody fields in a quarter of an hour reached a small chapel erected on the spot on which Tell shot Gisler. A painting representing it on the front of the chapel. From the steps we saw the lake of Lucerne. Descended in a few minutes into Kussnach. A very small & pretty town. An old Lady in her finery at mass. Embarked on the Lake of Lucerne. Lovely shores—Rigi in clouds. Passed several churches—& the gulph of Stanstadt in gloomy grandeur, the town not long visible—& the ruins of an old castle, once, we were told belonging to a *Grand Autrichien*. A gay young man in the boat, & so large in proportion to its small size, that it rocked when he took snuff or shook the ashes out of his pipe. Alarmed, & most when he & his friend rowed. They stopt to drink p[err?]y at a house vis a vis the chapel of St Nicholas, & we came on in a larger boat by ourselves. Magnificent night scene—up Ury. Table d'hote. Heavy rain.—

[1] In the landslide of Sept. 1806, which buried Goldau.
[2] *v.* introduction, p. 54.

23. Three covered bridges for foot-passengers at every five yards presenting pictures to the eye over an arch. In two they were historical & the subjects national, in that which led to the cathedral & was the longest, the subjects were from the bible. In every one there were windows upon the lake & mountains. In the cathedral mass performed with violins & bass-viols. In the square was a parade. French horns played a slow, sad & touching air. Peaches & figs in the market. No grapes. Returned to Sursee. Ladders & baskets full of apples in every orchard, some of which were now purple with crocusses—the road overhung with boughs full of apples of the deepest red. Lake of Sempach, blue as ultramarine, tho' the sky did not seem bluer than in England. Drove along it to Sursee. Till yesterday we had had no rain—bright sunshine all day long. This morning before eleven the sun shone out again. A succession of green & wooded vallies. A small lake & on its island a chateau with its round tower & extinguisher-roof, its terraces & draw-bridge. A high hill, the ruins of a castle upon it. In an hour we counted ten chapels & crosses by the way-side but in a few minutes afterwards we saw the sign of the black bear, & the horse-hair wings of a Bernese cap, & found ourselves in a protestant Canton. The road had a very altered character, & the appearance of a by-road, but the villages were numerous, & in every field were many peasants, who far & near became statues at the sight of us, nor stirred from the attitudes they were found in while we continued in sight. Passed thro' many woods of fir, in which they were collecting the cones in baskets, & were struck with the catching lights & deepening shadows as the sun set. To-day we had long a parting view of the Uri Mountains &, as we came on, the Glaciers of Bern rose in the sky. No more beggers. At Schweiz the beggar-girls pursued us into the Inn & up stairs. Slept at Sumiswald where two little Bernoise, the eldest twelve years old, filles de la Maison, entertained us with singing & playing on the piano-forte in their Psyche caps & long plaited tails. Walked in the church-yard by Moonlight. In France here & there a chateau, but no cottages, no farm-houses are scattered over the country; in Swisserland every where; if cottages indeed any can be called; for in the Protestant Cantons, in Berne particularly there is scarcely a house below the rank of a first rate English farm-house;—most of them being enormous & of a

151

neatness & solidity never seen in England. The prodigal use of the fir in building, & its being so often left in its natural colour give great warmth & beauty to the landscape—& that they last long in that state Dr Zay's house at Arth is good evidence, which appears to be still more modern than many in excellent condition up & down Swisserland. Our postilion lit his pipe continually with a flint & a key from his pocket, as he rode on in the saddle; a usual custom with the Swiss.

24. Continued thro' a rich woody & uneven country. The Houses still larger & more numerous, & still built entirely of wood, roof & all, & within, floor, wall & cieling; nor were they white-washed, as too often in Switzerland, but in the rich natural hue of the deal. In the vallies we saw yesterday, many of the peasants are said to be richer than the citizens of Berne. At Bern in the public walk read Rousseau's account of himself in the Isle de St Pierre,[1] & proceeded to Arberg, walking a few yards along the upper public walk of Berne. The river beautiful, & thro' the day, particularly the latter part of it, the snowy Alps—among which the Screckhorn, or Peak of Terror was most eminent—were grand & striking beyond every thing we had seen, particularly as we left Berne. Uneven road. Fir woods. Rich & extensive view of the vale of Arberg & the Lakes of Bienne & Neauchatel. Arberg. A Landlord who let his wife wear the Bernois dress, tho' it cost 60 louis, & who thought the English were fondest of veal.

25 *Sunday*. A summer mist clearing up into Bright Sunshine. Soon reached the Lac de Bienne & for half a league went along it to Logna. Embarked & in twenty minutes landed on the Isle of St Pierre. It consists of a high ridge on the N.W precipitate & hung on the S.E. each side with wood & vineyard. The Snowy Alps are magnificent in the distance; & the many little towns that border the lake & throw their white reflections on the water give a cheerfulness to the terrace, described by Rousseau. His chamber, its window looking over the lake towards the Alps. A flight of steps thro' the floor as in Dr Zay's house at Arth; by which he is said to have made his escape from unseasonable visitors. The terrace. The pavilion. Great numbers of Holiday-People from the Neighbourhood. Waltzes in the Barn & the Pavilion. Orchestra in the last, two violins played by men & a

---

[1] In book XII of the *Confessions*.

violin cello by a woman. A Romping game on the terrace. A military band with their colours marched in—as Amateurs [?]. Gaiety of their departure. The lake busy with boats. M^r & M^{rs} McDonald. When all was still, sat in Rousseau's room by moonlight & walked on the terrace. The reflections nearly as bright as before. A Heavenly Ev^g. & warm as Summer. Read the Heloise in the Wood in the Afternoon. A bad Table d'hote. Several Guns fired in the course of the evening produced a very grand reverberation behind the Hills to the N.W.

26. Came upon the terrace, & thro' many noble trees, the blue lake, the blue sky, the mountains in that thin haze which precedes a hot day, the five or six villages glittering along the water's edge, the singing of the Autumn birds, the musical murmuring of the church-bells over the lake—that came to the ear like the hum of a beetle or a great bumble-bee, than which there is not a finer note in nature—altogether made so chearful & enchanting a whole, that no wonder Rousseau speaks of it as he does, & Ld Camelford[1] desired to be interred here. Two boats were crossing, & the voices first drew my eye to them—then, but not directly, was heard the dashing of the oars. Two very delicious attractions are possest by the Isle de St Pierre, cheerfulness & seclusion; & the quiet, neatness & civility of the family in the Grange cannot fail to make it a charming residence. I shall often wish myself here. We slept here by means of an order from L'Hopital de Berne. The vault for Lord Camelford is at the farthest end of the terrace where the ground falls suddenly to the lake. Four small bits of wood in the midst of some young trees mark the Place. The mason who made the vault pointed it out to me. To the Hospital he left £1000. to be paid when he is interred there; & they are impatient for his arrival. Crossed the lake to Ceclier, & went by land to Neuchatelle, a very neat & picturesque town, capt towers & steeples & hanging terraces & chateaux & maisons d'eté innumerable by the lake-side. Continued along the lake to Concise by a most amusing road, winding up & down among vineyards, & orchards in which last all

---

[1] Thomas Pitt, 2nd Baron Camelford, 1775–1804. The war prevented this request—made in his will—from being carried out, though the body was embalmed and packed. By the time hostilities ceased, it seems to have been lost sight of.

the country were out, filling baskets & little carts with apples & walnuts;—nothing but climbing & shaking boughs, & raking the fruit together under the trees upon the grass—Passed thro' several steep & very picturesque little towns with chateaux & chateaux-like towers, & romantic glens running up Jura & down to the Lake, which was full of beautiful reflections from the evening clouds that hid part of the Alps—Thro' a forest scene arrived at Concise by moonlight. The village being much excited by a Noce, & we were received as the Bride & Bride-groom on their return home, as we entered the village. Pistols had been before discharged to salute us on the road. Women every where sitting out at their doors dressing flax in the moonshine.—It is remarkable how much gayer & better peopled the Northern side of a Lake is than the Southern! The SW shore of the Lake of Neuchatel combines in a high degree the wild & pastoral character of the Savoy side of that of Geneva & the gaiety of the Pays de Vaud. We were delighted beyond measure, & under the illumination we saw it, preferred it to almost any thing of the kind we had seen.

27 At Concise slept at a small inn kept by a Widow, & for neatness, comfort civility & cheapness, superior to any inn I ever met with abroad, I believe I may say at home. Passed the bride-groom's house. A very pretty garland of flowers suspended over the gate. The bride an heiress. Continued along the lake to Yverdun—At Orbe walked on the Castle Hill—When within two hours of Lausanne the country became beautiful, being tumbled about & full of woods, houses, orchards & picturesque villages. Deep glens full of wood—Peasants in all the fields— every basket full of fruit & every hand dark with walnuts. Many people shaking the trees by the road-side—Ploughing—gather-ing potatoes, weeding the vines—the women in their large straw hats & dress of many colours, the Alps resembling faint clouds in the distance. The sun now shone out at parting & threw a faint gleam on the lake of Geneva. Gaiety, richness & beauty of the environs of Lausanne. Walked in the upper public walk, a double row of noble lime-trees, commanding the lake & moun-tains. Dusk. Walked by the Lake again.

28 Left the pleasant environs & continued by the Lake, more or less. Morges, Rolles. A Chateau with its round & square tower. Joseph Bonaparte's house elevated on a terrace with a full view

of the Lake & Mountains. In the wing was a screen of limes
with loop-holes. Copet.[1] Walked in the avenues & square
lawns behind the house. Saw the plantation in which the
Mausoleum stands. A mist hung thro' the day over the lake &
mountains.—Chateaux—villas—Geneva—Walked in the Public
Walks.

29. Orfevres. Saw a cage, designed for Persia in which two birds
fluttered & sung. Set off for Italy. Beautiful Environs of Thonon
& Repaille. Richly wooded hills, & valleys or glens—Lake in
sunshine. Meillerie in Moonshine. Incomparably the finest side
of the Lake. Girls under a tree weaving fishing nets.[2] All eating,
as they walked, apples or walnuts; even the postboys on their
horses. Every peasant, as you pass, uncovers his head, &
addresses you with the words, 'Je vous salue.'

30. Warm & cloudy. Rain at intervals. Walked along the lake
towards Geneva & Martigny. Cattle feeding & ringing their
bells, in the open chestnut-groves. Goats descending to be
milked. Boat, laden with casks, under sail from the little harbour.
The opposite shore soft & beautiful. Vevay, Clarens, Montreux
& Chillon lay in deep repose under the Mountains—The rocks
advancing & receding clad in the richest wood, here & there
even to their summits, the lively verdure relieved frequently
with dark fir, here called the Sapin—I believe it to be universally
the spruce. A magnificent woody promontory to the right of St
Gingoulph. Moonlight Night—No moon visible—Walked by
the lake. The inn deliciously seated over the lake, & very quiet
& comfortable. Shall stay another day. Excellent Perch &
Wood-pigeon for dinner. Breakers were discernible today on the
other side of the lake, tho' no leaf stirred on ours. Read the
Nouvelle Heloise.

Oct[r] 1. Walked along the shore, the rocks & woods involved
partly in Mist. The objects on the other side very distinct. A
herd of goats browsing among the rocks in very picturesque
groups, two fine boys one with a horn, watching them—attitudes of the goats & the boys. The boy blew his horn, one of the

[1] The home of Mme. de Staël.

[2] 'weaving' changed in MS. from 'netting'. This becomes in *Italy* ('St.
Maurice')

> Still by the LEMAN *lake, for many a mile,*
> *Among those venerable trees I went,*
> *Where damsels sit and weave their fishing-nets. . . .*

155

goats had a bell. A diligence drawn by two mules & a horse, with the pace of a snail. Majestic woods sweeping from rock to rock. Every man & woman you meet have a billet or wood-knife slung behind them. Looked into the Church. Wherever I have gone particularly since I left France & never perhaps so much as in Savoy, the poor peasants have every where struck me with their unaffected courtesy, with their gentle, humble & cordial manners. *Oct 2ᵈ* Walked by the Lake. Set off & passed by the Castle of the Rock on the banks of the Rhone. A Magnificent array of rocks, the chain extending from Evian, retiring & advancing, & clad almost every where with woods of the richest verdure. In England we boast of our green fields. Swisserland may boast of hers too. The approach to St Maurice. A *most romantic* town. The bridge with its single arch over the Rhone, its castle & watch towers, the abbey church, the convent, the chapel & hermitage on a ledge of the Rock, & the overshadowing Mountains, hemming in the town on each side. It is built in a narrow pass, & the street & the River fill up the space. The Pissevache. Guided to it by some fine boys. The women hereabouts wear a small straw hat obliquely, so as to give them a coquettish air. It does not cover the head, & is ornamented with ribbon round the crown, that is frequently fringed with gold or silver. Martigny. Its round tower. Walked up the vale towards Chamougny by a snow-torrent & found there two beautiful little villages of the true grey tint. An Excellent trout &c at the Castle. Drank the wine of La Marque, & thought it not unpleasant. Its first flavour is sweet with a lively acid, but its fare well is sulphurous. Bury Pears.

Oct 3. Came to Sion. The valley & sides of the Mountains sprinkled with villages. Every where much more populous than any County in England. Sion, a very romantic town, with its hills & castles. Where we stopped to give the horses water & slices of bread,[1] looked into the church, in which mass was performing (the priest well drest, the two boys kneeling & ringing the bell behind him like boys from the plough) was much affected by the silence & humble attitudes of the people, particularly the women there. Gathered some black grapes hang-

---

[1] A common continental practice. It is to be suspected that many visitors, besides Dr. Samuel Butler on his tour in 1819, scored off the natives by asking them why they did not first butter the bread.

ing from a trellis roof behind the church. Breakfasted & walked up the hill at Sion to a convent & church & ruins of a Castle. In the church saw a pair of crutches left by a cripple cured by some relics there lately. He is said to be now living below in the town. Went in a charabanc a little league to a hermitage across the Rhone. Stopped at a little village at the entrance of a Mountain Glen like Dovedale,[1] & saw a path winding up it like a shelf along the mountain-side, planted with trees. Were told it led to the Hermitage. Ascended by it, passing a cross, & continued gradually ascending, a snow-torrent descending far below us along its rocky bed. Passed ten or twelve oratories like small sentry boxes, each containing a rude painting not ill-designed of our Savior's passion, inscribed Station XII & XI & X. Each with a text in German—& at length the path made a sudden turn & went up zig zag, leading thro' a small gate near which was his well of water & another oratory, & an image of Christ on the cross, small life & coloured to the life. Higher up was the Hermitage—a very old one, 13 hermits having lived & died there. They are buried in the chapel—a small house of two stories with a chapel adjoining, hung with many rude paintings ex voto, & an altar piece. A poor cripple was kneeling against the railing of the Altar, a figure for Rembrandt. Found the Hermit—un veritable hermite—an old shrivelled figure but still active, & cheerful—I may say merry as he laughed much & unaffectedly. He wore a bib & apron of leather, & his hands were black with walnuts, which he had been peeling for oil. Looked into his cell heated by a stove & in his room up stairs. were offered some honey & bread black as jet. A young man a noviciate, was as merry as he. There had been three—but one died last winter, & one was gone thro' the country to beg from village to village & was not expected home before the spring. Our friend in an ashy habit of frize & a bushy beard with eyes but half open & skin shrivelled like burnt parchment, not unlike Barry the painter[2] or Jobson in the farce had been crushed by a stone from above, last year, while working in his garden (indeed many they have & many patches of vineyard walled & locked &

[1] Rogers's Highland tour of 1812 led him north via the Lakes. He visited Dovedale with Tom Moore before going on to the Wordsworths.

[2] James Barry, 1741–1806.

guarded at the door by a cross, above & below)—& he lay
singing psalms & recommending himself to God till relieved by
the neighbouring peasantry. A picture of the miracle, if it may be
called one, in the church. An image also of the Virgin. She had
been a blonde, but on the french soldiers levelling their fusils at
her she became black as an Etheopian. Found when we returned
into the chapel a young man on his knees Curé of a church on the
opposite mountain, the point of its spire just discernible over the
ridge. A very cheerful modest & sensible looking person, who
stood by while the story was told us, & who came back with us
to the village. The hermit dismissed us most courteously, saying
he should pray for us. Walked up the glen again along the river-
side & the hermitage & its little oratories & crosses scattered up
& down among the rocks had a picturesque effect; went up till
the glen closed & left no spare bed for the path & the river. The
view from the hermitage was striking. the torrent so far below
—the broken & projecting rocks, the winding path seen in so
many directions, the mountains shutting all in, & a distant view
of the mountain without the glen, on which was a small church
& no human dwelling. The village on our return half hid among
trees—the hills of Sion, the castles of grey stone, & the grey
rocks & mountains in a rich tone of colour. Walked again up the
castle hill—the sun was not visible, but the sun-beams were
thrown across the mountains, & the mountain-vista from Martigny the river returning thro' it, exceeded any thing I ever saw
—near 20ᵐ long & not a mile wide, the march of the mountains
being nearly in a parallel line. The river was the Rhone, the
passage was the passage over the Alps! & Night descending
gave new breadth & solemnity to it. The Mountain-vista towards the Simplon was similar in length & breadth & distinguished by two small appennines one behind the other, each
seemingly bearing a castle on its summit, but the evening light
was less favourable there. Walked till dusk, the clocks striking
six. Dined on Red Partridge, Chamois & Marmot. The Chamois
has a slight taste of the Goat.

Oct 4. The valley more interesting as we advanced up it. Woods
of fir & holly. Along the north or sunny side villages innumerable, every cottage festooned with vines; & a spire always in
sight. Vast rocks up & down the valley & on the highest & most
irregular the ruins of a castle & church. The square & round

watch towers & wandering battlements! A scene for a romance. The castle of Udolpho & the church of Otranto. As we proceeded, the country grew wilder & snowy peaks more & more discovered themselves, the Rhone still our companion & villages where in England we should have seen only single cottages. The tall narrow watch tower of Italy now & then rose among Swiss cottages, which appeared like bird's nests where trees could scarcely grow. (A church or espece de Calvare & a path that led up the mountain-side like a *Wall* to it, at every turn an oratory containing images in groups that represented the Life of our Saviour. Found a peasant at prayers in the Church the altar of which was entirely gilt & learnt that two villages were still higher up the Mountain.) Met Mackintosh & his Daughter. They had seen the Lago Maggiore. To-day we had continued up the same Mountain Avenue, every turn presenting a Vista more or less wild & grand. Now the wildness seemed to prevail & the dreariness; & now the industry of man made new efforts, & beauty & cheerfulness resumed their place in the desert. romantic towns & villages every where.—trellisses covered with vines, houses hung with vines, planks thrown across a lane clustered over with vine branches. The first view of Brigue striking. Its many turrets bearing globular & bulbous pinnacles gave it something of an eastern character. A convent of Benedictines with its church the principle object. Visited a convent of Ursulines, who visit the sick & who showed us their refectory, church & cells; & walked on a bridge over the Rhone. The sun shone to-day without a cloud, but the black & cold shadows of the Mountains lay much along the road. The valley always seemingly about half a mile wide, the Mountains running nearly parallel with each other & the meadows often as flat & smooth as a bowling-green.

Oct. 5*th* Ascended by a Calvare. Formerly the traveller on his mule, pursuing the bed of a torrent, wound up a deep & narrow valley, till in two hours it terminated; & by a zig zag path up the mountain he ascended in another hour to the Hospice. A road, wide & smooth as any that lead from town to town now winds like a serpent up the left mountain &, by continual turnings, bridges over chasms & passages thro' the rock, gradually arrives at the same place of destination. It is itself an object for wonder running up & down—often like a road from another country—sometimes to the eye in almost parallel lines & after an ascent of six hours we looked directly down that narrow valley on Brigue the town we had left. The magnificent woods of pine that hang upon the mountains, each in the very figure of its cones, seen at a distance, & all sloping in flakes where the soil or the shelter encourages them, appearing in form like the crystals & petrifactions in a grotto, & shagging, as it were the sides of the precipices. The scales of the trunk have a grandeur; & even when dead & shattered, they strike as they stand erect, or lie in confusion up the steeps. As we approached the summit & looked down upon the white road carried along these black & desert tracts like the great wall of Tartary; now disappearing & now issuing as it were out of the mountain below us when by the road-side we saw from the carriage-window small cateracts rushing into tunnels under the road among icicles & blocks of ice, the water congealing as it fell—& the dust at the very same time rising from the road, we could not but wonder at the boldness that planned, & the genius & industry that executed it. Passed several waggons heavy-laden, & herds of goats without inconvenience; a strong rail, painted of a dark colour, running by our side, tho' in some places it seemed to be going to ruin. Passed thro' a gallery cut in the rock, & hung with icicles above a foot & a half in length & of great beauty. The roof of the carriage shattered several as it passed & they fell with a shrill sound. Ascended for 4 hours, & at a small stone house had a delicious breakfast of strong coffee, cream, eggs &c. The man, who attended upon us, in a courteous & gentle accent, said he passed the winter alone, with only a single attendant. At almost every mile was a strong stone building inscribed Refuge I or II. —Passed the Hospice, a Convent, in which are only two monks for the relief of Travellers. It stands in a little valley & was once of signal use. At the top a deep silence—no murmuring—no whistling of winds—No extensive view—no distant gleams of inhabitd countries—a chaos of rocks & snowy peaks rising, one behind another—the sky of a blue almost black—no foliage to blow thro'. Ran down to Semplon, a little town or village, & there changed horses, taking 3 instead of five. Fell suddenly into a deep valley, & now opened or rather shut upon us one of the most extraordinary scenes in Nature. For twenty miles we went rapidly down thro a pass so narrow as to admit only the road &

the torrent that fell by our side. Often the road was hewn out of
the mountain & three times it passed thro' it—leaving the
torrent to work its way alone—the passage or gallery as I believe
it is termed by the French Engineers being so long as to require
large apertures for light. The road was so smooth & gradual,
that our wheel was never locked—indeed the drag-chain had
given way & the horses galloped, nor turned aside for the
peasants & their carts drawn by mules whom we met in our
descent. The torrent was white with foam, leaping & tumbling
along, now & then lost in a channel that to us had no bottom,
& sometimes not three yards wide. On a rock near a bridge are
etched the names of some French who leaped across it by means
of a cord on a rapid march from Italy. In this descent passed a
church & then an Italian Chateau or something like one & then
the scene opened & discovered a gay scene of white houses
scattered on the mountain, a dream—but soon it closed again &
Night came upon us, a night among the Alps, & by the river-
side we continued till we found ourselves on the edge of a wide
valley & looking down from a bridge on the river far very far
beneath us, & houses glimmering along it. At length we drove
into Domo D'Ossola & found ourselves in an Italian Inn, waited
upon by a smart little boy & girl, children of the house. Supped
on Trout & Black Cock. Sometimes the road seemed resolved to
enter the Mountain, & to say, in the language of the Arabian
Nights 'Open Sesimæ'—& ever it appeared winding before us
thro' these rude regions, as if thrown by a Fairy wherever we
went—like the velvet carpets unrolled before the Great—& in
like manner it conducted us along the Lago Maggiore, so even &
smooth & of such equal breadth—like a white ribbon when seen
at a distance, & lifted above the level of the meadows in the valleys.
Oct 6. The environs of Domo D Ossola are very beautiful, the
mountains covered with woods; villages churches & country
houses seen every where among the trees. At Vagogna left the
road and driving in under a trellis hung with large clusters of
black grapes to the door of a small albergo where we breakfasted on coffee, partridges grapes & excellent cream. At a turn
of the road, the Lake suddenly broke upon us. At Bavino found
the Count Boromeo, wrapt up in his mantell in the remios[1] with

[1] ? =*remigio*, the space between the rowers' seats. *v*, Jal, *Glossaire
Nautique*.

his son, in waiting for the Princess of Wales[1] with his gilded barge & colours & awning. Went with four oars to Isola Madre (The Simplon wind blew & it was rough & cold) where are gardens & terraces orange & citrus trees full of fruit & the old house of the Boromean Family. From the windows saw the Barge rowing towards Isola Bella, which, after being at our departure, met by a little girl with fruit & another, a fairy with flowers we visited tho' in heavy rain. Walked thro' the house & gardens. Ragged children peeping in the hall & up stairs the maids waiting to see the Princess—a vast dinner preparing for three or four days. The views from the Islands are beautiful & ever varying. White towns, white as built of marble, with high towers, under the dark mountains lie along the lake, & sails & boats with awnings, some from Como, some even from Venice are every where passing. The Islands themselves are almost always to be wished away, except the fishers' island—tho' sometimes they are amusing objects—

Slept at Bavino & on *Friday Oct* 7*th*. continued along the shore, the sun on the lake & mountains, vineyards (trellisses hung with vines & clusters of black grapes) every where—peasants with long baskets on their backs full of grapes & women & boys gathering. Our terrace led us in front of Belgirate that runs along the shore where stood the Milan stage & under a chain of hills or continued hill covered with vineyards, woods, & houses. Breakfasted at Arona at the feet of the colossal statue of the Cardinal,[2] & from our windows had so enchanting a view of the castle—Anghiera—& village on the opposite height, & of the lake & its mountains that we gave up all thoughts of Milan for that day & resolved to pass the day there. The little town of Belgirate glimmering in the sun under its mountain stands out into the lake, & is nearly met by a woody promontory over against it, & the strait of water between them almost every minute discovers three or four white sails advancing or retiring, as in array—the horizon bounded by distant mountains—At this

[1] Caroline, wife of the Prince Regent, who had deserted her when Prince of Wales in 1796. Much scandal had accumulated about her by the time she decided to travel abroad. She returned to London in 1820, but died in the following year after having been excluded from George IV's coronation.

[2] Carlo Borromeo, 1538–84, saint and cardinal, archbishop of Milan. The statue is 75 feet high.

moment I see from the balcony six or seven towns & numberless villages along the shore & directly in front an extensive woody campagna, glittering with villages up to the hill-tops & Above all, the sacred mountain of Varese with its convent. A region for a refined & elegant people. Yet where are they? Every peasant you meet is the same slouching sauntering figure you see in an Italian caricatura. The handkerchief wrapt round the female head reminds you of better things; & you see finess & intelligence in almost every face.

Two ragged barefooted little boys are now singing buffo songs together before the window to a laughing audience & would give pleasure any where. In the evening walked by the lake towards Belgirate, & saw the Night come on. The vineyards were, some of them, a busy scene on both sides of the road. Wains, laden with casks, & drawn by oxen. In the road they were weighing grapes in tubs, & the principal person called out of the Vineyard a gatherer with a fresh basket & begged our acceptance of some. Went up into a Vineyard, full of women & a man gathering, & stood under a trellissed walk hung with black clusters. When we came out, a little boy well drest presented my Sister with large bunches, & his father urged her to take them all. At dusk the scene was very solemn from the breadth & deep tone & repose around us. No walk was ever so full of contrast, such gaiety as we went, such an awful stillness as we returned. This morning as we returned from the Statue, we met the Princess of Wales in her walk up to it. Caught a winged Grasshopper there.

Oct 8. Soon left the lake. Near Sesto had a sudden view of a town on the other side of the Tesino immediately below us, & soon afterwards were ferried over in the carriage, driving into the boat & out of it. The road & the country now greatly degenerated. Overtook the Princess & her guards. Breakfasted at Rho, & came into Milan at 3. & lodged at the Albergo Imperiale. Went to the Opera, or Teatro della Scala a magnificent Salle, a deep & splendid stage. Over the curtain the hour, exhibited in illuminated figures, changing every five minutes thus   45   0

  IX   X

The house vast, & simple in its design, the boxes circling in parallel lines hung with blue or yellow silk alternately from the floor to the roof; & all receiving light only from the stage;

except in a few instances; where, the figures being illuminated from within, the glimmering & partial lights had a very visionary & magical effect. The Pss. of W. sat in Gen[1]. Bellegarde's[1] box. Went up stairs with Lord Holland[2] to a Rouge y Noir table, which is said to maintain the House, the man, who keeps it, paying dearly for the licence. Horses in the ballet.

Oct 9. Called on L[d] Holland. The Cathedral. A Sermon. Painted Windows. Rich cieling of the Dome. Rich & elegant beyond all others, but not so grand as many. Its filigraine work, its multitude of statues & reliefs—Numberless statues without & within. Palace of the Viceroy. David's Picture of Bonaparte on Mont St Bernard. Rich velvet in the Salle Du Trone. Cathedral. High Mass. Leonardo's picture of the Last Supper in the refectory of Santa Maria degli Grazie. Great sweetness & repose. No quaintness as in the Easel Pictures ascribed to him. The grandest style & the sweetest! Not a step below Raphael! & evidently copied by him. The hands, the attitudes, the air of the heads! Was greatly affected by it, faded & disfigured as it was. No Print gives you any idea of it. The countenance of the Christ almost worthy of the Original & beyond any of Raphael's in his cartons; & the figure sitting at the upper end of the table & that rising with his arms half-folded on his breast admirable—as well as the Judas. At the other end of the Room a large crucifixion of a very early date, the helmets of the Soldiers in actual relief. It must have been esteemed by Him, or he would not have been so stimulated. Round the ruined cloisters are antient paintings, representing the death of many a pious monk half perished but some of them excellent. The exterior of the Dome of the Chapel by Bramante, of red brick of the richest tone. Its many parts & singular projections form a whole that struck me exceedingly with a certain antient grotesque grandeur, small as it is, before I knew what it was & which I can never forget. The sacristy of the Church of St. Satyro by Bramante is in a little manner, but the alto relievos, particularly of the boys, are very beautiful. Walked with the rest of the World in the green

[1] Heinrich Joseph Johannes, Count von Bellegarde, 1756–1845, led the Austrian armies in Italy 1813; 1814, governor of Milan, defeated Murat in 1815. His residence was at this time the Villa Bonaparte.

[2] Henry Richard Vassall Fox, 3rd Baron Holland, 1773–1840.

avenues near the Villa Bonaparte. Saw the Forum Bonaparte. & the Ampitheatre[1] built by Bonaparte for land & water exhibitions after the example of the Coliseum, & after dinner drove out in the Corso, a broad raised avenue, commanding the town & part of the Country to great advantage. Cavalry-guards were stationed there, & many Carriages, more than I supposed to be in Milan, but of no beauty or elegance, tho' very gaily painted were there. The balconies were full of people & before the coffeehouses they were sitting out & drinking coffee & sherbet, as in Summer. The air warm & mild & soft as in a Spring-day. The narrow streets, the houses of a pearly-white, the balcony to every window from which a female figure is almost always looking as in P. Veronese & Tintoret, the open turrets on the roofs, & the statues on the churches & palaces all give one back what I have seen so often with pleasure in Italian paintings. In the streets there are a double line of smooth flag-stones to receive the wheels of the carriages, & they run along as smoothly as in an iron railway—or as the coach wound up to go round with the Bella Catherine.[2] No road can give so easy a sensation. Am I in Italy? have I said to myself

[1] The forum was begun in 1801, the Amphitheatre in 1806. They formed a vast project to celebrate Napoleon's victories in Italy by providing a parade ground—entered from the north by the great triumphal arch of the Simplon, which was never finished—and an arena where horse and other races could take place; it could also be flooded and used for mock naval combats and pageants on classical lines. The birth of the King of Rome was celebrated by a naumachia there, and the amphitheatre was flooded at intervals thereafter. In 1828, for instance, there was a boat race between gondoliers brought from Venice. *v.* Lord Broughton, *Italy* . . ., 2v, London, 1859, i, p. 51. There is a good account of the games given there in 1814 for the Archduke of Austria, at which the Princess of Wales was present as a great honour, in Lady Charlotte Bury, *op. cit.*, i, 395–6.

[2] This may possibly refer to a sort of switchback. Tom Moore described one in *The Fudge Family in Paris* which he had seen in 1819:

> *Last night, at the Beaujon, a place where—I doubt*
> *If I well can describe—there are cars, that set out*
> *From a lighted pavilion, high up in the air,*
> *And rattle you down,* DOLL,—*you hardly know where.*
> *Those vehicles, mind me, in which you go through*
> *This delightfully dangerous journey, hold two.*

This is in Letter V. In a note to a passage about the amusement park in Letter X, he says 'The cars, on the return, are dragged up slowly by a chain'.

a thousand times. Am I crossing the Alps? Am I on Lago Maggiore, am I in Milan? Do I at last see the Last Supper of Leonardo da Vinci, & the Works of Bramante? How often in this manner shall I question myself before I have done. These very words have been said again & again by others & *will be* again & again. Went at night to the Teatro Italiano or della Canobia. The Water-carrier.[1] A beautiful Theatre on the same plan; but less. The same obscurity—even greater. The acting good, but not very good. The scenery in both houses bad. Looked afterwards into the Opera house, lighted up—illuminée au Jour— for the Pss of Wales. A thousand & thirty candles. Each loge having suspended over it from the wall in a glass bell (inverted) five candles. A blaze of light, more than three times as much as in the Opera house in London. From the top, the parterre from the scarlet & white dresses of the women sitting there, very rich & vivid. The boxes not brilliant—Parisian bonnets prevailing there—but the silk hangings concealed in some degree the poverty of the dresses. Walked about & sat in the parterre. After dinner to-day a poet introduced himself with much grimace & gesticulation—Mons[r]. Mad[me] J suis Poete—Repeated a stanza in our praise as an impromptu—Presented a printed address to the Allies, a MS. on the English—& solicited the name of our first Minister begged to have it in writing & repeated *Liverpool* many times to himself in a plaintive & desponding tone.[2]

[1] or *Les Deux Journées*, Opera in three acts by Cherubini, first performed Paris, 1800.

[2] A recognized part of the tourist industry. When the English traveller Lemaistre arrived in Milan in 1802 a poet called who spoke impromptu verses of welcome and later sent round a sonnet in honour of the English nation. (*Travels* . . . , i , 257). Among Rogers' papers is a little book with a patterned paper cover containing a sonnet in MS. presented by a similar poet on his arrival in Florence. It begins with the following greeting:

'Happy Omens of Felicitation to the most distinct and illustrious noble Gent[m] Myster Rogurs England and Company on the auspicious arrival in Florence—the Accademician, and Poet Angel Schiantarelli in testimony of his dutiful respect presents to your Lordship, with the most sincere desire, his following poetical compositions, with hope that your Lordship, will not disdain to place them under your powerful protection, and flatters himself that with the usual generosity of your Lordship will not fail to be rewarded.' The names are inserted in a different ink. Another English visitor at Schneiders, earlier in the same season, received an identical

Oct 10. Saw the Basilica de San Ambrosio Entering by the cloisters of the ex-monastery, the work of Bramante, in red brick, & striking, the mosaic domes, glittering with silver, the pallium of the high altar, work of the 9th Century, & in the Chapel of St Satyro, a little monumental bas relief in stone low on the left of great beauty. Saw also the miraculous statue of the Virgin in the Sanctuary of Notre Dame; a good marble statue— The vestibule, Bramante's in red brick, is full of paintings illustrative of her interpositions. A boy tumbling unhurt from a garret window, a carriage overturned, &c. Saw the body of St Charles Borromeo in a chapel under the Cathedral, by many wax-lights; & a tomb of John James Gabriel de Medici said to be designed by M. Angelo in a small chapel on the right. The two female figures bending in marble on each side & the eagle on the top are in a grand manner. Went to the Gallery of Arts. The Frescos by Luini & Gaudentio are admirable. The Preaching of St Mark in Alexandria, by   a Supper   by Paul Veronese   by Tintoret & an early Raphael. A good collection of casts in a noble salon.

Went at night to the Puppet Show, Theatro de Girolamo, & saw a Comedy & Ballet well-performed by Fantocini. Marionettes.[1]

Oct 11. In the Cathedral before 10 oClock were three women confessing. The kneeling attitude of a young woman, her face hidden, the affected or real mystery or delicacy of the Priest, his ear turned towards her, his face to us, but half hidden— Went to Belleguarde for a pass-port. The Lazaretto. The Corso, from which there is a noble view of the Alps. The Last Supper of Leonardo da Vinci lost none of its effect upon me. The Refectory arched. In the centre of the Cloisters a marble well. On the

salute, and 'the waiter of the inn afterwards told me, that this man had similar sonetts for everybody that went that way, no matter from what country'. (T. Baring, *A Tour through Italy* . . . 2nd ed. 1817, 169). On his second tour, in 1821, Rogers wrote to Sarah 'I received a visit from our old friend the poet with his book'. *Contemporaries*, i, 323.

[1] The Girolamo was a small theatre designed especially for marionette shows. The puppets were nearly as large as life, and there was dialogue, spoken behind the scene. People of fashion, and tourists, made a point of going once a season, but there was a regular clientele among the poorer classes. Girolamo was the name of the principal puppet, who in Milan had something of the fame and following of Punch elsewhere. *Fantocini* = *Fantecini* = little men.

wall round the cloisters richly coloured paintings, the figures as large as life, & as closely crouded & as irregularly arranged as to size as in a Dutch Cabinet. The martyrdom of saints, the deaths of pious persons, Satan as an Ape removing the candle from before a Father writing a copy of some holy book, the candle becoming all flame & burning his fingers—A Monk dragging him along in triumph by his horns—& various holy figures in white habits variously employed—The tower of the church—Its rich ornaments, its numberless projections & fan-like roofs jutting out above & below, & the red tone of the bricks & tiles give it an Alhambra air, as indeed have most of the old brick turrets & cloisters of this town. Saw a row of roman Columns fluted with Corinthian Capitals. The Hospital. Walking thro' the Piazza del Duomo, the open space in front of the Cathedral saw a busy scene. Stalls of wine—Acquavite Rosoli & other liquors. Chestnuts boiling. Book-stalls. Dog-shearing. A puppet-show in which was a smart dialogue & many blows between Harlequin & Punch. A raree-show, the showman saying much of *'cardinals'* to a boy peeping thro'. A Conjuror, breaking an egg into his hat, stirring it round with a spoon, sugaring it; & then exhibiting round to a laughing circle of 200 at least—a pancake! Another Conjuror with more pomp & less humour but with nearly as large a circle. In an adjoining street a bass viol, two violins, a guitar & a dwarf in a gay Eastern habit, the two last singing to the Accompaniment, the last with much gesticulation. Two violins, a tambourine & two female singers in the next Street, the tambourine-player first striking on his instrument & announcing a 'Canzoncina'. And in the court of our Abergo Imperiale when I returned a band of four wind-instruments making very sweet music.—Went to the Teatro di Re—& saw tumbling & dancing.

Oct 12. In the Cathedral saw a woman confessing. The shutter of the Window between them, opening inwards hides the face of the Priest from the passenger. A Mass in the chapel of St Charles Boromeo. Walked in the Piazza del Duomo—The *Pomposo* conjuring. Two female & two male voices, the two men accompanying with Guitars, performing a ballad delightfully, a cap going round for *sous*. Troubled by the Passport. Set off at 2 for Venice. Level country. Long Avenues. The Alps visible on the left. From our windows at Cassano had a good view of them, & the most crimson sky after sunset I ever saw, a sky without a cloud. An excellent inn.

Oct 13. Long avenues. A populous country, the Alps still on our left at a short distance, the Bergamesque running along at the foot of them, the birthplace of Tasso & Harlequin. Mulberry trees. Brescia Semiramide per Signor Di Voltaire announced on the Walls of the Theatre. Its environs beautiful, the mountains behind it covered over with white villas, their terraces & vine-trellisses. Purple figs remarkable for their bloom & flavour. Before we came to it, un bel convento dei Fratri on a lofty hill under the Alps hung with vines. Its porti[c]oes & galleries. As we left Lonato a file of military in a narrow avenue winding up the hill. Descended to the Lago di Garda & slept at Desenzano. An excellent Inn with spacious apartments & a balcony over the lake. Size of the boats told us the size of the lake indeed.

Oct 14. The sun not visible, but the water in a golden glow from the reflection of the clouds in the east; Rivoltella throwing the shadows of its turrets on the lake; which, to the North, is hid in the clouds that have come down upon it from the Mountains— were it clear, we might see into the heart of the Alps, as the lake is 35m long, & we look directly up it. To me it seems like a dream that I am to be at Verona today, the town of Romeo & Juliet;—& to-morrow at Padua & the next day at Venice. Yesterday my thoughts were wandering, when they were suddenly called back by the sight of a direction-post 'To Verona, To Mantua!' On the right on a reach of land lies Sermione, near which are some ruins said to be the House of Catullus. We are now looking upon a lake mentioned by Vergil & sailed upon [by] Catullus. Went down & saw the women kneel along the beach, washing, each on a small wooden board—her banco de lavora—their various attitudes. A Girl holding a bunch of grapes as she knelt, & eating them grape by grape. Sermione & its turrets as we looked back upon them. The morning-mists heavy on the mountains & the lake. Crossed the Mincio! that issues from the lake. Verona, a towered City under the mountains. descended to it thro' meadows, planted with rows of mulberry groves. Triumphal Arch. Tombs of the Scaliger Princes, (Roman) Bridge. Ponte del Castel Nuovo. Roman fragments. Saw in a Convent-garden with the eye of faith Juliet's stone coffin, the niche for her lamp, the spiracle for her respiration.

Lessened they said, by the zeal of the English for fragments.[1]
Three or four times a year the story is represented here on the
stage & all the World go to see it. Love no child's play in this
town. The day before yesterday a man in a fit of Jealousy
stilotted his wife & her lover, his friend. All were very young &
the woman, as we were assured by all, excessively beautiful. He
had told her he was going out of town & came suddenly upon
them. The house in which the deed was done was pointed out to
us. The door barred, the windows thrown open, as for purification. The Man is in prison. Everybody said 'They deserved it'—
tho' their tone changed a little when they said how beautiful she
was! We passed it afterwards behind, as we returned by another street. Then it was entirely shut up. Young men, silk
weavers, in a work shop singing in parts a chorus in an Opera
familiar to my ear & in a style that there seemed delightful.
Vespers at the Cathedral. The chanting solemn, all chanted
response in the litany, & the white veils of the women became
them kneeling. The Opera. A tragedy. The house on the principle of those at Milan, but faded & darker if possible.
The performance seems every where to begin at 8 oClock.
Rain.

Oct 15th. Rain. The same level country. Distant hills, here &
there topt with a castle. Villas as we approached Vicenza. A
pretty town. Ascended to the Madonna del Monte by the
colonade of Palladio, & from the windows of the Convent had the
most enchanting view of a Campagna, scattered over with villas,
their orangeries & vineries. A Venetian Casa on the nearest
hill with its galleries & porticoes & hanging vineyards—the
Casa Capra, from which Ld Burlington took his idea of Chiswick, & beneath it a thousand others of a pearly whiteness;
beyond which fading into blue, the richest of all countries, the
garden of Venice, rich & level as a carpet, the domes & turrets
of Padua on the horizon & in the haze of distance, grand &
visionary to our eyes as those of Delhi or any City of Romance.
From the windows & balconies we were in, the ground falls

[1] Byron, who had already gleaned one of Lucrezia Borgia's hairs from
the Ambrosian Library in Milan, wrote to Rogers from Venice, Ap. 4,
1817: 'thence on to Verona, where I did not forget your story of the
assassination during your sojourn there, and brought away with me some
fragments of Juliet's tomb. . . .'

precipitously into the valley, we seemed almost to hang in air, so lofty was the terrace, & the town of Vicenza, with its public buildings, & its suburbs, was laid open beneath us as in a bird's eye view. No scene was ever at once so riant & magnificent; & in an evil hour must the Benedictines have left it. Setti commune,[1] along the side of the Alps. The Olympic Theatre, esteemed the master-piece of Palladio a very beautiful interior (with solid & immoveable scenery, splendid perspectives of a city), & his own dwelling-house rendered so important for its size by the variety of its ornaments—but I must confess that I was better pleased with one or two of his little villas on the road-side to-day than with all his greater efforts. Modern Architecture is but a jumble at best & as inferior to the Greek when in its purity as a Monkey to a Man. From Vitruvius downwards they have not borrowed the thoughts to improve upon them or to make them their own, they have not invaded like a conqueror but a thief & have altered only to degrade the divine original. Their imitations give pleasure only so far as they remind us of their models, & it is a pleasure mingled with pain. Were a Writer to borrow as these Builders have done, would his works live a day or an hour? But these things obtrude themselves at every step you take. The same level country to Padua, the olive married to the vine[2] which hangs from tree to tree in the most elegant festoons now turning into scarlet & gold rendering the fields on each side most gay & beautiful. The vine branches shooting from a tree give it the air & spirit of the laburnum in blossom. Came into Padua after dark & walked under its arcades. Coffee houses— Drafts. Cards—Music on the Guitar & Violin. Barbers shops. In almost every shop facing the door, an altar or Holy Picture decorated with nosegays &c in a recess & lighted with a lamp. Supped on Beccafici; & eat to-day the grapes of the vine of the vino santo, as sweet as sugar & as yellow as amber.

Oct 16. Saw the Cathedral, & the Sta Justina—Their domes over the trees of the botanic garden. Saw a Gondola. The Pisani Palace on the Brenta, half refurnished by Eugene Beauharnais.

[1] The *Sette Comuni*, a Venetian resort, on a high plateau near Asiago, in the mountains of Vicenza.

[2] In MS. over 'vine' is the number '1' and over 'olive' the number '2', Rogers' usual way of indicating the substitution of one word for another. The sense seems clearer in the order given, however.

171

The Old part, a hall, & a salon, in antient or rather old-fashioned magnificence. Passed many villas & palaces of the Venetian Nobility, Foscari & &c, gay with columns, statues & paintings in compartments, & overlooked their gardens full of citron & orange trees. Met many gondolas & passed a passage-boat towed along the Brenta by horses, a tide river between high banks. The sumptuary law with regard to Gondolas must have blackened Venice. At a turn of the road the Postilion pointed with his whip & cried 'Venice!' & there it was just above a low horizon & shining in the sun. Left Mestre in a Gondola & soon afterwards Venice with its long line of domes & spires & turrets, one clustering behind another, & all rising immediately out of the water in bright sun-shine gave us an image of beauty, beauty rather than grandeur, but of extreme beauty. As we drew nearer, the line became irregular & broken, & at a rapid rate we entered the City by a narrow, & then the great canal, passing under the Rialto. St Mark's Place a dream! A beautiful Evening.—In our voyage three turks pointed out to us by the boatman in an upper portico conversing together said to be grandi mercanti. Looked into the Opera—It begins at 9 & is over at 1. Took ice before a coffee house in the Piazza.—All the men booted! Half the pavement wet in an evening.

Oct 17, 1814 Venice.

Met the Host as it was conveyed, at a quick pace, along under a canopy with many tapers. All the people knelt down as it was passing.

The Cathedral. Its five domes & almost every vault & archway glittering with representations of Saints in gold mosaic (glass blue or gilt. Not a blank space for the point of a needle; a religious light (not from painted windows) sobering the whole, & massing the many parts into harmony. Its interior small; its mosque like roof & singular front affecting the mind greatly as the work of some unknown people. St Mark's place a wonderful combination, the great church, the Ducal palace, the square tower or campanile with the angel on the point of it—the wind's attendant (see Gibbon)—from the gallery of which Gallileo frequently made his observations; these neither Greek nor Gothic, nor Saracenic, transport the mind to those regions of antient fable so dear to us in our earlier days. The turk, the greek & the polish Jew, the Venetian muffling his chin in his cloak, his wife in her white veil—fasciole & antiently her zendeletta[1] all black, the Jew formerly in his red hat—not to mention the black gondolas assembled before the steps of the vast platform, & the various cries [illegible]   of the gondoleers, the sellers of zucca & of every eatable under heaven— Crossed the inner court of the Palace, & ascending the scala di Giganti, so called from the colossal statues at the top of it, saw the hall of the senate, the walls & cieling full of splendid paintings of the history of the republic by Titian, Paul Veronese, Tintoret, Bassan &c, the atchievements of Dandolo, the submission of Barbarossa, the taking of Constantinople &c. Saw also the chamber of the Council of ten into which the state-prisoner was brought up for examination—from the piombi or the pozzi his cell in the roof or under the canal of the Palace the first cruelly hot in summer—the closet lined with a black wainscot in which he received his sentence of death, before he was led thro' the narrow winding passage down the steep & narrow winding staircase (a staircase resembling a well dark as night & seemingly as steep as a precipice) & across the Ponte de' Sospiri to be strangled in the first dungeon on the left. Saw also where the bocce di lione had been; & the apertures thro' which the denuntiations were received into the Palace.

If Venice is no longer Venice, as every body says, one can however see what was not seen before—at least in the way one would like.

Went up the great canal in an open gondola, visited the Ghetto the district of the Jews, saw il magazin del Gafforo, a small wine-house which Goldoni is said to have frequented to see the manners of the lower class—returned & walked in the public gardens—many gondolas, it being a jour de fete, on the wing for Lido.

18. Saw in the Cathedral just within the threshold the square piece of porphyry on which Barbarossa knelt to the Pope. Breakfasted & from the gallery of the square tower saw Venice *in the sea* without a wall or a rampart, the canals not visible. Walked on the Rialto, embarked there in an open Gondola, saw some works of Canova in the Palazzo Albrizzi & rowed over to Lido, a small island where is a house of the Council of ten, still

[1] Veil of fine silk.

inscribed Consilium decem; where the common people go for recreation, & near which the Doge from the Bucentaur threw his ring into the Adriatic. The many Gondolas always going & coming in that direction & the lively & spirited action of the men, as they row standing, make it a busy & chearful scene. Went to the Opera at night; the ballet Macbet—but, alas, a King of Persia! On the shore the house of an Apothocary was pointed out to us close to the Ponte del Sepolcro in which Petrarch is said to have lived; tho' when I enquired, the tenant knew nothing of it.

19 In the cathedral lay in state under a crimson pall & among lighted tapers the body of a noble. Walked to the Rialto & in a covered gondola went to the Palazzo Barbarigo in which he is— Titian is—said to have painted. Many of his *best* pictures & in their original state. Nothing at least but Time had touched them. The other apartments full of Doges & Cardinals, ancestors of the Family. The cieling, deeply channelled as are most roofs in Venice—beams across the cieling or under the roof—& richly painted with small japanlike ornaments; brown & gold. The walls a light green. Went on to the Church of Sta Maria di Frari The vault of the Pesaro Family & over it a magnificent picture of Titian's—still theirs. The Virgin & child in the clouds, an ancestor of the House & his children, & many of his friends below. Engraved. Several more by Titian & others of that school. Near the wall on the other side a small slab of white marble in the floor thus inscribed—

Qui giace il gran Tiziano di Vecelli
Emulator de Zeuzi & degli Apelli.

In the church of St Sebastian saw several paintings & frescos of Paul Veronese & his epitaph on a stone in the Floor. Returning by the Place of St Marc, rowed under the Ponte di Sospiri & behind the Palace of the Doges. Landed on the very threshold of the Palazzi. In the hall of the Barbarigo were the cabins—Felzi —of their two gondolas in all their blackness. They are removeable at will & here looked like Palls for the dead. A Venetian Count copying Titian's Magdalen there. As you row up the great Canal the palaces are without number, of different styles & ages; some with saracenic windows, & arcades below & above. On the Rialto, or in it, as Shakspeare says, you may walk

to & fro along *the breadth* of the bridge, & there only could
Pierre & Jaffier[1] have walked. The ballustrades are low, & the
view is up & down the great Canal, but not extensive. Many
shops but of an inferior sort; opening to the walk up & down the
steps in the middle. Behind there is a narrower ascent on each
side. The Jews were obliged by law to dwell in another quarter.
In the Cathedral the mosaics consist of coloured figures on a
gold ground. Saw a Priest very cooly take snuff from the box of
a man who was praying on his knees. The giant's staircase of the
finest marbles as are the cisterns there. An electrical machine
in the middle of the Piazza. For a sol you are electrified for your
health.

20. In the Palazzo of the Casa Grimani saw some fine marbles;
particularly in the chamber or Tribuna designed by Sansovino,
a small circular room; among others the bust of an Amazon one
breast uncovered, of exquisite beauty. It is difficult to conceive
any thing more splendid than such a House. A Gallery full of
ancestors, Doges, Cardinals, Generals by sea—Generales de
Mer—painted by Titian, Paul Veronese, Tintoretto at the door
of it planted on each side two of those ensigns of command that
distinguish the prow of the General's ship, richly wrought &
gilt, ensigns of two of the Family, held out from the wall by a
golden hand. This cieling was painted by Giorgone, & that by
Raphael who was a guest of the Family's for 15 days; the ornaments in fresco are by Gio. di Udine, & the armorial bearings of
the family on that Table are all of precious stones. Yet after all,
the ancient marbles are the glory of the House. There in the
court were two Feligi, or covers of the Gondola. The Arsenal.
Two colossal lions from the Piræum at Athens—are at the gate
in different attitudes & a lank & grim lioness of a striking
character. An antient armoury. Coats of mail, belonging to
Doges & Generals. Turkish Standards. Antient Dock-yard. The
Bucentaur degraded by the French into a hulk. The Rope-walk
by Palladio, a double range of Tuscan columns & what, I con-

[1]   '*Pierre*.   On the Ryalto every Night at Twelve
                I take my Evening's walk of Meditation,
                There we two will meet, and talk of pretious
                Mischief—
       Jaffeir. Farewell.'
Otway: *Venice Preserv'd*, Act I, Sc. i. Otway's name was on the lips of
the traveller to Venice at least as frequently as Shakespeare's.

fess, has pleased me the most of his works, exhibiting a grand vista diminishing almost to a point. Models of vessels from the gondola to the ship of war. Afterwards to the Fraternity of St Roch—Scuola di S. Rocco; a wonderful exhibition of the Invention & Noble Daring of Tintoretto. The Crucifixion alone a treasure of Art! What a strange thing is fashion! Almost every man in Venice but myself walks about in a pair of boots. How inhuman to rob them of the only four horses they had.[1] Would not the Milan stud succeed on the stage here! As you row up the Great Canal many a half ruined Painting, Giorgione's perhaps, broken not faded, surprizes you with its rich colours wrought up with gold, the colours alive, the images scattered & gone; & many a frieze of common workmanship, but in a better time. And in other parts of the city the tinklings of a guitar accompanied by a female voice are frequently heard thro' an open window, interrupted only by the dashing of the oar below. Nothing can be more gentle than the gliding motion of a gondola—no jerk—no plash as on the Thames—no feathering the oar—& nothing can be more well-bred & attentive & silent than a gondolier. He never looks back. He dips it & lifts it up again without noise his back towards You—With or without the felze you lie & read at your ease on a black leathern cushion that rises to your head. It is a conveyance refined & improved upon by the experience & study of the most sensual & luxurious people for many ages. You move rapidly & the motion is soothing & pleasureable to the nerves. Saw the island of St Christoforo della Pace, now the cemetery of Venice, inclosed with a wall. A boat lay at the gate, that had brought a body.

21st Octr. Went to the Church of San Giovanni & Paulo; along the walls are the monuments of most of the Doges & Foreign Generals Servants of the Republic; four equestrian & as large as life. Those against the West Wall are by Sansovino, & Canova used to call them his garden for there he came to study. So much excellent sculpture is seldom to be seen within consecrated walls. Saw the monument of Admiral or in the language of Venice, General Emo—by the Master of Canova Torreti[2] in the

---

[1] The bronze horses from the façade of St. Mark's: taken as trophies by the French. Rogers saw them being taken down by English engineers in Paris after Waterloo, in preparation for their return to Venice.

[2] Giovanni Torretti, 1744–1826.

8. A tourist at Tasso's cell, Ferrara

9. The Arno and Ponte S. Trinita from a point near Schneider's hotel

Church of San Martino In the dress he wore & a most admirable statue his figure recumbent—great simplicity & sweetness of character. In the Arsenal a monument to his memory by Canova himself. Petrarch's house. Sansovino speaking of the monastery called Il Sepolcro, says, Poco discosto vi si trova un altro portone dove era la casa nella quale habitava il Petrarcha &c. p 24. b.[1] & a great gate answering to this still exists close to the Convent.

The mosaic paintings on the outside in the concave spaces over the doors of the great church certainly very ornamental, the splendour overflowing from within—

Piazza di S. Marco, described by Petrarch in 4 dell suor Senili— Ep. 2. p. 782. orbis parem habet.[2] In the place are bronze pedestals or columns richly relieved [in which] are three standards, those of Cyprus & Candia & Negropont, that formerly bore on solemn festivals golden banners & silks of great value. The angel in the attitude of benediction on the top of the campanile—AD. 1490—turns with the wind after one said by Vitruvius to have circled on a tower at Athens. AD. 1517.[3]— once gilt, &, when the sun shone upon it, to be seen at sea 30 miles off. The two granite columns from Constantinople, on one a Lion looking to the East, the seat of their empire emblematical of St Mark, on the other a marble statue of St Theodoro, standing on a gilt crocodile, antiently their Patron, his shield in his *right* hand, to signify that the Republic would act always on the defensive. There the nobles used to walk. Their walk called Le Br[o]glio. Le torre delle hore. Within the circle of the dial-plate are the signs of the Zodiac in an azure field; above our Lady, gilt, & large as life—& an Angel followed by three Magi who, moving, do her reverence, entering at one gate & going out at the other. A Lion winged, & two bronze statues, called

---

[1] In *Venetia descritta in XIV libri* . . . , Venet, 1604. 'Not far away is another gate where was the house Petrarch lived in &c.'

[2] In this Epistle Petrarch describes the festivities which took place in the Piazza after a victory over the Cretans, and exclaims that in his opinion no other square in the world could compare with this, for its beauty, and for the view of St. Mark's, resplendent with marble and gold. Rogers is using the 1581 Basel edition *Francesi Petrarchiae . . . opera . . . omnia.* The phrase *'orbis parem habet'* occurs on p. 783, not 782.

[3] The top of the Campanile was struck by lightning in 1489. The angel was placed there in 1513.

Moors—Mori—*dal volgo*, who strike the bell by turns with their maces, made in 1496. The Rialto. In 1252 a ferry there. bridge built in 1400 enlarged in 1450 & two rows of shops added. In 1524 repaired with an opening at top to let the Bucentaur pass—see Vasari 742.[1] In 1570 resolved to build it of marble & Sansovino's plan adopted—but a war with Turkey prevented its being done. The island, *di Rialto*, highest of the sixty. The piazza di Rialto, *la prima piazza d'Europa*, before the existance of the bridge or the Place of St Mark; a square, round which ran porticoes, & under them every morning, as it were a festival, not only merchants, painters & musicians, but many of the nobility assembled for Conversation. This place was in Shylock's mind, when he said What news on the Rialto?

> *Signor Antonio, many a time & oft,*
> *In the Rialto &c.!*

—The Jews, by the laws of Venice were formerly obliged to wear a red hat. Should not Shylock?—The Bucentoro, so called from a word in the decree for building it 'Quod fabricatur navilium ducentorum hominum—' Saw in the Casa Manfrini a multitude of pictures, some good particularly a groupe of three heads ascribed to Giorgone, but the woman's appeared to be that of Titian's Mistress. In the evening eat ice in the Caffé. It is served in squares & often in strata of different colours. A guitar & two violins discoursed very agreably. A Sirocco, as for some days past; & a very overcoming atmosphere. Nothing in activity but the fumes of Venice. Resolve to establish a snuff-box. The nobles live in the third story. Their rooms of representation are on the second.

Oct 22 Walked in the Palace. Saw the Santa Maria della Salute, & Santo Giorgio Maggiore. Walked in the Porticoes of the Piazza di Rialto, where Shylock walked. The Houses over them are now of a reddish colour. (In the church of St Lorenzo on the island called Gemelle lies the body of Marco Polo, called Milione, the traveller, under the angi-porto)[2] The Church of Santi Giovanni e Paolo. Above 30 doges there, most of them in sleeping attitudes; & for the most part sculptured admirably.

---

[1] The reference is to Giorgio Vasari, *Vite de' piv eccellenti Pittori, Scvltori e Architetti*, 3v, Fiorenza, 1568.

[2] ?*Anti-porto* =porch.

Mestre: October 23rd

The walls white & the windows perhaps too light for effect; but
the monuments, looked at one by one, must affect every mind, &
as night comes on, are most solemn. One of the Equestrian
figures in a *severe* taste & admirably seated on the horse. Rain.
Sirocco. Heard music at night in the caffé—ate ice—& walking
to the Great Canal went home by water. It was amusing to
observe the moving lights of the gondolas; to see now & then
one shoot across the stream at a little distance & vanish into one
of the lesser canals. Passed the steps of [the] Theatre, where
many were drawn up with their shining prows of white metal in
array—in waiting for the company. One man remains in your
boat, while the other stands at the door of your loge. When you
come out, he attends you down, & calling 'Pietro' or 'Giacomo'
is answered by his companion & away you go. The gliding
motion would restore composure after any agitation in an Opera
loge or a casino. They dip their oars, as if they were afraid of
disturbing you behind the curtain, yet they fly. Looked into a
casino this morning on a first-floor in the Place of St Mark, a
billiard room, two card-rooms & a ball-room. The walls gayly
papered & the ceilings painted; the furniture slight & showy, &
the ensemble bringing to mind a second-rate assembly room in
England. A square, all Window, thrown out & cushioned large
enough for two persons to sit in & look up & down the Piazza.
From without, these Windows very frequent in Venice have the
appearance of a lantern & are like some seen in London to catch
a side view—the projection generally being confined to the
Window. Met the English Consul's Gondola & an Austrian
Minister's. Each had the National colours planted low behind
the felze.

Oct 23. Walked to take my farewell of St Mark's place. Looked
at the piombi & counted 12—each large enough for a man, some
rising, one behind another—Then from the bridge looked towards the Ponte de' Sospiri & on the water of the canal of the
Palace, sluggish & black between the high walls—Who but
must shudder when he reflects that human beings have languished perhaps for no fault—for a virtue under it—What an
alternative! the Piombi or the Pozzi—a brain-fever or suffoca-
tion! Left Venice crossing the great Canal near the Rialto—
Passed again our Lady of the Sea, a small oratory on piles.—
Mestre—the Palaces on the Brenta—statues without number—

179

paintings fading fast, or rather crumbling from the walls—
Orange-trees full of Oranges—Innumerable statues of dwarfs
round a garden—Moon-light—Padua—ate ice in a Coffee-
house. Gallileo gave lectures here and Petrarch was a canon of
the Cathedral. Some playing on guitars or drawing their swords
—or orating in a great wig.

Monday. Oct 24. Forgot to drink last night of the vino del
Petrarco, described to us as a *delicious* wine, first made by him at
his house at Arquà. A picture of the Virgin by Giotto in the
Cathedral was Petrarch's; he valued it highly & bequeathed it to
F. da Charrara. Gothic & faded. Ego nihil aliud habeo dignum
se. Vasari 129[1] Giotto. What a scene of magnificence & horror
was Venice in the old time! Who could pass along the Canal of
the Palace, whatever his schemes of pleasure might be, & not
think of his fellow-beings under that black & sluggish stream
with nothing to interrupt their meditations but the falling of
water-drops or the heavy plash of the oar that went over them.
Who could enter the Palace-court, & not shudder when he lifted
up his eyes to those 13 narrow cages on the leads (I have stood
& counted a dozen at least) most of them measured, as it would
seem, just to admit a man; &, under a sun nearly vertical, so
intolerable! Venetian Gardens. Statues. Vases. Vistas lengthened
by a painted landscape at the end. Apropos of gondolas at night
—Oh if you had any love-affair, how nervous would it make
you, not knowing its contents or its destination—& how
infinitely more interesting, as more mysterious, their silence
than the noise of carriage-wheels. Nothing can be more luxurious than a Gondola with its little black cabin in which you can
fly about unseen; the gondoliers so silent all the while, they dip
their oars &c.

Oct 24. By several Venetian houses, empty & falling into ruins,
their statues grown grey with moss, & their paintings crumbling
from the walls, went by a canal-side to Monselice, where was an
old castle with its wall, & watch-towers running up the hill from
the base to the summit—breakfasted & went along a hill-side,
the valley full of olives & vines in scarlet festoons from tree to
tree till the little village of Arquà with its high church-tower,
the houses one above another of grey stone, discovered itself on
the side of an opposite hill, the hill-tops round it wild & scat-

---

[1] Vasari quotes from Petrarch's will.

tered over with olives. The morning had spread itself heavily upon it, it was a heavy rain, & a cloud like a curtain hanging over it gave a grandeur to it not its own. We wound round & crossing the valley, ascended again into Arquà. By a rocky path among the walls & houses we went up to the highest house in the village the front of which was plain & low, but respectable. Thro' a large room, or covered court we entered a smaller—the the ceiling was divided into small squares, each containing a rose, & the beam that crossed it was painted in like manner of a dark colour. The upper part of the walls was painted round & not ill-painted, in compartments or rather a series of pictures, in a slight manner & in light or faded colours, faded from Age, but most probably of an after-time, representing his interviews with Laura, his grief, & the progress of his passion. In the next room, the ceiling the same, over the door was his cat dried in a glass case with some lines written under it in latin hexameters. A third room less than the second & much less than the first contained behind some old wire trellis his arm chair & ward-robe half-perished. Above lay his ink-stand in bronze—the form very elegant. A winged Cupid formed the stopper, sitting on the top, & the vessel, a circular vase with the heads of four sphinx-like women at the corners each terminating in a branch or flower, the feet small, & scarcely discernible. The chair was an arm-chair & sitting in it in a closet 6f. by 5f. into which another door led, with his head upon his hand he was found dead. The windows mostly down to the floor & opening each into a small iron balcony that looked over the valley. The ground fell precipitately into the valley which was wild & confined but covered with olives & vines, with not a habitation in view the hills rocky & rising round it. It stood on the side of a steep hill. A pomegranate tree full of large fruit near the house. Went again down the hill & in the church yard saw his tomb—a large stone sarcophagus on four short columns resting on a double stone base. On the sarcophagus was sculptured his bust, his head wrapt round in that close head dress he usually wore, the fashion of the time, & such as he is always represented in—the features too the same—A laurel tree, probably often renewed, being of no age, grows at each corner.—The tomb, according to the Inscription, was raised by Francisco da Brossano, who had married Petrarch's natural daughter.

Thro' a long strait road went on to the Adige & were ferried in the carriage over the Adige, here a very wide river, with tame banks; the road sandy & almost impassable. Are threatened with oxen to-morrow. Slept at Rovigo.

Oct 25 Rain. A Fair at Rovigo & the road scattered over with people. Arquà,[1] The Po, a noble stream, but muddy; & its banks low, edged with poplars. Ferried over it, & continued along it for some time, the Alps now appearing on the other side wrapt in snow. Two little towns fronting each other, & a ferry & a string of boats between them. Passed thro one of them, & thro' a street partly covered; & on a Pavement proceeded to Ferrara, leaving a road so deep & heavy, that we had almost always gone at a foot's pace with six horses. Ferrara. A beautiful street, with a long perspective. The three Moors, a magnificent Inn, exhibiting on each side of the gate a long list of its imperial & royal guests, from the Emperor Joseph downwards. Saw in the Cathedral, antient without, modern within, an admirable painting of Benvenuto Garofolo, subject St George, & the Last Judgement by him. The Ducal Palace, walled & moated, with its four massive towers. The Hospital of St. Anne, in which Tasso was confined under the pretext of his being mad (we were shown a grated window as the window of his cell) & the house of Ariosto, with his old motto renewed on the front of it, 'Parva sed apta mihi &c.' an excellent airy & roomy house. Looked into the room in which he died, 20 feet wide, with a high raftered ceiling, the ornaments still on some of the beams looking backwards into his court & his garden. We now tread on classic ground; every hill & valley, every bit of pavement in every town 'by sacred poets venerable made!' The natural politeness & anxiety to please of the young Lady at the house of Ariosto. Many grand palaces & extensive gardens. The theatre beautifully constructed on the same principle as the rest in Italy; the boxes in circles to the cieling; some with green drapery, some without. Lighted from the cieling, a thing unusual in this country. When you turned from the stage, the tone of light was soft & beautiful. But one box lighted within. A comedy of three acts. Andolfati's Company. Several sedan-chairs at the door, with round paper lanterns, like melons that had a pretty effect. Began at a quarter past 8, & all over at half past 9.

[1] Arquà Polésine.

Ferrara: October 26th

Oct 26. Round the cathedral door papers requesting you to pray for the souls of such & such persons.—The Library of the University. The courtesy & intelligence of the Custode. At the end of a long apartment the monument of Ariosto, made of various marbles. Within are his bones much perished. His chair, plainer than Petrarch's, entire, & very low & easy. Sat in it. Would I could have said 'Ed io sono anche[1] &c. Manuscript of the Pastor Fido with Guarini's corrections. The writing beautiful, the lines clear & regular as in print. Manuscript of the Gierusalemme Liberata. The writing another's & the corrections by Tasso in a careless heavy hand—yet there were some passages of his, small & still more beautiful than Guarini's. Many whole stanzas struck out with his pen, whole pages at a. time. Single Sonnets also of his on seperate papers & exquisitely written—

The Orlando Furioso. In a thick & careless hand but very clear & intelligible, & the lines in great order. Several corrections as in the rest—All on small quarto paper, the size of the time; & but little changed. The standish of Ariosto in bronze.[2] Larger but of the same pattern nearly as Petrarch's. A Cupid sitting cross-legged, his finger on his lip. A masque between the Sphinx's heads, A tripod. The chair & standish very ill-drawn & given, in the Venice Edition of his Works. The air & grace & proportions, entirely lost; particularly of the last, which is very elegant, & the parts massive & grand. No cast in plaster or clay ever taken. A bronze medal of Ariosto found in the coffin. Not such regular features as in busts & paintings—but with more countenance. The Casa Quatango,[3] in which Guarini lived, & the Pastor Fido was first performed, is now levelled with the ground. The library a handsome suite of rooms, well-filled, the tops of the books carefully papered, & a line of portraits above them. The booksellers shops of Milan were some of them excellently furnishd with French, English & Antient Books. At Venice also excellent classics, & Pope Shakespeare, Bayle &c. At Molini's particularly; & another Bookseller unlocked his

[1] Does Rogers mean 'would I could have said that I also am such a poet. . . .'?

[2] Lord Grenville gave Rogers a copy of this inkstand, in silver gilt, with the inscription 'Samueli Rogers hoc amicitiae Pignus W.W.B.G. 1826'.

[3] Palazzo Gualengo.

183

drawer, & showed me a Boccacio, of the famous edition, for which he asked me forty louis. Molini's Catalogue was numerous & valuable. The shop-keepers there civil & more than reasonable, willingly restoring the money the next day, if you return with a fancy-article. My Sister met with two instances. The vendors on foot wander every where, & seem far to exceed the rest of the moving population. Criers of Zucca, two bearing it between them on a board, hissing hot, slices of which all sorts eat greedily. Criers of its dried seeds—of pomegranates—of biscuits, of thrushes, &c. The piazzetta, formerly appropriated as a walk by the Nobles, & called Il Broglio. Left Ferrara in heavy rain with four horses—& arrived at Bologna after dark; in our way ferrying over the Reno, a narrow rapid & muddy stream, between low sludgy banks. At supper of course the Mortadella of Bologna. said to be made of ass-flesh.

Oct 27. The arcades light, & well contrived for shade & shelter. Il Duomo. The cieling of the choir rich, & the Deity in the centre, whoever conceived it, sublime. In the chapter St Peter & the Virgin over the body of Christ—by Lud. Caracci. In San Petronio the meridian of Cassini traced along a long brass in the floor. The Asinelli, a high tower; & its neighbour, the Garisenda, mentioned by Dante, remarkable for its inclination—both brick. The comparison of one with the other increases the effect. The last appears to be falling, & in some points of view, when seen together, they give you the idea of an earth-quake, when the towers of a City are toppling to their fall! The bronze Fountain of J^no of Bologna in the Piazza del Gigante. The Neptune full of energy, as are the boys; & all the parts grandly conceived; but the subject not pleasing. The Palazzo Zambicari. Many of the early Masters. A Ludovico Caracci, death of the Virgin, admirable for breadth & beauty. Seemingly without varnish. A female head. One of four. Name of the Artist & the young Lady unknown, but evidently a portrait, the features the expression beautiful; all the gentle gaiety, the candour, the diffidence of Youth—a delicious light playing over the eyes, the mouth. Exquisite beauty, yet with the life & reality of Individual Nature. Her hair full of curls, seemingly intermixed with hair of a pinkish colour. Canova, according to the Custode, spent half an hour before it; & well he might! Passing thro' the Piazza found a circle formed by a Story teller.

He had spread a painted or canvas cloth before him, to throw back the croud, & with his hat on the cloth & a stick in his hand & much gesticulation he was chanting in rhime a story of St Luke & the Virgin. Bologna was a word for ever on his lips, Bologna more in his eyes than the rest of the world put together, & at every mention of the Evangelist of our Lady, every listener touched his hat or bowed. With his stick he continually kept back intruders, & all seemed to treat him with respect. When a sol thrown on the cloth rolled away, some hand was always ready to throw it back again. In his story he continually introduced a couplet or two improviso with great effect. A little Theatre opened last week in the cloisters of the Convent of St Martin's. Beautiful! almost white with bas reliefs in delicate shades; the cieling concave & yellow with gilt network; the boxes with green silk hangings & divided by white columns reeded but of doric dimensions. Over the stage 4 winged women dropping garlands, all white, an exquisite voice in the Comic Opera, all delicacy & sweetness, Signora Marcolini!!! The house lighted from the centre, & the broad & soft lights thrown round, & into the boxes gave a visionary effect that was enchanting. Never since I came into Italy have I been pleased before in a Theatre. This delighted me. The dancing here, as at Venice, in the lowest stile of burlesque. It being for the benifit of the Prima ballerina, she sat in her rouge among the receivers at the door.

Oct 28. Some of the cries not unmusical. Went to the porticato of the Madonna di San Luca 3ᵐ long, commanding the environs, & the country. Went also to the New Cemetery & saw the tomb of Banti.¹ & to the church of St Michel in bosco, commanding a view of the town & its towers & of the little hills round it covered with vineyards & villas,—Smith's point of view I believe.² The corso new & not worthy of notice. the Palazzo Mariscalti full of pictures. A beautiful Correggio, three Saints— a noble Titian, a Portrait of a Venetian. Saw the four cielings in the Zampieri Palace. One by each of the Caracci & one by

¹ Brigitta Giorgi Banti, ?1751–1806. Daughter of a Venetian Gondolier, she became an opera singer of international fame. She was dissected after her death in an attempt to account for the extraordinary power of her voice.
² *v.* John Smith (1749–1831), frontispiece to his *Select Views in Italy*, 2v, 1792–6.

Guercino; Frescoes small in size, but in a great manner. In the Piazza children tumbling, a woman discoursing about it in the intervals of some noisy music with much pomp of elocution. Near it was another circle & the reciter again at work, his story comic & a new picture unrolled before him—his broom lying by; Bologna still much on his tongue & an allusion to the fountain just by him. Went to another, the largest Theatre a Concert. Large & heavy. Rain. Slept here in the same chamber as the Emperor Joseph. His portrait hung here to record the circumstance.

Oct. 29. Set out at point of day with a muleteer & his three mules which we were told would walk a grand pas over the Apennines. Passed the Fountain & under the towers, admiring the vegetables on their way to market, particularly the cavolifiori—cauliflowers—piled into a cone on the head of the bearer; as at Venice we had admired the baskets of black grapes. Went along the valley, villas & palazzetti on the hills on each side till we were joined by the Savena, a river evidently subject to floods. The hills beautiful; almost every one with its white building, & hung with trees, & vines thrown over them, that with their yellow leaves threw so many brilliant lights over the landscape. Soon were lost in the clouds, a heavy mist & small rain continuing thro' the day, during which we were slowly ascending, with relays of oxen, that came out two by two at a minutes notice as we passed thro' the villages. Slept with quiet sensible people at Scarlicalasino. The house full of traders.

Oct 30. Mist, that soon cleared away. The Apennines rather wild than grand; at most always woody, & discovering a crater or wide circle of bare ridges, the vallies within diversified with little hills cultivated or leafy to the summits & rendered still richer by the morning lights. At Pietra Mala or evil rock (near which, under the church, is a steep rocky precipice from which many may have fallen) the congregation were issuing from mass (9 oClock) & descending by a winding path into the village. Soon afterwards saw a mile off across the valley on a green hillside a bright flame with a tremulous motion. No trees were near it, but the ground was green, & it seemed like a small clear intense fire. It was volcanic, rising from no aperture, & gives the name to the Mountain, Monte di fo.[1] Thro' this wild region

---

[1] Mountain of fire. Sir Humphrey Davy had investigated the nature of the flame a few days previously and had decided that it was due to fire damp.

were escorted by two of the Tuscan Cavalry in long white cloaks & white helmets. Met another carriage, & were overtaken by a third, both so escorted in broad sunshine. The Mail was robbed on this very spot in the day-time the week before. Had again recourse to Oxen & at length from a summit (having left behind on our left hand Giogo the highest of the Apennines & Firenzuola a little village at the foot of it) had extensive view of a Tuscan valley. Descended to the Albergo delle Maschere; & had it to still greater advantage. A long valley, full of little elevations, & innumerable groves, yellow as gold. White villas, almost every one with its tower & its cluster of cypresses scattered up & down & along the side of it. It realized all my dreams of Italy. Visited the old avenues & garden-terraces of the Villa Gerini, & wandered about till dusk. Slept at the Albergo.

Oct 31 Descended & went along a valley that gradually contracted & grew wilder & wilder; yet full of beauty dove-coloured oxen ploughing in the intervals between the vines, & young women washing in the river; villas every where appearing, each with its cypress, its long roof, its tower & open gallery, the Appennine Mountains shutting in the scene behind us, & every thing reminding us that we were still among them. Passed Caffagiuolo a castle-like villa of the Grand Duke's, & Pratolino another, on an eminence, looking up the valley towards Florence. The foldings of the mountains in front, their outlines half fading into a warm sky, the conical hill of Fesole & its convent closing up the valley & the winding of the road upwards, these things as they appeared to us, gave us a high idea of its situation. Went up—& from the summit, the Valdarno & half Tuscany opened at our feet & to the right, where the river discovered itself winding along in its course towards the Mediterranean, Florence with its domes & turrets immediately under us. Entered & passing along its flat pavement by the Cathedral, came with our mules to Schneider's hotel[1] on the Arno. Our driver, a young man, had pulled off his hat to almost every Madonna on the road. His exhortation to his mules a

---

[1] The most famous and expensive hotel in Florence, and the most popular with wealthy English visitors. It was also known as 'The Arms of England', or 'Locanda d'Inglaterra'. English food was served. It was on the north bank of the Arno, near the Ponte alla Carraia. See Introduction, p. 87 ff.

double note & most barbarous. Dined at Ld Holland's. At night went to the Princess D'Albany's,[1] Alfieri's Widow, where was Luchesini[2] & returning home drove thro the Piazza di Gran Duca.[3]

Nov. 1 A heavenly day. Walked on the Arno. Violets, Roses of Provence, & Orange-blossoms offered every where in baskets for sale. Saw the Chapel de' Medici, & the tombs of the Medici in the Chapel de' Depositi, by Michael Angelo. The sitting figure of Lorenzo, a noble & striking Phantom! In the Cathedral under its octagon dome by Brunellesco heard the service on the Eve of 'the day of the dead'. Giotto & Brunellesco himself lie here. The Campanile, designed by Giotto. A Picture of Dante. Painted Windows that even excelled those of the Cathedral in Bologna. No rainbow ever richer. Saw a child christened in the Octagon Church of St John Baptiste. Returned thro' the Piazzo di Gran Duca. What an assemblage of Sculpture. The Equestrian Statue of Cosmo I. The Samuel. The The Perseus. The Hercules & Centaur. The Rape of the Sabines! The bells are now tolling for The Dead; & the bells of the Campanile, as they are heard over the River, are 'most musical, most melancholy.'—

Novr 2. The Day of the Dead. All the bells tolling & the chime is singular & mournful, went to the Church of San Lorenzo, where Mass was performed by the Prior in the Mitre & Pontifical habits. The Service began with an Anthem, accompanied only by the Organ & Singers in a Galery over the Altar; after

---

[1] b. 1752, Princess of Stolberg-Gedern. Married in 1772 Prince Charles Edward Stuart, the Young Pretender. Left him and settled in Florence with, but not married to, the dramatist Alfieri. On his death in 1803, she remained in Florence until her own death in 1824. She derived the style Countess of Albany from her marriage with Charles Edward. She held a salon in her house at No. 2 Lungarno Corsini, and from 1814 every visitor of rank or culture found his way there. She made the most of her connection with the blood royal, wore the arms of England on her carriage and ruled her circle with an etiquette said to be stricter than that of the Grand Ducal court. She received a pension from the English government.

[2] Girolamo Luchesini, 1751–1825. An official at the court of Prussia from 1779. From 1806 he was *gran maestro della corte* to the Baciocchi at Lucca. On Napoleon's fall he returned to Florence and offered his services to the Countess. Though he had served a Bonaparte, he was very tactful to the English, and told Tom Moore that he was *'uno dei pilastri delle arte'*.

[3] Piazza della Signoria.

which, with many waxen tapers, followed by the congregation with wax lights, they proceeded into the Cappella dei Depositi, & there in a circle sung the   . The statues seemed to become animated the while. That of Giuliano looked on with a mild & sorrowful look, while that of Lorenzo seemed to say with a stern & haughty air 'Tis well! Proceed!—' They then descended, singing, into the vault beneath, where are the bodies of those that sleep, & again sung the   as before. Again the vaults of the Church (preceded by a banner of black & gold, exhibiting a flower & a scull crowned, in alternate squares. 'Oh Death where is thy crown?') burning frankincence & scattering holy water along, in those dark & silent chambers. It was finely imagined once a year with light & choral music & frankincence & holy water to descend, if I may say so, into the dwelling-places of the dead. The strain was heavy & monotonous & perhaps too loud; saddening not soothing. (The Palazzo Gerini: Many Pictures, none very eminent.) Palazzo Vecchio, built by Arnolfo di Lapo, disciple of Cimabue; who began the Duomo. Piazza del Gran duca. Equestrian Statue of Cosimo I by Jno of Bologna. David, by M. Angelo, his sling on his shoulder (in his hand). Hercules overcoming Cacus by Bandinelli. Judith by Donatello. Perseus with the Medusa's head in Bronze by B. Cellini, with bas reliefs of the history of Perseus & Andromeda. Rape of a Sabine by Jno. of Bologna, with historical bas reliefs. Thus has Vasari described the Medici. Due Capitani armati—l'uno il pensoso Duca Lorenzo nel sembiante della saviezza—l'altro il Duca Giuliano si fiero—Duke Lorenzo is a living man among marble Statues. 741. Grato mi é il sonno —Pero non mi destar'; deh parlar basso.[1]—un Davit giovane, con una frombola[2] in mano.

[1] In answer to some verses of Gio. Battista Strozzi on his figure known as Night, Michelangelo replied, according to Vasari, with these lines:

> Grato mi è il sonno, & piu l'esser' di sasso,
> Mentre che il danno, & la vergogna dura,
> Non veder' non sentir', m'è gran ventura;
> Pero non mi destar; deh parla basso.

'I am glad to sleep and still more to be of stone. I am fortunate neither to see nor feel while loss and shame endure: so do not wake me—speak softly.'

[2] *Frombola*=sling. Rogena is describing Michelangelo's David, now replaced by a copy.

Well might Milton speak with delight of his gathering violets on the banks of the Arno.   Epit. Dan.[1]

Nov. 3. The Gallery. The Wrestlers, the dancing Faun. The slave listening & whetting his knife. The young Apollo, his hand on his head. Canova's Venus[2] is in noble company!— The Raphael's—the two holy Families, the St John, & Titain's Venus, all in a day! in an hour! Dined at Ld Holland's & went to the Opera Charlotte & Werter.[3]

Nov 4. The Academy of Arts. Frescoes & Oil Paintings from the Suppressed Convents. And. del Sarto. Fra. Bartolomeo. Raphael. A miracle. I have a wash-drawing of it, of the same size. The Piazza de S. Marco. Here, in the Garden of Lorenzo the Magnificent, M. Angelo, among others, distinguished himself.—the loggia & alleys adorned with marbles & pictures. (The casino now there was built by Francis I. in 1470,[4] four years before the birth of M. Angelo & was afterwards inhabited by many Princes. Was not its small garden, not   an acre, within high walls, the spot?) Over how many doors is the bust of Cosmo Pater Patriae.

The Convent & Church de S. S. Annunziata de' Servi. (In the church lie Politian & Pico della Mirandola.) In the vestibule— cortile or cloister—a series of frescoes, miracles, three or four by A. del Sarto. Some of the detached figures etched by Zuccarelli. Beautiful vases for holy water in bronze. Over one of them 'Virtus ex alto.' The cloisters magnificent; an urn of holy water next the door into the church. A well, as usual, in the middle. Monumental marbles in the floor & on the four walls. Over those on the last, splendid Paintings. Many more than respectable. Here over a door into the church A. Del Sarto's Madonna del Sacco!

The Father is reading aloud. The Boy in the mother's lap

---

[1] *O ego quantus eram, gelidi cum stratus ad Arni*
   Murmura, populeumque nemus, quà mollior herba,
   Carpere nunc violas, nunc summas carpere myrtos,
   Et potui Lycidæ cercantem audire Menalcam!
   Milton, *Epitaphium Damonis*, ll. 129 ff.

[2] This took the place of the Venus de' Medici while it was away in Paris, and was transferred to the Pitti on its return.

[3] Perhaps the name of a ballet.

[4] In fact later, by Francesco I, in 1574.

endeavouring to snatch at the book, while the mother is lost in deep attention, yet, as tho' unconscious of it, calmly & gently keeping back the child. A story told with great simplicity & quiet & sweetness. Greatly admired by M Angelo & Titian— (Piazza near it. An Equestrian Statue of Duke Ferdinand by Gio. Bologna in bronze. The two fountains of bronze by Tacca. Boys in singular masks.)

Nov 5th. The chapel of Brancacci in the Carmine The Life of St Peter in small figures, principally by Masaccio (engraved in parts by Patch)[1] Buried there 1443.!!! In this chapel M Angelo received the blow on his nose from Torregiano, as I am told by Fabre[2] Heard mass sung for the soul of a Noble Florentine. One of his servants standing at each end of the Pall.

Saw the Life of John the Baptist by Andrea del Sarto in the small cortile or cloister.[3]

(Saw also a Painting (many of the figures designed by M Angelo) by [Bugiardini] in a small chapel on the right in the Church of Sta Maria Novella called by M[ichael] A[ngelo]. Sua Sposa). I have a drawing of a single figure there. Walked in the Gallery & looked at the Bacchus of M. Angelo.

The Baptistery. The Sacristy of San Lorenzo. Ortolans at dinner. White as snow & wonderfully rich & delicate.[4] In the evening at Lord Holland's saw Col. Campbell from Elba.[5]

Nov. 6. Saw again the Chapel of Brancacci, & at eleven set off

[1] Thomas Patch, d. 1782, *Life of the Celebrated Painter Masaccio*, 1770.

[2] The painter, F. X. Fabre, 1766–1837. He was the companion of the old age of the Countess of Albany, and painted a portrait of her which is in the Uffizi.

[3] Chiostre dello Scalzo.

[4] The taste lingered. Mrs. Jameson met him on his second visit to Florence, in 1821. 'Samuel Rogers paid us a long visit this morning. He does not look as if the suns of Italy *revivified* him—but he is as *amicable,* and amusing as ever. He talked long, *et avec beaucoup d'onction,* of ortolans and figs; till methought it was the very poetry of epicurism.' *Diary of an Ennuyée,* 1826 ed., p. 98.

[5] Sir Niall Campbell, 1776–1827. It was he who escorted Napoleon to Elba and remained there in a very vaguely defined position. He was looked upon as a sort of 'policeman' and was subsequently blamed for Napoleon's escape. But he had no power to hinder the Emperor, nor even to see him unless he was specifically allowed to.

among the sunny hills & white villas of Florence; continuing for three hours along the Arno in its descent from the mountains. The country grew gradually more & more appennine as we ascended to Pelago; a small town on an eminence in the bosom of the Mountains. Found the street full of women, a young man, one of a large family, having just received the stiletto into the region of his heart. He died in half an hour. The murderer had escaped. They had been playing together. Slept at Signor Marconi's. Cards & Backgammon at Night. Fowls, hare & small birds at Supper. Two Priests & three Chasseurs, & a young man returned from serving as a Conscript.

Novr 7th. Rain. Set off at ten on horseback. went down to the bridge & then ascended by a road of flat pavement for two hours along the side of a mountain. Distant views. Cottages. Italian villas. Oxen ploughing in the vineyards; & women every where hoeing, & weeding. A River below us. Passed thro the cloister of a small convent, having first passed thro' a gateway, & observed every where a higher cultivation. Sweeping mountain-lines, wave above wave—Were now in the domain of the Convent. Crosses with latin mottoes. Sanguis Pretiosa. Crucem Tuam adoramus. A town (Atosi) on the opposite height. Crossed the glen by a bridge & again ascending, entered a majestic wood of pines, from which we emerged on the Convent, seated on a lawn among these mountains, oratories & crosses up & down in the hanging woods. Lodged in the Convent, in the Apartments of the Superior. A Priest a very gentlemanlike man the only Religious in the House. Conducted by the Custode & Superintendant of the forests, saw the cloisters, the dormitories (each Padre had two large apartments) the church—from which Andrea del Sarto's Altar-piece is removed to the Academy at Florence—, the theatre & *green room*, the refectory in which there was a pulpit, the kitchen fitted up with stoves, with an oven for confectionary & a hearth in the centre with a circular dome over it, sufficient to roast an ox in, & a window thro' the wall to convey the dishes thro' into the refectory, the ward-robe, the college, the prisons in the fortress (a tower enlarging at top like most in Italy) each with its stone seat & table & aperture to convey the food thro' the wall, the Bakery, &c &c. In a chapel were the tombs of several Abbots, Moderators, & other dignitaries.

10. The cathedral, Florence

11. The arcades of the Uffizi

Vallombrosa: November 7th

D. O. M.
Venerabili Patri Matthiae Passanthio
In collarum deserto eremitae austeriori
Humili affabilitate conspicuo
Oratione et ierniis summe verendo
Queis daemonas superavit, fraudes delusit, spectra non metuit,

Of another it is recorded
Annorum quam plurimum spatio odorem jucundum corpus afflaverit. And of another, an Abbas Vallumbrosianus it is said, & no wonder, that he died Apoplexiae ictu. In the Cloister are many paintings of miracles & among others[1]   .

The first of these worthy men lived, I conclude, in the Sagro Eremo, or sacred desert, beyond these mountains. Mr Eustace[2] mentions his apartment at Vallambrosa, as admirably adapted to the spirit of the place & the order; the walls being merely white-washed, without either paper, wainscot, or tapestry; their only decorations a few prints of subjects taken from Scripture. Had he supped in the Abbot's apartment as we did, most splendidly decorated with oil-paintings in gilt pannels & landscapes & magnificent architecture in fresco—the cieling a sky full of boys showering down roses, the doors with paintings & gilt frames & hinges—had he seen what I have already named & other apartments painted in the richest arabesque like so many Parisian boudoirs, he would have cooled a little on the subject. But we were admitted behind the scenes as at Venice, some reparation for our losses in other respects, as the drama is over.[3]

Il Padre Abbata Fornaini. Dined & the Clergyman entered with coffee in his hand; & recommended an evening-walk. Walked up a noble avenue thro the forest, the blue mountains breaking thro' them in mist. Passed two oratories. The Paradisino high on a rock among these vast forests of fir. The blaze of a fir-fire; the noise & splendour, like those of a firework & as short.

---

[1] The following passage is crossed out: 'of an incident that occurred to one of the order roused from his bed di Mascheto troppo sontuosamente. Nothing less, I imagine, would have roused him.'

[2] John Chetwode Eustace, author of the most famous work on Italy of the century to that date. See Introduction, p. 57. He died in Naples of Malaria in August 1815.

[3] The monastery had been suppressed in 1810. It was re-constituted in 1817.

Catherina, the Custode's little wife. We were here in the season that Milton must have been here after the fall of 'the autumnal leaves that strew the brooks in Vallambrosa.' 'The Etrurian shades' of Milton were thinned, but we saw 'the autumnal leaves &c. Nothing can exceed the grandeur of these forests of abate, rising every where into the clouds, whichever way we turned. The convent is almost shut in by them, & its vast quadrangle being seated on a small lawn, most beautifully undulating & green as an emerald. It has a high campanile; & its fortress is nearly as high. The sala we sit in has this inscription very ornamentally wrought in the cieling. A D. M.DCCLXVII. & the Superior was in all probability reposing here, with half-shut eyes, while E was admiring the plainness of his Apartment. The next is larger. The walls are painted with landscapes in the style of Vernet. Cameos in the cieling.

Nov. 8. Heavy rain & impenetrable mist. At ten it drew up like a curtain in front of the convent & discovered a distant valley & a mountain-side sparkling with white buildings in the softest sunshine. A beautiful vision. It was but for a few minutes. Again the curtain dropped, & all was impenetrable as before. Yet this accident was enough to repay us for hours of darkness. What glimpses of heaven, what elements for the imagination to work with in such a country as this! The regularity of a pine-forest, such numberless lofty stems or shafts rising one beyond another perpendicularly, & to such a height, wherever the eye turns, endless to the imagination, the grave & still light discovering a depth almost unfathomable.

'Vallombrosa, the name of an Abbey, says Ariosto, rich & beautiful & holy; & courteous to all that came there.'[1] & beautiful it is—tho' in decay for it is now a place for owls to hoot in. Politian mentions the susurrus of the Pine.[2] Its music in a high wind is dear to the lover of wild nature. From my window I see

---

[1] *Orlando Furioso* XXII, 36, lines 3–6:

. . . *Vallombrosa*
(*così fu nominata una badia*
riccea e bella, nè men religiosa,
e cortese a chiunque vi venia):

In *Italy*, 'The Great St. Bernard' this becomes:
. . . *that house so rich of old,*
So courteous. . . .

[2] *Rusticus*, line 11: '*Hic resonant blando tibi pinus amato susurro.*'

garden-walls & terraces & stone pillars & gateways without
end, where many a garden flower grows wild.' See Eustace, II.
306. small, plain & unadorned as the private apartments even of
the richest abbies invariably are!!! all the windows double. Went
up along a broad flat pavement by the garden walls, of grey
stone & pillared gateways, & turning under the hill & passing a
cataract that tumbled headlong from rock to rock thro' the hanging wood, ascended rapidly (no steps seemingly in this country)
to the stone recording the miracle of St. Jno Gualbert & the
Arch-fiend & from thence to an oratory or tabernacle now shut
up. Here another of those visionary scenes, clad in the lawn of
almost naked light, presented itself; the vale of the Arno winding almost down to Florence, the vale in sunshine, the river
bright as burnished silver, & the villages & villas, thro' the thin
veil, shining with a soft lustre not their own. Again before a man
could say   the mists rolled over it—the river
alone still visible—still splendid in its course up the valley—but
the storm drew nearer & nearer, & I withdrew.

Vallambrosa stands on a small lawn, full of beautiful undula-
tions, half encircled with sweeping pine-forest, shade above
shade, a woody theatre,[1] rising one above another, & from its
height among the mountains commanding the vale of the Arno
& the opposite mountains, & the windings of that river to
Florence. From the rocky paths above it, not a five minutes
walk, you see the course of the river &, when as far again,
Florence itself. The cloisters small & probably little used. No
appearance of any tomb-stones here. The cloisters arched, the
arches filled with paintings & walled on both sides with open
windows to the court.

(I am no longer my own master. I am become the slave of a
demon. I sit gazing, day after day, on that terrible phantom, the
Duke Lorenzo in M. Angelo's Chapel. All my better feelings
would lead me to the Tribune & the lovely forms that inhabit
there. I can dwell with delight on the membra formosa of the
Wrestlers, the Fawn & the Apollo, on the sunshine of Titian &
the soul of Raphael; but the statue loses none of its influence. He

---

[1] *Cedar, and pine, and fir, and branching palm,*
   A sylvan scene, and, as the ranks ascend,
   Shade above shade, a woody theatre
   Of stateliest view.
   Paradise Lost, Book IV, 11. 139. ff.

sits, a little inclining from you, his chin resting upon his left hand, his elbows on the arm of his chair. His look is calm & thoughtful, yet it seems to say a something that makes you shrink from it, a something beyond words. Like that of the Basilisk, it fascinates—& is intolerable! When you shift your place to the left his eye is upon You.)[1]

The monastery of Vallambrosa, a low quadrangle distinguished by its campanile & fortezza, is seated on a small lawn, green as an emerald, & undulating beautifully, & half encircled with sweeping pine-forests, one above another, a magnificent ampitheatre,

Insuperable height of loftiest shade.[2]

In front opens the vale of the Arno—Valdarno—stretching away to Florence, the river visible in all its windings, among the farms & villas & convents that glitter up & down among the hills—

Went up again with my sister, passing the cataract that hurries into the valley below; that valley now as brilliant as ever in the sunshine the Arno, & the little town of Pont a Servi shining in the sun & many farms, convents & villas as far as Florence.— The Mountains folding beyond them—The valley seemed to rise before us; but, it was an optical deception, the Arno running rapidly towards Florence from these Mountains, among which it takes its rise. Meanwhile the clouds of mist were rolling over the landscape, now opening, & now almost entirely shutting it up. Ascended to the Paradisino, a small house & chapel on a perpendicular rock commanding Florence on one hand, Livorno & the sea on the other. In the church was an Inscription on an antient Cellarum custos.

A vitiis ad virtutes
Ab uxoratu ad continentiam
A strepitu Platearri ad silentium solitudinis
Redactus.

[1] This passage in (Rogers') brackets is copied in ink from a pencil version on the opposite page, subsequently covered over in ink with the passage 'Went up again with my sister', etc. There is no indication as to when the pencil entry was made. The handwriting shows the ink copy was written at the same time as the passage that follows. 'The monastery of Vallambrosa', etc.

[2] *Paradise Lost*, Book IV, 1 138.

Florence: November 9th

Approached it by a broad pavement, & turning to the stables on the left, were glad to remain over a cottage-fire, while our guides went to open the Abbey. We were then led thro' the arched & richly painted cloisters & up a staircase, when we were met by an elegant young person, the wife of the custode who taking my Sister by the arm, led her to a warm hearth in a sala full of gilding & arabesque; & there we spent nearly two days, experiencing every polite attention from the Padre Abbati Fornaini who came regularly twice a day with the caffettiéra[1] in his hand. While dinner was preparing, the custode, with his bunch of keys, conducted us over the Abbey. The Fratri were buried in the vaults under the church without any memorial. In my room were three kneeling desks for prayer & a Salvator Mundi hung over the bed.

Nov. 9th From a window in one of the passages a view of the fall, the Paradisino & the dark woods, shade above shade, now whitened over with snow. Left the Convent seated immediately under mountains almost perpendicular & hung with antient fir-trees, a small lawn undulating on the left & in front of it; & passing thro' the grove we had entered by, descended rapidly into the vale below, torrents crossing the pavement continually, & now & then streaming down it. Nothing could be more beautiful than the retrospect—the Convent, the Paradisino, the hermitages, & their dark back-ground; a little frosted over with snow. A deep glen & foaming cataract, our road winding along a precipice far above it. Sheltered in a blacksmith's cottage. Pelago half way up a craggy mountain—Its romantic appearance. Left our friends there. The Arno full & rapid. The sunbeams played divinely among the mountains & discovered & relieved their waving lines. The gradations of an Italian sun-set; the full blaze, the last parting rays as from the eye of heaven, the cloud edged with a line of light & glorious beyond any thing of the kind in our northern climate, the flame-coloured, the golden, the rosy, & at length the pearly sky. As we approached Florence saw the dome, the belfry, & the watch-tower of the Palazzo vecchio—with many other turrets—black against the evening sky. The dome magnificent!—

(An Italian theatre is lighted only from the stage & the soft shadows (that are) playing over it), have a very visionary

[1] 'coffee-pot' crossed out.

effect. Here & there the figures in a box are illuminated from within, & the glimmering & partial lights are almost magical. Sometimes the curtains are drawn, & you may imagine what you please.)

Novr 10.*^th*. Saw the Santa Croce. Over the door, within, un Crocifisso grande in legno, by Cimabue. The tombs of Machiavel, Galileo & M. Angelo! A beautiful painting of Giotto's on an Altar in the Chapel of Baroncelli, the crowning of the Virgin, &c. the heads conceived & painted in the finest style—& nothing wanting but perspective!! A splendid painting by Bronzino. Himself, his wife, son & daughter at one corner of it. The countenances generally beautiful. A Cimabue, like my own.[1] Alfieri's monument by Canova. The dwelling-house of Michael Angelo. A plain front & broad overhanging roof. A small quadrangular court within, with inlaid fragments of antient bas-relievos. The tribune. The bronzes. A small Jupiter. J^no of Bologna's Mercury. The Pitti Palace. A noble Andrea del Sarto. Indeed many. The rooms magnificent & palace-like. The hangings green, & crimson silk. The cielings richly gilt. The Boboli Gardens. Green avenues, open & shut. Statues. Fountains & Terraces. Florence & its public buildings, & its hills on every side almost covered with villas & convents, cedars & garden-groves. The Cascine.

Eustace & Ld Brownlow[2] dined with us.

Nov. 11*^th*. The hall, in the Palazzo Vecchio, full of gilding, painting & statuary, & the noblest room I have seen in Florence. The rich cieling & the walls painted by Vasari. Two groupes by M. Angelo & Bandelli. The Ricardi Palace. A handsome quadrangular court full of frescoes & inscriptions on antique marbles. The memorable inscription of the Medici, 'Hospes &c'[3] Medals

[1] There were two paintings attributed to Cimabue in Rogers's Sale Catalogue. No. 597, The Virgin enthroned with the Infant in her lap; St. Francis, St. Bernard, and four female saints standing at her side. From the Collection of the Right Hon. C. Greville. And No. 611, An evangelist writing, from the same Collection.

[2] The Rt. Hon. John Lord Brownlow. Eustace dedicated his work of Italian travels to him. They were travelling together; en route, like Rogers, for Rome.

[3] 'Stranger . . . Once the house of the Medici. In which not alone so many great men, but knowledge itself had her home. The house which was the nurse of all learning; which here revived again. Renowned also for its cultured magnificence, a treasury of antiquity and the arts.'

on sale in the upper rooms. Saw the Sasso di Dante—stone-seat.
Along the wall over against the south side of the Cathedral,
runs a long stone seat. A small slab of veined marble, white with
blue veins, & serving as a foot-stone, distinguishing that part on
which Dante is said to have been used to sit. It is said to be the
coolest place in all Florence in a summer evening: & there
probably he sat with his friends. The cathedral; the octagon
dome with its 3 galleries, the portrait of Dante, the painted
windows—M. Angelo's chapel. Lorenzo in deep thought—
Pietro with a scroll open in his hands & in conversation. Maria
Novella. Giotto, M Angelo. Arrived too late. The host entered
from the sick, proceeding with a quick pace. Many figures in
white, with eye-let holes. Went instantly into one of the chapels,
& performed a mass.—Ortolans.

*Nov*ʳ 12 Carreggi Villa, built by Cosmo, afterwards the scene of
the Academy. Lorenzo died here. A small house, inclosing a
quadrangle on a small elevation in the level vale of the Arno. 3ᵐ
from Florence; commanding that vale, here as flat as a bowling
green & within a circle of hills; Fiesole a leading feature. The
gardens formal—wall under wall, with many orange-trees in
lines. The rooms recently ornamented. The view from the
loggio gay, Florence, its churches & towers, & the beautiful
suburbs—the Appenines in the distance. The dome of the
Cathedral, the Campanile, & the tower of the Palazzo vecchio
are every where the principal objects. The dome seemed to be
within half a mile of us; so clear was the air. Olives & Cypresses.
Madonna del Sacco. Rich Cloisters. The Cascine. A concert in
the Opera House. Bright Sunshine & a cold wind from Valam-
brosa. Snow on the Apennine Mountains.

The Campanile, designed by Giotto, & the prettiest thing in
Florence, forgetting the beautiful gates, & the bridge of the
Trinity. Giotto's life, Vasari. 128 The Faun in the tribune. The
head & hands by M. Angelo. The Brutus of M.A. The Herma-
phrodyte. restored by M.A. Qʸ? The tribune a small octagon,
hung with crimson damask & lighted from the dome inlaid with
mother of pearl. In a circle stand the Wrestlers, the Young
Apollo, the Whetter of the Knife, the Dancing Faun, & now in
the place of the Venus, Venus by Canova. A Titian, a Coreggio,
a Parmeggiano & two or three Raphaels are exquisite specimens
—Many there I must confess I should gladly exclude. The mix-

ture of statues & pictures here very agreeable;—filling the mind with delight from the assemblage of such various master-pieces. *Nov 13. Sunday.* Walked in the Boboli Gardens. Florence immediately under us; Fesole beyond it. It presents itself as a splendid cluster—as a village—in some points of view, the roofs of houses being concealed. The Opera.

Novr 14. Saw the pictures of M. Fabre Fiesole. The village-green. The cathedral. The Franciscan convent. An Inscription. Soldiers fight battles, we fight all our lives. The vale of Arno, the river, the city. The olives every where like lavander-bushes, with here & there a cedar. Came down on foot, an accident having befallen the carriage. A delightful walk. An evening mist, like the bloom of a plum, had overspread the mountains & the distant parts of the valley. Fiesole behind us, with its tower, & open buildings; forming one of a chain of hills; & in front seen over cypresses, the towers & domes of Florence! A heavenly dream. In the sky a red streak so often in Italian paintings; & which I used to think unnatural. What a life was a life passed in such a city—in such a valley—in such a country— with such people in the golden days of Florence! Here came in succession Dante, Petrarch, Boccaccio, Machiavel, Gallileo, M Angelo, Raphael, Milton—The dome against the bright sky noble; &, being less elevated than that of St Pauls is what makes it perhaps appear less. As we crossed the Arno, the glow on the water & in the sky; & the soft scenery in the West.

Nov. 15. I am released. The demon loses his influence. The beautiful forms in the Tribune & the Gallery have won me back to truth & Nature.[1] The tribune, a red water silk. The cieling & cupola shells of mother of pearl. The Niobe. The Venetian

[1] By 1821 the Medici Venus had taken the place of the Lorenzo. 'Rogers may be seen every day,' wrote Mrs. Jameson (*op. cit.*, 98–9), 'about eleven or twelve in the Tribune, seated opposite to the Venus, which appears to be the exclusive object of his adoration; and gazing, as if he hoped like another Pygmalion, to animate the statue; or rather perhaps that the statue might animate *him*. A young Englishman of fashion and as much talent as espiéglerie, placed an epistle in verse between the fingers of the statue, addressed to Rogers; in which the goddess entreats him not to come there *ogling* her every day;—for though "partial friends might deem him still alive," she knew by his looks he had come from the other side of the Styx; . . .' She added that 'Rogers with equal good nature and good sense, neither noticed these lines, nor withdrew his friendship and intimacy from the writer'.

School. The Annonciata. Andrea del Sarto. The church of San Marco. Casino & Garden there, with Eustace. Returned by the Palazzo Ricardi (Medici) read the inscription over a red porphyry cistern in the court full of bas reliefs busts & antient inscriptions, saw the statues in M. A's chapel & returned by the Maria Novella. The Cascines. A beautiful evening corso. The sky the colour of flame, thro the light branches. The Campanile. Well might it be mentioned on the tomb of Giotto, & well might Charles V[th] say, 'it was prophaned by the public eye & deserved a case!'

Nov. 16. The Laurentian Library. A long Convent-like Apartment, discovering few book & full of reading desks in double rows as in a church. Illuminated Missals, not of the very first Order. A fac-simile of the Virgil, gone to Paris. The Petrarch on Vellum. His portrait with a pleasanter expression than in the copies. Hers a beautiful countenance, with her eyes cast down. The MS written in a round & clear character. At the end on a seperate page & in the same hand that singular relation of his interview with her at church, told as by himself in the first Person & suspected to be an invention; after which follows a life of him.

In the Strozzi Palace saw Titian's portrait of a child (a whole length) fondling a dog, as engraved in Sandrart.[1] Clear & pure from his pencil. The face a little faded. A green curtain hangs before it. Saw the gems in the gallery, the Brutus of M. Angelo, & the master-pieces in the Tribune. Saw also the Chapel of M.A. The visage of Lorenzo under the shade of that scowling & helmet-like bonnet is scarcely visible. You can just discern the likeness of human features; but whether alive or dead, whether a face or a scull, that of a mortal man or a Spirit from heaven or hell, you cannot say. His figure is gigantic & noble, not such as to shock belief, or remind you that it is but a statue. It is the most real & unreal thing in stone that ever came from the chissel. Eustace, Lord Brownlow at dinner.

Nov[r] 17. The Carmine, to see again the chapel of Brancacci. The San Spirito, a light, well-built church in the Italian Style. The Corsini. Many Pictures; but none very good. The noblest Palace in situation. St Maria Novella. The tomb of the Greek Patriarch

---

[1] Joachim von Sandrart, 1606–88. Painter and writer on the history of art.

In the chapel on the left a rude altar piece by   & in
the same chapel[1] on the right of it a large painting of the
Martyrdom of St Catherine. Diva Catherina Sacra. The Picture
by [Bugiardini] many of the figures said to be designed by M.
Angelo. Is not this the best in Florence? The Saint herself & the
light from heaven upon her exquisite. The story admirably told.
The consternation of all, blasted by excess of light. A boutique
for Odours in the Convent. Very elegant & the most so of the
kind of any thing we have seen. The Academy of Arts. Paintings
of Andrea del Sarto, from Vallambrosa. His life of J^{no} the Baptist again, in the Cloister of the Frate. White, shaded. Bronzes.
The Gallery. The Tribune. The Camoes &c. The Strozzi
Medusa, &c. The garden of the Ferino Palace. A Fountain in the
middle. Full of Flowers in the Spring, tho' in the town. Oranges,
Lemons & Citrons in abundance. Discovered by it, that many of
the streets have the same odour, as we drive thro' them. The
Cascines. Walked along the Arno. A glorious Sunset. The whole
sky in a delicate bloom or faint rose-colour. Dined at home.
Nov. 18. Sun-rise. Vale of Arno. At the gates found country-
people with carts & mules & horses & asses, a long train that
had assembled without, before the opening of the Gates. The
Arno. A distant view of Florence. Mountainous. Many villages
& towns & castles. Bright sunshine. Nothing could be more
beautiful than such a vale at sunset. The chain of hills on our left
in full splendour. That on our right in black shadow, every
church & convent with its tower & belfry, every villa with its
gallery & cypresses, with its long roof its dark & clear outline
against the brilliant sky. A young moon. Levane. Passed thro a
town full of shoemakers, & overtook many people carrying on
their heads a vast cluster of Florence Flasks, some full of wine,
some empty. Slept at Levane, lacrymoso non sine fumo.[2]
Nov. 19. Set off by star-light, & as the dawn came on, the woods
on the horizon discovered against the kindling sky their waving
& various outlines; every leaf & twig being dark against it, &
as distinctly made out as the fibres of moss, or the ramifications
of sea-weed in a hortus siccus. As the blush strengthened in the
east, the stars faded, & at length the sun came up without a

---

[1] This appears to be the Capella Rucellai, but it is not likely that Rogers
would refer to the great Cimabue altarpiece in those terms.
[2] Horace, *Satires*, I, 5, 80.

cloud. A wild rocky & romantic road. A broken bridge. Deep
ravines. Arezzo. The Prado. The cathedral. The market. In the
chapel of the Vasari Family in the old church of La Pieve are four
heads of the Family, forcibly painted in the old style. In an
abbey-church of Monte Cassino a cupola well represented.

Wound along the side of a chain of hills, covered with vines &
olives, the green corn springing up every where in the open
spaces. Met now & then a pedlar transporting his wares on an
ass or two, from town to town, his wife & a boy or two in his
train. Passed under Toricella & Cortona, an extensive level
valley on the right, 20^m at least in breadth, bounded by Radicofani & a line of hills. The Valley seemed full of trees under the
beams of the evening sun, & as he set in a cloudless sky beyond
it, the horizon not much higher than at sea, nothing could be
grander; his broad disk, full to the eye, unobscured by mist, &
only now & then lost to the eye in a blaze of glory. Then came
the colours of evening, till the moon shewed itself higher up in
the sky. Earlier in the day, the innumerable groves of olives, &
the mountain-ridges beyond them, line waving beyond line, gave
what Claude has so often given. The olive-tint also reminded of
G. Poussin, & of what used to disappoint me in his paintings,
but what disappears under a full illumination. Slept at Camuccia;
& at supper sat down with a Spaniard, Col. Palafox,[1] an Italian
& an Englishman, who with their mules had followed us thro'
the day, & had hastened to overtake us from Florence. Their
dreadful confinement for three days in a house of refuge on their
way down the Simplon, during a heavy snow storm, & the fall
of an Avalanche.

Novr 20. A grey morning. The country still beautiful, but wilder
& wilder. Cortona left behind on its mountains. Well might it be
called the *Nest* of   . A forest. The field of battle of
Thrasymene. Rumours of Banditti. Three banditti-like figures.
Gigantic Olive trees, like antient oaks, stunted by time. The lake
of Perugio, once of Thrasymeno. The little town of Passignano
on the lake. Nets & fishing-boats. Continued winding along its
shores to Torricella with its narrow streets, where we dined on
some pike just caught. The opposite shores mountainous &
covered with wood, that appears to rise precipitously from the

---

[1] ? Jose de Palafox y Melzi, 1780–1847. Capt.-General of Aragon, Duke
of Saragossa.

water. On the left a castle on a promontory, the distant Mountains folding behind it, & far away on the right the romantic town of Passignano descending from a height into the lake. On one of its islands—there were three—among trees rose a church-tower; & perhaps in wild beauty it is equalled by few. Walked up the hill thro a forest-like wood, & met a singular figure coming down with a brisk step; a young man about 18ʸʳˢ of age in black, a short brown oil-skin cloak over his shoulders, a staff with a cross on the top of it in his hand, & a crucifix hanging from his neck under his coat. He said he was on a pilgrimage from a village near Rome, to the church of San Antonio at Padua, fulfilling a vow he had made in consequence of his escape from the Conscription, & he held out his hand for charity. On the summit saw the extensive walls of the castle we had seen in the valley; & looked over a vast plain bounded with mountains, several castles above & below us—the wildest scene & the noblest we had met with among the Appenines. Descended & traversed it till Perugia appeared; & with *bovi*[1] before our mules we entered it, Passing a convent with its cloisters overhanging a deep chasm.

Nov. 21. Left Perugia by star-light. Crossed the Tiber, a broad & rapid stream. The valley we now descended into, level & still richer than those we had passed thro'. Assisi with its magnificent cloisters & churches on the hill-side; the church of Madonna degli Angeli, the [Porziuncola] of St Francis, like the house of Loretto, a small rude chapel-like structure, its shrine lighted up & full of kneeling figures under its low roof, like an ark within a magnificent temple. Two Franciscans kneeling on the out-side, & a woman of middle age with an expressive countenance. She wore an oil-skin cloak, & over it a woolen one. It was the habit of a female pilgrim; & she said, as she knelt, that she was on her way from Rome to Florence. Foligno in the vale. Its cathedral. Its corso; the mountains just above it, & a Monastery just discovering itself as in the very bosom of them. It was a striking contrast to walk on this terrace, which skirts so gay & busy a little town, & let your eye wander up these wild & rugged barriers that swell immediately from it. Such transitions are only to be found in Italy. Coasted these mountains, castles & castle-

---

[1] Oxen were used to assist horses or mules when roads were particularly steep. See Introduction, p. 76.

like towns, hanging high above us on either hand, Montefargo & Trevi the most distinguishable. Sowing & ploughing every where, the ploughman alone guiding the plow & the oxen. People returning from a fair. A Lady in lace & gold & scarlet with her maid, both riding astride. To the Temple of Diana over the little river Clitumnus, & immediately under the road. The ground falls before it, & it is accessible only on the sides. Its pediment too high, its four corinthian columns (two with spiral flutes, two wrought like the pine-cone) within pilasters; yet from its size, situation, minute ornaments & general effect most beautiful. Spoleto soon appeared before us on a high mountain. Portafuga. The gate of Hannibal. The Aquaduct traversing a deep & almost immeasurable chasm. Saw it by moon-light; & its vastness & entireness, connecting us at once with some mighty people, affected me deeply. So magnificent a work to supply the little town of Spoleto with water! Built probably by Theodoric. by some is ascribed to the Romans, by some to the Goths. Its piers seemed to descend into a bottomless gulph—into the centre of the earth

Nov. 22. The sky almost starless. Left the deep glen and Monte Luco alas, invisible, on our left, scattered over with white hermitages, & when day broke, found ourselves in a long & narrow mountain-valley, shaded by antient trees, & here & there unfolding a lawn of great beauty; the road winding along by the broad & stony bed of a river, now like many others without a drop of water. From hence we were drawn (by bovi, driven by a woman, whom we found waiting for passengers in the road) to the Somma, the highest ridge of the Apennines here, & by a long descent came among numberless olive-groves with their twisted & mossy trunks, & their thin & light foliage resembling at first leafless trees in the white frost of a winter's day. Passed several travellers, who courteously saluted us from their cabriolets as we passed & it was a pleasant thing in these high & lonely regions. At the bottom a Castle in ruins. Three Salvator-like figures, probably chasseurs, pointed out mysteriously to us by Ferdinando, our Servt, as Ladri.[1] Terni. Up a glen ascended rapidly to the summit of the Cascata delle Marmora. First saw the Velino rushing to its fall. Then from the very brink saw it dissolving into mist, & afterwards from a

---

[1] *Ladro* =robber.

summer-house (thanks to Pius VI) saw it in front, precipitating itself into the under-world, & discharging its thousand currents breaking, as it were, into serpents, like the fires of a rocket, after its explosion in the air. It was all whiteness, & well answered its name. The rocks around it are grey & twisted, & hung with luxuriant foliage. The sides of the fall stream with vegetation & well relieve its whiteness. The sun shone & threw a vivid rainbow across the foam below, & the cliffs on either side. A shower of rain rose & filled the air tho' at the vast height at which we stood. Near this spot looked up another valley, & counted no less than four castles among the mountains; Monte-franco lay lower, while Castelargo, seated on a rude eminence, but half seen in one of those dark recesses, seemed built for Romance.

Crossed a wide valley—une trés plesante plene, says Montaigne,[1] ou la riviere Negra se joue & s'enviloppe estrangement —castles & towns on the heights at a distance, Narni a castellated city on the mountain in front. Under it is the bridge of Augustus, & by the grey light of evening contemplated the vast & splendid ruin. It stands in the Nera with its piers & broken arches, discovering thro' them the high & woody shores of that River, an old castle overhanging it. The situation becomes the place. At Florence we thought only of Modern Italy & of its golden age—As we approach Rome, Antient Italy rushes on the Imagination. Italy has had two lives! Can it be said of any other Country? Overtaken by a Signor returning from an afternoon's airing, & who begged us to visit the bridge in a cabriolet he had hired. Thunder & heavy rain in the Night. Little Cities of antient renown upon the mountains, where the eagle would chuse to build his nest, shew like little lights where you would least expect them, & break out under a morning or evening-sun in places seemingly inaccessible; four or five at a time. Wood every where on these Appennines.

Nov. 23. Set out at day break. A magnificent glen on the right, the Neri with its white current running down it. Along the edge of this glen, & fronting the valley we crossed yesterday, is

[1] *Journal de Voyage en Italie*, *s.d.* 20 April, 1581. 'Narni . . . au pied duquel roule la riviere Negra, *Nar* en latin; et d'une part ladite ville regarde une très plesante plene où ladicte riviere se joue et s'enveloppe estrangemant.'

Narni seated, with its cathedral its churches, its fountains of great beauty, & a castle of walls of great extent, yet in the inn, & probably in the town there was not a candle, or a drop of milk. Thro' a forest-scene we continued till we descended into a wide & woody valley, here & there rising into volcano-like elevations, & thro' which the yellow Tiber was winding like a Serpent below us. Here we left the Appenines, & soon afterwards Umbria; crossing the Tiber into the Sabine Country by a noble bridge built by a Roman Emperor & repaired by a Pontiff. Civita Castellana. Its Cathedral. Rich fragments of antient foliage in a modern wall near the Piazza. A low level plain; rushy fields, sulphurous fumes, an old aqueduct at Nepi, Montenosi, passing a dismal exhibition of the foot & arm of a robber. Came in, in a procession of six vetturini so gregarious are they from fear towards Night. A crowded Inn. No chimney in any chamber.

Novr. 24 Break of day. Soon came on the Appian Way, a good pavement that left off now & then & then began again. Met Two Pilgrims on their way to the Santa Casa in the Church of Loretto. Each with his staff, his flask, & wallet; & a silver cross wrought on his oil-skin. They said they were to get their cockle-shells at Loretto. They were both, ruddy in the face, tho' a little wrinkled. Went up a hill & were told between the 15th & 16th milestone to prepare for a sight of Rome. Left the Carriage, & ascending, in less than a hundred yards, thro' the haze of the morning & across a dreary & uncultivated plain saw in the horizon what we had longed so much to see! The dome of St Peters, the castle of St Angelo, the *thousand* churches, & the smoke like a light over the rest of the line, tho' the houses were undistinguishable. Rome herself lay before us with all her nameless associations. High mountains on the left. Met a Clerical Gentleman in a travelling coach & six—Dined at 11 at & drove rapidly down to Rome! entering it by M'Angelo's Gate.[1] St Peters seen almost always till we came to the gate. Passed an antient sarcophagus on the right, commonly called Nero's tomb.

Nov. 25. The Pantheon! What a walk from the Vatican to the Coliseum! So long a spectacle of ruin and of scorn. St Peter's. Vespers.

[1] Porta del Popolo. The north face was built by Vignola, to a design by Michelangelo.

Nov. 26. The Pictures & Marbles of the Capitol. Tarpeian Rock. Forum. In Carcere. The dungeons, upper & lower, into which the prisoners were let down by a cord thro' an aperture in the floor—Qy Were the Catiline Conspiritors lodged there & put to death?—& into which Jugurtha, after being led in triumph, was let down to perish, his ear-rings having been torn as perquisites from his ears. Scala Gemonia. There is something very delightful in reflecting that the dismal cell in which an unbroken spirit had languished for nobly asserting his freedom of opinion should afterwards become sacred & be visited by pilgrims upon their knees. The Capella Sistina. St Peters. A Thunderstorm at Night Streets lighted by the lamps of a few Madonnas. Men & women walking & sitting at their doors with a little earthen vessel full of charcoal on their laps hanging by a cord—

Nov 27. Mass in the Capella Sistina. The Pope knelt before the Altar, & ascended his throne under the canopy crimson & gold. Ceremonies. The silver mitre put on & off. The reverences of the Cardinals. Other dignitaries kissed his foot & received his benediction. Delicious singing in a gallery. No organ or instrumental accompaniment. His dropping frankincense into the censer—Exposition of the Sacrament, borne by the Pope bareheaded under a silver Canopy into the Capella Paulina splendidly lighted up. There the Sacrament being administered with singing, he returned into the Chapel of Sextus & again into that of Paul III, where he remained kneeling before the altar half an hour. Many cardinals & others at different distances behind him. All rose & went away, one by one, before him. A feeble old man. Seventeen Cardinals. The Glorious dreams of Raphael in the Vatican. His Arabesques in the Loggie. The last much perished & almost entirely painted over. His tomb in the Pantheon. St Maria Maggiore. It was striking & unexpected to find oneself in an antient chapel; a venerable figure kneeling in rich habilaments before an altar burning as with the fires of the firmament, two or three halberds such as Raphael has painted on his left, a few scattered figures in purple behind him, & scarcely any others—all kneeling—there but six or seven english standing or sitting along the wall. Had I seen it in a dream, it would have greatly affected me. Had I been assured of seeing it realized, I should have disbelieved it. Every habit & figure & implement (the Greek bishops how imposing in their long beards)

12. The Martyrdom of St. Catherine, by Bugiardini.
'Is not this the best in Florence?'

13. The entrance to Rome from the north: Porta del Popolo

such as Raphael saw & gave us! The Coliseum, by moonlight.
Slept in the Palazzo Rondinini.[1]

Nov 28. Canova's workshop. Antonine Column. Doria Palace.
Colonna Palace. Compared to these in extent & splendour what
are the houses of England? The small gallery that runs round
the quadrangle of the Doria, hung with red silk & full of
pictures, more captivating in my eyes than even the splendid
hall of the Colonna—209 f. by 35 f.—full of pictures & marbles!
The Chigi Palace now half unfurnished.[2] In the Doria large
landschapes by Gaspar Poussin; as also in fresco are many in the
Colonna. In the gallery or hall of the last a slight sketch of
Titian's. Four half-figures, evidently portraits their hands joined
in prayer, a mother, her son & two daughters; the dove, within a
circle of cherubim shedding light upon them. Admirable for
grave simplicity of design, & light & exquisite execution. At the
end of the gallery the garden, terrace above terrace, to the top
of Mont Quirinal, full of cypresses, orange-trees & antient
marbles.

Nov. 29. Bright sunshine! The fountains before St Peter's
forming splendid rain-bows. Walked in St Peter's. View from
the towers of the Capitol! The Forum. The aqueduct of
Claudian. The tomb of Cecilia Metella. Titus's baths. Tivoli,
in the cleft of a mountain, & Soracte behind it, wrapt in snow.
Frescati. Tusculum! It was a brilliant day, & the scene interesting beyond all others, yet melancholy rather then beautiful,
& grand rather from association than reality.

The arches of the Coliseum! Vastness; Solidity; & masonry
grand & simple. Why, had we not known otherwise, should not
it last for ever? Thousands of years hence will some of its stones
be found, one upon another. Its masses are like so much rock.

Nov. 30. The Pantheon. The Justiniani. Antient Marbles. The
He Goat. A bust of a Boy (inscribed I believe Amori). A sleeping nymph. View of the Pantheon from the window. The Farnese Palace, by M.Angelo. The Gallery! Annibal Caracci &
his scholars, Domenichino, Albano, Guido. The Spada Palace.

---

[1] Via del Corso No. 518–9, opposite No. 20, where Goethe stayed. It
later became palazzo Sanseverino and is now the seat of the Banca
dell'Agricoltura.

[2] The family had been penalized for criticizing the French administra-
tion and were forced to raise money by the sale of pictures.

Pompey's Statue, at the base of which Cesar is said to have fallen. In a grand hard style. The Farnesiana in an orange garden on the Tiber—civil oranges gathering 4 baskets full. In its hall the Cupid & Psyche of Raphael; or rather of his scholars; & the redness that prevails here as in his bible in the Loggia, &

Panorama of Rome from the tower of the Capitol

indeed in many of J. Romano, leads one to suspect it to be original & untouched. The back of one of the Graces is a charming exception & is ascribed to his pencil. Beauty of the countenances. Spirit of the birds & butterflies. The Galatea. Appears to be well-preserved & wins upon You the more you look upon it.

Orange-trees full of fruit, & as high & spreading as the Mul-

berry-trees I knew in my youth. We had here a good view of
the Farnese Palace. Its loggia & its attics grand & beautiful.
(Had Rome stood alone in the desert like Balbec & Palmyra,
unmixed with baser matter, fewer pilgrims would have trodden
its pavements, yet some from the ends of the earth!

Decr 1. Fonte di Trevi. A magnificent profusion of marble &
water—the water the celebrated Aqua Virgo.—Before it is a
semicircular stone seat on which the citizens sit round to enjoy
the water-breeze in a summer evening. The Rospigliosi Palace.
In the garden, in a summer house or pavilion the front of which
inlaid with many rich friezes in long pannels is the prettiest I
ever saw, is Guido's Aurora. A Thing, so often copied, always,
I think, falls short of your expectation; it soon however if truly
fine, recovers its rank in your mind, & so in a great degree does
this. The fullness of the compartment, the size of the figures &
vivid colouring, especially in the sea & the sky, the beauty of
some & grace of many of the group, cannot fail to strike you.
Military music on Monte Cavallo, while we were here.

In the next room, Adam & Eve in Paradise by Domenichino—
full of flowers, & birds & other animals—Spotty as a whole, but
admirably painted in parts. Monte Cavallo. The Colossal
figures! The column of Trajan. Perfect in its proportions, & full
of rich sculpture. The Baths of Titus. Arabesques in its walls &
caved ceilings; particularly the last. Colours still alive. Landscapes. Dancing figures. They bring you nearer to the Romans
than all the rest. The interior of their baths, & houses! A foretaste of Herculaneum & Pompeii. The passages lofty & narrow
& vaulted; & painted to be seen only by torch-light. Church of
San Pietro in vincoli. The tombs of two Cardinals. Their portraits by Domenichino admirably painted. Tomb of Julius II.
The Moses of M.Angelo, bold & rather extravagant. A Virgin
& child above it, all over beautiful!

St Martin. Landscapes in fresco by Gaspar Poussin the figures
by Nicholas, his brother. All the frescoes of Gaspar that I have
seen are crude, cold & unpleasing.

St Gregoire. Near it are three chapels. In that of St Andrew, face
to face, are grand frescoes by Guido & Domenichino representing the Martyrdom of the Saint. The last has been the happiest.
Guido's is full of men. Domenichino's of women & children; &
he has outdone himself! It is perhaps the most beautiful of his

works. From the terrace before St Gregoire there is a noble view of the Ruins of Rome. In a field, thro which you pass to the Baths of Titus, you are arrested by the Coliseum! It is seen in all its grandeur; discovering itself there in size at least nearly as a Roman must have seen it.

*Dec*ʳ 2. The Fountains of St Peter's scattering rainbows in the Sun. The Capella Sistina. David slaying Goliah, round & finely coloured in a silver manner, as are the women bearing the head of Holofernes. The colouring indeed of many of the angles solemn & suitable to the subjects. The last Judgement, least pleasing in every respect, & as a composition faulty; but in expression invention & anatomical truth unrivalled. The cieling altogether grand, & arresting the attention. From the loggie of the Vatican built by Bramante there is perhaps the richest view of a Metropolis in the World.

> *The City which thou seest, no other deem*
> *Than great & glorious Rome, Queen of the Earth*
> > *There the Capitol*
> *On the Tarpeian Rock—& there Mount Palatine*
> *The imperial Palace,*
> *With gilded battlements, conspicuous far*
> *Turrets & terrasses, & glittering spires.*
> *Many a fair edifice besides, more like*
> *Houses of Gods—*[1]

(7 oClock. The bells are now tolling the suono di Morti—& a loud chant is heard at a little distance, & the Corso is full of lights from one end to the other. It is the funeral of the Marchesa de Caligula, & her body uncovered on a golden bier is passing under the windows. Most of the procession is moving under umbrellas for the rain is heavy; Many white dresses. It is now gone like a dream!) The Arabesques. Some of these that remain are painted with so light & delicate a pencil, that the bible-histories must have been retouched. So red & heavy a complexion could never have been Raphael's. The arches & little domes very rich in perspective. The Arabesques said to be by J. de Udine. The Pictures by J Romano. The Incendio del Borgio. The middle & right of the picture beautiful; the left evidently by an inferior hand. The central group, the woman

---

[1] *Paradise Regained*, Book IV, ll. 44 ff.

kneeling, & the boy instructed by its mother, to kneel & pray, preeminent. The figures in the distance on the upper steps exquisitely coloured.

The Mass at Bolsenna. The Priest in his crimson vest kneeling at the Altar as rich as Titian himself! & so are many parts of the Attila. Leo X & his white horse most splendidly painted.

What a glorious composition is that of the Sacrament. Heaven & Earth! & how sweetly painted!

The Heliodorus. Here perhaps on the left is the loveliest of all his groups. How his pencil delights to run into women & children!

The St Peter is perhaps the coldest of the series; the rest being as rich & in many parts richer than any of his oil-paintings. But how well is the story told. An old man asleep (& in sleep how affecting is his attitude, how full of humble resignation) his hands & feet chained to the hands of a soldier on each side, both leaning on their spears. In an instant an Angel illuminates the dungeon, & in another instant, conducted by that Angel he is out of the prison. The attitude of the Apostle in his sleep is above all praise. The Jurisprudence, sweet & beautiful in thought & execution. In the School of Athens the figure of Empedocles surpasses M Angelo himself. The Mount Parnassus, I must confess, affects me least of all, tho' the Homer & Dante, & two or three of the Muses are transcendent. Exposition of the Sacrament at St Peter's.

Decr 3. The bells ring the suono de Morti. Three treble notes in quick time; then after an interval three base notes.

We dwell above the clouds, & look down on the seven hills of Rome. We are in the Rondinini Palace, distinguished for its possession of the celebrated Mask of the Medusa,[1] & from the windows command a little world. That hill, covered with gardens is Monte Pincio, antiently the collis hortulorum, the abode of Pompey & Sallust & Lucullus; that white building with its turrets & garden & cypresses is the Villa Medici; there is the Castle of St Angelo, Adrian's tomb, by Belisarius made a fortress, there is the dome of St Peter's! In half a minute You are on a terrace at the top of the House, & there you see all Rome & its campagna!

Decr 3. St Pietro in Vincoli M A's Moses. Grandeur of his limbs

[1] Now at Munich.

& his drapery. St John of Latran. Statue of Constantine in the Portico. Porphyry Sarcophagus before the monument of Clement XII from the portico of the Pantheon. Columns of gilt bronze. Tomb of Andrea Sacchi. Cardinal's hat suspended.

Holy Staircase. Kneeling figures ascending it, saying a prayer on every step. From the balcony behind it a noble view of the Aqueduct of Claudian! extending along the valley far & wide.

Santa Croce. Temple of Venus & Cupid, a wreck. Porta Major. Temple of Minerva Medica in a garden. Arch of Gallien Baths of Diocletian. Sta Maria delle Angeli Salvator Rosa's Tomb. Martyrdom of St Sebastian, a magnificent fresco of Domenichino! A boy, full of fear & curiosity. Another kneeling!—A cardinal's hat. The Meridian in brass. The cloisters of the Chartreux by M. Angelo.

Fontana Felice. Vast volume of Water Two noble lions in Basalt, Egyptian Workmanship; their plinths rich in hieroglyphycs. Place of the four fountains, the centre or meeting of four grand avenues or streets, perhaps the best view of the City. Monte Cavallo. Church of the Apostles. Tombs of Ganganelli & Volpato by Canova. Concert & Exposition of the Sacrament in the Church of Jesus.

*Dec*ʳ 4. Went among villas & white walls to the Villa Albani, on a declivity, on the left overlooking the vale, now purple, & the hills beyond it of the same tinge—Frescati in full view. Statues & Friezes & precious columns unnumerable. No fireplace; & a mal-aria in the summer. An orangery. Pavilion in the Rospigliosi Gardens. Aurora of Guido. Capitoline Marbles. Pliny's doves. St Peter's.

*Dec*ʳ. 5 Went on the Via Appia to St Sebastian's which you approach thro a grove of cypresses & thro' which you pass into the catacombs; sand-quarries, branching out in narrow ways & now & then enlarging, now & then contracting; cavities for the dead on each side one above another; like the beds in a shipcabin. Here the first believers assembled to pray, & here often they were martyred. Human bones were mouldering in many. Tomb of Cecilia Metella. Its perfect masonry rich frieze & beautiful inscription. The three names so interwoven; her father's, her husband's & her own. Stables, house of exercise & Circus of Caracalla. a small antient temple, now the church of St Urban, & almost immediately under it in the side of the hill the grotto of Egeria. A spring overhung with aquatic plants, falls into a cistern within it, a statue of a nymph in a recumbent posture lies over it. Another little temple of brick, called the Temple of the God Rediculus. The Arch of Drusus. Returning by the Coliseum; the tomb of the Scipios; & St Stefano Rotondo. Nothing can be more affecting than these excursions from Rome, the fields uninhabited, almost uncultivated & covered with ruins; the Aqueduct of Claudian crossing the valley & every where the principal feature; as well as the battlements & watch-towers of the City Wall.

Decr 6. A funeral procession along the Corso; the mourners hid, the dead uncovered; a young woman who died in childbed yesterday, & seemed in the bloom of life. The hymn sad & un-pleasing came up from below us.

Temple of Juno. Arch of   Theatre of Marcellus. Temple of Charity. Ponte Palatino. House of Pilate Temple of Fortuna Virilis or Senatorio Temple of Vesta. Round. Temple of Pudicitia

After the Region of the Forum, perhaps this is the most inter-esting spot in Rome. As you walk the narrowest streets how often do you see wedged in the wall of a house a fragment of rich foliage or the fluted shaft of a column! Went along the Tiber under the Mount Aventine, & by the cave of Cacus. Basilica of St Paul. Its beautiful columns. A cloister of the age of Constantine, contiguous. Its small pillars inlaid with various marbles. & its mosaic friezes. Tomb of Caius Cestius, half within, & half without the wall. A pyramid. A painted vault within it. A square pannel or compartment formed by black lines, a dancing figure at each corner. Burial ground of Foreign-ers, not of the Catholic Religion. Macdonald's tomb.[1] A small column, now green with vegetation. Pathetic inscription, in English & Latin. Some withered elms skirt the ground. The day was mild, the air Bright, & the melancholy stillness & character of the scene far from unpleasing. The arches of Janus, & Septi-mus Severus; the last tho' small, rough with sculpture & retaining its inscription. The cloaca. The Corso, excepting twice before a column & a church, not so wide as old Bond street. Here the carriages parade at a quick pace. The old King

---

[1] Sir James Macdonald, *d.* 1766. The tomb was erected by Piranesi. Rogers is of course referring to the Protestant burying ground.

of Spain,[1] Lucien Bonaparte,[2] & Roman Ecclesiastics & nobles, some in phaetons drawn by sleek mules. Well-drest men are often standing to see them. The poorest people carry about embers in earthen vases—a scaldino. A Roman girl of low condition often elegantly drest, with scarlet sleeves & bright green bodice & yellow petticoat. The men of the country with white hats & very high tapering crowns. No wind & no mist since we came here. A pouring rain, like our summer showers every day, but clearing up suddenly, & the air soft & bright as in our Autumn. Almost all the men with umbrellas & jockey capes to their great coats; the sleeves hanging down & seldom used. A poulterer's shop, people plucking feathers from dead fowls, living ones on all the shelves side by side as if they were roosting. Qy. tied? Oxen with very large wide horns, & much larger themselves & less handsome than those in Tuscany.

Dec[r] 7. Church of San Pietro in Montoria in which hung the Transfiguration.[3] Circular Chapel by Bramante; introduced by Raphael in his carton of St Paul. Fountain of the Water Paulina. From these regions—Mont Janiculus—a magnificent view of Rome. Repeated Milton's lines here, & found them wonderfully accurate. The roofs of Rome how green with vegetation! Villa Pamfili Doria. The most beautiful & enviable I have yet seen. The Casino rich with relievos, the flower-garden broidered with flowers in *arabesque*, or after the fashion of a Grecian scroll, the cypress avenues, the orangeries, the lawn shaded round with pines & other forest-trees; the fountains—& beyond all the Sabine mountains blue as ultramarine, Montecelli, Tivoli, Frescata shining in the sun—& St Peter's alone in a single frame—thro' the pines. Palazzo Corsini. An endless vista of rooms hung with silk & velvet of the richest fancies. The sheep browsing on the pavement of the Court! Box cut into the best ornamental borders yet seen here. It is in La Lungara, a hand-street Palazzo Farnese, wherever seen the noblest private building.

[1] Charles IV.

[2] Prince of Canino, 1775–1840, the second eldest of the brothers. His political disagreement with Napoleon and his stubbornness in marrying a wife of whom the Emperor did not approve led to his fleeing to America. He was caught at sea by a British ship and lived for a while as a country gentleman in England. He had lived in Italy before his flight and returned there in 1814.

[3] Then in the Louvre.

Decr 8. High mass in the chapel on Monte Cavallo. State
Carriages of the Cardinals. Long tailed black horses. Cardinals
in scarlet with scarlet hats. Grand music, like the most solemn
& simple parts of Handel's chorusses. No light & quick movements. A gilt mitre. The Cardinals kissed his hand—Continual
bowing to each other. An embrace & salutation sent down from
one to the other. The Pope knelt, leaning on the same stool as
in the miracle at Bolsenna. Vatican Library. Music in St Giacomo de Hispanioli—Lady Westmoreland's[1] concert. Lucien
Bonaparte. Cardinal Fesch.[2]

Decr 9. Villa Mellini, on the Monte Mario, antiently Clivus
Cinnæ. Thro' a wild grove you wind up to it, discovering thro'
the trees continual glimpses of what is in reserve for you. St
Peter's immediately under you, appears alone & separate thro'
the loop-holes. The house was once inhabited by Ld Bristol,[3] &
is now empty, & of little value; but the height & abruptness of
the hill & the pines & brushwood that adorn it & furnish fore-
grounds that render it delightful. From the house runs a woody
terrace, commanding the Tiber & the Emilian, or Flaminian
way issuing from Rome like an arrow; the Sabines & Soracte
bounding the valley & in an opposite direction you trace (by
Cecilia Metella's tomb, & other ruins) the Appian on its way
towards Naples. No where could Milton's lines be pronounced
with such effect as here. The Capitol, Mount Palatine (there
among others Cicero had his house & there was Nero's golden
house—now cypresses mix with shapeless ruins) & those
cypresses are threatened with the axe. The noblest feature is the
Coliseum, a wonderful fabric here standing apart, tho' in the
midst. The Tyber runs a yellow naked stream! Behind St Peter's,
extends a level desert & as we descended by another path a
silver line shone beyond it. It was a sea, & that sea the Mediterranean! We had never seen it before. The villa Madama lies
immediately under the Villa Mellini. At sun-set saw both from
the roof of the Rondinini, the sky being crimson & gold behind

---

[1] Jane Saunders, wife of John Fane, 10th Earl of Westmorland.

[2] 1763–1839. Napoleon's uncle. He returned to France in 1815 but came
back to Rome after Waterloo and lived in retirement amid the splendid
collection of paintings he had amassed.

[3] Frederick Augustus Hervey, 4th Earl of Bristol, bishop of Derry,
1730–1803.

the Pantheon. What a pleasure to recognise objects that have been before unnoticed, & that now stand forth in a new light!

Decr 10. The Vatican. A mile of Marbles. Marbles rescued from the darkness & silence of a second sleep in the earth.[1] A Malaria there in summer; & in winter an intense cold.

Decr. 11. Walked in the Medici gardens. Avenues of cut box. Terraces overlooking the Villa Borghese on one side, & on the other almost all Rome. Thro' the Porta del Popolo, & by the Muro Torto—to the Villa Borghese. Its friezes its statues & vases are gone from the front, & from within are vanished the master-pieces so known & admired,[2]—Its pavilions & fountains, its circus & aviaries are mouldering away, yet it is still the most splendid Villa in Europe. Its inequalities & its ilex groves, & its fading splendours at the gates of such a City as Rome! Met Louis Bonaparte[3] there. On the Antonine column in the third round of the Spiral & on the fountain side rather inclining towards the gate of the Spada Palace saw the Jupiter Pluvius. It is small, & scarcely distinguishable but well-given by Bartoli.[4]

Eleven Corinthian Columns, said to have belonged to the Temple of Antoninus Pius, now wedged into the front of the Dogana di Terra.[5] Fluted, & sustaining a rich intablature—A Majestic Ruin. The Solar Obelisk transported from Hieropolis

[1] This is a form of self-quotation. v. *An Epistle to a Friend*:

> *Here chosen gems, imprest on sulphur, shine,*
> *That slept for ages in a second mine:*

[2] The statues and pictures had in great part been purchased by Napoleon in 1809. Finch, who was there in May 1815, reflected: 'Little did the fond founder of this Villa suppose that the philosophic traveller would inscribe upon his journal, after viewing it, one striking and strongly allusive word, "Fuit".' Tom Moore disliked even what was left, 'some tasteless and fussy works of Bernini,—the David flinging the Stone, and biting his under lip with the exertion; and Apollo and Daphne, with the toes of the latter most frightfully elongated into leaves and roots.' Journal, Nov. 5, 1819.

[3] 1778–1846, the third Bonaparte brother, for a time King of Holland. The happiest part of his life was spent in Rome, where he led a quiet and studious life. He was the father of Napoleon III.

[4] This is plate 5 in *Columna Cochlis M. Aurelio Antonino Augusto . . . brevibus notis Io. Petri Bellori illustrata et a Pietro Sancte Bartolo iuxta delineationes in Bibliothecâ Barberinâ asservatas, ac cum antiquis ipsius Columnae signis collatas aere incisa . . .* Romae M.DCCIV.

[5] The custom house, to which travellers had to drive on arrival. Now the Bourse.

to the Campus Martius by Augustus, Red Granite & inscribed
with Hieroglyphics. Mount Palatine. Hence the word Palatium
or palace. The house of Cicero was at the foot of it, a little
elevated. Augustus lived here 40 years, never changing his
room, winter or summer. & here was ever afterwards the
Imperial Palace. Caligula connected it by arches with the Capitol, & Nero, covering the Mountain with his embellishments,
dwelt here in his Domus Aurea. It was laid low by the Vandals,
& now in the Orti Farnesi you see fractured capitals & rich
cornices half hid in the long grass;—Vast masses of Wall &
Tower here & there mouldering along the declivities. The Orti
Farnesi have now themselves given way. The terraces are dis-
mantled—the aviaries a ruin, & the fountain designed by M.
Angelo no more to be seen—but its situation is unrivalled. The
Capitol, the Forum & the Coliseum are striking objects here. In
the baths of Livia are rich ornaments on the vaulted cielings.
Golden flowers on a white ground—& pictures, & single figures
in frame-works of blue & gold. Scala Santa. A croud ascending
continually. Many descend, & again renew their journey upwards. A monk at the gate receives the canes & umbrellas of the
devotees; &, strange to relate, there are chains & collars fixed
to a pillar for their convenience. We saw a Lady releasing her
lap-dog after having accomplished the pious labour. The noise as
they mount together is like that of horses in a stable. On the
highest step is a cross of brass, which they kiss with more or less
fervency; some salute it all over. In our return met a funeral. In
the coliseum a Franciscan-like-figure had been preaching, &
others in the same habit, their eyes only visible, & attended by
numbers of people, went from Passion to Passion[1] round the
area below, kneeling & chanting a hymn, the notes of which
were simple & not unpleasing.

Of Antient Rome its roads, & aqueducts its walls & watch-
towers, its seven hills its campagna, & the mountains that skirt
it, the river that crosses it & the sea that opens beyond it, still
remain to us. Many of these things are not only unchanged but
unchangeable. The snow at this moment shines on Soracte, the

---

[1] Clement X had altars built round the arena, and a larger one in the
centre: it was part of the attempt to secure respect for the building as a
scene of Christian martyrdoms. The altars were repaired by Benedict XIV
in 1750.

Tiber winds along from the Apennines to the Tyrrhene sea, & the sun still continues to rise & set in the same places. What materials then are left for the Imagination to work with! Of the churches some were temples—like that of Vesta & the Pantheon, & the Church said to have been the temple of the God Rediculus —& many were basilicæ or halls of Public meeting.

*Dec*ʳ 12 Thro the gate of the Popolo designed by M. Angelo, went along the Flaminian way & over the Ponte Milvio; then returned along the other side of the Tiber by the via Felice & ascended to the Villa Madama, so called from Margaret of Austria, daughter of Charles V. It stands on a declivity half way down the Monte Mario, commanding the Tiber, the Sabine Mountains, Montelice, Tivoli & half Rome. The house or casino is small & unfinished; but the garden-front is beautiful, & ascribed to Raphael. A loggia of three noble arches, the cieling vaulted into many sections & richly arabesqued. Niches full of fairy-painting & mouldings & recesses such as a Painter would introduce to catch the playing lights; much of the foliage in stucco, & white on a dark blue ground. From it extends a short terrace. A fountain, the water gushing from the trunk of an Elephant. Within are two rooms, painted after the fashion of the baths, in the cieling & cornice by Julio Romano. A bushy path leads along the hill-side to a wild recess now overgrown with wood, a sort of rural theatre, where are a grotto & a spring, now choked up with vegetation, & open only in front to the campagna. There in better days were plays performed, & among others the Pastor Fido; some say the Aminta—& there the massacre of St Bartholomew it is said, was first conceived. It is by far the most beautiful casino, robbed, as it is, of its friezes & statues; & does honour to Raphael himself.

In the Farnesina, another villa belonging also to the King of Naples saw again the Cupid & Pysche, & the Galatea, works of the same divine Master. The best light here is now at one oClock. An Assembly at the Princess Massima's.[1] A dark staircase & on a landing place, half discovered by a faint glimmering, a couple of beggar-women, their hands held out with cries of supplication. A gallery or corridor—then a hall & then the

[1] Christine de Saxe, wife of Don Cammillo Victor Massimo, granddaughter of Frederick Augustus III, King of Poland. One of the Roman families most hospitable to the English.

voices of servants waiting in an antichamber—all darkness visible At length you enter a room in which are four gentlemen two of them eclesiastics playing at cards; then another in which are three or four card-tables & in which the Lady of the House receives you & then the last more crouded. All were elegantly painted in Etruscan, or hung with Silk, walls & cielings; & well-lighted. A fire in the last of them. The card-tables uncovered—the brown wood. Lucien & Me Bonaparte. Coffee, tea, ice & lemonade. No names of the English were given in, but you were introduced as a Cavaliere Inglese.

Decr 13. High mass in the Church of St John of Lateran for the repose of the souls of the Kings of France. An annual ceremony. The French Embassador, representing his Master who is first Canon of that Church sat elevated in a chair. Several canons were present. A fine soprano voice. Saw the Villetta Olgiati, a small house in a garden behind the Villa Medici, rudely painted after his[1] designs & said to have been inhabited by him. As Cameos in the angles of the cieling are some female heads, said to be those of the Fornarina & other ladies of Rome. Saw afterwards the Tomb of Augustus, now an ampitheatre for bull-fights.[2] At Ld Holland's Cardinal Ruffo.[3]

Decr 14. Saw the Marbles of the Vatican & walked in the Gardens; among orange-trees glowing with oranges, the hills in the neighbourhood topt with snow. The Bronze Pine Apple there from Adrian's tomb. The long gallery of inscriptions, & the multitude of human beings here assembled in stone, most of whom bustled away their hour on *this very stage*, the precious marbles, the jasper, the alabaster, the porphyry red green & grey, the parian; the rosso, the nero, the giallo antico, such a blaze of marbles the light of day never shone upon. The mosaics under your feet are alone enough to arrest you, & whoever sees the red porphyry in a mass, as in the vast basin there—41 f. in circumference—under the dome on the pavement from Otricoli & in the tombs of St Constantia & St Helen, will confess it to be

[1] Raphael's.

[2] The mausoleum was fitted up for public spectacles in 1780. The bulls were first teased by unarmed men who had two barrels to jump into in case of need, and then by dogs. The arena was also used for concerts and fire-work displays.

[3] 1744–1827. Leader of the Neapolitan revolt of 1799. He had returned with Pius VII from Paris.

the richest purple in nature. The imperial chamber at Constantinople was lined with porphyry; & was called the purple chamber. Saw Canova among his marbles, being introduced by Davy.[1] His Hebe holds the cup with her finger & thumb only, because it was regarded by the Antients as a mark of respect to the person waited upon.

Decr 15. The Borghese Gardens. A warm sun. A green lizard, with bright yellow spots basking on the trunk of a tree. Met Louis Bonaparte walking, & afterwards Lucien & his wife, il Principe & la Principessa de Canino.[2] A duel with sabres there the day before yesterday. Saw the sun set from before the Church del Trinita & the Medici villa. A glow thro' the windows under the dome of St Peter's. That, & every other object in deep shadow. A rich glow on that Church at half past 5. Duchess of Bracciano's Assembly. Punch & ice & Music. The ladies sat round, the men stood behind them. A servant in livery in half boots, a rueful figure at the door within the room. Church of St Maria del Popolo. Chapel of 'Agostin Ghigi amico suo caro' the work of which was superintended by Raphael; who died before it was finished. The cieling is in mosaic from his designs (see Dorigny's prints)[3] & the statue of Jonas must have been modelled by him, it is so full of sweetness. The head, says Canova, is that of the Antinous.

—What a pretty idea is that of a family-chapel, decorated by successive generations, & receiving them into its vault!

16th. *Friday*. Colonna Gardens. Terrace above Terrace to the summit of the Quirinal. Gigantic cornices of the Temple of the Sun, at the foot of a noble pine, a landmark almost every way. View of Rome. Orange-walk. From a summer-house a view of Monte Cavallo & the horses. Church of St Clement. A chapel full of Masaccio's paintings—beautiful, & in the same manner as those in the Carmine at Florence, tho' evidently of an earlier date. St Stefano Rotondo. Villa Mattei. Egyptian Obelisk. Saw again the Domenichino & Guido in the chapel near the Church of St Gregory. Were the Martyrdom equal to the Spectators,

[1] Sir Humphrey Davy, 1778–1829.

[2] The papal title conferred on Lucien Bonaparte, referring to his estate at Canino.

[3] Nicolas Dorigny, painter and engraver, 1658–1746. He lived in Rome for 20 years. These prints were published in 1695.

the first would be one of the finest in the World. From the terrace a majestic view of the Palace of the Cesars, the aqueduct that supplied it, the Coliseum &c. In the third chapel, that of St Barbe, a statue of St Gregory sitting, designed by M. Angelo, & worthy of him! tho' the subject is singular. The Dove is whispering in his ear, & his right hand is lifted as with emotion. Saw the sun set from the Monte della Trinita, every pine tree on the horizon, every electrical wire on the churches visible against the glow.

Decr 17. *Saturday*. Went with Mr Millingen[1] & purchased a bronze foot of greek workmanship.[2] Antient cornices & capitals from the Borghese Collection in the street before a Stone-Mason. Faded Frescoes on the front of St Vital, said to be Domenichino's. Called at Mr Tolwaltzern[3] a danish Sculptor of singular merit. Sun-set from the Trinita. Red streaks in the sky. Party at Mrs. Rawdon's.[4] The Lucien's went down with a lanthern.

18. *Sunday*. Loggie & Stanze of Raphael in the Vatican. St Maria del Popolo. Borghese Gardens full of company. Two card-players on stone-seats at a stone-table in the shade; another leaning over & looking on. One wrapt up in his great coat, the other without his hat & without great coat. Sun-set from the Trinita. Not a cloud. Concert at Lucien Bonaparte's. The Car

19. Saw Statues with Mr Dodwell[5] & afterwards with Mr Millingen. Saw the Prince Poniatowsky at his villa[6] & the stair-

[1] James Millingen, 1774–1845, archaeologist, a resident in Italy for many years, bought antiquities for collectors in England and elsewhere, including Rogers.

[2] Sale Catalogue, No. 191. Bought by W. H. Forman.

[3] Bertel Thorwaldson, 1770–1844, lived in Rome continuously from 1797 to 1819.

[4] A friend of the Hollands. Her daughter married Lord William Russell in 1817.

[5] Edward Dodwell, 1767–1832, traveller and archaeologist. Lived for many years in Rome, where he died. Like Millingen, he helped collectors with the choice and purchase of antiquities.

[6] Stanislas Poniatowski, 1754–1833, ex-Grand Treasurer of Lithuania. Lived in Vienna, then Rome, where he amassed his collections, then in Florence, where he died. The villa was outside the Porta del Popolo; his collections, which Rogers visited later on, were in Via della Croce, off Piazza di Spagna.

case of the Braschi Palace. Cardinal Rufo at Lord Holland's. Mad^me Massima's Assembly. Lucien & Mme Lucien Bonaparte at cards, Cardinal Fesch at the corner of a card-table.

20. Visits. St Onufrio. From the terrace a view of Rome; the Sabine Mountains in deep shadow, the snowy mountains beyond them all couleur de rose.

In the Room in which Tasso died, saw his cup (Etruscan ware, Black Nola, a fellow to one of mine, the foot broken, & his towel). On coming out the snows were colour of flame. A broad sunshine on the side of one of the Sabine hills. L^y Westmoreland's. A Girl leaning out of the Window, with her scaldino— her marito[1]—in her hand; a pretty subject for a picture.

21. St Michael & Satan by Guido in the Church of the Capuchins. Saw the chambers—sculleries—below in which the bones of so many monks of that order are ornamentally disposed on the walls & ceilings, & where the dried bodies of so many Frati in their corded habits of ashy brown are to be seen lying & sitting in the attitudes of prayer & meditation. A scull in a cowl is indeed a mournful spectacle, & by twilight as it came on, or by the glimmerings of the bony lanthorns suspended there, what nerves could resist the influence? Saw the Colonna & Justiniani Palaces, & walked in the Pantheon & the Vatican, how beautiful, how awful is the former, tho' the hands of time & violence have lain heavy upon it. The Corso.

22. Marbles. Rain. The Justiniani again. No Installation of the Roman Senator to-day. The bag-pipe plays in the streets by night & by day for nine days before Xmas, like our Waites.

23. Went with Sir Humphry Davy to Titus's Baths. Vermilion the most expensive colour of the Antients; & not lavished even by the richest. None of it in the apartments of the Servants. Delicacy of some of the Paintings. The Emperor's bath. The Room adjacent in which the Laocoon was found. The niche in which it stood, coved & with a vermilion ground as are also the walls. The painting that remains most elegant. The most splendid of all the chambers. 40 f—by 20 f. Livia's Baths. Beautiful painting on a deep blue. The villa on the ruins of Palace, itself swept away. Remains of the Aviary. M. Angelo's, & also the fountain under it. Walked thro' the forum to the Capitol. Columns half-buried & arches but just extricated.

---

[1] *Marito* =husband, a popular term for the *scaldino*.

14. A side view of the Coliseum

15. Tourist being shown the baths of Livia

24. Bought the Ruspoli Marbles.[1] Albani villa. Mountains in bright sunshine & full of velvet lights. Exquisite bas-reliefs. The large marbles of no great merit. The small numerous & beautiful. Saw the sun set from the Trinita del Monte, & heard the guns announce Christmas. What if such sounds had been heard here in the old Time. The Auspices would have come out & Livy have recorded it, as an Omen of dreadful import. (Christmas Eve. Dined with L⁰ Brownlow & Eustace.) Heard high mass in the Chapel on Monte Cavallo. The Pope & many Cardinals present. Sweet voices. The music lasted 3 hours, the service four, & concluded at 12 oClock at Night.

25. *Christmas day, Sunday.* High mass in St Peter's. The Pope officiated. His public entry. A hymn before he appeared, then a silent procession. The banners, the cap & sword, priests in rich habits & long order, himself in his triple crown & in gold habits borne aloft in a state-chair, & moving his hand lightly here & there in benediction. He sat first on the side, then in front of the Altar, after having ascended to it & elevated the host, which levelled the innumerable croud with the Pavement. Prince Ruspoli presented him with the sacramental wine, which he drank thro' a gold syringe. Celestial voices singing all the while. The Queens of Spain & Etruria[2] in an elevated box. Sat under the dome. Rain. Walked in the afternoon in the Medici Gardens. Dined at Lord Holland's.

26. Went in Torlonia's[3] Carriage to the Palazzo Bolognetti &

---

[1] 'Jan 24, 1815. . . . We went to an artist who has all the valuable pieces of the famous Ruspoli gallery. . . . The English purchasers are getting some good things out of this collection.' Mayne, *Journal* . . . , p. 251.

[2] Wife and Infanta of Charles IV.

[3] The wealthy parvenu Roman banker Giovanni-Raimondo Torlonia, 1754–1829. Most English visitors used his bank and he entertained widely. Thackeray felt very strongly about him. In Ch. LXIV of *Vanity Fair* he writes thus of 'Prince Polonia'. 'It happened at Rome once, that Mrs. de Rawdon's half-year's salary had just been paid into the principal bankers there, and as everybody who had a balance of above five hundred scudi was invited to the balls which this prince of merchants gave during the winter, Becky had the honour of a card, and appeared at one of the Prince and Princess Polonia's splendid evening entertainments. The Princess was of the family of Pompili, lineally descended from the second king of Rome, and Egeria of the house of Olympus, while the Prince's grandfather, Alessandro Polonia, sold wash-balls, essences, tobacco, and pocket handkerchiefs, ran errands for gentlemen, and lent money in a small way.' There is more to the same effect in Ch. VIII of *The Book of Snobs*.

saw his chambers courts & galleries & his statue—or rather groupe—of Hercules Furens by Canova. He is dashing one of his children to the ground. throwing Lica into the sea. Then saw near the Corso his apartments full of statues antient & modern & his *cemetery* full of fragments.

27. Walked in the Corsini Gardens & heard music in the chapel at St Peter's. Went up & down a very gay Corso & walked on the Trinita del Monte at Sunset. Ropes & pullies from the upper windows to the well, for the bucket to go up & down. & thro' the landing places to the latch at the gate. Called on Prince Poniatowski & saw his precious stones. The Moors—Moriscoes—of Spain could abjure their religion, but their ears could never endure the ringing of Bells. What a drawback on the pleasures of Rome that perpetual clang of iron against Iron.

28 *Wednesday*. Saw the costly gems of the Prince Poniatowsky. In our daily journey thro' the City, what various scenes have taken place where our wheels were unconsciously rolling. Who but must consider it as a vast theatre in which the human passions have acted. Here Cesar fell, here Cicero pleaded, here the Roman Matrons went in longa ordine. Here Brutus saw his sons die, here Virginia received the knife of her father, here Cornelia received her boys from school, & Sylla walked the streets after his abdication. Here Virgil & Horace wandered together & Scipio Africanus passed in triumph—& how many kings have ascended to the Capitol to be strangled after the shew.

Who could not fall in love during the celebration of high mass Petrarch with Laura in the Church of Stª Claire Boccaccio with Mary of Arragon in the Church of the Cordeliers of Naples in the jour de Paques—[1]

Thursday 29 *Decʳ*. Bought the bust of Valerian from which Canova had taken a cast. The villa Ludovisi. Guercino's ceiling of Aurora. Spotty; but rounder & more solid than usual, & altogether worthy of its fame. Not done justice to by Volpato.[2] The ceiling in an upper chamber well-painted by him & full of

---

[1] This passage comes after the List of things to be seen more than once in Rome and between a pencil and the ink versions of the similar List for Florence (see App. 1). There is no further Journal text in this note book, and the passage might have been made at any time the note book was in use.

[2] Giovanni Volpato, engraver, *b.* 1740, *d.* in Rome in 1803.

Atmosphere. In the first casino, the Architecture of which is Domenichino's, many marbles, among which a sitting statue of Mars, with a cupid at his foot, preeminent for expression, repose & dignity. The gardens confined in their view, but in high order, & an excellent example of the Italian style. Long walks between cut hedges; statues, temples, pines & cypresses intermixed—& the lights & shadows over the small lawns, & under the green trees (it was a clear, bright, & warm day) enchanting. A more pleasing mixture of stone & verdure, & playing lights in a small compass I never saw. Met the Cawdors[1] at the Villa Albani. Delicious distances. No snow on Soracte.

The young lady Odescalchi,[2] jilted, can no more be seen in the Corso (at Corso time) or in Company, till again affianced. Her fortune £7000. Can read a little, write a little, & knit a great deal. Mr Dodwell's attendance on her. Never dared to be absent from the Corso,—for two years. Had refused many dinners to be there. A side-glance in passing, all he had. Never in her company but with a third person. She says she never did like him but her maids persuaded her to go to the window, & to fancy herself in love with Mr D. He had abjured his faith for her—but, tired & cured, is now said to be in love with another. She put up la novena (a prayer for 9 days to the Virgin) to be released from her love (she & all her relations) & it had answered. Hoped much from the prayers of her brother a saint —She had chosen her brother for tutor, a young jesuit, 23^yrs of age, who passes his life in preaching & confessing nuns, & who is said to have refused a Cardinal's hat. Orsi's[3] Comedies, very descriptive of Roman Manners.

Friday 30. dec^r. Went with Allen[4] to the Palatine, famous in the days of the republic for the Temples of Apollo, Vesta, Juno,

---

[1] John Campbell, 1st Baron Cawdor, *d.* 1821.

[2] Daughter of the Duke of Bracciano. Finch mentions the same piece of gossip and it was still going the rounds when Moore came to Rome. Dodwell 'used to be a great favourite with the Pope, who always called him "Caro Doodle". His first addresses were paid to Vittoria Odescalchi, but he jilted her; and she had six masses said to enable her soul to get over its love for him.' *Memoirs*—ed. Ld. John Russell, iii, 64.

[3] Does Rogers mean Giovanni Gherardo di Rossi, 1754–1827, referring to plays like his *Il Calzolajo Inglese in Roma?*

[4] Possibly John Allen, 1771–1843, then warden of Dulwich College, and an intimate of the Hollands.

Victory, Minerva & Fortune, for the houses of Hortensius, Gracchus, Catullus, Crassus, Scaurus, Clodius, Cicero & Cataline; & afterwards for the Golden house—now covered with weeds, & shapeless ruins & bushes. Augustus built on the east side, towards Mount Cœlius—Tiberius extended it to the south & west; Caligula towards the Forum & Capitol, by a bridge passing to the senate, without entering a street—& Nero towards the North, occupying parts of the Esquiline & Celius. In the Orti Spada saw a casa di Campagna, painted in Arabesque & said to be Raphael's—Hereabouts Augustus is said to have built his Siracusa, his house of pleasure—& here we saw spacious subterraneous apartments, lighted from the centre & from the brow saw the Campagna, the Appian & Ostian ways &c— Afterwards vis a vis St Gregorio saw other remains of vast size & extent, being conducted over them & into them by a missionary of the English College—thro' the garden of the College— From the summit had a magnificent view—saw the Claudian aqueduct & three of its branches one of which came to the Palace of the Cesars, the Baths of Caracalla, the Tombs of Metella & Cestius, the Coliseum & innumerable objects of great interest. Descended to the Baths, & walked thro the Hall of the Sun & other chambers, the walls of which were full of niches for statues above & below. A magnificent suite of three apartments, in the cove at each end were found the Hercules Farnese & the Farnese Bull now at Naples. Saw also the cove in a small chamber in which was the Flora. each facing the other, & visible thro' the doors. Music in the Church of San Sylvestro—

Saturday. 31 *dec*[r]. Saw Dodwell's drawings done in the East.[1] Drove by the Fonte Pauline to the Villa Pamphili. Pine trees. Noble distances seen thro' the trees. St Peter's a single object in its grandeur below. A brilliant day. A Te-Deum in the Church of Jesus. Sixteen Cardinals entered in procession, each preceded by two lights, & knelt in a row before the Altar. The congregation falling down as with one impulse, & singing as with one voice the alternate verses of the Te-Deum, the Choir singing the others—the chant rose like *the sound of mighty waters*. Piccolo Ballo at the Principessa & Principe of Canino's. Many children there.

Sunday. 1 *Jany* The Borghese Gardens. Home scenery & small

---

[1] He travelled in Greece from 1801 to 1806.

16. The Stations of the Cross in the arena of the Coliseum

17. Daniele da Volterra: the taking down from the Cross

distances. Carpets & tapestries, green, red & yellow, from the windows & balconies, along the streets thro' which the Senator was to pass. The windows & balconies full of animated figures. A balcony near us full of Nuns; & many eclesiastics every where. Many open carriages in the open spaces. The streets full of orderly quiet & well-drest people. Military Music. Cavalry with helmets. Silken Banners of many colours. Ecclesiastics & other Seniors—Lawyers—, some on led horses. The Senator uncovered in gold silk robes, his hair flowing & bien-poudré— on a white horse—bowing to all—In the evening the Capitol illuminated—Bands of music in booths—the basalt lions pouring wine.[1] A full-drest assembly of Romans & Forestieri in the central building of the Capitol. Ices & iced Punch. The statues illuminated. The streets full of walkers, an unusual thing in Rome, & nothing could be more quiet & silent than the happiness of the People. A beautiful day—bright, & not cold. Saw the Procession from Dodwell's.

Monday, Jan 2ᵈ.—The Marbles in the Vatican. St Peter's. Torwalson's Studio.

Tuesday. Jan 3. Bought the Torso in the Convent of San Carlo. The Frescoes in the Vatican. Tomb of Paul III. by Giacomo della Porta. said to be M. Angelo's design.

Wednesday. Jan 4. From the top of Trajan's column saw Rome. The elevation too small, & the view much inferior to that from the Capitol the Vatican & the Lateran; but the Coliseum, the temple of Peace, the Palatine—now overspread like a rock with earth & verdure—, & the Capitol are seen in all their grandeur! the last rises above all Rome; it stands on a precipice, & answers to every antient description. You here look upon the Asylum from the Gauls, & upon the hill from which on the other side the criminals were thrown! Saw again the Marbles of the Capitol, the Lex Regia in bronze, which according to Gibbon was created by the fancy of Ulpian or of Tribonian himself (See Gibbon, c 44. p. 344), & what remains of the taking down of the Cross by Daniel da Volterra. What is left of it justifies all its

---

[1] These then guarded the bottom of the steps leading to the Capitol. When Corinne first spoke to Lord Nelvil, and in English, '*Quel fut l'étonnement d'Oswald en l'entendant! Il resta d'abord immobile à sa place, et, se sentant troublé, il s'appuya sur un des lions de basalte qui sont au pied de l'escalier du Capitole.*' Mme de Staël, *Corinne*, bk. 1, ch. 4.

fame. A sublime composition, deep & solemn colouring, & a pathetic sentiment throughout. May it live in Mosaic; & supplant one of the many Usurpers in St Peter's! Saw the tomb of Leo X—unworthy of him, & a statue of our Savior of no great excellence by M Angelo, in St Maria sopra Minerva. Walked in the Pantheon & again saw Torwalson's Studio. He & Millingen dined with us.—

Thursday, Jan 5. Palazzo Massimi. The Discobolus. The same as Townley's,[1] but more perfect. The Palazzo Spada. Exquisite Bassirelievi. A man watering his horse! The Farnese Gallery.—

Friday. Jan 6. Twelfth Day. Went with Abbé Taylor[2] to Monte Cavallo. That magnificent Titian, part of which is engraved in wood—which, I think, is criticized by Sr Josh[a] Reynolds.[3] A beautiful holy family by Andrea del Sarto in the Room in which the Pope takes his solitary dinner under a Canopy. Walked thro' the rooms of the Palace,[4] now unfurnished. A view of Rome from the windows. Thorwalzern's basso-relievo. At last the high mass in the chapel was over, the Roman nobles & many Cardinals withdrew thro' the hall, & by Mon Signor Doria, the little Master of the Ceremonies, we were led thro' a narrow passage-room into that in which the Pope was standing, in his white cloth habit, buttoned up to the chin & his shoes of scarlet velvet, embroidered with gold flowers. He received us most courteously & we formed a circle before him—said much of the Inglese—that he was now too old to travel that he would rather have gone to England than where he did go—that he was going to receive some English ladies in the Garden—To each of whom he gives a rosary—When we knelt to kiss his hand, he seemed distressed, & affected to shrink back from us, & made many efforts as if to assist us to rise. His manners however were very simple, his courtesy equal to the most refined, & the sort of

---

[1] Charles Towneley, 1737–1805. His collection was purchased by the British Museum.

[2] Since the Reformation the introduction of English visitors to the Pope was usually performed by a Scots or Irish ecclesiastic resident at Rome. Taylor was an Irishman, who arranged times, advised on clothing, etc. He died in 1821.

[3] The S. Sebastian in the chapel of the Quirinal on Monte Cavallo, mentioned by Reynolds in his eleventh Discourse.

[4] The Quirinal palace had been prepared as an official residence for Napoleon in case of his visiting Rome and was being reconstructed.

hysteric laugh half subdued with which he spoke generally to us, as we were named to him, discovered a modesty & anxiety to please, which were very engaging. It lasted about 5 minutes. Went out with the Hollands to two Presepio's[1]—& in the Ev^g to some music at the Dss of Bracciano's.—

Saturday. Jany 7th. Went to the Villa Lanti—from the garden of which is an admirable view of the City. The Lateran, the Vatican, & St Peter's;—above all the Coliseum a half circle & much elevated—the Pantheon—& the Aqua Paulina with the various villas, & the Mountains beyond them, the Corsini & the Farnese immediately under us. The bells were now & then chiming far below in the sunny morning. Walked there near an hour & then to the Vatican. When two or three women are thrown together, how delightfully are they painted by Raphael! What can be more enchanting than the two groupes of the Muses in the Mount Parnassus! In the private chapel of Pope Nicolas V, where he used to hear Mass, saw a Fresco of S. Lorenzo by J^{no} of Fiesole. Fra Giovanni da Fiesole—exquisitely sweet & simple, equal to the very best of his Master Masaccio— & much admired by Raphael. see Italian Guide.[2] Saw Lady I. Montague[3] in St Peter's. Twelfth Night at Ld Holland's. The Italians afraid of sitting near the fire. The Marchesa de Capranica (Principessa) leaning out of a window in the Rondinini Palace with her scaldino in her hand; an earthen jar—full of wooden embers that send forth, they say, no smoke .

Sunday. Jan 8th. Camuccini's collection of Pictures & Marbles. Casts from the Antique in the French Academy at the Villa Medici. The Doria Palace again, & the first chapel on the right

[1] A *presepio* is a large scale model of the manger at Bethlehem, with its appurtenances.

[2] The most up to date Roman guide books in general use were four: 1. Mariano Vasi, *Itinerario instruttivo di Roma antica e moderna*, 2v, Roma, 1814 (based on the ed. of 1763. There was an ed. in French in 1803. The first in English was in 1819). 2. André Manazzale, *Itineraire instructif de Rome et ses environs*, 2v, Rome, 1802 (1st ed. 1794). 3. Angelo Dalmazzoni, *L'Antiquario o sia la guida de' forestieri pel giro delle antichità di Roma*, Roma, 1804 (ed. in English in 1803, in French in 1804). 4. Michelangelo Prunetti, *L'osservatore delle Belle Arti in Roma*, 2v, Roma, 1808–11. It appears to be the last that was used by Rogers, and to which he is referring here, though it is impossible to be certain.

[3] Jane Montagu, daughter of William, 5th Duke of Manchester. She died later in the year, at Geneva.

in the S. Maria della Pace (belonging as it appears to Agostino Chisi) over the arch of which, without, are sybils, prophets & children by Raphael—but much damaged. The Borghese Gardens.

Monday. Jan. 9. Villa Mattei. Shady walks. Views of the Ruins; & the Mountains. A Palm-tree. The Obelisk small & pieced. Walked under orange-trees in the sun. Gathered oranges & eat them. St Maria della Navicella, the front designed by Raphael. simple. the arches like those of the Villa Madama. Walked thro' the Forum to the Capitol from the Coliseum.

Tuesday. Jan 10 Called on Canova. Saw his picture of a girl alarmed in her nakedness & pressing her clothes—the first idea of his Venus—She may shiver with cold which the Venus should not do. Mentioned his loves. Said the rules of Aristotle assisted him in his art, as much as if they had been first applied to it. Saw his Religion—his horse colossal now without a rider. Went up to the ball of St Peter's. a high wind & wild music there. Looked down upon Rome. Saw the Cupola from the Gallery. Raphael's frescoes. J^{no} of Fiesole's frescoes—Looked into the Pantheon. How much grander than the dome of St Peter's! Vaster to the eye & flatter. More like the dome of heaven.

Wednesday. Jan 11. Sat in the sun at the door of the Villa Melina, the soothing hum of the flies, the green leaves of the ilexes & cypresses, & the bright blue sky made it a summer's day. Below, St Peter's the Pantheon, & the Coliseum in its vastness & its elevation. How constantly it preserves its character of greatness! Yet the Romans were barbarians after all. They subdued Greece, & said to the Greeks, Build us vast ampitheatres for men & beasts to worry one another in; vast aqueducts (not knowing that water rises to its level) & What else did the Babylonians, the Egyptians of old time? They said also—Take our likenesses in stone; & almost instantly Rome became as full of statues & busts as of men! Walked thro' the fields to the Villa Madama. Its loggia how grand & how rich, above all others; small as it is. Walked to the dell—thro' the thicket which must have been always wild. The ornaments of the fountain on the lower terrace gone, as are those in the dell. Dined at $\frac{1}{2}$ past three at the Prince Poniatowski's. His cabinet of bronzes,[1] &c. His apartment warm & chearful. The Senator at

[1] Some of which came into Rogers's possession.

his prima sera. Dinner, three & three. Called in the evening at Mad.^{me} Massima's. The children putting the map of France together; a little abbé sitting by.—Afterwards to Lady Westmoreland's.

Thursday. Jan 12. Wet morning. Dined at Lady Westmoreland's.

Friday. Jany 13. Palazzo Buonaparte. Pictures & Marbles. Vatican Gardens. Coffee house.[1] Bas Reliefs without. Arabesques within. Vatican Museum of Marbles, & Library. In returning called on Ignacio.[2] in front of St Carlos. A Man was just dead, who would never suffer his vineyard to be dug. & there is to be a digging. Saw a bushel of bronze collected yesterday from the farms & cottages hard by. A bull, a sheep, a dolphin, a key, the bracelet of a gladiator, an adder's head with silver eyes, many human figures &c &c. What an inexhaustible mine is Rome! Dined at Ld Cawdor's. Cardinal Fesch at the Dss of Braschiano's Concert. Every Cardinal wears a scarlet cap on the bald crown of his head. The circular tonsure, says Gibbon, was sacred & mysterious. It was the crown of thorns; but it was likewise a royal diadem, & every priest was a king.

Saturday. Spent two hours on the brow of the hill within the grounds of the Villa Medina. A brilliant day, & not an object unseen & unnoticed but the Column of M. Antoninus—On my left the threefold fountain—Fontana Paulina—, & church of S. Pietro in Montorio—where once was the Transfiguration—, the Tomb of Caius Cestius & the two towers of Belesarius (the Ostian Gate) the tomb of Cecelia Metella, the Claudian Aqueduct, St Stefano Rotondo & the Villa Mattei & the St Maria della Navicella built by Raphael, St J^{no} Lateran, the Coliseum, the Capitol, the Column of Trajan, the Monte Cavallo, the Pine in the Colonna Gardens, the Pantheon, the Church of the Trinity, in which was the taking down of the Cross by Daniel de Volterra, the Villa Ludovisi, the Villa Medici, the Pines in the Borghese Gardens, the Villa Melini, the Castle of St Angelo, the Vatican & St Peter's—& immediately below us the Palazzi Corsini & Farnese—these, & no doubt to a learned eye, a

---

[1] 'Coffee-house'—sometimes spelled 'Caffeous'—was an alternative term for 'Casino'. Thus Vasi's guide of 1813 says of the Quirinale, 'au milieu il y a un gracieux caffè-house.'

[2] An art dealer?

thousand more, stand out distinctly & relieved—Went down to the Vatican, & again saw the Stanze of Raphael—Surely these frescoes, in colouring, composition & expression, & in every excellence, surpass all the Pictures in the world. The defeat of Attila strikes me the most—but in sweetness the Miracle of Bolsenna, the St Paul, the Fire, the Parnassus, the Jurisprudence—the Sacrament, the School of Athens (most injured, alas)—what can equal them? The Attila, the St Paul, the Fire in the Borgo are in his last & grandest manner. Dined at Fazaquerly's.[1] A fricassee of frogs & Porcupine in sweet sauce. The Opera from Lady Holland's Box.

Sunday, 15. Spent the day at Torlonias. & in the Borghese Gardens.—Dined at Sr H. Davy's. Canova shewed how he kissed his bed, three times, when he went into it after dinner. His bed regularly warmed.

Monday, 16 *Jany*. Mr Millingen at dinner.

Tuesday. 17. Early visit from the Cawdors. Letters received. Saw Marbles of no value with M. Heavy Rain. Dined with the Hollands. Canova sate by at dinner. Then came Macpherson, President of the Scotch College here, Lucien Bonaparte, & Rose[2] introducing a Bp. The B^s & M. came to us in the Evening.

Wednesday. 18th. Day of the Establishment of St Peter as B^p of Rome. High Mass in St Peter's. The Pope, borne in & out, preceded by the Cardinals & blessing the People.—Saw from a gallery under the dome. A bird's eye-view. The voices of the choir came up in a full stream of harmony. Raphael's Frescoes. Masaccio's Chapel in St Clemente. St J^{no} Lateran. St Maria Maggiore. Dined at Torlonia's. The Chief of the Inquisition, the Grand Ecurier—& a knight of Malta there. Went to the Teatro Argentino with Tolwalzern. Millingen's Converzastione. Waltzing at L^y Westmorland's.

Thursday. 19th. Walked in the Medici Gardens. A little snow seemingly on Soracte. S[arah] visited some nuns in a Convent. Ld Holland ill.

Friday. 20th. Saw Camuccini's[3] paintings. Walked thro' the

---

[1] John Nicholas Fazakerly, 1787–1852, M.P.

[2] William Steward Rose, 1775–1843, translator of Ariosto and friend of Rogers, was in Italy at this time.

[3] Vicenzo Camuccini, 1771–1844, the most famous native painter of his day. A visit to his studio was on Vasi's itinerary.

forum. Went to the tomb of Cecilia Metella. Snow & hail & gleams of sunshine. Severe cold, of which the Italians complain incessantly. Called at the Church of St Antonio of the Portuguese & had our horses blest. Two candles were lighted before a head of the Saint; & the Priest, standing on the threshold, read four short prayers in latin & sprinkled them with holy water, our coachman sitting on the box with his hat off, & crossing himself two or three times. Yesterday two donkies & a set of horses were seen there. A harmless superstition & better than most, as likely to inculcate in the minds of the people humanity & respect for animals.[1] The church was strewn with green leaves, & the walls hung with crimson cloth: on account of the festival of the Saint. Millingen at dinner. Mr Bergen & his greek wife at tea. Sat with Ld Holland & went to Music at the Dss of Bracciano's.—From the balcony behind the Scala Santa saw again that striking view of the Aqueduct & the Walls of Rome—

Saturday 21st Marbles of the Vatican. Vespers in St Peter's. M. Angelo's Chapel of the Virgin. Church of St Augustin. Raphael's colossal figure of Isaiah in fresco.—Ball at Lucien Bonaparte's— Alas, the Anniversary of Louis XVI's execution. Roman Beauties. A Doria, a Ruspoli, an Odescalchi—Cards—

Sunday. Jany 22. Camuccini's Marbles & Pictures. Borghese Gardens. Church of San Antonio. The roads to it lined with multitudes of people. The Priest in a square black cap & white surplice standing on the steps & scattering holy water on the various animals that passed before him, the drivers & those in the carriages with their hats off. Humble donkies, whiskies, barouches—Caratelli—full of people, coaches & *eight*, in swift succession. Among others, a horse entered to run in the Corso, a plume of feathers on his head, & many circles on his haunches, danced up to receive the benediction nor was led away till it had been repeated three or four times. The Priest continually returned for holy water into the church which was crouded, where many bought masses of a Priest who sat receiving the pauls, & registering the number. For 16 days after that of St

---

[1] This same sentiment was attributed by Charles Reade to the Pope himself in Ch. LXII of *The Cloister and the Hearth*. Finch, who was there on the 17th, said that the animals received not only the benediction but a piece of cake.

Antonio the ceremony is said to continue. You received for half a paul a portrait of St Antonio & his pig, & a small lacquered cross—

Monday. Jan 23. Met the Abbe Fea[1] at Dodwell's concerning the Marbles. Saw the statues in the Vatican, & walked in the Forum & the Villa Mattei. The Post-horses of Rome were blest to-day.—

Tuesday. Jan 24. First day of Carnival. Rain in the Morning. Tapistries hung from some of the windows. Some carriages parading in the Corso. Soldiers foot & horse. Shops open as usual. chairs before the windows. Soon after 4, the Corso was full of people, & guns were fired to clear it of the Carriages. At a $\frac{1}{4}$ before five some cavalry soldiers galloped along it to open the avenue for the horses; & a little before the Ave Maria, five started from the Piazza del Popolo—for the Piazza di Venezia in each of which, scaffolds were erected. They appeared black & small as rats at a distance running on thro' the narrow channel, the people shouting, & the spiked balls urging them along. When they had passed us before San Carlo, guns were fired there to heighten their fears, & lend them new wings. The street being strait, we saw nearly from the starting place to the goal. The croud forming but a thin line on each side, & the windows exhibiting no show? Is this the population of Rome, & is the Carnival to produce nothing better? After dinner at the Duke of Bedford's,[2] the Dss waltzed, & danced with castanets before Canova. Looked in at Ld Holland's, & went to a splendid ball at the Marchioness of Mariscotti's. Silk hangings. 60 lights in each of the two rooms. Dancing in one—Cards in the other. The Princess Doria a Neopolitan. Lemonade with snow in it. How much more elegant than our ice. The Wafers every where superior to ours.

Wednesday. Jany. 25. A bright day. Walked in the Villa Pamphili Doria. A Lake. Fountains, terraces, pine groves. The Snow-mountains sun-gilt, & green lizards peeping out every where. Blue or Purple Crocusses in the lawns springing up & with the freshest fragrance. View of Rome from the fountain

[1] Carlo Fea, 1753–1836, archaeologist and author of a number of books on Roman antiquities. Pius VII made him *Commissario* of the Antiquities of Rome.

[2] John Russell, 6th Duke, 1766–1839.

18. Blessing the horses of Rome

19. The Carnival: pelting bystanders with starch

Paulina, & from before the Church—St Pietro in Montorio. The Chapel or Temple of Bramante, seemingly suggested by the Temple of Vesta. In St Peter's heard an Anthem & visited the Bronze Foundery near the Vatican—

Thursday. Jan 26. Went to Canova's studio with Lord Cawdor, & walked in the Borghese Gardens. In the carriage went up & down the Corso, crouded & full of carriages & then, from a scaffold in the Piazza del Popolo, saw the horses, five in number, brought up before a cord breast high, which they endeavoured to leap over—a live coal between the shoulders of each. The cord falling away they went as before; plumes of feathers on their heads, & gold paper or cloth of gold fluttering from their backs—& a cracker bursting in sparks from them—& their hoofs striking fire from the pavement—In the Ev^g at L^y Cawdor's & Lady Westmorland's.

Friday. Jan^v 27th. Went to Vitali's,[1] & walked in the Medici Gardens, & the Corso. Beautiful Masques in the Shops. The Carnival properly begins to-morrow, the Carnival having been reduced from 8 to 6 days. The races were only by permission. The fire on the horses is inclosed in a brass ball. & the moccoli[2] forbidden—formerly after the race of the last day—the corso was a blaze of light, balconies, carriages & the streets, every hand holding a lighted taper to celebrate the funeral rites of the Carnival. The Roman who described it to me laughed for joy at the recollection of the merriment it produced; every voice crying out 'Moccoli, moccoli!' Music in the corso to-night—A guitar & violins—always moving along—

Saturday, Jany. 28. Heavy Rain. At one oClock a masque in white, passed under the window with a panier of flowers on his back. Went with Ld Cawdor to the Vatican Marbles. Afterwards went up & down in the Corso. Several Masques in the crowd; & in two or three of the Carriages. A great disposition to be merry every where. Four horses ran. Saw them from Ld Holland's balcony. The children there in masks & fancy-dresses. Dined at Lord Holland's. Went afterwards to the Dss of Bedford's, & to the Canino's ball.—What a statue is the Minerva.

[1] I do not know to what this refers.

[2] Lighted tapers. The end of the carnival witnessed scenes of wild excitement when everyone tried to extinguish his neighbour's taper while keeping his own alight.

A depth of thought, a sadness in her look & figure, a calm solemnity, that penetrates the soul, & disposes it to silent meditation. So indeed is it with all that is truly sublime in Art & Nature.

Sunday. Jany 29. Walked in the Albani Gardens & saw the Casino. Boys lectured in St Peter's. An Anthem there. Made a Giro or two[1] in the Corso. The Corso full. The Tyber overflowing. Met with a flood & a boat, & turned back again. Water in parts of the Corso.

Monday. Jany 30. Rose before 7. Went to the Church of St Egidius, to see a Nun take the veil. At half past 8 she came out of the convent & went away with two ladies who called in a carriage for her. At Nine Cardinal   a Genoese arrived & entering the Church which was strewn with bay leaves, as well as the steps, went immediately to offer up his vows in silence at the high altar. Presently afterwards came the Sposa, 22^yrs of age & knelt down her fan in her hand before a side altar on the right, attended by her little sister on her right & on her left the Marchesa Grimaldi her relation in deep mourning. Her mother was said to be there. She was drest in a rose-coloured silk, her hair in a turban white & gold with ostrich-feathers & many jewels. Her diamond ear-rings were also very splendid. Her little sister was in a sky-blue vest, her hair in a wreathe of flowers, & on her shoulders were long wings shaded with blue. The eldest seemed calm & even cheerful. She looked about her with composure tho' heavy sighs at intervals came from her—, while her sister looked chiefly upon her as she knelt & with the spriteleness of a child, when pleased with something that is going on. In a few minutes the Cardinal went up to the Altar & performed many ceremonies, & soon afterwards the young Lady & her sister removed to the desk he had left & knelt there, a boy in a white surplice kneeling on each side with a taper. The Cardinal turned round more than once extending his arms & then joining his hands in a dignified manner to bless her. She then went & knelt on the lowest step behind him & received into her mouth the wafer from his hands, after he had held it up before the People. She then knelt again at the desk, & then retiring to a chair on the left, between her sister & the Marchioness, heard the sermon in Italian addressed to her by the

[1] Took a turn or two.

Rome: January 30th

Cardinal sitting on the highest step of the Altar, often address-
ing her as Louisa. She heard it without emotion, & as soon as it
was over, the Cardinal in his silver mitre & with his golden
crosier as Bishop descended & advancing down the church (the
Sposa on his right hand holding a rich crucifix in one hand, &
with the other by the long lappet of his robe, white & gold)
turned thro a passage on the left to the Convent-door. There she
was met by the Abbess & the Nuns with lighted tapers who
received her, & returned before her chanting to an altar lighted
within. The Cardinal came back into the Church & went up
to the Grille or Grata on the left of the Altar, behind which
the Nuns & several Ladies richly drest had stood during the
service & where the Noviciate now appeared kneeling. The
Cardinal asked her if she was resolved, & prepared to discharge
the duties of her new character. She answered in a firm voice, &
a black curtain was dropt & a bell sounded the suono del morte.
(Behind it & before the Altar within she had thrown herself
down as dead, & the Nuns sung the Miserere round her, all
present holding tapers. They then removed her rich attire, her
hair was cut her brow bound with the fillet, & her white veil
thrown over her) In a few minutes the curtain was drawn up &
she appeared in a nun's habit, & with a crown of gold on her
head, but unveiled. She knelt before the Grille, her little sister
by her side, & the Cardinal thro' the grate pronounced his
prayer & benediction. All the congregation joining loudly in the
Amen. He withdrew to say his prayer in silence before the high
altar & in a few moments the curtain fell again while she knelt &
prayed.—The Nuns kissed her by turns, & she preserved her
composure, but her little sister threw her arms round her neck,
sobbing & saying, my dear Sister, do come home with us—
don't stay here. She had yesterday been in the corso, & at night
at the Opera. She was certainly plain, but in bon-point & her
eyes had the light of Youth, & in the habit she had the lustre of
youth, a lustre that almost never fails. The Cardinal afterwards
breakfasted on Coffee & Chocolate in the Convent. My Sister
was there behind the Grille & in the Parlour & saw the Cells,
& miserable beds—An old man plainly drest in an old fashioned
wig sat above her during the sermon a little removed nearer the
Altar—& was perhaps her father—The Carmelite Nuns rise at
one in the morning & at five. She had wished, she said to be a

nun, from five years of age. Her youth, her ornaments, her composed features & heavy sighs, the unconcern of her little sister at the beginning & her grief at last, her entrance into the Cloister, conducted by the Cardinal, the doors closing upon her for ever—never more to be opened to her in her life—or even after her death—the nuns meeting her & singing before her— her responses thro' the grate, the falling of the curtain, the bell & the miserere, & her reappearance as a nun with a crown of gold upon her head, (how like a victim for sacrifice!) her receiving the kiss from each of the Nuns, each & all calling her *the Sposa* the Sposa!—her still kneeling before the grate, her sister, her ministering angel by her side till the curtain fell. She was the only young person in the Convent A very pretty young girl in full dress in the Convent.

The Corso full, the balconies, the windows, the foot-way, the street—a band of music playing in the Piazza Colonna—a double line of carriages—some full of masques, coachmen, footmen & all—some with a woman driving & two pantaloons behind—throwing a storm of starch like the smallest sugar-plumbs on their unmasked friends & into the unmasked carriages—many pretty young women in the croud & sitting among the masks with the most delicate complexions—Who should be there in a carriage but the Mother & Sister of the Nun?—Many as gentleman of the old court, hat in hand. many as quack doctors—some in romantic cavalier-like dresses—a car full of children & drawn by a donkey—several persons with masks of paper, written or lined for music,—some fringed up & down with parsley & brocoli & cabbage-leaves—some with a clean shirt over all—some with boots of laurel leaves, & every fancy that frolic or economy could suggest in this hour of madness. To sober the joy, alas, a new cord was strung for the corda, & the executioners were ranged before it;[1] & the foot & horse every where. Masks of Monks & Nuns & Eclesiastics forbidden.

Tuesday. Jan 31. Saw some modern marbles, Nero Antico &

[1] 'It was then the horrible custom to carry out the extreme penalty of the Law upon criminals in full view of the Carnival crowds, and the scaffold was often erected in the centre of the Piazza del Popolo, at the head of the Corso, where the maskers gathered. Thus, it was no uncommon sight to see the executioner and his assistant perform their dreadful task disguised as *Pulcinella* and *Traccagnino,* and then go down to enjoy themselves with their friends.' F. McLaughlin, *Rome* . . . , ii, 19.

Porphyry of great beauty. The Corso full of masques, notwithstanding the rain. A Carratella full of Turks. A Turk alone in
his carriage smoking his hooka. Carriages full of waxen masks,
that did not look as if they were alive. Africans, Banditti-
figures, but mostly grotesque fancy-figures. Groups of Harlequin & Columbine & Pantaloon. A fidler, a guitar-player. A
man in the rain with periwig & chapeau-bras, holding over his
head with great importance the skeleton of an umbrella. A
seller of dressed Macarone (a mask) running after a Poulterer's boy (sober reality) with some picked ducks in his tray.
The former offering to ladle some of his lime & white-wash into
the tray—the latter running in a real fright. A mixture of real &
fictitious character to be seen only at a carnival. Three horses ran—
At 8. went to the Masquerade at the Teatro Nobil d'Alberto.[1]
A noble theatre indeed when seen from the stage; & illuminated
from the parterre to the roof. Few attempts at character. Most
were masked, & almost all in fancy-dresses. Some women of
inferior rank in their best attire, as like the invention of the
moment as possible. Quadrilles & Waltzing. A Master of the
Ceremonies. The same tremulous treble heard every where.
Young men representing old ones, & others in the attire of old
women. Soon after 10, the lights began to be put out, & a line of
soldiers gradually contracted the area till all were gone. Less
noise than in an English Masquerade. The Dss of Bedford's
harp master went with his guitar in mask.

Wednesday, Feb 1. Raphael's stanze. Dante's Portrait twice in
the same chamber. What a beautiful example of the old manner
is the Dispute of the Sacrament! It is as rich as a flower garden.
How lovely the Jurisprudence, how sublime the release of St
Peter! Perhaps the picture I should most wish as an altar-piece
for my chapel would be the Mass at Bolsenna—The story is so
sweetly told—but that which comes home most to human
feelings is the fire; &, were it all alike well-painted, would be
the noblest picture in the world. At present the Attila surely
deserves that title. The School of Athens has suffered most of all;
&, tho' admirable in its groupes, makes but an uninteresting whole.
The Chapel of Sixtus. The cieling is unrivalled in grandeur.

---

[1] *recte* Aliberti, the largest Roman theatre, used almost exclusively
during the Carnival, for operas and balls. It was burned down in the
middle of the century.

When the eye is lifted up, a multitude of majestic forms break upon it, but what they are & what they are doing, is not learnt so soon. Perhaps the awe is increased by the obscurity. The oftener I have looked at it, the more I feel the sublimity of the colouring & its fitness for such a composition. In its place it is perfect! A gloom that gradually breaks away, & discovers more & more the mind of the Author. What a roundness, & what splendid lights glimmer here & there, without disturbing the solemnity of the whole. The Last Judgement I cannot yet admire as I wish. Walked in St Peter's. Dined at the D. of Bedford's. *Thursday Feby 2.* Purification of the Virgin & Presentation of Jesus in the Temple. (Candlemas Day.) The Pope entered his chapel on Monte Cavallo at ½ past nine. 17 Cardinals present. He consecrated the candles, sprinkling water over them with his blessing, that, as God taught the bees to make wax for the use of man, so he would look with favor &c The Cardinals, Bps, Nobles of Rome, &c all came up one by one, & kneeling, kissed (the first his hand, the rest his foot) & then receiving a candle from his hand, kissed it & passed on to their places. They then lighted them, & following the choir preceded him in his chair (himself holding up a lighted taper & blessing the people) round the adjoining hall, & back again—in their rich golden episcopal habits as Bps—Then he knelt before the altar with his taper, & resuming his seat, read parts of the service with a loud & clear voice. High Mass in all its solemnity. The Music as usual entirely vocal. It was over at 12.—Walked afterwards in the Medici Gardens, The air balsamic, & the sun bright. The chequered shade & sunshine in the green allies. At 2 it turned to Rain. Heard an Anthem in St Peter's. The candles so blest, are much sought after in cases of sickness. St Peter's conceived by a great man & executed by little ones. When the dome became conical, it lost half its grandeur; & what meaness in all the details. The statues, the reliefs, the mosaics with but how few exceptions, below criticizm. The mean heat of Italy is said to be 70. that of England 57—& the heat of the church is the medium heat. The thickness of the walls, double windows, the double doors & burning lamps &c give it also an advantage over St Paul's, not to mention its being larger. In Summer it is as much colder than the external air, & the cold is said to be intolerable. *Friday. Feb 3.* St Pietro Montorio. An admirable station, &

particularly for the Ruins (tho' far inferior in that respect to the capitol)—but to me far less striking than the Lante. There the town lies so directly at your feet. The Fountain, the botanic Gardens, the Pamphili Villa. Hot sunshine A long avenue, a little stripe of shadow down one side of it, & all were glad to take it. The sound & sight of the water very grateful. Sat long by the Fountain. The Campagna seen thro' those noble pines whose crested heads form an uninterrupted canopy—one crest. Magnificent view of St Peter's & the mountains behind the house—as of Frescati & the Alban Mount in front. Lawns purple with crocusses. The Stanze of Raphael. How exquisitely coloured are those he did himself entirely, before he called in his scholars to his assistance! The mass at Bolsenna, the dispute of the Sacrament, the Jurisprudence, &c—! Walked in St Peter's with Allen, & saw the Chapel of the Strozzi, the second on the right as you enter, designed by M. Angelo. There are three admired above the rest in Rome, That of the Corsini in St Giovanni di Lateran—that of the Ghigi in St Maria del Popolo, by Raphael & this by M. Angelo. Here or hereabouts was the Curia of Pompey, in which Cesar lost his life.

Saturday. Feb 4th. A bright day. The Farnesini. Cupid & Psyche. Galatea. More of female beauty here perhaps than any where, & perhaps accounted for in his Life by Vasari.[1] Went up the Corso in a Caratella. The high tide of the Carnival. A may-pole & dancers. A seller of frogs, his frog-basket on one arm, & some skinned frogs in a wooden bowl in the other, which he offered for sale. Bravos. Spadassins with swords—Many peasant-women walking or in carriages, in rich dresses red & gold. Two fantastic figures forced by the military from behind Mr Lee's Carriage for throwing bon-bons, unmasked—their clothes torn from them, & they were hurried away nobody knows where. Seven horses ran—A perpetual fire of starch from the carriage of the Zartowisky's[2]—all Masked. A car of bay leaves, full of

[1] Vasari tells the story of Raphael's being so much in love at the time that he was unable to get on with the Marriage of Psyche. Agostino Chigi solved the difficulty by installing the lady in his palace.

[2] ? Prince Adam Czartoryski, who had known the Hollands when in London with the Czar in the summer of 1814. He already knew Italy, and had been in Rome in 1800. The ardour with which he plunged into classical studies there, characteristic of the educated visitor, is engagingly described in his *Memoirs*, ed. Adam Gielgud, 2v, London, 1888, i, pp. 211 ff.

masks—demons with horns—A bear & his leader—A large dog-like head behind a carriage, to which the mob spoke as to a dog. 'Begone.'—A Mask with a long snout—The corso gay & not noisy, a very amusing scene—singular & grotesque figures every instant appearing on foot or within & without the Carriages. Much practical humour & innocent madness in the people. Along the sides in chairs among the croud sat many people of condition in mask. Cardinal Rufo & the Dss of Feano at a window together. An old gentleman in rich clothes, a pococurante[1] figure.—So gay, yet so quiet croud—in their mirth too there was something, if I may say so, of a seriousness it was to be at an end so soon! When the line was formed for the race, many white masks ran wild till driven in by the laughing soldiers, & one with great humour danced sideways down the line, driving in the croud with his back—till compelled to fly by the soldiery. The Ball of il Duca, e la Duchessa Sforza Cesarini. Rooms hung, the first with white, the second with red silk, & together with the staircase splendidly illuminated. Large bougies as you went up. The Ladies formed a square till the dancing began on the carpet. A profusion of refreshments, Tea, coffee—ices, iced cherry water, iced punch, lemonade, citron &c—Cards. Guards at the Gate—A Canopy & Portrait of the Pope as usual, the chair under it turned to the Wall. All the Ladies as usual well-drest with diamonds & flowers. No french bonnets as at the theatre. When the Austrians attempted to light up the theatre at Milan, they desisted from a fear of a disturbance. The Italians like to sit in the dark, some that they may go undrest, others perhaps from other motives.

Sunday. Feb 5ᵗʰ. Palazza Sciara. Half of the Barbarini Paintings, belonging to the Youngest Brother.[2] The Gamesters of Caravaggio. Modesty & Temperance by Leonardo da Vinci. A Portrait by Raphael—Qʸ of himself—. A Titian, three men bearded with a little boy, Half length. A small & beautiful collection. The Spada Bas Reliefs. The Farnese Cieling, which gives less pleasure, the more we look at it. Its colouring sandy &

[1] Nonchalant, carelessly dressed. By 1762 the term was naturalized in English, and led to the forms poco-curantish, pococurantism. (*N.E.D.*) Moore dedicated his *Rhymes on the Road* to members of the Pococurante Society.

[2] Half the Barbarini collection passed to the younger brother, who lived in Palazzo Sciarra, as a result of a lawsuit settled in 1811.

approaching to foxy. An anthem in St Peter's, & the exposition
of the Sacrament there. Called at the Feano Palace on M^rs
Rawdon. Two men playing vehemently at Mora,[1] three or four
men standing by—Dodwell saw the servants behind a Cardinal's Carriage playing at cards on the top of it. A Cardinal's
umbrella red, a Prince's blue.

Monday. Feby 6. Carnival. In the Corso at ½ past 2. Masks innumerable. One Car or stage, shaded with boughs & full of
revellers, eating macaroni & drinking wine. A carriage full of
masks with the head of a bird. A mask with a gigantic butterfly
on his head. Many Pococurantes. A shower of confetti from two
balconies of Palazzo Feano—& from one at the Palazzo
Corda—Dss of Bedford, Miss Rawdon, Me Zartowiski L^y Davy
L^y Westmorland—A mask with his brush offering to brush our
clothes—Saw the race from a booth at starting—5 horses—live
coals on their backs—Dined at the D. of Bedford's. Called at
the Prima Sera of the P. of Canino's. Found the Grand Inquisi-
tor there. Ball given by Madame Ord.[2] McDonald's fall in
dancing with the Dss of Bedford. Dancing of a daughter of the
Dss of Feano.

Tuesday. Feby. 7. Saw Canova chissel the marble of the statue
of Victory designed for Russia, & the mould taking from his clay
model of Religion for the nave of St Peter's. Saw his own
paintings & his terra-cottas. Put on a mask & domino & went
into the Corso. Heavy rain of confetti from the balcony of the
Cawdors [?]. Gay & busy perspectives of the street full of
masks & carriages full of masks; tapestry hangings from the
balconies full of masks & fancy-figures. A cocked hat stuck
round with radii of turkey feathers—the face ochred, the feet
fringed with brocoli leaves. Two men in a bull's hide driven
along by drivers. Saw the race from a chair before the Ruspoli,
where the Ladies were sitting masked in a row, & tormenting
their friends as they passed. At Night went to the Masquerade.
View of the Theatre from the stage! every box full of rich &
grotesque habits. The House overflowing. Many lovely women
in fancy-dresses. People of every rank crouding one another,

[1] A popular game for two which consisted of flinging out a number of
fingers at the same time shouting out the number each anticipated his
opponent would extend. The game was commonly played with considerable vehemence.

[2] ? Mrs. Orde, sister of Lady Oxford.

Death & Time. Called at the Marguerita & found the Duke & Lady Jane alone; till the boys came & L^d J^nol & Lady Davy, masked.

Wednesday. Feby 8. Ash Wednesday—High Mass at Monte Cavallo. The Pope dropping ashes in the form of a cross on every head, on cardinal, bishop, noble, &c 'Ashes thou art, & to ashes thou shalt return!' each kneeling before him, & kissing his hand or his foot according to his rank. Two english nobles said to be there, one of them Lord Clifford[2]—The music particularly fine when the censers went round, tossing & diffusing incense. A divine day. Bright sunshine, & the air vif, not cold. Passed St John Lateran. Beautiful views of Frescati & Castel Gandolfo on one hand; & the Mediterranean on the other, with not a ship upon it. Passed many sepulchres in ruin—aqueduct stretching across the campagna to the mountains. Ascended to Albano, & walked up to a small convent of Frati above it, who would not admit my sister. From the green behind it a delicious view of the Lake of Albano hung round with groves, the black shadows of ev^g spreading over it, & a flock of goats drinking on its brink— the convents round it on the Alban Mount, the Rocca di Papa &c & the town of Castel Grandolpho the favorite spot of Gangan-elli[3]—its dome & roofs & pinnacles immediately over it & black against the sky, as it had been cut out in Paper—of the campagna, far & wide & level as a vast floor, the Tiber winding & entering the sea at Ostia, the sea itself bright in the sun, & the Moun-tains on the right appearing thin as a vapour. Saw the sun set for the first time in the Mediterranean, the sky afterwards red as a ruby; &, immediately the distant tinklings of the ave-maria died away in the air. The scene gave every variety that Claude has given, & how divinely. The Capuchins in their brown corded habits, & six sbirri descending armed from the mountains, a drove of goats & another of asses with water-casks & here & there a lying figure on the bank gave animation to it, & the Sbirri with their guns, weary perhaps with wandering threw themselves down among some brushwood on the brow of the hill over Albano, & lay there conversing till the day was gone. Walked till dusk & came in at 6 oClock.

[1] Lord John Russell, later 1st Earl Russell, 1792–1878.
[2] Hugh Charles, 7th Lord Clifford, 1790–1858.
[3] Lorenzo Ganganelli, Pope Clement XIV, *d.* 1774.

Albano, where we sleep to night, is, it is said, the scite of the magnificent gardens & villa of Pompey.

Thursday. Feby. 9. Sunrise. Tomb of the Horatii. Descended & rose again into   . Mountainous & woody. Aricia. Gensano; passing unseen the lake of Nemi. Velletri. Via Appia. Pomptine marshes. Mountains & mountainous towns on one side, & sea on the other. Aquatic fowl innumerable on the pools & flying over them. Kites & cormorants on the wing—Seagulls—the air resounding with their cries. Buffaloes in herds—their rueful looks, shaggy hair, & barbarously ringed horns—Circean Promontory—Two sails on the sea—rough roads—shady avenues—cork groves & little lawns intermixed like an english park—Slept in the sun with impunity—A Country full of history & fable—Here stood the enchanted Palace of Circe—Here Cicero embarked to cross the bay on the day he died—Terracina its hanging orange-gardens glowing with the richest yellow in the sun, like the gaudy representations of fruit-trees, I remember to have admired when a child in a penny-print. Walked under the perpendicular rock & along the sea-shore—the road winding round the bay—Many sails in the offing & many boats on the shore—An English or Irish Soldier in the garrison—A noble bay hanging woods—The bay across which Cicero had gone the mountains on which he had looked so often —Sunset—Lady Heathcote[1] supped with us.—

Friday—Feb[y] 10th Sun-rise behind the Point. Mountains ridge behind ridge—melting—their vallies full of sunbeams—Mountain-towns—Vapours blue & violet—orange-orchards—as many oranges as leaves—groves of cypress like so many Turkish burying-grounds—Roman tombs by the way-side rough with bushes—Olives—fishers with their nets on their shoulders like shrimping nets—probably for crawfish—many large figtrees without leaves—many peasants on the road—girls carrying baskets of oranges intermixed with leaves—priests on an ass—woods along the sea—fig-trees their silvery & smooth bark—Fondi—the Orange orchards on both sides of the road full of fruit. Cypresses against the mountains. Appian way thro' a mountain-pass—sent up thro' an extensive olive wood—Stations of cavalry at the foot of it—Retrospect of the valley we had left. Itri a romantic village & castle on a shelf in

[1] Catherine-Sophia, wife of Sir Gilbert Heathcote. She was born in 1773.

the bosom of the mountains—Stations of soldiers at every mile
—Long among the mountains—olive woods—the air sweet
with myrtle—discended from the carriage & gathered myrtle
with its dark berries—large old figtrees bare of leaf—Sea on the
right—Round tower on a square base said to be Cicero's tomb—
near it Nausicaa's[1] fountain—Promontory of Gaeta—Ischia—
Procida—Mola—Embarked on the Mediterranean from a cave
of what is called Cicero's Inferior Villa now in an orange-
garden—The bay—where Scipio & Lelius gathered shells on
the shore—The Mountain-screen on the left—Marano, a town
seated on a shelf among the mountains, said to be full of
Bandits—castles along the shore—Vesuvius beyond the point!
Landed in an Orange-garden & walked up under a trellis by a
long flight of steps to a Villa inscribed Joannus Andreas
Laudatus. A D. 1581. & from the terrace long contemplated the
scene, while my Sister coasted the bay & went round by Gaeta.
Warm sun—Small ships of War stationed to guard the fishers
from the Turks, the yellow orange-trees below, yellower at a
distance than heath in the fullest flower, & intermixed with
cypresses Lemon trees less crisp & more pendant—a sea without a tide—Vesuvius!—
Returned by sea & found the women washing in a fresh spring
on the sands. Found others in the narrow street washing in a
fresh stream in the narrow street,—The shadows, as I looked
from the terrace darker, the tints richer than I had ever known
before—We now feel ourselves in Italy! Crakenthorp supped
with us. The air mild & the scene splendid as in a Northern
Summer!—The inns at Terracina & Gaeta da Mola on the Shore.
Saturday. Feby 11. Rich streaks in the orient—Went thro' a
wood of olives along the shore & under the mountains, the sunny
sea glittering thro' the trees. Myrtles every where in the hedges
—& aloes, some of them gigantic, but cut down—road full of
peasant people, & women working in the fields in pretty
dresses red & blue, their heads in white linen—desolate towns
here and there halfway up the mountains—like long lines of
white stones with not a leaf of vegetation about them—a
church tower alone denoting them to be houses, the snows
immediately above them—At Garigliano an old aqueduct of

[1] Nausicaa is crossed out, with a carat underneath, but nothing has been
written in its place.

Minturnian Q^y—runs to the mountains—Passed the Garigliano on a bridge of boats. Left the Appian Road & thro' low &
level marshes, in which Marius was found, & by St Agato,
leaving Sessa high on the left (q^y did Horace & Virgil meet
there, or at Rocca di Mondragone see Lalande. 5. 196. & Vasi.
5)[1] crossed the Volturnus at Capua & thro' a level plain among
vines hung from tree to tree came on thro Avasa to Naples; the
long avenue gradually filling with passengers of all sorts—& the
mountains receding—The Strada di Toledo—Noise & bustle—
& went directly to the Locanda del Sole—into a large room,
with columns & coved cielings, but without a fire-place, the
windows looking directly into a Piazza as busy as the Palais
Royal, & up to the summit of Vesuvius—Walked in the Chiaja
& went at night to the Teatro de Fiorentini.—
Sunday, Feby 12. The Place of St Lucia. The Chiaja.—Saw M^r
Giuseppe[2] Vases & Bronzes. Went in L^y Oxford's[3] carriage & saw
her children. Dined & in her box at St Carlo saw an Opera & ballet.
Monday. Feb. 13 Mr Honey[4] at breakfast. Went with him—to
Herculaneum—to the theatre there—seen by snatches[5]—,
(semicircular & with a permanent scene, like Palladio's at
Vicenza) encrusted with marbles—& overwhelmed, according
to Dion Cassius, by the grand eruption in the year 79, in the
hour of representation, an eruption so fatal at once to Pompeii &
Herculaneum. The rest of the City is again interred.—Saw also
the Palace, & the Museum, so full of antient Paintings. Dined at
L^y Oxford's with Ld Clare[6] & Ld Fred^k Montagu[7]—& afterwards
went to M^r. Vaudricourt, who sung very charmingly in duo's &

[1] Referring to Lalande, *Voyage en Italie*, 7v, Geneva, 1790, and Marien
Vasi, *Itinéraire instructif de Rome à Naples*, Rome, 1813.

[2] An art dealer. *cf.* p. 258 l. 27.

[3] Jane Elizabeth Scott, married Edward Harley, 5th Earl of Oxford in
1794. She was separated from her husband and her lack of means, and the
rowdy behaviour of her children ('the Harleian miscellany') gave rise to a
good deal of gossip in Naples.

[4] He is mentioned in *Contemporaries*, ii, p. 45, as telling Rogers how
when in Paris during the 1830 revolution, he was forced to save himself on
one occasion by jumping into the Café de Paris through an open window.

[5] Because it was partly underground, and had to be seen by torchlight.

[6] John Fitzgibbon, 2nd Earl of Clare, *b.* 1792. A contemporary of Byron at
Harrow, he appears in early poems, e.g. 'Childish Recollections' as Lycus.

[7] Frederick, *b.* 1774, brother of William Montague, 5th Duke of
Manchester.

trio's—& from the top of the house saw Vesuvius at intervals discharging red flame. An awful sight! At this moment from my window I see a column of white smoke like a cloud (the other evening at sunset it received the richest lights) issuing from its crater & rolling off to the South East.

Tuesday. Feb 14th. Went with Honey & the B[oddington]s[1]— thro' the Grotto di Pozzuoli & along the sea to Solfatara—& the Temple of Serapis at Pozzuoli—looking across the water to Baia—Rich colours of the sulphur, its bubbling sound—heat of the earth—beautiful white heath blossoms, violets & myrtle every where,—ampitheatre & aqueduct Coming down, met in a lane some merry-makers accompanied by a guitar & a violin that played beautifully a lively air called the Manfrano, the party, all young men, dancing.—Fell on my knee.

Wednesday Feb 15. Five or Six Girls in a brown habit & in a black veil, the foremost holding a cross ornamented with flowers —singing in a chorus with a tin box to collect money—Le Orphini di San Vincenzo Ferrara—Another band of the same kind had just passed under the balcony.—Orphans of charity. What a source of amusement is the Largo del Castello—in which we live, How many trades are carried on under our window—One man is making & baking small white cakes with honey, & sending boys out with them for sale, as fast as they are made. Another is peeling oranges & squaring them on a board for sale. Here a group of boys is engaged at Chuck farthing, & countless groups are in conversation—A stand of caratells is close to us—On the right is the Castle—A square mass flanked with battlements & round towers—& in front the cloud of Vesuvius is shifting its form every minute—now rising in a curve into the sky—now diffusing itself along the Mountain.— Here comes a train of white habits preceded by a crucifix & two priests uncovered & now they return with lighted tapers & a body inclosed in a richly carved & gilt case—

[1] Samuel Boddington was a partner in Richard (Conversation) Sharp's business. Sharp wrote to Rogers on Dec. 2, 1814: 'Boddington tells me that at Florence he got a glimpse of you as you were setting out for Vallombrosa, where, in November, you would find, I guess, the leaves strewn about as in Milton's simile. What present pleasure! What future recollections! Your Muse must have become already a fine Italian Lady.' *Contemporaries*, i, 175. Boddington had already been Rogers's companion in Paris both in 1791 and 1802.

Ball at the Princess of Wales's. Duca & Ducessa di Gallo.[1]
March[a]. di Berrio[2] & his accomplished daughters. M[e].
a Polonese last from Elba.—

Thursday. Feb[y] 16. Two bands of the Orphans. A very pretty
girl threw up her veil & with many smiles & gestures of supplication held up her hand, singing to the balcony of our Locanda.
Went to the Lago d' Agnano—the Grotto del Cane & the Sulphur baths—such as are called by Pliny the spiracles of Pluto—
& along the new Road towards Puozzoli, overhanging the sea.
From the platform before the church & its little convent built by
Sannazarius on the site of his beloved villa had a magnificent
view of Naples, of Vesuvius & the bay.—Dined at B[s]. & at San
Carlo saw the King.[3]

Friday, Feby 17. A heavenly morning. Under Niscida a ship
with its white sails, as we passed it. Embarked at Puzzuoli in a
boat with four oars, & coasted the shores of Baiæ. Perhaps the
Forum Romanum alone affects you more with its vestiges of
antient splendour. Arches above arches, half-sunk, broken, &
honeycombed by water & fire, chambers, caves, these in continual succession, as the boat moves silently under them, remind
you of Cicero, & his questiones Academicae, of Lucullus of Piso,
Hortensius, Marcellus, Augustus, Pompey, Cesar & Marcus.
Landed near the Lucrine Lake, & thro' a cavern by torch-light,
went to the Lake of Avernus, shut in among the steep mountains. A temple on its banks.—Returned & reimbarked for
Baiæ—Baiæ, famous for its myrtle groves & sulphurous waters
(Hor[ace]. Ep. I. 15.)—Temple beyond temple—a dome
lighted like the Pantheone, half a one like that of Peace, a round
temple like that of Vesta—vaults reticulated, & sculptured in
squares & circles & diamonds, The Piscina
The Mare Morto, the Elysian fields—Walk thro' a vineyard—
Cape Misenus from which the elder Pliny set sail with his fleet
for Vesuvius, where he lost his life—Baoli—antient tombs—the
blue sea every where breaking in, as we walked, on both sides.

[1] He was minister for foreign affairs first under Joseph, then under
Murat, and had travelled widely in Europe. He died in 1833.

[2] The Marchese Berio was an Anglophile, an entertainer of the English
and an admirer of their literature. He wrote an Ode to Lord Byron,
stimulated by a reading of the 4th Canto of *Childe Harold.*

[3] Joachim Murat, married to Napoleon's youngest sister, Caroline. He
succeeded Joseph Bonaparte as King of Naples in 1808.

As we went, the blue transparent mist along the surface under the dark mountains & discovering the dark sails thro' it. A carousing party before a Vinetto on the bank as we were returning—Dined at Princess of Wales's—Went to L^y Oxford's, & afterwards to the Pss of Belmonte's,[1] where was Pharoah &c— *Saturday. Feb^y.* 18. Rain. Dined at 3 oClock at the Archb^p of Tarentum's[2] in the house formerly Sr Wm Hamilton's.[3]—Gems Vases—A long suite of Rooms looking on the bay—terraces full of shrubs & flowers. Dinner in Switzerland—in a landscape room, looking on a cavern—Cinders from Vesuvius found on his terrace here—His Cats—The Presidente—Sitting on the table with his back to the company.—L^y Oxford M^r & Mrs Rose, Ld F. Montagu.—Opera at the Fiorentino—
Sunday. Feby 19. The Palace. Waited in a Gallery—The Marquis de Berrio—Duke de Gallo, Archb^p of Tarentum. Presented to the King. Spoke of the Weather—of Rome as triste—of the Pope's enmity—The Neapolitans good Catholics notwithstanding—wanted nothing more than his benedictions—Of Bonaparte and Elba—A good-looking man & very courteous & seemingly diffident of himself—Met him afterwards gallopping in the Chiaja. A delightful afternoon—Cold—The Hollands at the Grande Bretagne—

[1] She was responsible for presenting visitors to the Queen and entertained them freely, both at home and at the Opera. Pharoah, of course, = the gambling card game, Faro.

[2] This venerable and cultivated man held a salon where visitors could meet the intellectuals of Naples. There are many accounts of him by travellers, e.g. Lady Morgan's *Italy*, George Ticknor, *Life, Letters and Journals*, N. P. Willis, *Pencillings by the Way*. The cats, which so much interested Rogers—he not only wrote about them in Italy, but acquired a portrait of one of them—came to play a rather larger part in the Archbishop's household in later years.

'While we were in the midst of a scientific discussion one of the cats came up to him, and made a significant mew, when the old man cried out to his chaplain and secretary, who was in the room:
'"—!"—calling him by his name—"mon chat veut shier;" upon which with an obedient start, the reverend secretary ran and opened the window, and let puss out into the balcony. "Est ce que mon chat fait bien?" demanded the old man. "Oui, Monseigneur, ce chat fait tout ce qui est convenable;" whereupon the old gentleman expressed his satisfaction, and resumed the discussion." ' *Private Diary of Richard Duke of Buckingham and Chandos*, 3v, 1862, London, i, 315.

[3] 1730–1803. Plenipotentiary at Naples 1764–1800.

In the Ev^g went to the House of the Minister of Finance, Monsr Moseburg   , where all the World danced, & the King himself in a quadrille with the Pss of Wales. Wonderful play with his limbs—too much so with his head & body—It gave him the balancing air of a Rope dancer—or of a dancing master teaching ease to his scholars. A very gay & elegant house— pretty vistas—It was delightful to drive home along the shore— the moonlight on the sea—smooth as glass—& bright as an illuminated mirror.

Monday, Feby 20th. A brilliant day—Went to Pompeii, winding along the shore & round Vesuvius, thro' Villages, one half desolated & rebuilt, (Torre del Grece) one (Portici) built unknowingly over a town swallowed up & lost in liquid lava that has hardened into stone. Passed thro' fields of indurated lava, & among the richest gardens, the mountain, like a gloomy tyrant above, sending forth his displeasure, & seeming only to withold destruction from those who lived beneath him—We had no intimation of what was coming—when, alighting at a small door, we descended a few paces, & found ourselves in the forum, the columns of its portico standing, & on some of them scrawled by the people names, a horse galloping in red chalk—then came the theatres, the basilica, the temples, the streets—after passing the Apothecary's, who can stand at the fountain—Ganimede— where the three ways meet paved with lava—& look up & down near the oil-merchant's door & the miller's, & not feel a strange & not unpleasing sadness. Who can walk thro' the better houses—one of these is bounded by Vesuvius itself—particularly those in the borgo, their baths, & courts & gardens unmoved? or stand near the gateway & look down the street of tombs, one by one, so vast, & of marble so white, so ornamented, so entire —What an idea do they give us of the Via Appia?—Looked into one of them (Venii) & saw the Vases of red earth in their niches, & in the centre the glass vase full of bones—the very elegant seats by the way side—Coved, painted red & in arabesque— What a labour to grind the flour, a labor once from which Kings were not exempt—

Grind, Mill-stone, grind—

Mora played by some peasants in the *Basilica* The ruins round the base of Vesuvius may be compared to the bones that strew the ground at the mouth of a Lion's den; who is only sleeping within—& growling in his slumber—the lava-streets, the wheel-tracks, the stepping stones, the names & figures scrawled on the columns in the forum, the worn steps, the stone-seats by the way-side, the iron hooks in the door posts for the hinges to move on, the stone-counters & earthen jars in the oil-merchant's shop, the circular stains of the cups on the marble slab in the liquor shop—Salve on the threshold of the villa. the oil-merchant's jars, the miller's mill-stones, Looked towards Capri on what Tacitus calls 'pulcherrimum sinum' —L IV. c 57[1]—Went to L^y H^d—& to Me Vaudricourt's & from her terrace looked over the gardens & the bay by moon-light.

Tuesday. Feb 21. Cold & overcast. Saw the Papyri unrolled in the Studio, being first strengthened with something like gold-beater's skin or ising-glass. Saw the Bronzes & a crown or garland of gold lately discovered in a tomb & the Pictures & Vases. Went to the Opera at San Carlo.

Wednesday. Feb 22. Went in a warm & bright sun, the sky with-out a cloud, & the sea breaking along the shore, thro' the Grotto of Posilippo, where the lamps are always burning, thro' the vineyards & orchards, & along the coast to Puzzuoli—looked down on Avernus—, to the Reservoir, the Temple of the Giants, Casino Reale on a lake—the Arco Felice (one of the antient Gates of Cuma, of all the Cities, says Strabo the most antient); Cuma, says Virgil, the germ of the Roman Power, so reduced afterwards as to be called by Juvenal, vacuis Cumis— Tarquin retired & died there. (From the monte di Cuma is an extensive view of the Golfo di Gaeta, in other times Seno Formiano, seperated from the Golfo di Napoli, formerly Seno Campano by the Promontory of Misenus. The country over which the eye wanders is that of the antient Campania felix— the first object that rises there is the Torre now called di Patria—about 6^m off, precisely in the Place where was Liter-num, by many wrongly called Linternum. Scipio Africanus—It is close to the shore—)

Walked over a hill & looked down on Baiæ & its busy port & its ruined temples—the Temple of Venus now a cooperage for wine—horses laden with wine passing over the hill—goats on a

---

[1] Annalium, Lib. iv, *recte* cap 67. Rogers owned a copy of Taciti *opera quae exstant*, 2v, Amster., 1685. The reference is to p. 518, vol. i.

building covered with brushwood—Sat & ate grapes & oranges,
borrowing a knife from some men singing in the vineyards—a
delicious hour—

(We began under a convent, & are now over a church. Last
week we moved round a brazier like so many weird sisters—
& saw no flame but the flame at the top of Vesuvius. The old
Romans talked much of their hearths, but in modern Italy such
things are thought unhealthy, & shunned like the Mal'aria.)[1]

Thursday, Feb. 23 Went up Mount Vesuvius—its furrowed &
channelled sides—channelled by floods of lava—Sunshine. A
hazy morning. No cloud. Wind North East. Mounted a small
horse at Portici. A mountain road, rough & stony. A church. A
vineyard wall—a cottage—a cross—Lizards sunning themselves among the stones—with their short quick motions—very
tame & a quick pulse in each side—& the cicada flying across the
road like a little bird—when it settled, it appeared to be a large
grass-hopper—from the hermitage an extensive view of the
campagna, the bay, & the mountains, far & wide, some of which
are still topt with snow. Descended into a valley of cinders, &
now what stood before us but a black Mountain, a Mountain of
Cinders—travellers ascending & descending like small white
spots—Atrio dei Cavalli—Left our horses at the foot of it &
gained the summit; & as you drew near it, sulphur-stains
appeared on every side, & smoke rose here & there; & the ashes
felt warm to the feet.—Proceeded to the crater; nor heard nor
saw any thing till we had gained the utmost height that inter-
cepted all sight & sound; then we looked down a small but
dismal hollow, an inclined plane beyond which appeared the
gulph, the opposite side of which, black & sulphurous, rose
precipitately, & considerably above the nearer side. Then it was
that we heard & saw—& we descended to the edge of the gulph
—The noise was not continual, but by fits—The silence that
came continually, rendering it still more awful—a noise now
deep & hollow, like the rolling & dashing of waters, or of a
metallic fluid, much heavier & harder than water—now sharp &
clattering like that of a Forge such as Virgil places in Etna—
Volcani Domus—& now like the explosion of great Ordnance,

[1] It is not clear when this was written; it is characteristic of Rogers'
disconnected interpolations. The first sentence presumably refers to their
lodgings.

or of thunder among mountains—the noise instantly followed by a discharge of large substances, most of them red hot, many of which fell back into the abyss, & many against the sides with a violent crash—& some at our feet & behind us. In the air they appeared like shells thrown by an enemy, & the danger was not small my two guides continually pulling me by the arm, & crying 'Andiamo, Signor.'—Those that fell near us were lighted cinders, near a foot square, & red as when dropping or shot out from a fire. The sound increasing, & a greater explosion having taken place, & the wind shifting against us, we retired to our first position, above a hundred yards from the crater, when another still greater succeeded, throwing vast cinders even to the place we had reached. From the extreme edge it was indeed most horrid, the substances continually thrown half-way up resembling in the darkness lumps or masses of red flesh, like so many drops or 'gouts of blood', & now & then a flame lighting up, as it were, the darkness. Stood awhile on the brow of the mountain, now looking down on Herculaneum & Pompei & Stabia & now on the horrid gulph. It was an awful & an interesting thing to connect them in one's mind, the Sun shining on the sea & the shore, on Portici, Resina, Torre del Greco, Castello del Mare—Annonciata—all so lovely & smiling so near the mouth that may devour them all. Met many pilgrims on our descent—Pears among others—going to visit it by night—A beautiful evening—Took some refreshment on the stone seat at the hermitage—the sun set without a cloud behind the mountainous island of Ischia—the sea a sheet of silver—the sky a rich orange, shifting into a thousand tints—till the full moon rose majestically from behind the crater of Vesuvius, silvering its smoke now like a fleecy cloud—& the stillness & sweetness strangely contrasted with what we had left passing below. It was night when we came into Portici—Two men kneeling on each side of a cross A flame on Vesuvius as we came home—Bright Moonshine. Found the Archbp at Cards. Sat with Ld Holland. *Friday. Feb* 24. Marquis of Berrio's Library & Garden. Mass in his chapel. Venus & Adonis by Canova. The new Road—The King there—also L^y Oxford the Hollands, the Duchess of Gallo —&c—Water beautiful—deep blue, fading into a light blue under the mountains, that transparent mist or rather light so happily imitated by Claude. The Villa Reale. Group of the

20. Naples and Vesuvius from above Virgil's Tomb

21. Tourists in the street of tombs at Pompeii

Farnese Bull.[1]—Dined at the Princess of Wales, called afterwards on L^y Holland & played a game of chess with L^d H^d at the Duchess de Gallo's ball.

Saturday. Feb. 25. A dead Lazzarone found on the staircase of an English Lady here one morning—Saw the Villa & Garden of Mr Heigelin[2]—high, uneven ground looking over the bay & city—artificial rock & ruin—coloured statues—the prettiest thing was the family-burying place planted with cypresses— with urns in niches & affectionate inscription to the memory of a son & a brother. Went to the Campo Martis a vast plain—with a magnificent distance—12000 men there horse & foot—the King on a black Arabian—then on a white—almost always in full gallop—the Queen came to the ground in a Postchaise & removed into a barouche with an umbrella—The King came in a curricle & four—many evolutions, a sham fight—the horse charging squares of infantry, one of which inclosed the royal carriage while taking their luncheon—The road to Naples (when finished to be the approach from Rome) presents a noble view of the bay—& city—

Sunday Feb 26—Heard mass in the royal chapel before the King —a fine concert that lasted half an hour. Visited Virgil's tomb. From the vineyard thro' which you pass to it, a full view of the bay, the city &c a romantic situation. Two children, one the child of English, the other of Genevese Parents lie buried there. Went along the new road towards Puzzuoli.—Delicious views across the bay, a transparent blue medium seemingly diffused over the surface of the sea, rare as ether, a bloom—rather suddenly changing into a lighter colour along the horizon & the opposite shore under the Mountains—a bloom, if I may call it so, a blue light I had never before seen but in a Claude. It was Sunday, & great numbers of carriages & people on foot were in motion, a chearful sight—Card-players by the road-side. Several parties dining on the grass among the ruins of an old house—Colonna's—near the sea—The King & Queen in a curricle & four.—In the Evening a ball at Court. A presentation of the English to the Queen. The King & Queen, with the Princess of Wales between them in chairs at the top of the room —all the pages in array behind—A Quadrille danced by them—

---

[1] This then stood in the open, in the public promenade of the Chiaja.

[2] Mr. Heigeln, formerly Danish consul.

The Queen dancing with her son, the King with the Princess of W. The Queen afterwards waltzed, & the King danced country dances. The King played at chess with Lord Holland. At length the pages were called in to reinforce the dancers. The ball-room mesquin—the colours gaudy—the music in a recess—the other apartments, belonging to the Queen, magnificent. Eat an ice, & had the glass carried away by a man in full dress with a sword. The King richly dressed in a Kemble-habit, such as Kings seen on the stage are wont to wear. His countenance mild his features handsome—the Queen still beautiful, tho' une peu maigre. very graceful & wreathed with diamonds from head to foot. The Queen danced like a Gentlewoman—the King like a dancing-master, perfect in his steps & affecting an ease not natural to him—the Princess of Wales like herself—Their son a boy 14^{yrs} of age, with a pleasant expression, not handsome. His sister a year younger said to be beautiful.

Monday. *Feb^y* 27. Embarked at Puzzuoli & rowed thro' the rock into the bay of Misenum—of an immense depth, says Strabo— then landed at the Cape & ascended the hill, commanding the Mare morto, the Elysian fields &c—not those of Virgil & called so afterwards, probably, from their beauty—but the day was misty—& the Portici shore scarcely visible—reimbarked on the sea now a little freshened, & the mist darkening over Baiæ returned directly to Puzzuoli—The sea-views in our way home along the shore beautiful . . . Junketting parties at the Vinetti as we passed them—Walked in the Villa Reali, & looked at the Farnese Bull. In the Ev^g. Giuseppe called with a lamp, a vase, & several fibulæ & amber ornaments.

Tuesday. *Feb* 28. The Strada Nuova. Walked in a vineyard, & thro' an orchard among fig-trees, & cherry-trees in blossom. Lizards. The sea, blue as ultramarine, & the sails white as snow, breaking in every where. A great smoke from Vesuvius. It rose like the sacrifice of some Patriarch, of Abraham himself on the summit of the Mountain. A mist over the distant shore. Card Parties & dinner-parties within the ruinous walls of the Un- finished House of the Colonna Family. Walked in the Villa Reale; & dined with the Archb^p. who made me kiss him on both cheeks. The Hollands, Allen, Charles & Dr Holland[1] there. The

---

[1] Sir Henry Holland, 1788–1873, medical adviser at this time to the Princess of Wales.

President, the Chambellan, the Dame d'Annonce,[1] & the Grey
hound. A beautiful day—& a brilliant scene from the terrace &
the windows. The King gone to the Chasse—The H^{ds} drank tea
with us.—

Wednesday. Feb. 29. Two English Gentlemen Mr Leigh & M^r
Prime, went to Pestum on the 27th—at 4 in the morning—&
returned at 12 at night, spending two hours there!! The courts
& fronts of the Palaces here at a ball are lighted with high
braziers.—

Wednesday. March 1. A horse killed at the Chasse yesterday by
a boar. Bright Sunshine. Went to Pompei. Saw again the armed
man scratched by some idle hand on the column, the horse, the
boar, the fish, the ship scratched on the wall—the wheel-tracks,
the stepping stones—the meeting of the three ways—the 'Salve'
on the threshold, the name on every door-post, the serpent on
the Physician's, the smokiness of the baker's oven, the stain of
the liquor-glasses. As we looked down into the vintner's-shop &
on the jars inclosed in the counter cased with various bits of
Marble, I thought I saw the man serving his customers—& as
the shadows of evening came on, & standing alone, I looked up
the street of tombs towards the city-gate, the strange silence &
deserted air of the place almost overcame me. My companions
were gone into the villa, & my time was well-spent. A single
horseman was coming down the narrow street, & the hollow
reverberation of his horse's hoofs made it still more dreary to
the ear—Took some refreshment in the Basilica. The tombs are
marble & as white & as fresh as from the quarry. Saw Castell à
Mare on the shore under the Mountains, where Stabia stood &
where the elder Pliny lost his life. A great smoke from Vesuvius
to-day. As we returned in the dark, the lights in the water
reflected from the Mergyllina shore, the light-house & the
lights burning in the fishing vessels at sea, rendered the scene
lively & amusing. Men digging on the high ground above the
tombs, & a single swarthy figure wrapt in a dark cloak, sitting
by & looking on. When we turned away, it was still as motionless as before. It seemed preternatural, or rather as just dug up.
—A lovely sun set. A light from Vesuvius—
A ball at Pss of Wales's. King & Queen danced in a quadrille &
the Queen waltzed.

[1] Presumably more of the Archbishop's cats.

The Italian Journal

Thursday. March 2ᵈ. Briliant day. Bought the bronze handles of a Vase.[1] The Chartreuse. View from the balcony. You seem there to hang in air—like a bird, or an adventurer in a balloon—the city, like a model, immediately under you, the sea & the mountains & the islands—men like ants—a file of muskets sparkling like water in motion—Capo di Monte & directly over it a red mass under the hills, Caserta—A Piety, by Spagnoletti, the best he ever painted—in the Sacristy. Cheerful Cloisters.

Walked in the gardens & over the house of the Villa of the Prince Caraffa de Belvidere. Sea-views—Anemonies—Lʸ Oxford & her children. A fine evening. Crakenthorp & Davenport[2] dined with us—The Opera.

Friday. March 3ᵈ Sunshine. White reflections in the water under the Mergyllina Shore. Pompei. The street of tombs. The stains of the cups. The miller's. The Oil-merchant's. The wine-merchant's. The Apothecary's. The lizard, & the cicada (in conjunction) were in the lonely street. The stepping stones. The foot-way on each side. The little theatre. The forum, full of weeping willows in green leaf. Left Stabia on the right & soon afterwards entered the mountains. Many travellers, and houses up & down every where. At length met again the blue sea, &, by a rapid descent along it entered Salernum. The bay of Salerno, almost encircled by mountains.—Under those on the left lie the temples of Pæstum, to be seen thro' a telescope. Those on the right discover their broken summits, ridge above ridge; & those immediately behind it are finely tumbled together. White houses every where. The Quay full of idle people. Several cards parties. Many coffee-houses & traiteurs.—Walked for three hours in the public walk & along the fields. A sunset. An excellent dinner at the Albergo. Steeple hats worn by all the Peasantry.

Saturday. Mch 4ᵗʰ. Figs, oranges, mulberries, white thorn in blow, olives, neat tillage—between the sea & the mountains—two beautiful palm-trees—pursued the mountains leaving the sea—when under Eburi turned from them across marsh & forest-like ground—innumerable lilies & myrtle-bushes—herds of buffaloes rough & rueful—a man on horse-back in a cow's hide—a man & boy on foot in a capote made of the skin & fleece

[1] Sale Catalogue, No. 181.

[2] ? Edward Davenport, *b.* 1778, son of Davies Davenport, M.P. for Cheshire. He was a friend of Foscolo and Sydney Smith.

of a sheep—Palace of Persano on a river—Peasants in Sr W. Raleigh's hats—high-crowned & tapering—marshy roads—a stable wall swarming with lizards in the sun—a green one in the sun, large & most vivid in its colours & motions—green with black zig-zag lines—on the heath where we stopped to refresh the horses, a cottage conical & circular thatched, fire in the middle—a board over it—a hole above to let the smoke out— four beds—spacious & almost comfortable—no light but thro' the door—black with smoke—capottas of cows hides—black as jet—hung out in the sun—a guitar—In the farm-yard a cistern & an altar of white marble, now used for rural purposes. ferried over the river—country open & level—did not see the Pestum temples till we approached them—the temples in a plain on three sides shut in by the mountains—on the fourth open to the sea—& the sea itself half shut in by them—by the Promontory of Surrentum, within which are the Isles of the Syrens—A magnificent theatre worthy of such objects. the columns almost bare, broken & of an iron-brown like iron-rust—the floor green with moss & herbage—the columns & cornices of the richest tints & climbed by the green lizards that flee into a thousand chinks & crannies at your approach—the snail adheres to them— the butterfly flutters among them, & the hawk is sailing over them—fluted fragments of columns—& mouldings of cornices among briars strew the middle space between the temple & the basilica—& no noise is heard but the rustling of the lizards or the grazing of the silvery-grey ox just released from the plow— Many twice-blowing roses here not now in blow—There are some still near the walls.—innumerable violets in blow among the fragments—the air sweet with violets. In cork the hue & crumbling texture of these ruins (I may add of the Coliseum) are exactly given—Nothing wanting but the size.[1]

How many suns have risen from behind the mountains, & set in the Tyrrhene sea, throwing these gigantic shadows aslant the green & briary floor! since in these temples gods were worshipped—Is it true that they remained buried for ages in the night of woods, till a young painter or a shepherd fell in with them? Was it on such an evening as this, after a sleep of 2000 yrs, the sun's disk just shining thro' them—Now the sea-breeze,

[1] There was a cork model in the Naples Studio, and others could be bought on the spot.

& the mountain-breeze sweep thro' them—Now the fisherman of Salerno as he passes, sees them standing on the desert plain under the mountains, & pilgrims visit them from the corners of the earth, & the little towns—Capaccio old & new—that hang upon the mountains like an eagle's eyrie look down always upon them—Still is the solitude awful from the vastness & grandeur of the theatre—the lizard & butterfly within, the choughs & daws with their lonely cries without—the plough passing up & down under them, drawn by silvery grey oxen, cannot affect them—

To muse by moonlight in the temples of Pestum, to gaze on the shadowy mountains thro' those gigantic columns, & the dark blue sea

Walked towards the sea, gathering anemonies, & the iris & periwinkles—a lonely round tower on the shore—a herd of buffaloes coming slowly home—Walked within the great temple after sun-set—warmth of the air there—& the solemn gloom was nearly such as I had felt in Tintern Abbey by twilight[1]—but what a scene! Who could stand half-way & look up & down without emotion thro' those enormous & majestic masses first to the sea—then to the mountains, as night came on—Who ever saw them elsewhere thro' such a frame-work?—

Came with a letter from the Arch^p—Miserable quarters. One of the columns of the largr temple struck with lightning—& afterwards repaired—The walls remain, & some of the watch-towers, but what has become of the city. No ruins, no inequalities—the plain is level, & the temples stand as if they had just been built there. Buffalo eggs & Buffalo Ricotta at supper.

Sunday. *Mch 5*. Slept well on six chairs—Rose before six & revisited the temples, just as the sun, rising from behind the mountains clad in vapour, threw his beams thro' them, & his strong & catching lights on the columns in long array. A multitude of rooks & small birds in the great temple, the air filled with their cries, the hawk already wheeling round them on his wing. Capaccio in a cloud. The long level line of the sea & land contrasted with the broken & varied outline of the mountains tumbled together one behind the other. Walked in the

[1] Rogers first saw Tintern in the course of a tour through the West of England and Wales in 1791, and wrote a richly romantic account of it in his journal—July 20. *Early Life*, 199 ff.

great temple & the basilica. How heightened their effect by broad lights & shadows thrown across the columns—As the eye wanders within while you stand without, the intricacy & grandeur strike you far beyond the most majestic grove—Never saw the Morning vapours spread with more effect on a chaos of mountains than when standing in the smaller temple—the mists luminous & thin as gauze—behind was a darkness wrapping up all—a depth of mountains & mountain-gulphs— far away in the mist Eburi—Went into the church—devotion of the people—linen on the women's heads simply & gracefully folded—men in sheep-skins—one kneeling with his crook in church a most picturesque figure—

From the city-walls behind the Basilica clustered the columns of the temples together—a forest of columns—& immediately under the walls saw the river rushing to the sea thro' lilies green as an emerald—a woman washing among the loose fragments of stone Square towers on the walls which towards the sea exist no longer. A little Girl at the well drinking out of her mother's hands joined together. The temples much improved by the breaking lights—their crumbling forms—broad deep & broken shadows within among their many columns—green leaves here & there on the plinths of the columns. Bright sunshine—a warm & lively air. A chirping of birds—the plain strewn with fragments—corn here & there—The columns of the richest & warmest tint—like metallic rust that relieves the bright verdure with which Nature has touched them above— gashed severely in many places—but just enough to give the freedom & spirit an Artist would like to give.

Drove thro' the gate—myrtles & white thorn in blossom—the ferry—battle between two lizards—velvet lights on the mountains—birds of prey—olives—wild asparagus—Eburi—Orangegroves—parties of gatherers sitting under them—baskets of oranges—ladders against the trees—Now coasted the mountains, ridge beyond ridge, their vallies full of sunbeams— beautiful palm-tree—The views much more striking than as we came—the promontory of Sorentum, the birth-place of Tasso, within which are the isles of the Syrens, & the various mountains in front finely contrasted—the lowest in deep shadow—the highest melting in a sunshiny vapour—parties sitting under the trellisses before the doors—Salerno—the quay crouded with

Sunday people—The vast granite tazza in the court of St Matteo from Pestum. Walked on the sea-shore—A well of warm water there. Many came to drink, & fill their pitchers. The Planets very bright. Looked back to the shore on which the temples are visible in a clear day to the telescope.

Monday. Mch. 6. Walked on the shore. Bright sunshine. Set off at nine, winding up round the bay. Vietri & its hanging citron-gardens—terrace above terrace. La Cava, its arcades its convent on a summit, its antique, romantic bridge of tall narrow arches, its terrace-gardens—long seen among the hills—banks of primroses & violets—orchards white with daisies—Goitres—crouded road—guard of honour for Lord Holland—Pompei—many visitors there—its lonely streets—its many liquor shops—names on the walls of the houses—street of tombs—looked up it by a delicious light—a melancholy to be found no where else . . . —Naples—Ld Holland's Duke de Gallo there—Bonaparte gone from Elba—Fainting of his Sister the Queen—many conjectures—Un peu d'espoir, says Mosbourg, et beaucoup de desespoir.

Tuesday. Mch 7. The Archb^p. The Strada Nuova. Walked down to the Shore near the little village of Marechiano. Orchard trees in blossom. Wild flowers. Green Peas. Villa Reale. Dined at the Pss of Wales's. St Carlo.

Wednesday. Mch 8. The Studio.[1] The Farnese Flora! A Venus & Cupid from Capua, the Farnese Hercules. Walked in the Villa Reale. The Farnese Bull. Dined with the Archb^p of Tarentum. Craven[2] there. The Princess's Ball. King & Queen danced together. Sat with L^y O[xford] in the Ante-room & observed the quick gestures of two Speakers near one another, each standing over a sitting audience. The Fine weather continues. Sunshine. Mist. Cool Wind. Dusty in the high roads.—

Thursday. Mch 9. A Fine morning fading away. Puzzoli . . . A little boy sitting against a stone, his bundle of sticks by him. Many children carrying bundles of faggots. Avenues. Arco felice the eastern Gate of Cumæ. Ascended by it & looked along that fine sweeping shore towards Gaeta, 6^m off stands the Torre di Patria—& along the sands Scipio & Lælius used to wander,

---

[1] The Museum.

[2] Keppel Richard Craven, 1779–1851. Resident at Naples from 1805. He acted as Chamberlain to the Princess of Wales on this visit.

gathering shells & sea-weed—the subject & occasion of Cicero's dialogue on Friendship—As the eye runs along those sands, who can help thinking of them with reverence & affection? Crossed over to Baiæ, & turning back along the cliff towards Puzzuoli, followed on foot the Mule-path, looking down on broken arches & vaults & columns, immediately under us in the sea. Mules & asses laden with wine-casks, stained red with wine passing to & fro, in a long train. Romantic gallery thro' the rock cut by Pietr' Antonio of Arragon for the Vetturali—lighted here & there, by loop-holes to the sea on one side & on the other opening to a length of vast chambers full of darkness—from the last of which issued a hot vapour—Our Cicerone entered it & descending by a staircase in three minutes returned, profusely heated, & bearing a jar full of hot water in which we boiled some eggs. Those he visited are called, I believe, the Baths of Nero. In our way waited for two trains of mules & asses, & the strange songs & noises of the Mule-drivers made the grotto re-echo.—Returned along the cliff, admiring the deep purple of Niscida, and the hills of Puzzuoli, the blue sea & the delightful little harbour of Baiæ, so busy & so distinguished by the circular temple of Venus. Went to a Pavilion of the King's on the Lake Fusari—& there found a large Party at dinner—Heavy rain—tempestuous sea. White breakers, dark blue sea. Returned to Naples.— In the Evening a thunder-storm & a violent hail-storm at Midnight.

Friday March 10. A Fine Morning that soon passed away. Walked thro' the streets, & bought the small terra-cotta lamp of Actæon,[1] & some glass-bottles. The shops without windows— as in other parts of Italy. A miller smoking with the sang froid of a Dutchman—his man grinding. Went to the Queen's Museum. Etruscan Vases. Bronzes, Terra Cottas. An exact representation of a Tomb. The Walls copied, the Contents original. Catalano's vases & medals. Walked in the Villa Reale, the Clorinda frigate in sight. Dr Holland dined with us.

Saturday. Mch 11. Went to the Studio. Saw the Marbles. Took leave of the Pss of Wales. Strada Nuova. Walked down to the sea thro' the ruins of the house of Queen Joan. Along the water towards Puzzuoli—a succession of casini & coves in the rock,

---

[1] Sale Catalogue, No. 210. 'A lamp, with Actaeon attacked by a dog, the spout broken.' It sold for 5s.

some in ruin. Du Kane[1] dined with us. The Opera; with L^y Eliz^th Forbes[2] in a box given to her by the King. The King at the Opera.

Sunday. Mch 12th. Mass in the Chapel Royal. The King & his attendants, his ministers, his grand marshal of the Palace, the Cardinal   , the Archbishop &c. appeared in the galleries above, & a concert vocal & instrumental began & continued for twenty minutes; the Priest consecrating the wafer & performing his various kneelings below. The King then made his bow—a circular sweep—& retired. Walked round the Lago d'Agnano— within a circle of hills—almost covered with water-fowl, the cries of which are most dreary & wild. A scene of great retirement. Found a marksman on his face in the path, his gun in his hand. Passed the Grotta del cane. Walked with Lord H^d. in the Villa Reale. Dined at the Comte de Mosbourg's, Ministre Sécrétaire d'Etat. A magnificent dinner 70 lights. A chandelier over the table & lights upon it & round it—No lamps. 15 persons. a dinner without end. Fish broiled in the second course; boiled in the first. Tea served round after the fruit & the confectionary. The Opera. Henri, the first dancer, in the ballet his foot caught by the trap-door. Returned to the ball at Mosbourg's. An Excellent band. Few Neapolitans there. Many rumours & much anxiety.

Monday. March 13. The air hitherto seldom sweet with flowers; nor have I heard any singing of birds. The women of the lower order often handsome, tho' their complexions are generally dark & of one colour. Among the girls there is great liveliness of expression, & certainly whether from feature or countenance I cannot say, there are more faces to remember in Italy than in England. The dresses of the Women much more Picturesque. The red & blue, & yellow cloths fold well upon them, & the ass & mule they ride on are often very ornamental to the landscape, the head of the animal being fringed & tasselled with rich colours. & the women sitting picturesquely with a graceful bend of the head.

Tuesday. March 14. The Posilippo Road. A haze on the sea.

[1] A friend of Creevey (*C. Papers*, ii, 230) and Sydney Smith, who called him 'Little Du Cane . . . a very amicable pleasing person'. (*Letters, ed. cit.,* i, 415).

[2] Lady in waiting to the Princess of Wales.

Little sun. Called on the Davys & Lady Heathcote. The Bod-
dingtons & Du Kane at dinner. Green Peas now every day &
Red Mullet. Mme de Vaudricourt's. Sweet singings in duets &
trios.—

Wednesday. March 15th. Museum at Portici.[1] The Stocks. The
Paintings. Rise in my opinion. The figures very beautiful in the
conception, & some well-executed particularly the animals. L^d
J^no Russell went on with me to Pompei. Entered by the tombs.
Went in to the family inclosure of Arria. The vases & glass urn
full of bones removed from that on the other side by the Queen
From the little theatre returned alone thro' the vineyard & up
the streets. Four or five mill-houses. As many liquor-shops; a
stone seat at the door of each, & a scale of steps for the cups. The
stains of the cups, the smoke in the ovens, the wheel-tracks—the
stone steps at the doors worn hollow by the feet—Walked all
alone up the streets, looking up & down, now to Vesuvius, now
backward to the Mountains along which many towns were
scattered aloft—now to the sea—Stabia in full sight—the shops
—the private courts & houses—the street of tombs—looked up
it from the very end—its dreary & desolate character—its pavement worn & bad; & what shews its antiquity, & its bad condition for many years—where the lava stones had sunk into a
hollow—a deep rut had been worn by the wheels labouring out
of it, the rut ceasing when the wheels had gained the level again.
Many lizards on the walls—large & beautiful, green & brown
equally so—Walked on the City walls, thro' six or seven arch-
ways, looking down into the country on the left, into the town
on the right. The air warm, the sun bright, tho' the day rather
windy. Returned thro' the fields of lava, winding round Vesuvius, up which Allen had gone to-day. As we passed by Davenport's leap[2] the usual croud by the Teatro Fondi. A man on a
stage exhibiting a magnet & an iron-weight adhering to it—
two pantomime figures scuffling with one another on a second
stage—& on a third a man haranguing—A stall hard by serving
out glasses of ice-water from many jars. In the ice is squeezed a
little lemon. Dined at Lord Cawdor's, & called afterwards at

[1] The most valuable parts of the collection had been taken to Palermo
by the royal family when the French invaded Naples, but numbers of
papyri and pictures remained.

[2] Perhaps a joking reference to some feat of Davenport's. I have not
found the expression elsewhere.

L^y Holland's & L^y Oxford's. L^y H. in bed, Ld H. with the Duke of Gallo. L^y O's children at blind-man's buff.

The Lazzaroni—a name for that class of people, here more numerous than in any other City I have seen, who hang loose upon Society & live from hand to mouth. They seem to be a noisy, gay & harmless race, retailing fish & fruit, & crouding the quays & streets with their stalls & baskets, & offering their little services on every occasion. Their principal luxories are macaroni & iced water. Goitres in Portici & even in Naples.

Wednesday. March 15. Fine morning, blue sky not without clouds. Puzzuoli. Walked down to the Lake Avernus. Flowers. Lizards. A Farmhouse on the Lake. Arco Felice. From the height looked towards the Torre di Patria. Walked across the Isthmus & looked down upon Baiæ. A vessel from Elba there. Conversed with the sailors, who asked us with great simplicity if we wished for a passage. Strong lights & shadows. Flying Mists. Vesuvius in streaks of snow (as in a half-mourning) went in & came out instantaneously. It appeared with long downward streaks of light. Purple shadows & catching lights. Nisida with a splendour & importance I never saw before. As we returned, the silver waves, the white surf on the shore, gave great spirit & beauty. Walked thro' the Villa Reale. L^y Davy called & drank tea—

Thursday. Mch 16. The Grotto[1] dark as night. No opening at the end visible. Lamps glimmering. A scene for an Arabian Tale. It seemed interminable. The end blocked up by passengers or obscured with dust. Embarked at Puzzuoli. The shores of Baiæ. Masses of brickwork—fragments of walls—arches above arches —reticulated brick-work—chambers in the rock foundations in the water—arches covered at top with corn & bushes & wildflowers—vaults—in long succession—the pack-horses in a string along the cliff above. Landed at Baiæ—conversed on the pier with the commander of a little squadron of gun-boats setting sail at night for Gaieta. Had just dispatched a boat to Naples & its sail full before the wind—Eat Grapes & oranges & biscuit in the Octagon temple of Venus. Scuffle of Sailors there. Walked along the shore & embarked under the Castle. Ruins still greater & more perfect above & below. Stood over for Nisida. White sails, sails bright as silver against the distant

[1] Of Pozzuoli.

mountains of a deep purple—along which the three various towns Castele di Mare &c were distinctly visible. Puzzuoli seen on the Baiæ side like a town of Albert Durer's—Houses in a cluster above houses, every window & gallery & ledge clear & exactly given to the eye.

Landed on Nisida at the fort & by a path walled on each side, winded up to the house on the top—Walked in an olive grove & among vines, a pine standing here & there. Views of the bay & the Mountains thro' the trees. The Island rises precipitously on every side with little variety & is cultivated only on the high ground. Brutus & Cicero. Returned to the Main Land, having just visited an island in the Mediterranean, as we had before done in the Adriatic. Plantations of flax green as Spring, among the vines. Grotto of Puzzuoli. Dined & went to the Opera. The King & his two boys there. In the Morning saw the Archbᵖ. & found him languid & in pain. Received his Apostolic kiss. How beautiful is Old Age in him. He is thought to be declining; & may his gentle & courteous spirit pass away without a sigh. Long, long will he be remembered with tenderness & veneration.

The little port of Baiæ, from which the eye discovers only a circle of mountains, its little bustle, its various ruins, its distant mountains so broken in their lines, & so multiplied in its lines— Nisida, on one of its sides is an exhausted crater—a volcano burnt out.

Friday. Mch 17. Called with S[arah] & saw once more the Archbᵖ. Lord Frederick Montagu with him. He seemed in better spirits & stronger. The Chaija. The Strada Nuova. That azure bloom on the sea, & light pale edge under the Mountainous shore. Drove into the Toledo & drank snow-water & lemon water cooled with snow, & lemon, pulp & juice, squeezed into it; at the most famous stall—painted & carved, a virgin at the top with two candles burning before her. Casks or wooden flasks that move up & down at will. Snow Water without lemon cheaper—Drove to the Cathedral. Singing & Instrumental Music there, it being the day of our Lady of Loretto. Returning, met her in full procession with wind-music, & instrumental music, & banners, & figures in white dominos as in a funeral with lighted tapers. Dined at Lady Oxford's, & went afterwards to the Dss of Gallo's. All the shops are decorated with plate &

artificial flowers & various images—for the approaching festival
of Easter. At Night they are full of lights, & as there is no glass
to obscure them, they shed a full blaze. At the orange & ice
stalls—Sorbettario—or rather snow-stalls—where Acquialo is
sold—, strings of oranges like onions, are suspended & intermixed with green leaves on each side—Snow comes every day
from the mountains.

Saturday. Mch 18. Left Naples. A band of music playing God
save the King & other tunes at our door. Thro' vineyards, vines
carried from tree to tree, green corn springing under them—
many people busy there, went to the Aqueduct that runs from
mountain to mountain, a noble pile of three-fold arches—with
less grandeur & simplicity than those I have seen of the Antients. Walked up the Mountain towards Caserta—& gathered
myrtle—myrtle so near the snows. From the summit looked
down on the Palace, a noble square mass, noble when seen up its
own avenue from the foot of the cascade. The Belvidere & its
orange & flower-garden. Jonquils, violets, carnations, poli-
anthusses. The Palace. Endless suite of rooms in the old-
fashioned style. New Rooms fitting up for Murat. The stair-case
very handsome in the old style. A mist over the distance, con-
cealing Naples, Vesuvius & the sea. A delicious grove of ilex,
interlacing bay & laurel, closing & imbowering like a summer-
grove. A lake, an island, a castle.—freaks of the last King. Bleak
Mountains in a semicircle behind all.—Old Capua—Passed thro
a double arch—& left great remains of an oval ampitheatre
between us & the mountains which ran along within a mile of
the road. Monumental Ruins here & there among the vines.
Rome & Carthage, Hannibal & Scipio Africanus. Entered Capua
at dusk. Ice in a Coffee-house & supped by a brazier.

Sunday Mch 19 Rose at 6; & standing at the door of a Macaroni-
shop saw it in every stage of the process. Every shop being
lighted by the door, all are laid open as by the Diable Boitu.[1]
First came a lawyer's, a man in a broad hat & black habit among
many writings in close conversation, with him—Then a lottery
office numbers crouding to learn their fate, a country-man coming out with a handful of copper-money & joy in his eyes—

---

[1] In Chap. 3 of Le Sage's *Le Diable Boiteux*, Asmodeo, the devil, takes
the hero up to the housetops of Madrid and removes their roofs to show
him what is happening inside.

then a cook-shop, fish & sallad displayed, & a little officer at breakfast with a silver fork—then the macaroni shop, where it was selling by the weight, then the next, where it was making, & hanging in both from the cieling, like sheets in a printer's ware-house, then a coffee-house where two men muffled in their cloaks were drinking off rapidly their coffee, all this in the little town of Capua—Went thro' a level plain, rich in bread & wine & oil, a chain of mountains a mile off on the right—Walked up from the first post-house, Larks singing—picturesque farm-houses with their open porticoes at a little distance in the common-fields—Beautiful heath-blossoms—St Agatha Sessa a town well-situated on an eminence—the ground tumbled about it—Here Horace is said to have met Virgil, & into it I went, attracted by its beauty; & leaving unknowingly the road to Rome—

Soon fell in with the Garigliano, & crossed it by a bridge of boats, a mountain-town—Traieti—hanging high above us. Indeed as we proceeded, others appeared—Little towns, that first appeared like a line of grey & broken crag near the summit & then sha[r]pen into houses,—I have often looked at them with wonder as places of human dwelling—no sign of cultivation the ground about them grey as themselves—At the Post-house, the remains of an ampitheatre, a grey mass of stone here & there, & a magnificent aqueduct running to the hills—those hills in purple—Reliques of Minturnum, in a semicircle of hills— Gathered the leaf of an Aloe, variegated—under the Aqueduct— Entered a wood of olives intermixed with fruit trees—Peaches & Pears—What a gay & beautiful moment all the fruit trees in blossom—& the beans & peas—the bay of Gaieta—Embarked & rowed along the shore—aloes—a road—Gardens—Mountains—Tomb of Cicero in a wood under the mountain—Traieti —Gaieta—the fleet of gun-boats from Mola—returned & landed at the Garden, the Palazzetto of Prince Capuccelli— Fruit in full blow—Vaults under the terrace—a sort of temple with eight Tuscan columns—4 on each side—oblong—& a coved cieling with squares like the Pantheon another vault with ornaments, in relief—evidently belonging to a villa, now said to be Cicero's—The view from the terrace enchanting as ever—& towards the town on the shore—orchard-trees in full bloom, their light branches red, & white with blossoms—orange-trees

271

& lemon trees full of fruit, such as a child would draw, who thought he could never put in fruit enough—the Seville Oranges rich as gold—& noble cypresses rising below against the blue sea, or against picturesque buildings under the mountains—Saw a composition of the last kind—perfect & beyond all my dreams of Italy. Walked up & down for two hours, thinking of times past & persons never to be forgotten—The Evening delicious— The B's came by in a boat. The scene much richer than before— combining the elegance & youthful beauty, of Spring with the splendours of Autumn. The soldiers gone, & no moving figure but the gardeners. A Blackbird singing. Return on foot thro' the town—busy fire-light & lamp-light scenes in the houses— Moonlight on the sea. The elements of the scene—Mountains, woods, rich garden scenery, Italian houses—& the blue sea with shifting sails, the latin[1] sails of the Levant, & mountains, like a thin vapour, almost shutting it in—

Monday. Mch 20 Rose at 5. Sunshine soon after six. A well in a dingle. Many girls with pitchers on their heads or in their hands coming up out of it. Aloes, Portugal laurel in blossom, black thorn, pears plums, & woods of myrtle every where—hedges of myrtle—& myrtles overspreading the ground every where— the air sweet with myrtle—military stations—Itry—Fondi & its cypresses & orange-groves—Terracina—Here with regrets we took our last leave of Orange-gardens—Walked up a narrow foot-lane between hedges & there saw a tesselated pavement of white marble in the path—trodden perhaps for ages unknowingly by the Peasants. The Circean Promontory on our left like an Insulated Mountain in the Horizon—visible for miles & miles. a dead flat—mountains on our right hung with small towns—three in sight at once—A church with its marble columns converted into a stable—B's spring broken—Had proceeded with two gens d'armes from Itry towards Fondi—& from Torre Tre took four sbirri to Veletri—From Cisterna to Veletri a long line of bright light on a hill in front said to be an illuminated convent but found to be charcoal burning—Slept at Velletri in the Ginetti Palace now an inn, rich in marble staircases, gilded cielings painted cornices, busts & statues; & from the gallery in the morning saw the Circean Promontory across a vast extent of marsh fading into a thousand tints; the little

[1] i.e. lateen.

22. Pæstum

23. Tivoli

town of Cora with its antient temples on the grey mountain in
front.

Tuesday, Mch 21. Many women in red bodice & blue petticoat,
& white head-dress flat as a tile, washing in a public cistern
below us. Thro' vine fields & between hedges full of flowers to
Gensano. The little lake of Nemi in what was evidently once a
Crater—Nemi high above it with its tall tower, & Gensana
Vecchia above it too on a precipice of rock, shattered stone &
brickwork & luxuriant vegetation,—& the Franciscan convent a
a low roof on the opposite height with its many cypresses &
pines—a little path along its shore—the ruins of the temple
lying there on a low eminence—Larks singing in the sky—old
women & children wandering up & down for faggots, & boys
following you with bunches of violets—not a house or roof but
in harmony—Winded up & down among large old oaks over
the sea thro La Riccia, a little town very well-built & romantic
—(the Aricia of Horace)—to Albano—The Lake—A Crater too
—the little towns of La Rocca di Papa & Castel Gandolfo—&
three or four Franciscan Convents upon it—Passed & sat before
one shaded by enormous ilexes—a monk in his spectacles
walking & reading before the church-door—What can surpass
the little walk to Castel Gandolfo—& back again—
You wind along a lane among antient trees & banks of violets &
periwinkles & anemonies—the lake beneath you & its perpendicular banks—its Convents—& its grey towns—You return
along another lane no less rich & overshadowed, the Mediterranean in all its beauty & grandeur breaking every where in
upon You—picturesque figures—a man on horseback—another
who offered us his asses to ride upon—Repose, Seclusion, in the
highest degree—leading to the Magnificence of the Ocean & to
as much beauty tho' of another character—& all within the compass of an hour. Returning into Albano, saw 8 or nine girls in all
their finery returning from Communion for the first time—they
went into a dark little church & knelt huddled together in a
close group, whispering, adjusting their flowers & half suppressing their titters, while they turned their heads to steal a
look at us—They then walked up the town—Drove down into
the Campagna—tombs increasing number—aqueducts stretching far away—St Peters—gibbets exposing legs & arms by the
way-side—St John Lateran—the Coliseum, wall flowers along

its ledges, the Arch of Constantine, the column of Trajan, the corso crouded with impatient news-mongers—Via Belsiana— The women certainly handsomer than in Naples—& all better-drest & quiet—

Wednesday. March. 22 Waked by a blackbird in a Cage. The Borghese Gardens. Met Louis Bonaparte there. The Ghisi Chapel in Stᵃ Maria del Popolo. Heard the Miserere sung in the Capella Sistina, all the candles being extinguished & all kneel-ing. The voices dwelling long on every note, nothing could be more pathetic, nothing more solemn. The soprano voices every now & then vibrated thro' the frame like musical glasses & had the effect of the Harmonica. In the Evening saw Lucien Bona-parte at Lord Holland's.

March 23. Thursday. Received the second part of Charlemagne.[1] The Marbles of the Capitol. Walked thro' the Forum & the Coliseum. The Strozzi Chapel in St Andrea della Vallé. The marbles of the Vatican. Heard again the Miserere. Its force beyond eloquence. The three Masters, whose music is sung on the three days, are said to be Pergolesi, Sarti, & Jomelli. Tol-waltzen called in the Evening, & Irwin.[2] To-day only one Cardinal was present. Yesterday 22, but not the Pope. He had set out an hour before the Ceremony, for Viterbo, whither the old King of Spain, & the Queen of Etruria had fled. The Nea-politan troops at Terracina on the Papal territory. His notifica-tion on leaving Rome. In the holy week no bells ring, no clocks strike, all wear mourning, & the images of our Lord are covered with a black veil. For 3 days the tomb on an altar is illuminated in every church. In the capella Paulina it is most splendid In St Peter's elegant in the highest degree. The back-ground scarlet, & the dark circle of kneelers round the rails of the Altar, the silence, the devotion, scattered figures behind all, while the glittering exposition of the relics from a high gallery drew

---

[1] *Charlemagne, ou l' Église délivrée,* epic poem by Lucien Bonaparte, pub. in Paris, 2v, 1814. Translated into English largely by Samuel Butler, headmaster of Shrewsbury. It was not a success, though Byron praised it. Hazlitt wrote: 'I believe I am the only person in England who ever read his *Charlemagne.* It is as clever a poem as can be written by a man who is not a poet.' *Notes of a Journey through France and Italy,* 1903 ed., p. 254.

[2] v. Commonplace Book, p. 290, 'Two landscapes by Gaspar Poussin— boᵗ of Mr. Irving at Rome—in 1822.'

another croud under the dome—all at the present moment most impressive. The lamps round the Sepulchre of St Peter extinguished.

Friday. Mch 24. Rose early & walked in the Medici Gardens. Met Ld Ebrington[1] smoking a hooka, & Du Kane. A brilliant morning, & warm as summer. The Pantheon. The Villa Pamphili. The lawn covered with anemones of every colour. Walked by the water, & round thro' the pine-grove. The Mountains seen thro' the trees; the water sparkling in the sun & now delicious to the ear. Walked & saw the marbles of the Vatican, the tapestries representing the cartoons of Raphael, & the Stanze, a walk of unrivalled grandeur & beauty. What a volume of antiquity is unrolled in the first sala—what divine beauty in the stanze. To-day & yesterday open to all Rome, the only days in the year. Heard the first miserere again. Another was sung at the same time in St Peter's. An exquisite evening. The air balmy & full of sweet odours on coming out of the chapel, & transparent, discovering the moving crouds at a little distance with a black & clear outline. No atmosphere In the Evening walked thro' the Coliseum & the forum by Moonlight. When under the high side of the first, its breadth & heighth almost overcoming.

Saturday. Mch 25 . . . Called in the evening on Lucien Bonaparte.

Sunday. Mch 26. Went thro' the desert, & among the tombs to Tivoli, turning up in to it, thro a wild grove of olives. The temple. A deep glen winding into the Mountains, hung with magnificent olive-woods & opening to the campagna & the sea, a circular temple on a rocky precipice—a river-fall, a cataract— The view of Mæcenas's villa from the other side—A long classical building full of arches above a white fall, the valley, the mountains beyond it, cypresses, rock, foam, catching lights & brown shadows, & the noise of waters dashing along at your feet—But the many falls, & the many turns of this magnificent glen presenting a thousand pictures, have been so often painted, why add more? Foam illuminated by sunshine, rain-bows, & every charm of rock & water! The Grotto of the Syrens. Surely the water white as snow bursting thro' the darkness of the cavern, is the first thing of the kind in the World. Met a girl going bare-shod to a chapel of our Lady among the Mountains,

[1] Hugh, Viscount Ebrington, *b.* 1783, eldest son of Earl Fortescue.

gaily drest. It was Easter-Sunday, & many young women, in their best attire, were sallying forth. 'Look there, said our Guide, those people on the top of that Mountain, 'they are gone up to eat something.'—Large buckles, exceeding all we had seen. Descended, leaving the ruins of Adrian's villa among the cypresses on the left. How rich in associations is Tivoli. Horace & Catullus, Claude & Poussin have given it a lustre not its own, yet in itself it is a gem of the first order. Sat half an hour in the olive-grove over against Mæcenas's Villa, the most classically beautiful, the most romantic, the gayest scene in the world!

Monday. Mch 27. Left Rome at noon. A Summer's day. The Mountains always beautiful. Snow on many. Sun-set. Stars rising & setting, & coming out by degrees.

Tuesday. Mch 28.—Slept at Ronciliogno, & now before light. A noble view of the Appenines on the right, in dark mist; the Tiber, a line of silver, sweeping along their bases. The Lago de Vico, & its woody shores. Viterbo. Detained there six hours. Interview with the Governor, a Bishop in his purple stockings. —Petrarch arrived here lame from the kick of a horse. Sermon. Benediction. Beat of drum without, ringing of a bell within; the people kneeling. A singular assemblage of scarlet hoods. Sat on the grass in a field near the Florence-Gate, & looked at the Mountains. Set off at 3. following a coach full of ecclesiastics. Left them behind at the first Post-house. Lago di Bolsena; its islands & its hanging woods. A beautiful evening. Bolsena. Smart girls at the well. Rich sun-set on the Lake. Star-light. Guards with the carriage before & behind. Slept at Aquapendente.

Wednesday. Mch 29. The Mountain. Radicofani on the summit. Larks singing. A bleak prospect on every side. Proceeded with mules; descending by degrees into a softer country—meeting a file of soldiers, & afterwards the Grand Duke's Courier, all asking for news. Walked on the bridge & slept at Ponte D'arbia—The sky rose-colour at sun-set! The stars brilliant!

Thursday. Mch 30. Rose at 4. Splendid Moon-light. Sienna & its towers soon appeared on an elevation under the hills as we advanced along the Val D'Arbia. The Casino of the Nobles. The Piazza pleased me greatly. The Palazzo Publico, the torre della Mangia, the Palaces of the Sansedoni & the Ghigi & Saracini, with pointed windows, reminded me of Venice; & had an eastern, a Saracenic look. Antient Fresco Paintings in the Palazzo Publico. The Cathedral of marbles black & white had a very antique, solemn air. The floor by Beccafumi, inlaid with marbles white & black representing sacred history. Mass performing & the organ playing. Saw in the Baptistery rich & venerable within, without of the same complexion as the Cathedral, a Lady & a little girl confessed, & the communion administered by the Confessor. The Public library small, neat & with eclesiastical figures in it, like a Weanix or a DeNeuf. The public walk gay with statues & looking towards the Mountains. The country, at first full of country houses scattered up & down, grew more & more mountainous; convents & castles, & little towns here & there under the afternoon-sun. A romantic & hilly stage from Poggibonsi to Barbarino where we slept, just without the walls on the mountain-top—In the West the hills of Pisa & Lucca—in the east Radicofani, mountains on every side, ridge beyond ridge, & many villas & casinos of the Ricardi & other Florentine Nobility in sight with their turrets & loggie & cypresses. The sun set gloriously, & an intermediate glen lay at our feet, broken & winding & solemn in the highest degree. What colours above the horizon in an Italian sky, when the sun has just gone down!

Blue
Rose-colour
Pale Yellow
Amber
Deep Orange

The 'Celestial rosy red' diffused far & wide, such as I never saw in our Northern sky, never in an Italian Painting—Nor am I sure it would please in Painting—yet in Nature who could turn his eyes from it? It went; & the orange & the blue remained, & the stars came out—

Friday. Mch 31. A Heavenly morning, Walked out & saw the sun rise nearly opposite to where it had set. It rose as it set without a cloud. Continued among the mountains, many farm houses & convents in sight, till from a brow we had a rich view of the Vale of Arno & its cypresses, the domes & towers of Florence breaking thro' the trees below. A Carthusian Convent magnificently seated on the left. Schneider's. The Tribune. The Cathedral The Medici Chapels. The Gate of Ghiberti.

Saturday. April 1. The Chapel of Masaccio in the Carmine. Saw a Lady at prayers with a lighted taper in her hand. After breakfast called on Faber[1] & the Tribune, & the different chambers—the Bronzes, the Vases &c. Went halfway up the hill of Fesole. Silvertop, Du Cane & Fazakerly at dinner & Lord J^{no} Russell.

Sunday. April 2. The Church of S^a Maria Novella, The Altar Piece of St Catherine. The Cross of Giotto.

The Church of St Lorenzo. The tombs of the Medici. Took leave of the Phantom! the organ & choir at a distance. The Church of the Annonciata where in the Cloisters are the Madonna del Sacco—& the history of The Beautiful Gate of Ghiberti by A. del Sarto also.—Sat on the Sasso of Dante behind the Dome of the Cathedral, & visited the monuments of Gallileo, M. Angelo & Machiavel in the Church of Santa Croce. The Bridges, the reflections on the River, the Mountains. Set off at 3, having been told by Orsi, when getting up, that the Neapolitans would be here to-morrow night. Very sultry. Multitudes of Primroses & Violets every where. The Pratolino. The Colossal Figure of the Apennine, shaggy as with petrifactions. A wild boar in a cavern. his bristles. small & rather wild than fierce. View towards Florence from the balcony. Wood-full of Primroses—behind the house.—Mountain-valley. River. Villages. Castle of the Grand Duke. The Maschere. The villagers there at Cards. Sultry as the Dog-days. After all Florence strikes me most. I acknowledge the Grandeur of Rome, the Beauty of Naples; but Florence has won my heart, & in Florence I should wish to live beyond all the Cities in the World. Rome is sad, Naples is gay; but in Florence there is a cheerfulness, a classic elegance that at once fills & gladdens the heart.—

Monday. April. 3. Waked in the Night by the baggage & carriages of the old King of Spain passing under the Window. A bright moonshine. Overtook them afterwards in a state of hesitation—some returning—those in advance having been seized at Bologna. Men at house-doors called to us, saying the Neapolitans were at Bologna; & even at Lojano. Saw the fire at Pietra Mala. like the flames of a lime-kiln—very hot to

---

[1] ? Fabre. *v.* footnote on p. 191.

approach—the air in a liquid undulating state over it—a foot high—the rock or fragments of rock on which it seems to prey black with smoke—wherever with a stick you form a small furrow—& carry a flame into it, you kindle fresh fire—Fresh news along the road—that the Enemy were advancing, that war was begun. Extensive view among the hills—& from the summit towards the Adriatic—A delicious evening—Slept at a lone house within twelve miles of Bologna. the blackbird singing—& the night-jar's voice like the grass hopper's or the frog's in the hedge.

Tuesday. Ap. 4th. Rose at half past three. Saw the Moon-rise. A beautiful halo round it, not unlike that on which the dove is represented in the Dispute of the Sacrament. Raphael must have had such a thing in his mind. Saw the sun rise, round & without beams. Descended into a valley. Bologna in full view. Met a Pilgrim who said no horses could enter the town & that the bridge was shut. Met others who confirmed it, & others with their mules, having left the waggons at the gate; their mules being liable to seizure. Crossed the bridge, & stopped at a small house without the gates. Sent in a scout (D. Cane) who saw the King get into his carriage & set off with his staff. Went in, myself, the gates open, the streets silent & almost empty. Saw the Compte de Mosebourg. 'Je'm'engage pour vous, Monsieur. Officers in calashes, & baggage-waggons passing continually. Rumours of a battle. Music in the Grande Place. Ice in the Caffée—Crouds in the Arcades.

Wednesday. Ap. 5. Troops filing thro'. A battle last night. A wounded officer leaning on his servant in the street. Gen¹ Filangaie[1] dangerously wounded. Called again on Mosebourg. Said he would write to the King to-night, & asked us to dinner. Lord Jⁿᵒ Russell & Fazakerley arrived. Went to the Chapel of St Luca. An immeasurable plain lost in mist. The Apennines & its numerous ridges rising immediately on the south side. Bologna & its high towers at our feet. The Cavalry discovered by a long cloud of dust proceeding towards Ferrara. The Custode of the Church saw the flashes of the guns yesterday. The Pictures of the Zambeccari Palace Frescoes of Ludovico Caravaggio & Guido! The former divine. Mat-screens from the

[1] Carlo Filangieri, 1784–1867, Prince of Satriano, Neapolitan soldier and statesman.

sun over the stalls in the Grande Place. All the world sitting out of doors night & day. Figs in leaf. Horse-chesnuts in full flower. The vines beginning to open their leaves from tree to tree. Dined & went to St. Michele in Bosco. A view of Bologna & its towers & the houses in its environs. Thro' the trees along its winding walk upwards the town appeared by glimpses with rich effect. Prisoners marched into town to-night to a convent— & wounded soldiers bandaged up—on Cars. Saw a Pilgrim, his shoulders hung round with cockle-shells.

Thursday. Ap. 6. Went to an Antiquarian's & saw the Great Mogul's pipe & the Pope's slipper. Walked to the Public Garden, where the guns had been heard yesterday in the direction of Ferrara. Lilacs in full blow. Saw some Correggios in a Palace & eat ice. Dined at Moseberg's. A good dinner of one course with removes. The Commandant there. The Archb^{ps} Palace. Off to-morrow.

Friday, Ap 7. Set off at half past 5. Soldiers on the road. New graves. Fresh earth. Straw spread. Fragments of cloth. Men raking the ground smooth. A house full of bullet-holes. Tête du Pont shattered. Soldiers bivouacking before the gates of Modena.—Much conversation in the streets. The Commandant half drest. Breakfasted & saw in the Guirlandina (a tower all marble near the Cathedral) the Secchia rapita—a bucket borne as a trophy from Bologna in a surprize assault, & if we may believe Tassoni[1] the cause of a long war. It is inclosed with iron hoops to preserve it & the handle is iron, being very like an English pail. Saw also the Museum of Pictures. Neapolitan Soldiers filing thro' the town. Went thro' a garden, the festoons of vines just shooting into leaf—the young corn between the trees; & the eye wandering every where as thro' the lightest & greenest grove of feathery foliage. Laburnum in blow in the hedges. White houses of great neatness belonging to sub-stantial Yeomanry, appearing continually at a little distance across the fields. Women & children in groups spinning at the cottage-doors. Reggio, Ariosto's birth-place. Walked in a cloister, while the horses were changing. An Austrian Guard. Red whiskers red noses, light eyes & an erect figure, instead of the dark features & subtle expression & easy air of the Nea-politan. The plough & oxen at work, young girls with wicker

---

[1] Alessandro Tassoni, 1565–1635, in *La Secchia Rapita.*

baskets, at their waists dropping seed into the furrow. Carriages with Ladies & children taking their evening airings as we approached Parma. The Cathedral. The dome of Corregio. Exquisite grace & colours dipt in heaven faded, crumbling & fading away & seen as thro a glass dimly. Light & faint colours flitting, melting away, leaving little more than their memory, like witherd flowers. His angels all his own. A figure of a man on each side of the door by Corregio & by Parmagiano (in Italy called Parmagianino) to distinguish him as I conceive from others of Parma. The first very admirable & noble—Both strongly & firmly painted. The Steccata, built by Bramante. Moses breaking the tables, by Parmagiano, in an archway full of force. The Theatre, very noble & classical. The Studii The garden of the Ducal Palace.—

Saturday, Ap. 8. Saw again the Cathedral, the cieling of Sta Giovanna & the Madonna della Steccata, by a better light. The Colorno, the country residence of nostro Duca, said the driver, a handsome square building in a flat country, surrounded by a dyke. The Po. The bank, full of Austrian sharp-shooters. Sentinels before their straw huts on the bank. Fell down the river to a little town, 3ᵐ. off. Landed & proceeded among vines & mulberries, the country degenerating as we drew near Mantua. Soldiers scattered along the roads, & bivouacking in the fields. Waggons of bread—& ammunition—A lake—Gateways—Bastions—Bridges—The guard-house—the Pass-port—The Opera-house—pretty—elliptical & lighted only from the stage—glimmerings in three or four boxes—A comic opera—

Sunday, April 9. The Gonzagua Palace, belonging to a younger cadet branch of the family—Its front has a barbarous grandeur. built & richly painted by J. Romano. His own house—the front in a little style, but very gay & elegant—1695—Belonging to the Municipality, who have often refused to sell it. The Palazzo T. built & richly ornamented by J[ulio]. R[omano]. Story of Cupid & Psyche. Beautiful room filled with busts & frescoes in small compartments—The Battle of the Giants—A small square room—a cube—with a coved cieling—all the angles smoothed off & painted entirely over, leaving only a door & a window—Jupiter's throne left empty in the centre of the cieling has a fine effect. A cieling of the Sun in his chariot & the Moon in hers admirable for force. The Cathedral built by him after the fashion

of the Basilicas at Rome. Two men confessing—Left the town
thro' a covered gallery—Waggons of wounded soldiers. Retrospect of Mantua, with its dome, & spires & towers; the first
spires I have seen in Italy—a long line just above the waters of
its lake—more like a dutch town than any other. Rice grounds
with their trenches for water. A fete at Roverbella. An old
priest at the Posthouse door asked what news in latin & would
shake my hand at parting. Proceeded thro' vineyards & mul-
berry-grounds till we fell suddenly to the Adige in its rapid
descent from the Alps, & ferried across it. We were soon on the
threshold of that awful portal thro' which we were to pass
towards the frozen regions of the North. Farewel Italy! & am I
never again to see its blue skies & sunny fields—the vines
festooning from tree to tree, the green corn springing under
them, the lizard basking under the ancient wall—never again to
gather wild myrtle—or oranges or citron blossoms on a terrace
over the blue waters of the Mediterranean—never more to tread
its classic ground—I will live at least in the hope of it—[1]
We entered thro' a rocky mountain torn asunder perhaps at the
deluge. On each side it was steep as a wall, the Adige rushing
along by us. A grave with its cross upon it on one side, on which
I glanced the word 'Requiem' half obliterated, a small church on
the other. The valley afterwards widened a little & winded thro'
the Alps, discovering here & there on different sides of the
River little towns full of comfort & cheerfulness. A spire always
in sight, & almost always where it should be, where you would
wish to find it. many boats & rafts, & many a ferry with its line
across, & passengers waiting to pass. The magnificence of the
Mountains folding over one another, topt now & then with
patches of snow, the majestic motion of the river below, & the
beauty, the gaiety of the little societies on its banks presented a
combination hitherto unknown to me, & as night drew on, the
glimmerings of the last & the deep solemnity of the former
rendered the contrast still more affecting. Slept at Ala. At one
moment leaving a little town thro' which we passed, a line of
white houses & boats discovered themselves on the other side of

[1] This hope was realized (see Introduction, p. 108) in 1821. Rogers takes
the following route home: Trento—Bolzano—Brenner—Innsbruck—Ulm—
Stuttgart—Heidelberg—Mainz—Coblence—Cologne—Nijmegen—Amsterdam—Haarlem—Delft—Rotterdam—Antwerp—Brussels—Ostend.

the river—a scene as gay as Kew or Barnes, & reminding me
of them. The young people that ran from opening to opening in a
vineyard-paling to catch a sight of the carriage.
Monday. April 10. Many good houses with loggie & cypresses.
The Post-boy now began to wear his bugle, & blew it very
musically as we descended into Trent. Saw the Cathedral,
gothic. Before it a handsome fountain. Saw also the church in
which the Council was held; a representation of which, full of
portraits is there, & was explained with a loud voice by the
interpreter.—From Lavis to Salurn [Salorno] & from Salurn to
Bransotta the scenery was exquisite, the river sweeping thro'
the narrow valley, shut up behind with dark purple & rugged
mountains, those in front more distant & melting in the sunbeams; an old castle inaccessibly seated, a town white as marble,
a Swiss-like village brown as the fir it was made of, almost
always to be seen. The valley full of vegetation. A boy kneeling
barefoot in a chapel, by his mother probably, his dusty shoes
slung from his back. Night came on, & the glimmering lights up
& down the hills, sometimes, as one would think, above the site
of human dwelling, continued to Bolzano, where we slept. A
Watchman. Italian still talked, as well as German.—
Tuesday. April 11. From Bolzano to Brixen the scenery was
preeminent, heightened perhaps still more by the black shadows
of the morning. You soon enter a narrow pass by which the
Eisach issues, & you ascend nearly to its source. The entrance is
sublime & Dove-dale-like—on a greater scale—Rich vegetation
at first below & blue mountain summits seen thro the foldings in
front—glimpses of glens & their cataracts hurrying into the
Eisach—villages all neatness & tranquillity—old castles—chateaux with high towers—such as are seen in Paul Brill—romantic
wooden bridges roofed in—goats browsing in the woods &
peasants every where dressing the vines or raking the meadows
—yet the wildness, the air of seclusion is never lost—green
meadows—orchards—vineyards full of springing corn—every
pastoral image that a mountain valley can present, unfolds itself
afterwards; (sometimes 7 or 8 spires seen at once)—but when
you have passed Brixen the valley contracts, the river becomes a
torrent, woods of dark fir overhang it & strikingly contrast with
the snowy mountain that closes it behind you; & you drop down
into the little village of Mittinwald, where I slept at the bridgefoot

The glen that leads to the first Post-house from Bolzano, & another in which stands Mittenwald, recovering from the fury of the French, are first-rate; & vetturini on this road are to be preferred to the Post, as there are excellent houses for the traveller at every turn & he may rest where he wishes. The fresh verdure of the Spring relieving the darkness of the ever-greens gave a beauty not to be told—The vines on lattice-frames inclined like a melon-frame.—The Simplon is a stronger blow—The mountain-road from Brige is sublime—the descent to Domo Dossola is savage grandeur suddenly changing into beauty; but so much beauty mixed up with so much romantic wildness, so many places in which you would wish to stop wander & dwell with those you loved, I never saw till now. Walked up towards Brenner half a mile along the road—the Moon was rising over the glen, yet full of night the last gleam of day was on the snowy ridge that shut it up behind—the little church of Mittenwald with its red spire in the bottom—the noise of the torrent & its white foam—among the black firs—the noble & unconquerable spirit of the People shedding a sanctity over it—the solemnity of the hour in such a place—& my distance from home, all rendered it not a little affecting. I must confess that, except the Lake of Lucerne, I saw nothing in Swizzerland to be compared to the sublimer scenes in the Tyrol. A narrow winding glen, not a quarter of a mile wide, the steep sides grey rock half hung with dark woods of fir—a cataract along the middle of it thro' slips of meadow, cornfield & vine-yard, shaded with trees of the liveliest verdure—Wheels on the river for making salt—A snow mountain shutting it in at one end, & everlasting woods at the other, the little village—6 or 7 houses at most—with its wooden bridge, over which a herd of goats are now passing, & its tall church-spire now ringing its evening bell, in the bottom—such is what I should call the valley of Mittenwald. The road from Italy is not a little orna-ment, rising & falling among the trees. In the last retreat of the French, the village was set fire to & nearly burnt to the ground, & the poor woman the wife of my landlord, an industrious farm-ing man went out of her mind & still continues so.

Wednesday. April 12. Winded up the glen to Sterzing in a circular valley—an old castle on a summit & many snow-peaks round it. Inscribed on a chapel within an hour's walk of it—'The

Enemy came with his cavalry so far, & no farther.'—The torrent now becomes a cataract overhung with firs & larches that run among the snows & the road rapidly rises—snow lying in flakes along the sides, & men busy in breaking large masses of ice in the road—'Brenner'—In this stage rose twice the height of St Peter's—the descent rapid—a lake—a long chasm, the torrent far below & almost unheard among the firs—from a bridge looked down on their tops far, far below.

Schonberg. A neat house—a large family—the daughter pretty & in her dress & air, very like Richardson's Pamela or Fielding's Fanny, tho' perhaps a little too vive—Stoves—The kitchen fire on a high table-like structure, & no aperture over it—the cieling black with smoke—yet the room not smoky—Snow on every side—a chain of snow hills within a field or two—Their bustle & assiduity how different from the Italian, who leave you to yourself; a courtesy or something like it that gladdens & sweetens life. Snow lies hereabouts 9^{mos} in the year.

Thursday Ap. 13. A glen of great depth & breadth & hung with its firs, & echoing to its torrent opened soon on the left & was soon followed by another on the right. We descended along a ridge, a hog's back, each in its turn discovering itself thro' the trees—At length Inspruck appeared in a valley encircled with snow-hills. & seen as in a bright winter's day.—The Cathedral. The tomb of Maximilian, the Emperor. His kneeling figure, & marble bas reliefs. Black bronze statues of kings & queens round it had a singular & striking effect. View of the valley from the bridge. Public Walk. Table d'hote of Austrian Officers on their march to Italy. A mountainous & pleasant road up a third wider valley, a river, the Inn, accompanying us. Much timber lying about. Villages full of painted houses. A narrow mountain-pass. Left Inspruck with a pass-port for Lindau & were obliged to continue in that direction whether we would or not. Slept at Barbis, in a very comfortable clean house. Milk in a wooden dish to our heart's content, & butter & eggs. Our Postilion blew his horn, drawing his pipe of brass from his mouth as he approached the inn, & the high feather in his hat gave him a very chivalrous appearance. Posting slower here than in Italy. Their round fair fresh-coloured faces often very expressive, almost always agreable & sometimes very handsome. A strong large race. The weak, probably, die in rearing. The peasants always pull their hats off in passing & the children, if you notice them, kiss your hand.

Friday. Ap. 14*th* The same wild country. An extensive fir-wood —the wood-houses with their low roofs seen here & there under the trees. A small lake green as an emerald inclosed within steep mountains, the road winding up along a precipice by it, & in the midd[l]e a lofty island green with herbage & shaped evidently by art into a pyramid with the ruins of a castle on the summit. A singular scene of extreme seclusion—the mountains flaked with snow—flakes of snow drifted along the road side— A succession of vallies sprinkled over with neat roomy houses after the fashion of those in Berne, tho' less—villages full of painted & gilt fronts—a river of a dingy blue, the Leck, such as those from the melting of the Snows—forces itself thro' a long narrow chasm of rock with noise & fury near Fussen—a striking scene—Its chateaux above it—& on the other side the river widening into a Lake under black woods of fir, snow mountains glistering far above them, forms a noble scene. Rain came on & spread itself over this romantic country—Window-lights continually in view. Slept at Weisbach.

Saturday. Ap 15*th* Heavy fall of snow with little intermission all day. The country gradually less & less mountainous. Noble fir-woods—Wood-houses every where. Timber lying. Deal-yards. Glimpses of lawns thro' the firs of great beauty. Their silver stems. Went a Post stage towards the lake of Constance by mistake & returned on our steps. Neat villages; & faces in every window. Hop-Grounds. Slept at Memmingen—The servants of a house sitting round a dish, each with his spoon, & helping himself in turn—a stew or a sort of macaroni here called 'Italiano'.—

Sunday. Ap. 16. Another snow during the night. Went along a level plain, generally coasting the hills which were little more than a gentle elevation hung with wood, & varied with villages. —Ulm a little town—eat Asparagus there—with a large cathedral, gothic & singularly light but with no rich workmanship.— The choir dark & full of carved wood, rich & barbarous. Crossed a wide plain—like Runnimede, only much larger—circumscribed with distant woods on a gentle elevation—no villages now as before in sight—& few passengers on the road. A cross near it & a rail before the cross, a woman in a green dress kneeling before it. A vast area & she the only living being in sight. Fell into a deep rocky glen that afterwards opened; a stream running thro' it; & at the extremity of it slept in the little village of Geislingen & was there beset with sellers of work in bone & ivory. The head-dresses of the women—calls[1] of their caps—embroidered behind with gold & coloured stones— The belts of the men also embroidered richly, & ornamented with gilt or silver buckles of great size. The church-bell of a singularly rich & deep tone. In the room I slept in Prints from Stothard's[2] drawings of Going to School & Coming from School —German Copies, & two others with his name—La Marche a l'ecole Le Retour de l'ecole—Les Garcons Anglois en Promenade—Les Garcons Ollandois en Promenade—Our Postillions blew their horns very often going up hill—

Monday. Ap. 17. The country richer & more cultivated. towns every where in sight. orchards & vineyards along the hills. The trees in full blossom, the vines not in leaf. The environs of Stutgard a garden. A pretty little town. The Palace large & old fashioned. A German Play in a pretty theatre founded on a story in the time of the troubles in England. Began at 5, & ended at ½ after 8. Attention of the Audience.

Tuesday. Ap 18. Saw Taylor[3] our minister here. Music on the Parade. Walk in the royal gardens. The Menagerie. The camels as in a caravan—two zebras—ostrich, pelicans, beautiful goats, wolves, cats of the mountain—Dakrund the Sculptor.[4] Bust of Schiller, a friend of his. The stables. The Palace. Dined at 4. at Taylor's. Music on the top of the Church tower at sunrise, at noon & at sun-set. Solemn to-day, in consequence of somebody being dead. A trumpet & clarinet. Simple & grand. The Music in the orchestra last night excellent. The curtain never rose till the piece was finished; & the instant an act was over, the people in the pit stood up as with one impulse. The

---

[1] i.e. caul = back part of the cap.

[2] Thomas Stothard, 1755–1834. Rogers knew him well, and possessed several of his works. He made twenty drawings for the 1st complete ed. of *Italy*, thirty-five for the companion volume of *Poems*.

[3] Probably Sir Herbert Taylor, 1775–1839, then on a military mission to Bernadotte in Germany.

[4] Johann Heinrich von Dannecker, 1758–1841. Studied in Rome 1785 ff. where he was influenced by Canova. He became director of the Gallery of Stuttgart.

Chasse, the Court here splendid. The States, now assembled, having remonstrated against the Expenses, the first is to be laid down.

Wednesday, Ap. 19. Waked by the music on the tower, slow, & solemn in the highest degree. a little before six. Lasted about 3ᵐ. Repeated on the other side. Ludwigsburg. Royal Chateau & Gardens. Avenues. Towns & villages, orchards & vineyards. A stork in the fields—& another on a chimney Entered Heidelberg by moonlight. Drove along what appeared to be a lake under a mountain—White houses along the shore the Necker—

Thursday. Ap 20. Waked by a flourish of trumpets, & from the window saw the Place full of cavalry in array. All were gone in half an hour. The ruins of the castle—the hall of chevaliers, the statues of electors & counts Palatine on the outside, many in decay—the ton—the shrubbery walk & terrace, commanding the course of the Necker, Manheim, & a vast plain bounded by blue hills—Proceeded among orchards & cornfields under a chain of little hills thro' many villages—Darmstadt, like a new little city wide streets, broad squares—barracks—villas groves & gardens & garde-houses full of troops—a wide plain, the plough at work every where, & the air sweet from the fir-woods that encircled it. Thro' large woods of fir descended into Francfort—Two storks in the inn-yard—standing together—Good Burgundy—4ˢ a bottle—

Friday, Ap. 21. Walked round part of the town—thro' shrubbery-walks, little country houses of the merchants on one side, the castle-ditch now planted on the other—

Mʳ. Knatchbull, a Clergyman, attached to the Embassy at Stuttgard called & sat with us at breakfast. Thro' an open country to Hattensheim—Saw four hares coursing each other round & round at some distance till we lost sight of them—a flower garden at the post—Questioned by an old General there, as to Italy. His politeness. Passed us with his hat off—Mainz or Mayence a shattered town in a melancholy country, bare of wood & laid waste. Its cathedral—half of it a powder magazine. Its tombs. Its tower, of red stone, & richly wrought.—Soon had a view of the Rhine we had crossed by a bridge of boats near its confluence with the Mein at Mayence—an open country— Niden. Ingelheim—Ruins of Charlemagne's Palace there—now a mere wreck—The Rhine glittering thro' the trees in the

evening-sun under a green hill from the Post-house-garden—
Shewn to us by the Post-master who said Ld Wellington had
spent some hours there with his boys just before in his way from
Vienna—Descended—the Rhine a sheet of silver & losing itself
between the foldings of green hills—Johannisberg, a chateau &
vineyard, now Marshall Kellerman's[1] on the opposite height—
Three or four towns lying along the opposite shore. Bingen, at
the turn of the Rhine.—A castle perched on a point of the turn.
Walked till dusk. Military music, while we were at supper—
Slept there at the Post-house—Good cooking—the German
much more to my taste than the Italian. Good Rhine-wine—
Saturday. Ap. 22. The road runs along the Rhine, a magnificent
terrace-road in a ruinous state. The hills on each side steep &
every where covered with vineyard, but where rock breaks
thro'; their outlines heavy & monotonous—but the great entertainment arises from the towns, churches & ruined castles on
the borders.—almost always two or three towns are in sight, &
tho' nearly alike, throw great cheerfulness over the river—
several islands—people up & down at work in the vineyards—
no navigation—a raft with three men & a new built shed upon
it—three or four boats—the passage-boat returning—fishermen
drying their nets—castle-towers perched on the rocks—often
three or four miles of the river in sight & as many towns &
castles—yet after all the lumpishness of the hills & the little
business on the vast river under it dull & uniform—here & there
the road leaving the river—orchards full of blossoms inter-
vened, sometimes discovering the water by glimpses, sometimes
shutting it out altogether, the last no unwelcome change—the
vines being but half out in leaf, the season was certainly un-
favorable—the wind shifting, the stream rapid—a small boat
carrying a sail with some soldiers on board & two oars—kept up
with us for some time who were on a long trot—but disappeared
behind an island at last—The black tiles of the spires & houses,
& the black beams that seam the white houses disagreable—
Coblentz a large town at the junction of the Rhine & Moselle,
which last enters at a right angle—& seems to the eye to be
actually stopped by the current of the Rhine—It was so also
with the River at Bingen I believe still more remarkably—

[1] François-Christophe de Kellerman, 1735–1820, duc de Valmy, father
of Napoleon's great cavalry general, François Étienne de Kellerman.

Coblentz lies low, but from its many towers makes a good figure as you leave it. The ruins of Ehrenbrutsen, on a perpendicular rock over against it, very striking. A pleasant road across common fields, the right bank of the Rhine lofty & visible, as well as the towns along it, the river itself not so—At last came down to it & continued along to Andernach—a little town within castellated walls—Walked on the Rhine till dusk—more bustle than we had seen upon it before. A charcoal boat towed by horses—Two towns in sight on the other side—& the white reflections of the one, & the glow of sun set on the other very beautiful—The Rhine-salmon crisp & short as the best of the Thames. When caught it is boiled, sprinkled with vinegar & served up cold.

Sunday. Ap. 23. The left bank was let down a little, but the right continued as before—the reaches longer—& many villages & castles always in view—The church-bells combing [?] across the water most musically, & numbers on the other side seen in their best attire going to church; the mountains more rocky, more broken & often pyramidical—The Post-boy went into the house & lit his pipe—A boat with a single sail & eight or nine people on board kept ahead of us—who were at least going at the rate of 6ᵐ an hour—A ferry boat here & there plying. A hollow iron-tube at the Post-house to blow the fire thro'. Bonne. A view along the Rhine from the Elector of Cologne's garden-terrace—The Cathedral—Bones of saints framed & glazed. Half a mile from the town the Post-boy missed his pipe, & leaving his horses, returned on foot along the road to search for it—In half an hour he came back in despair—the Peasants armed with Pikes—now in Prussia Came along a level plain—a tree or two on the horizon & a wind-mill—behind us in deep purple the hills we had left with their broken summits, giving a promise far beyond reality, at least as far as we had experienced; but we wanted verdure & sunshine; & at last the sun breaking out, lighted up into great beauty what before had appeared to us but second-rate materials. The magical influence of light & shadow who has not known & felt?—At length the many churches of Cologne rose before us; & we entered it. The Rhine under our windows, the shipping, the yatchs that ply for Amsterdam, the colliers, the ferry-boat, & that gigantic ferry-stage which is continually shifting from one shore to the other, full of passengers horse & foot, each with his pipe, made a busy scene. The horse-men sat on their horses with pipes in their mouths—& the man, who watched the fire in our stove, stood by very cooly, smoking us with a very cloudy Pipe—A bridge of boats thrown across a quarter of a mile higher up for the allied army to pass over into France. From my window it looked like a spider's thread, knotted & spun across a sea. Exquisite Rhine Salmon. Walked on the Quay—Looked into the Coffee-house—& the Theatre—a comic Opera. The orchestra above the scale of every thing else. On each side of the curtain, gigantic figures of Attention & Silence—One with her hand to her ear, one to her lips—under-written 'Audi' & 'Tace.'—Returning, the vast Cathedral-Tower in the frosty light of the moon, looked like a cluster of Petrifactions. I have just gone to the Window, & the full moon is playing on the river divinely.—

Monday, April 24. Waked in the Night, & from my pillow, an elevated one in Germany, saw the great river under my window stretching away between its banks towards the Mountains. The country open & uninteresting, except when the orchards in full blow approached us, or the river, running along the valley below, doubled back upon us. Now & then we had a noble expanse of water, but entirely unaccompanied. The business upon it small, but rather increased. Passed thro' many large & well-built towns—but the villages (we were in Prussia) were clay-built—the peasants in wooden shoes—& a look of poverty every where. Pleasant walk thro' common fields, the larks singing; & people on foot returning from market. A Hail-storm. Rain. Night. Slept at Gueldres, arriving in the dark.—

Tuesday, April 25. Thro' the same sandy country—At
a procession of people, the Priest carrying a crucifix at their head, round & round the church, a saint painted on a banner preceding all—all with their beads & prayer-books, chanting. Cleves. Avenue of trees in the first verdure of Spring leading to & from it. From the high ground beyond it saw again our old companion the Rhine sweeping along at an hour's distance, ships in full sail on his surface. Nimeguen. From the public walks the river & all Holland stretching far away into the distance. Ferried across the river, & went along a winding causeway for miles, the river with its white sails on our left, orchards in blow, neat farm-houses & gardens full of cucumber-beds on the right.

291

A stork standing on his nest on the ridge of a house. Another stork flying across the road to his. The sun shone out before it set. Night came on, & we entered Tiel at half past nine. All neatness every where—bright window panes, white linen, carpeted floors—Wooden chauf-pieds under the table.

Wednesday. Ap. 26. Thro' an open country, planted with orchard trees & full of corn, went on to the Rhine, over which we ferried into what is properly called Holland—The high tower of Utrecht soon was visible—Chauv-pieds for the men under all the seats in their pews—up which we mounted & saw a circular plain, circled by no hills, intersected with canals—That to Amsterdam (as well as that also to Antwerp) was the most striking—the Treckshuyts upon it that ply to that City every day—at the town's end—At our feet the town with its neat streets, its canals lined with trees, & its bridges over which foot passengers were passing, gardens & groves in its suburbs; a scene of neatness, cheerful activity & comfort. The fish-market. Crossed a plain & came to the banks of the great canal, here winding with all the charm of a natural river, innumerable villas, gardens, wildernesses, & summer-houses Palladian, Chinese, & such as remain in England of the days of King William—along it on each side. Small canals, drawbridges, behind each—no fence to obstruct the eye in its wanderings— How superior to the Brenta! Many canals entered into it The houses small & unassuming, but with an air of comfort how grateful to the eye of an Englishman; the gardens plantations & banquetting houses large in comparison.—Several storks were flying across the water, generally in couples—on the wing they sometimes skim the air beautifully some seen at dinner, others afterwards at tea—Two on their nest on a sort of sarcophagus evidently built for the purpose on the roof of a house—In several trees also we saw their nests—Many aquatic fowls on the wing. Women rowing—& pumping—cows grazing & milking in the meadows—At length several towers & steeples were seen among windmills at a distance, & at length along a great canal resembling a noble river we entered Amsterdam. Its many wide streets, canals, & bridges—boats moving every where— Its universal propriety & cleanliness—ever chearful, ever busy —whiteness of the linen, & the red & white complexions of the women & children, many with good features—Most of the men with the orange ribbon in their hats[1]—An heroic opera in dutch—Between it & the farce, several national airs were called for & played, together with God save the King—some of the Audience beating time with their hands—A ballet—A small & dusky theatre—Not full—

Thursday. Ap. 27. Hail. Sunshine View of the City from the observatory at the top of the Institute, its houses all ridges & pointed fronts & chimneys surmounted with black fanes—its canals planted with trees now in the freshest verdure, & lightest of foliage—a circle of flat country—the sea on one side—with its shipping—The Palace as fitted up by Louis, now faded & in neglect—& the Museum of Pictures, many excellent, some exquisite. A Van Huysum of fruit, another of flowers, an Ostade with a window, a Gerard Dow, the subject a village-school by candle-light—a portrait of Admiral De Ruiter!!—Two, of the DeWitts, (& a picture of their bodies as exposed after death, very properly hung in a dark corner) fill the mind with regret. The new church in which is the tomb of De Ruiter—the old church in which are some painted windows, historical, but poorly executed, the Exchange broad & handsome, the Fishmarket, larger than Billingsgate—& in a similar situation—a coffee-house full of tobacco fumes, almost every man with his pipe—the Arsenal (went on board a frigate building & saw a boat with copper nails designed as a present for the Emperor of Russia—the Promenade, green allies—the Botanic Garden, no flowers in blow—the Neatness of the Women our constant theme—water every where, trees of a lively verdure every where—women as you follow them discovering full red cheeks beyond a cap of snow, & when you meet them, often handsome—No where can you meet Youth in such freshness, or age so blooming—all in quick motion all cheerful & stirring—more quizzical little bourgeois-like figures with a cocked hat & tye-wig with big curls, snuff-coloured coat & broad frills than in England—Such people wear out slowly here—Dined & drove along a pavement over many bridges—thro' plantations & between tea-gardens,

---

[1] The exiled prince of Orange was brought back to Amsterdam in November 1813 when a rising of the inhabitants, wearing the orange ribbon, had turned out the French. In March 1815 the prince became King of the Netherlands, as William I. The regime was now threatened by the return to power of Napoleon.

tea & coffee-rooms & alcoves without number. Drank lemonade in one, where some voices male & female were singing Orange Boven[1] & other songs very agreably. As we came back the lights were gleaming every where on the water. A wind-mill near the road against a western-sky, magnificently dark & such as Rembrandt has painted. The wind-mills here are elevated to a great height & in the twi-light may strike imaginations less fervid than Don Quixote's.—Wherever you go, at every turn you have a Teniers, a Cuyp, a Vanderveldt, a Gerard-dow, so faithfully have those enchanting Painters represented a Country that knows little or no change. Chariots drawn like sledges on the ground by a single horse. Men in deep crape & powdered periwigs announcing the death of a Person to all his acquaintance—

Friday, Ap. 28. Walked by the Canal side, for half an hour early. Milk-pails bright. Silent & persevering energy of a boy punting a barge along. It passed & turned down a side-canal under a bridge. A stall for selling slices of cucumber in salt water, & eggs boiled hard. Made a little excursion into North Holland & ferried with oar & sail across the Eye or Ye—All the boats & barges in motion—fish-woman in a boat receiving the fish from a fisherman's sailing vessel—Went in an open carriage along canals to Brock, a village like a succession of scenes in a new comic opera—the houses as painted yesterday—almost all wood & in various colours—the windows bright—the courts pebbled in mosaic figures—the public walks (all foot-ways) swept & smooth as in a pleasure-ground. The great doors richly carved & pannelled, nor ever opened but for a wedding or a funeral. Met the Burgomaster of the Village, a plain elderly man in a suit of ditto, very erect & with a slim waist & ruddy cheeks, with spectacles on his nose & a pipe in his mouth. Made a most courteous bow in passing. Had opened his great door last year for the Emperor Alexander, of Russia. A small lake or bay bordered with houses & gardens & chinese railings & pavilions, the path of the village running in & out among the little courts & gardens, & shop-doors never losing sight of the water gay with boats & a barge or two, all like a scene in a *Sterling* place, every

[1] i.e. Long live the house of Orange! A play called *Orange Boven* was produced in London in December 1833. It concerned the events mentioned in the previous note.

house like the cottages of the *rich* in England—Walked in three
Gardens—one full of box cut into chairs & tea-tables & stags &
dolphins—the others full of winding paths that double back upon
one another, their twistings well concealed by hedges—water
with wooden swans, a hermitage with a wooden hermit, another
with a man in a cocked hat reading, a recess with a man levelling
a real fowling-piece in your face—a white linen stock & gilt
buckle round his neck the girl our guide felt the buckle—(the
gardener seemed delighted with the surprize of one of the
company.) a tea-house with a servant-maid bringing in the tea-
things—& many temples, pagodas & obelisks—the paths—
strewn with broken shells—Went afterwards along the Ye to
Saardam—a larger place, dismal to approach—in a marsh intersected with ditches—& crouded with windmills—forlorn &
repulsive as a distant object, but the instant you enter it, a
magician seems to have waved his wand—houses all neatness &
comfort shaded by rows of trees run round a little bay full of
sails—you forget all you have passed, the brilliancy of the water,
the bustle, the groups on the shore, the church covered with ivy
—the gardens & plantations in & out—make you wish to stay &
sorry to go—Two young ladies came in a one horse-chair,
driven by a man—their dazzling complexions & singular head-
dresses—gold bandeaus, points & lappets & fillets of silk of
various colours, short jackets, & full petticoats—they seemed to
be shopping & they walked up the village together like things
from some new world. Vast wealth is said to be acquired in this
remote & comfortless corner of Europe—the wives & daughters
have fashions of their own—& the Goldsmiths of Amsterdam
form braids & circlets of gold, sometimes set with diamonds,
such are never worn in that city, for them & them only—Far
from adopting the fashions of other countries, their wealth
seems to be spent only in giving splendour to their own. Eat
Water-souchee Basse—an exquisite fish of the size of large
Tench—with the sweetness of Perch but with more crispness—
Returning saw several storks fishing or on wing & had long a
full view of Amsterdam, its roofs & towers intermixed with
masts—less in the water than Venice, & rather running along a
green level shore.—Went up & down the streets. Plate Glass
in the windows Magnificence of the Merchant's houses—M^r
Hope's—A snuff-seller in a cocked hat & spectacles & rich

banyan[1]—at his door. The shops richly furnished & from their neatness, & the brightness of the window-panes not to mention the propreté of the figures within, in many respects surpassing most in London, & far those of every other City, not excepting Paris—

The Dutch, by planting trees wherever water ran, have given a chearful charm to a Morass—Canals they love to a madness—they make them where they dont find them—along the side of every road—round every villa—every one has a canal of his own & builds as near the public canal as he can—& thro' every orchard, & garden—a passion fatal in Batavia—often productive of bad odours here—but not noxious, if we may judge from the faces you meet with. Their extreme neatness no doubt contributes greatly to their health. The water they drink comes in stone-bottles from Utrecht.—& their pipes[2] were first used in self-defence—The cows graze in the meadows with body-cloaths on.—

Saturday. Ap. 29. Pleasant houses & gardens on the Harlem Canal. Sea of Harlem. Harlem a pleasant town full of trees & canals. Fish market. Turbot. Bass & Dutch sauce at Breakfast. Gathered a nosegay of Hyacynths, Wall-flowers & Rynunculus's—all of a first-rate kind in the Garden of A. C. Van Eden & Cº. on the Wageweg. who sells all sorts of oignons a Fleurs. His hyacynths declining, his tulips coming on. Said not an Amateur of Tulips was in Harlem or Amsterdam. The Passion was over in Holland. A yellow hyacynth he valued at 50 Gˢ. Flowers in almost every window. A Statue of Michael [3] the Founder of Printing with a book in his hand in the Great Place—Mr Hope's house with a white front in the wood. Heard a Nightingale there. Saw in the town on a door the tablet of rose-coloured silk covered with rich lace to denote that the Mistress of the house was lying in. A slip of paper inserted between the silk & the lace announced it to be a daughter. In a village a stork's nest on a high pole erected for the purpose. Two upon it at the time we passed. On the ridge of a church a

[1] A loose jacket.

[2] *Pyp* = small dyke.

[3] It is Lourens Coster, 1370–1440, who is considered in Haarlem to deserve this title. The present statue of him in the Grote Markt dates only from 1856.

trough for the same purpose & the bird within it. Left Leyden within less than a mile of us—with its dome & its towers—the town-hall visible in which J[no] of Leyden's work-table is preserved, & the Pigeons that carried on the correspondence with the Prince of Orange during the siege—the Church of St Peter in which is Boerhaave's[1] tomb—Crossed the Rhine in a pleasant but very reduced condition this morning.

Villas & woods & gardens began now to line the road till we arrived at the House in the Wood.[2] Rooms richly furnished with China Paper & Japan-work. A noble Room painted over by Rubens & Vandyke & Jordaens. The last the principal performer. Great comfort—The Gardens not striking from the windows.—Thro' the Wood came on to the Hague; a very handsome small town, full of squares, wide streets, & shady malls—yet of that unassuming quiet character so striking in Holland; where all the villas are small, all the town-houses solid not shining. A dull dinner at the table-d'hote—Saw the chamber in which the deputies of the states assemble—& that in which they meet the Statholder, now King—Gravely Respectable, not splendid. Walked a little in the Wood. Eat delicious Gouffres. A comic Opera. The house rather below the rank of the town in plan, size & decoration. A little piece of 3 acts in which Henry V. was the hero.—To the windows in Holland—are fixed mirrors a foot in height & breadth, or wider & longer—generally an oblong or a circle that move up & down, & on hinges to reflect the moving pictures in the street. Sometimes another mirror reflects from the first & throws it right into the room! There are generally two to a window & sheltered called a Spiune or Specune[3]

Sunday, April 30. A pleasant road among villas & gardens & along a canal, treckschuyts full of company & barges with white sails passing by. At Delft a neat town, with a handsome place saw the tombs of Tromp, & Grotius & William of Nassau the founder. His statue in armour resembles much his picture in the chamber of the States at the Hague. At each corner is an alle-

---

[1] Herman Boerhaave, 1668–1738, surgeon and scientist.
[2] i.e. Huis ten Bosch, just outside the Hague, begun in 1647 and extended in 1734–37 by David Marot. Louis Bonaparte spent much of his time here during his reign as King of Holland.
[3] i.e. *Spion.*

gorical figure. One bears on her sword a hat inscribed the cap of liberty. It is evidently after his hat, being according to the fashion of that day. a spanish hat turned up & buttoned in front. His dog is there at his feet. Thro' the same succession of house & garden & wilderness & canal & orchard in full blow to Rotterdam—the streets & canals generally wider & fuller of shipping than those of Amsterdam. A handsome Exchange. The bronze Statue of Erasmus on the great bridge, in a doctor's gown; well-conceived & executed. He holds a book open in a thoughtful but chearful attitude. No painter seems to have done more justice to another, than Holbein to Erasmus, & Sr Thos Moore. The same cheerful scenery as before to the Meuse. Certainly no country exhibits such a succession of water, trees & shipping so agreably mixed up together as Holland, & the trees are just now of the liveliest verdure. Such a country in other hands would have been intolerable—Ferried across the Meuse twice, once with a sail, once with a rope—& sailed across a wide arm of the sea from Buitensluis to Willemstadt. The women to-day along the road & in every village & at every door in all their Sunday finery—Gold bandeaus on the forehead, gold ear-rings like a serpent or a ram's horn, a hat like a vast skimming-dish, straw on the upper side, a flowered linen on the under, & flat with a low crown. The shoes embroidered & like the Turkish Slipper. A warm Evening. Sun-shine & rain. Slept literally on the straw at Willemstadt, a lively & populous little village—Many talk a little English there.—Saw 8 or ten storks to-day flying sportively together at a considerable height. Saw a dog & cat at play together in a farm-yard.

Monday. May 1. Proceeded thro' a stiff clay at 6—Ferried over into a sand & continued to move slowly & sleep with little interruption till we rattled on the pavement of the road from Gorcum to Antwerp. Now in a Catholic Country. Women in a little chapel. Military in the road. Thro' a wood came into Antwerp. A multitude at work on the fortifications. A regiment of Hanoverians in the great place. The Church of St James's. Chapel & Tomb of Rubens. A charming Picture of his, there, engraved, I believe, by Jegher.[1] Collection of Flemish Pictures. Rubens's house—the view across the interior court, & thro' the

---

[1] Christoffel Jegher, a friend of Rubens, worked in the first half of the seventeenth century. The picture is the Altarpiece in the Rubens chapel.

archway into the garden, just as represented in the Print—evidently the work of a great Painter—no correct taste, no exact principles in the detail—but the richness the depth, the breaking of lights & shadows admirable. The sun was in the garden. The great church. The tower rich & light & peculiar. The number of the aisles—the height & elegance of the lantern—In the evening drove & walked on the river, the sunset a deep orange, & the tints on the water innumerable. The tackle & cordage of the shipping seen in the twilight against the western sky—fine as a cob-web—& intricacy itself—The coffee-houses in the Place Verte & the grande Place very gay at Night. Antwerp a very handsome town—the streets, places & houses give here & there a noble perspective.—

Tuesday, May 2. The country gradually improves as you draw near upon Brussells. The Palace, once inhabited by the Archduke, afterwards by Josephine, on an eminence among some woods on the right. Brusselles—Entered it by the Allée Verte. —high houses, narrow streets, the cathedral—the Park & its green allies, & its groves full of birds—white houses all handsome & some palace-like, fronting it on every side. The Concert. Catalain.[1] Lord Wellington. King & Queen of the Pays Bas. Full of Gaiety & Warlike Preparation.

Wednesday. May 3. The church. The Exhibition. The Museum. Rubens. Vandyke. The Park. Creeveys.[2]

Thursday. May 4. Avenues. Single houses. Ghent. Its turrets. People at work to prevent a surprize. The French King in the Prefet's house. The Cathedral, very handsome. High Mass there in great Pomp. The Place d'Armes. Its shady walk. The Theatre, small & shabby, but full to the cieling of the best company. Orange Boven. Henry IV. God save the King. Gretry's Music. Ami de la Maison by Marmontelle.[3]

Friday May 5. The Road full of English Cavalry. The promenade along the canal. Exchanged horses with an English Officer & some Ladies. Yellow heath in blossom. Larks &

[1] Angelica Catalani, 1779–1849, Italian opera singer. In 1814 she returned from a highly successful stay in London to take over the direction of the Théâtre-Italien in Paris. During the Hundred Days she toured Germany and the Low Countries.

[2] Thomas Creevey, 1768–1838.

[3] Opera, 1775. Words by J. F. Marmontel, 1723–99, music by A. E. M. Grétry, 1741–1813.

The Italian Journal

Nightingales. Boys tumbling by the road-side, to get money. Bruges a large town. Country desolate & sandy as you approach the sea. Ostend. Shipping. Soldiers. Large Market Place. English Theatre. Went on board two Packets. Coffee house. Contrary Winds—Billiards & Smoking & English tongues in motion.

Saturday. May 6. Music in the Great Place. Green Market. The Major in the Hotel de Ville. Walk on the Rampart. Saw the horses slung from three transports. Cannon balls landed on the shore. Wind. NNW.

APPENDIX 1

Passages omitted from the Text

─────────────⟨≋⟩─────────────

The 2nd, 3rd, 4th, and 5th passages are not part of
the narrative and there is no certain indication of when
they were written. They are signified in the printed text
by . . . at the point where Rogers appears to have written them,
or where they seem to relate most closely to the text.

page *line*

134 23 *Aug.*st 25. Museum! Pont Neuf. Notre Dame. High

Mass. Invalides. Fine singing. Ecole Militaire.
Champs de Mars. Pont de Jena. Gardens of the
Thuilleries. At night illuminations. Palais de Corps
Legislatif.
Aug. 26. Bibliotheque Nationale. Place Legislatif.
Pont de Jena. Palace of King of Rome. Museum.
Theatre Feydau. Palais Royal.
Aug 27. Monumens Francais. Chancelier L'Hopi-
tal. Thuanus. La Fontaine. St Sulpice. Musée.
Apartments in the Thuilleries. Salle de Trone.
Bed-chamber. Saw the King go out in his carriage—
'Je l'ai bien vue! said a Frenchman. The Opera,
Pelage
Aug 28. Jardin des Plants. Wild animals. Elephant.
Pantheon. Luxenburg Palace & Gardens. Rubens.
Le Souer. Vernet. Hall of the senate. Museum.
Thuilleries Gardens. Tivoli. Rope-dancing. Quad-
rilles. Fire-works. A ballet & scenery, concluding
with a cascade of fire.

226 26 To be seen more than once in Rome—
The Coliseum. The Capitol. View from the tower,
& walk thro' the forum. St Peter's. The Vatican.
The Arches & Columns. Capella Sestina. View from

the Ponte Rotto. View of the Aqueduct from a balcony behind the Scala Santa. View of the Coliseum from the upper path in the field thro' which you descend into the Baths of Titus. View from the Place of the four fountains. Farnese Palace. Farnesiani. Summer-house of the Rospigliosi. View from the Villa Mellini. View of Rome from the Loggia of Raphael in the Vatican, or from the loggia below it, at the entrance. The Doria & Colonna Palaces. The Villa Pamphili Doria. The Villa Madama. The Pantheon. The tomb of Cecelia Metella & the surrounding scenery,—Chapel of Nicholas V in the Vatican Fresco there by J^{no} of Fiesole. View from Trajan's Column & the Lante Villa. Palazzo Scha & Doria. Chapel of the Ghisi by Raphael in St Maria del Popolo   Chapel of Strozzi in St Andrea della Valle by M A   Altarpieces by Domenichino in the Church of St Maria delle Angeli & Chapel of St.

To be seen more than once in Florence—

The Gates of Ghiberti.

M. Angelo's Chapel.

The Tribune, & the Niobe.

Chapel of Bransacci in the Carmine.

Madonna del Sacco by A. del Sarto.

Vestibule of the Annonciata. Cloister of the Frate, painted with the life of J^{no} the Baptist. Piazza di Gran Duca. Ponte della Trinita. Boboli Gardens. Cathedral. Campanile. View from the Ponte Reale, particularly at Sun-set. Fesole. Vallambrosa.

Homer has peopled all this region with horrors— Virgil that of Avernus alone, throwing his tender graces over the neighbouring scenes. Marcellus died here, & here was he seen by Eneas,

Demanding life, impatient for the skies.

History has also ennobled what Poetry has consecrated.

Pompey, Varro, Lucullus, Cicero, Hortensius & Cesar dwelt here. (Lucullus on the Promontory of

Misenus, where Marius had lived)—the villas of
Marius, Pompey & Cesar were on the Mountains,
says Seneca—Then came Augustus & with him
Agrippa, Mecænas, Virgil & Horace—then, alas,
Tiberius came into the house of Lucullus on the very
summit, looking to the Sicilian & the Tuscan seas—
& from that instant Murder & Profligacy had their
reign, nor could Silius, Martial & Statius, tho' they
sung that shore, wipe away the stains. stains only to
be done away by earthquakes war & pestilence.—

264   15   Pompei & Stabia overwhelmed in 79—with Her-
culaneum—but before that City; the cinders, accord-
ing to Pliny, having been discharged before the lava.
more skeletons found in the two first, to the last
more warning having been given. Pompei 3ᵐ in
circumference.
A little theatre roofed.
A great theatre.
A great temple overthrown by the earthquake in 63.
Temple of Isis restored after the earthquake
Streets paved with lava, & furnished on both sides
with footways; & at intervals with stepping stones.
Many shops of perfumes, millers
Tomb of Mammia, the Priestess, & semicircular
seat
Villa of Pompei—near the tombs of the Arria
Family.
The Ampitheatre.
Pompei was the Emporium of many other cities.
The Sarno washed it on the western side, & the sea
came up to its walls. But on account of this iruption
in the reign of Titus, the sea withdrew itself to the
distance of two miles, & the Sarno changed its
course & its mouth.

264   32   The gulph of Puzzuoli—a league wide, a league in
length.
Tacitus calls it *Lacus Baianus*
Lake *Avernus*—from the Greek *Wanting Birds*.
Formerly hung round with forest,—now no longer

page   line

'A lake black with the darkness of woods, over which no birds can pass with impunity.'
A temple opposite the grotto. Lake Fusaro, called in Strabo *Acheron* & *that* on which Charon plied his boat. A royal Pavilion is now upon it. Near it the Villa of Vatia, described by Seneca.
Eneas, landing at Cuma, found a temple of Apollo. Sylla died in his retreat near Cuma. Torre di Patria, a league north of Cuma, at the mouth of the Liturnum or Clanio—the site of the retreat of Scipio Africanus.

275   23   The Same Walk thro' the Vatican. The Lanti Villa. View of Rome. The Groups on Monte Cavallo. The Barbarini Palace.

Books used by Rogers

Work and Edition used by Rogers	*Reference*	*page*	*line*
Sansovino, F., *Venetia descritta in XIV. libri, correcta, emendata,e ampliata da Giov. Stringa*, Venet., 1604	Sansovino, 240, 24	174	9
	Sansovino, 66	174	26
	Sansovino, 144	175	13
	Sansovino, 102	176	4
	v. also	177	4
De Sade, J. F. P. A., *Memoires pour la vie de François Pétrarch*, 3v, Amsterdam, 1764–7	De Sade, III, 674, 724, 799	181	40
	Petrarch, III, 74, De Sade	276	20
Gibbon, Edward, *Decline and Fall of the Roman Empire*, 6v, London, 1782–8	Gibbon, C 41, Note 4, 186	184	15
	See Gibbon, C 30, 26	205	16
	C 51, Note	233	20
	v. also	229	34
Vasari, Giorgio, *Vite de' piv eccellenti Pittori Scvltori Architettori*, 3v, Fiorenza, 1568	Vasari, 719 & 52	190	14
	Vasari, 164 & 5	190	30
	See Vasari, 298, 9	191	10
	Vasari, 84	198	6
	Vasari, 134	222	20
	Vasari, 208	222	31
	Vasari, 361	231	18
	Vasari, 73	304	1
	v. also	180	12
	and	199	32
		243	23

u

The Italian Journal

Work and Edition used by Rogers	Reference	page	line
Condivi, Ascanio, *Vita di Michelagnolo Buonarroti* (no indication of ed. The reference is to § LXIX)	See Condivi	191	11
Cellini, Benvenuto, *Autobiography* (no indication of ed. The reference is to Chap. 3)	See B. Cellini	191	11
Martialis Epigrammatum Libros XV, Parisiis, 1680, p. 219	Martial Lib IV. ep. 44 *tristi mersa favilla*	253	10

APPENDIX 3

The Evolution of 'Meillerie'

───────────────❦───────────────

The verses entitled 'Meillerie' were first printed in the 1830 edition of *Italy*. The Journal contains a rough prose preparation for them, and a set of verses that are fairly close to those finally printed.

(i) In pencil, upside down on two sheets at the end of the first notebook. The last lines are encroached on in ink by the end of the entry for Oct. 15th. One word is illegible.

(ii) In ink, upside down on both sides of the last sheet of the second notebook. Rogers went over this version in pencil, filling in blanks and making alterations. These pencil additions are printed in italics.

(iii) The relevant parts of 'Meillerie' as printed in 1830.

I

Enchanting Meillerie! Nature framed thee in her
    mood ~~moment~~
happiest ~~hour~~! Thy grey rocks that tower to heaven,
thy woods that fold & unfold, discovering a thousand,
                                   itself
thousand little lovely recesses & the lake ᴧ & its dark
                    that, like a bird, wings birdlike its way,
blue waters with here & there a boat   *its white*
                  its
with its   *vast with the hundred summits*
laten sails—& that ampitheatre of mountains,
shutting in the scene
 ᴧsome topt with snow, & all, sublime as they are,

307

softened into beauty by the mists & sunbeams of the
                            white scattered
morning, all exhibiting at their feet the ~~little~~
   above, & below,   shore
villages & chateaux along the ~~lake-side,~~—who could
                             of day
not dwell in thee for ever & bless the light ˄that
illumines the little world thou commandest—
but another light, the light of Genius has arisen
upon thee, the form of St Preux now wanders from cliff
to cliff, & among the chesnut groves that border thee
there under the D   there, Clarens, glitters thy
white front, that dwelling of Julia herself!

II

Thy grey rocks, Meillerie, that tower to heaven,
     glimmering
Thy fairy glades & open chesnut groves
That echo to the heifer's wandering bell,
Or woodman's axe, or steerman's song beneath,
As on he urges his fir-laden bark,
     far
Or shout of goat-herd boy above them all,
Who loves not; & who blesses not the light,
     thro' some
When from his loop-hole he surveys the lake
Blue as a saphire-stone, & richly set
With chateaux, villages, & village-spires,
Orchards, & vineyards, alps & alpine snows?
Here would I dwell, nor visit but in thought
     that chamber wont to ring
Ferney far south, silent & empty now
With wit, with mirth—refined

The Evolution of ' Meillerie '

As now thy Chartreuse & thy bowers, Ripaille;[1]
Vevay so long the exil'd Patriot's home.
Or Chillon's dungeon-floors beneath the wave
Channell'd & worn by pacing to and fro.
Here would I dwell forgetting & forgot
And oft methinks (of such strange potency
The spells that Genius scatters where he will)
Wander up these grey rocks like one in search
And say *exulting* Here St Preux has been
Then turn & gaze on Clarens, & again
Look round to find the traces of his passion.
Here would I dwell; yet know there is a scene
Far dearer to my better part of Man,
Thy lake, Lucerne, shut in among the Mountains
Mountains that flank its waves as with a Wall
some

Built by the giant-race before the flood,
Where not a cross or chapel but inspires
our

Holy delight, lifting the thoughts to God
From God-like men—men in a barbarous age
Who dared assert their birthright, & displayed
Deeds half-divine, returning good for ill;
Who in the desert sowed the seeds of life,
Framing that knot of
Founding those small republics
envy   the world

That still exist the wonder of mankind
Framing & knitting in the bond of love,
That
Who would not land on each & tread the ground,

---

[1] Towards the end of the first notebook these lines are written in pencil:
Ferney, thrice hail! That chamber wont to ring
With Wit, with Fancy; say, how silent now!
Ferney far-fam'd! Its chambers wont to ring
dark &
With Wit, with Fancy, ah, how silent now
Vevay, Lausanne!

Land where Tell leap'd ashore, & climb to drink
Of the three sacred fountains?

III

These grey majestic cliffs that tower to heaven,
These glimmering glades and open chestnut groves,
That echo to the heifer's wandering bell,
Or woodman's axe, or steers-man's song beneath,
As on he urges his fir-laden bark,
Or shout of goat-herd boy above them all,
Who loves not? And who blesses not the light,
When thro' some loop-hole he surveys the lake
Blue as a sapphire-stone, and richly set
With chateaux, villages, and village-spires,
Orchards and vineyards, alps and alpine snows?
Here would I dwell; nor visit, but in thought,
FERNEY far south, silent and empty now
As now thy once-luxurious bowers, RIPAILLE;
VEVEY, so long an exiled Patriot's home;
Or CHILLON's dungeon-floors beneath the wave,
Channelled and worn by pacing to and fro;
LAUSANNE, where GIBBON in his sheltered walk
Nightly called up the Shade of a ancient ROME;
Or COPPET, and that dark untrodden grove
Sacred to Virtue, and a daughter's tears!
Here would I dwell, forgetting and forgot;
And oft methinks (of such strange potency
The spells that Genius scatters where he will)
Oft should I wander forth like one in search,
And say, half-dreaming, 'Here ST. PREUX has stood!'
Then turn and gaze on CLARENS.
                                        Yet there is,
Within an eagle's flight and less, a scene
Still nobler if not fairer (once again
Would I behold it ere these eyes are closed,
For I can say, 'I also have been there!')

The Evolution of ' Meillerie '

That Sacred Lake withdrawn among the hills,
Its depth of waters flanked as with a wall
Built by the Giant-race before the flood;
Where not a cross or chapel but inspires
Holy delight, lifting our thoughts to God
From God-like men,—men in a barbarous age
That dared assert their birth-right, and displayed
Deeds half-divine, returning good for ill;
That in the desert sowed the seeds of life,
Framing a band of small Republics there,
Which still exist, the envy of the world!
Who would not land in each, and tread the ground;
Land where TELL leaped ashore; and climbed to drink
Of the three hallowed fountains?

Index

Aaberg, 152
Acquapendente, 276
Addison, Joseph, 49, 78, 101
Ainsworth, Harrison, 39
Ala, 282
Albano, 89, 209, 246, 247, 273
Albany, Princess of Stolberg-Gedern, Countess of, 122, 188
Albert, Prince Consort, 27
Alexander I, Emperor, 294
Alfieri, Vittorio, 188, 198
Allen, John, 227, 243, 258, 267
Allston, Washington, 57
Altdorf, 140, 148
Amiens, peace of, 55, 56
Amsterdam, 59, 282, 292, 295, 296, 298
Angelico, Fra, 231, 232, 302
Angoulême, Louis-Antoine de Bourbon, Duc d', 135
Angoulême, Marie-Thérèse-Charlotte, Duchesse d', 135
Annual Register, The, 58
Antwerp, 59, 282, 292, 298, 299
Arezzo, 203
Ariccia, 273
Ariosto, 102, 182, 183, 194, 234
Arona, 162
Aquà, 102, 180, 181
Arquà, Polésine, 182
Arth, 149, 152
Artois, Charles Philippe, Comte d', 135
Assisi, 86, 204
Auxerre, 137
Avallon, 137
Avernus, Lake, 251
Aversa, 249

Baccano, 72
Baiæ, 250, 251, 254, 258, 265, 268, 269
Bandinelli, Baccio, 189, 198

Banti, Brigitta Giorgi, 185
Barbarino, 277
Baring, T., 121, 167
Barnes, 283
Barry, James, 157
Bartoli, Pietro Santi, 218
Bartolomeo, Fra, 190
Basel, 54
Bassano, Jacopo, 173
Baveno, 161, 162
Bayle, Pierre, 183
Beauharnais, Eugene, 171
Beauharnais, Josephine, Empress, 69, 136, 139
Beccafumi, Domenico, 277
Bedford, Duchess of, 237, 241, 245, 246
Bedford, John Russell, 6th Duke of, 236, 242, 245, 246
Beer, G. R. de, 124
Belgirate, 79, 162
Bellegarde, H. J. J., Count von, 164
Belmonte, Princess of, 252
Benedict XIV, Pope, 219
Bentham, Jeremy, 142
Bergen, Mr., 235
Berio, Marchese di, 251, 256
Bern, 140, 145, 151, 286
Bernard, Hon. Richard Boyle, 122
Bernini, Giovanni Lorenzo, 218
Berrian, William, 97, 123
Berry, Mary and Agnes, 90
Bewick, Thomas, 38
Bienne, Lake, 140, 144, 152
Bingen, 289
Blake, William, 48
Blessington, M.P., Countess of, 27, 30, 39, 120
Boccaccio, 98, 101, 102, 104, 184, 200, 226
Boddington, Samuel, 41, 53, 120, 250, 251, 267, 272
Boerhaave, Herman, 297
Bois le Duc, 145

Bologna, 52, 59, 79, 82, 117, 184, 186, 278, 279, 280
Bolsena, Lake, 276
Bolzano, 282, 283, 284
Bonaparte, v Napoleon I, Emperor
Bonaparte, Caroline, Queen of Naples, 58, 68, 257, 258, 259, 264
Bonaparte, Joseph, 56, 154
Bonaparte, Louis, 68, 139, 218, 222, 274, 297
Bonaparte, Louis Napoleon, 39
Bonaparte, Lucien, 68, 106, 216, 217, 221, 222, 223, 224, 228, 234, 235, 237, 245, 274, 275
Bonaparte, Pauline, 68
Bonn, 290
Bonneville, 140, 142
Borgia, Lucrezia, 170
Borromeo, Count, 161
Borromeo, S. Carlo, 162, 167, 168
Bowdler, Thomas, 143
Bracciano, Duchessa di, 222, 231, 235
Bracciano, Giovanni Raimondo Torlonia, Duca di, 92, 225, 233, 234
Bramante, 106, 164, 166, 167, 212, 216, 237, 281
Brenner Pass, 83, 103, 282, 284, 285
Brig, 87, 140, 159, 160, 284
Brighton, 74
Brill, Paul, 283
Bristol, Frederick Augustus Hervey, 4th Earl of, 217
Brixen, 283
Broek, 294
Bronzino, 198
Bronzolo, 283
Brougham and Vaux, Henry Peter, baron, 34
Broughton, Lord, 165
Brownlow, Rt. Hon. John, Lord, 198, 201, 225
Browning, Robert, 34
Bruen, Matthias, 87
Bruges, 300
Brunellesco, 188
Brunnen, 147, 149
Brussels, 282, 290

Buckingham and Chandos, Richard, 2nd Duke of, 123, 252
Bugiardini, 191, 202
Buitensluis, 298
Burke, Edmund, 49
Burke and Hare (body-snatchers), 117
Burlington, Richard Boyle, 3rd Earl of, 170
Burns, Robert, 48
Bury, Lady Charlotte, 58, 98, 121, 123, 140, 165
Butler, Samuel, Dr., 72, 74, 82, 96, 123, 156
Byron, George Gordon, Lord, 21, 24, 30, 44, 45, 46, 49, 50, 52, 53, 60, 62, 67, 73, 101, 116, 117, 119, 124, 127, 140, 170, 251
Byron, Lady, 21

Cadell, W. A., 124, 125
Calais, 74, 75
Caligula, Marchesa di, 212
Camelford, Thomas Pitt, 2nd baron 153
Campbell, Harriet, 74, 78, 90
Campbell, Sir Niall, 191
Campbell, Thomas, 32, 39, 44, 120
Camuccini, Vincenzo, 67, 234, 235
Camucia, 203
Canino, Principe di v Bonaparte, Lucien
Cannes, 58
Canova, Antonio, 60, 67, 68, 134, 173, 176, 177, 184, 190, 198, 199, 209, 222, 226, 232, 234, 236, 237, 245, 256
Capranica, Marchesa di, 231
Capri, 254
Capua, 249, 270, 271
Caracci, the, 52, 93, 185
Caracci, Annibal, 209
Caracci, Lodovico, 184
Caravaggio, 279
Careggi, 199
Caroline, Princess of Wales, 59, 162, 163, 164, 165, 166, 251, 252, 253, 257, 258, 259, 264, 265, 266
Caroline, Queen, 26
Carrara, 77

Index

Caserta, 260, 270
Caserta, Duchessa di, 99
Casinate, 85
Castel Gandolfo, 246, 273
Castellammare, 256, 259
Catalani, Angelica, 299
Catullus, 102, 169, 276
Cawdor, John Campbell, 1st baron, 227, 233, 234, 237, 245, 267
Cawdor, Lady, 237
Cellini, Benvenuto, 189
Chaloner, C. J., 48, 120
Chamonix, 140, 141, 156
Champagnole, 138
Chantrey, Sir Francis Legatt, 26, 32
Charles IV, King of Spain, 216
Cherubini, M.L.C.Z.S., 166
Chigi, Agostino, 243
Chillon, 127, 143, 155
Chiswick, 170
Chronicle, The, 61
Cicero, 73, 219, 251, 265, 269, 271
Cimabue, 189, 202
Cisterna, 272
Civita Castellana, 207
Clanwilliam, Lord, 117
Clare, John Fitzgibbon, 2nd Earl of, 249
Clarendon, Edward Hyde, Earl of, 37
Clarens, 143, 155
Clary, Julie, 225
Claude, 38, 94, 96, 100, 102, 103, 138, 203, 246, 256, 257, 276
Clayden, P. W., 38, 116, 118, 120, 131, 133
Clement X, Pope, 219
Clement XIV, Pope, 246
Cleve, 291
Clifford, Hugh Charles, 7th Lord, 246
Cluses, 140, 142
Coleridge, Samuel Taylor, 43, 44, 48, 57, 119
Colles, John Mayne, 121
Cologne, 59, 282, 290
Columbus, 43, 47
Como, Lake, 82
Concise, 153, 154
Copet, 139, 155

Corneille, Pierre, 133, 134
Cornwall, Barry, 42
Correggio, 185, 199, 281
Cortona, 103, 203
Coster, Lourens, 296
Cowley, Abraham, 49
Cowper, Lady, 30
Coxe, Henry, 125
Coxe, William, 37, 89, 104, 147
Crabbe, George, 20, 44, 45, 47, 48
Crakenthorp, Mr., 248, 260
Craven, Keppel Richard, 264
Creevey, Thomas, 299
Cromford, 138
Crowe, William, 45
Curran, John Philpot, 134
Cushman, Charlotte Saunders, 39
Cuyp, 294
Czartoryski, Prince Adam, 243

Daily News, The, 34
Dalmazzoni, Angelo, 231
Dannecker, Johann Heinrich von 287
Dante, 98, 188, 200, 278
Darmstadt, 288
Darwin, Erasmus, 48
Davenport, Edward, 260
David, Jacques Louis, 164
Davy, Lady, 245, 267, 268
Davy, Sir Humphrey, 186, 222, 224, 234, 267
Deakin, Richard, 122
Defoe, Daniel, 49
De la Roux (Hotel), 133
Delft, 282, 297
Desenzano, 169
Devonshire, Duchess of, 64, 65
Dickens, Charles, 20, 50
Dieppe, 74, 133
Dijon, 100, 137
Dodwell, Edward, 223, 227, 228, 229, 236, 244
Dôle, 100, 138
Domenichino, 93, 209, 211, 222, 223, 227, 302
Domodossola, 161, 284
Donatello, 189
Donegal, Lady, 59, 122
Doria, Monsignor, 230
Doria, Princess, 236
Dorigny, Nicolas, 222
Dou, Gerard, 293, 294

315

Index

Dovedale, 157, 283
Dover, 74, 76
Dryden, John, 46, 47, 49
Dublin University Magazine, 116
Du Cane, Mr., 266, 267, 275, 278, 279
Dumont, Pierre Étienne Louis, 131, 142
Durer, Albrecht, 144, 145, 269
Dyce, Alexander, 118, 128

Eastlake, Elizabeth, Lady, 34, 118
Eastlake, Sir Charles, 125
Eaton, Charlotte A. (born Waldie) 73, 74, 97, 123, 124, 127
Ebel, J. G., 118
Eboli, 263
Ebrington, Hugh, Viscount, 275
Edgeworth, Maria, 78
Edinburgh Review, The, 19, 39, 119
Eisach, 283
Elba, 51, 57, 191, 251, 252, 264, 268
Epistle to a Friend, An, 43, 46, 48, 52, 218
Erasmus, 298
Este, Sir Augustus d', 39
Etna, 87, 255
Etruria, Queen of, 225, 274
Eustace, John Chetwode, 57, 71, 78, 121, 124, 193, 195, 198, 201, 225

Fabre, F. X., 191, 200, 278
Fazakerly, John Nicholas, 234, 278, 279
Fea, Carlo, 236
Ferney, 140
Ferrara, 73, 102, 182, 184
Ferrari, Gaudenzio, 167
Fesch, Cardinal, 68, 217, 224, 233
Fielding, Henry, 285
Fiesole, 199, 200, 278, 302
Filangieri, Carlo, Prince of Satriano, 279
Filicaja, Vincenzo da, 100
Finch, Robert, 64, 71, 76, 80, 81, 83, 84, 85, 88, 89, 92, 93, 96, 97, 99, 121, 126, 218, 235
Flaxman, John, 26, 38
Florence, 52, 58, 59, 61, 63, 78, 80, 82, 83, 85, 86, 87, 88, 89, 90, 100, 102, 108, 166, 187–202, 206, 250, 277–8
Accademia, 190
Baptistery, 73, 188, 191
Boboli Gardens, 198, 200, 302
Campanile, 188, 199, 201, 302
Carmine, 191, 201, 222, 278, 302
Cascine, 61, 198, 199, 201, 202
Cathedral, 97, 187, 188, 197, 278, 302
Laurentian Library, 201
Medici Chapel, 113, 188, 189, 195, 199, 201, 278, 302
Palazzo Gerini, 189
Pitti, 198
Ricardi, 198, 201
Strozzi, 201
Vecchio, 189, 197, 198
Piazza della Signoria, 188, 189, 302
SS. Annunziata, 190, 278, 302
S. Croce, 198, 278
S. Lorenzo, 188, 191, 278
S. Marco, 201
S. Maria Novella, 191, 199, 201, 278
S. Spirito, 201
Trinita, Ponte Santa, 199, 302
Uffizi, 52, 74, 75, 78, 81, 92, 94, 120, 125, 190, 191, 195, 198, 199, 200, 278, 302
Flüelen, 148
Foligno, 204
Fondi, 247, 272
Fontainebleau, 100, 136
Forbes, Lady Elizabeth, 266
Forman, W. H., 223
Forsyth, Joseph, 57, 65, 66, 78, 92, 121, 125
Foscolo, Ugo, 106, 109, 117, 260
Fox, Charles James, 20
Francesco Maria, Grand Duke of Florence, 190
Frankfurt, 288
Fraser's Magazine, 23, 25
Fuseli, Henry, 117
Füssen, 286

Gabrieli, Vittorio, 127
Gaeta, 248, 264, 271
Galiffe, James, 91, 93
Galileo, 101, 180, 198, 200, 278

Index

Gallo, Duca and Duchessa di, 251, 252, 256, 257, 264, 269
Garda, Lake, 169
Garigliano, 248, 249
Garofalo, Benvenuto, 182
Geislingen, 287
Geldern, 291
Geneva, 54, 58, 75, 87, 100, 136, 139, 140, 142, 155
Genoa, 59, 80, 89, 126
Gentleman's Magazine, The, 36, 37
Genzano, 273
Ghent, 299
Ghiberti, 73, 199, 302
Giambologna, 184, 189, 198
Gibbon, Edward, 54, 71, 146, 172, 229, 233
Gibson, John, 32
Gielgud, Adam, 243
Gilpin, William Sawney, 95
Giorgione, 27, 175, 176, 178
Giotto, 180, 188, 198, 199, 201, 278
Giuseppe (dealer), 249, 258
Gladstone, William Ewart, 20
Glenarvon, 21
Gluck, Christophe Willibald, 133
Goethe, Johann Wolfgang von, 20
Goldau, 149
Goldoni, Carlo, 173
Goldsmith, Oliver, 34, 45, 47
Gorcum, 298
Gower, Hon. F. Leveson, 117
Graham, Maria, 125
Granville, Harriet, Countess, 30, 117
Grattan, Henry, 20
Great St. Bernard Pass, 109
Grenville, Lord, 183
Grétry, A. E. M., 299
Greville, Rt. Hon. C., 198
Grey, Thomas, 49
Grotto del Cane, 91, 251, 266
Guarini, Giovanni Battista, 183
Guercino, 93, 186, 226

Haarlem, 282, 296
Hague, The, 297
Haller, Albrecht von, 144, 145
Hamilton, Sir William, 252
Hammersley & Co., 91
Hare, Augustus, 86, 124
Harford, John Scandrett, 113

Harries, Farquhar & Co., 91
Harwich, 74
Hattersheim, 288
Hayward, Abraham, 116
Hazlitt, William, 45, 88, 94, 124
Heathcote, Lady, 247, 267
Heidelberg, 282, 288
Heigeln, Mr., 257
Henry, Philip, 36
Herculaneum, 84, 111, 211, 249, 256
Hoare, Richard Colt, 121
Hobhouse, John Cam, 49, 71, 73
Holbein, 298
Holland, Henry Richard Vassall Fox, 3rd baron, 43, 109, 117, 164, 188, 190, 191, 221, 224, 225, 231, 234, 235, 236, 237, 252, 256, 257, 258, 259, 264, 266, 268, 274
Holland House, 26, 28, 43, 118, 119
Holland, Lady, 21, 30, 31, 53, 109, 117, 127, 131, 142, 234, 252, 254, 256, 257, 258, 259, 268
Holland, Sir Henry, 258, 265
Honey, Mr., 249, 250
Hope, Mr., 295, 296
Horace, 102, 202, 226, 249, 251, 271, 273, 276
Houches, les, 142
Huis ten Bosch, 297
Human Life, 27, 28, 38, 39, 43, 46, 107, 112, 119, 127
Hunt, James Henry Leigh, 45, 74, 89, 124, 125

Ignacio (dealer), 233
Ilchester, Earl of, 117, 119, 127
Immensee, 150
Ingleheim, 288
Ingpen, Roger, 124
Innsbruck, 59, 282, 285
Irving, Washington, 57, 70, 85, 116, 117
Irwin, Mr., 274
Ischia, 248, 256
Isella, 79
Isola Bella, 92, 162
Italy, 24, 27, 35, 47, 48, 49, 50, 95, 102, 103, 107, 108, 109, 127, 128
Itri, 247, 272

Index

Jacqueline, 43, 44, 46, 48
James, Capt. Thomas, 127, 141
Jameson, Mrs. Anna, 94, 108, 116, 191, 200
Jeffrey, Francis, 120
Jegher, Christoffel, 298
Johannisberg, 289
John Bull, 25, 42, 119
Johnson, Samuel, 20, 143
Joigny, 137
Jomelli, 274
Juvenal, 254

Keats, John, 63, 66, 89
Kellerman, François-Christophe de, 289
Kew, 283
Kinniard, Douglas, 117
Kippis, Andrew, 37
Knatchbull, Mr., 288
Koblenz, 282, 289
Küssnacht, 150

Lalande, J-J. Le français de, 78, 249
Lamb, Charles, 42, 119, 128
Lamb, Lady Caroline, 21
Landseer, Sir Edwin Henry. 118
Lapo, Arnolfo di, 189
La Riccia = Ariccia
Lausanne, 54, 140, 143, 154
Lauerz, 150
Lavis, 283
Lawrence, Sir Thomas, 32
Lee, Mr., 243
Le Havre, 74
Leigh, Mr., 259
Lemaistre, J. G., 105, 121, 166
Léman, Lake, 97, 140
Lennox, Lord William Pitt, 39
Leo X, Pope, 230
Le Sage, Alain René, 270
Levane, 202
Lever, Charles, 71
Leyden, 297
Lindau, 285
Lindsay, Alexander W. C. L., 25th Earl of Crawford, 86
Livy, 225
Loch Long, 133
Loiano, 278
Lonato, 169
Longmans (publishers), 108, 109
Loretto, 204, 207

Louis XVIII, King of France, 135, 301
Louvre, 52, 56, 60, 124, 134, 216
Lucas, E. V., 128
Lucca, 97
Lucerne, Lake, 54, 140, 146, 147, 150, 284
Luchesini, Girolamo, 188
Ludlow, Edmund, 143
Ludwigsburg, 288
Luini, 167
Luttrel, Henry, 30, 40, 42, 43, 117
Lyman, Theodore, 122
Lyon, 75, 76
Lyttelton, Sarah Spencer, Lady, 61, 122

Macaulay, Thomas Babbington, Lord, 20, 26, 39, 41, 111, 116
Macdonald, Sir James, 215
McDonald, Mr. and Mrs., 153
M'Donough, Felix, 123
Machiavelli, Niccolo, 101, 198, 200, 278
Mackay, Charles, 32, 39
Mackenzie, Henry, 37
Mackintosh, Sir James, 40, 49, 53, 54, 121, 131, 134, 142, 150, 159
McLaughlin, F., 240
Maclise, Daniel, 25
Macpherson, Paul, 234
Maggiore, Lake, 106, 159, 161, 166
Maginn, William, 25
Mainz, 282, 288
Manazzale, André, 231
Mannheim, 288
Mantua, 59, 106, 169, 281, 282
Marano, 248
Marechiaro, 264
Margate, 39, 74
Maria Louisa, Empress, 136, 140
Maria Louisa, Queen of Spain, 225
Mariscotti, Marchesa di, 236
Marmontel, J. F., 299
Marot, David, 297
Martigny, 140, 155, 156
Martineau, Harriet, 34
Masaccio, 60, 63, 67, 70, 76, 82, 108, 117, 158, 191, 222, 231, 234, 278

318

Index

Massima, Princess, 64, 220, 224, 233
Matthews, Henry, 66, 88, 89, 90, 95, 122
Maxwell, Col. Montgomery, 122, 123
Mayne, John, 89, 92, 121, 126, 225
Medici, the, 98, 108, 198
Medici, Duke Cosimo I, 102, 190, 199
Medici, Duke Ferdinand I, 191
Medici, Lorenzo de', 199
Medwin, Thomas, 24, 116, 119
Meillerie, 127, 143, 155
Memmingen, 286
Merry, Robert, 48
Messina, 80, 84
Mestre, 172, 179
Michelangelo, 93, 94, 113, 124, 167, 188, 189, 190, 191, 195, 198, 199, 200, 201, 202, 209, 211, 213, 219, 220, 223, 224, 230, 243, 278, 301
Milan, 58, 61, 66, 67, 68, 79, 82, 86, 87, 90, 92, 100, 103, 106, 163–8, 170, 301
  Amphitheatre, 69, 165
  Cathedral, 104, 164, 168
  Forum Bonaparte, 165
  S. Maria delle Grazie, 164
  S. Satiro, 164
  Teatro della Canobia, 166
    della Scala, 163, 166
    del Re, 168
    di Girolamo, 167
  Villa Bonaparte, 165
Millingen, James, 58, 70, 223, 230, 234, 235
Milton, John, 46, 47, 49, 102, 143, 190, 194, 195, 196, 200, 212, 216, 250
Mirandola, Pico della, 190
Mitford, John, 107, 117, 120, 121, 128
Mittenwald, 284
Modena, 59, 280
Mola, 248
Molini (bookseller), 183, 184
Monselice, 180
Montagu, Lady Jane, 231
Montagu, Lord Frederick, 249, 252, 269

Montaigne, Michel de, 206
Mont Cenis Pass, 82, 96
Monte Circeo, 247, 272
Montenosi, 207
Montenvers, 141
Montgomery, James, 46
Monthly Review, The, 37
Montolieu, Mme. J. F., 144
Montreux, 155
Montrond, 138
Moore, Dr. John, 37, 101
Moore, Thomas, 30, 32, 40, 43, 44, 45, 46, 48, 49, 50, 59, 60, 62, 85, 94, 107, 108, 117, 119, 122, 125, 127, 157, 165, 218, 227, 244
Morat, 144
Morez, 138
Morgan, Sydney, Lady, 83, 98, 118, 124, 252
Morley, Edith J., 116
Moron = Montrond
Morpeth, Lady, 117
Mosbourg, Comte de, 58, 59, 253, 264, 266, 279, 280
Murat, Joachim, King of Naples, 58, 68, 123, 251, 252, 256, 257, 258, 259, 265, 266, 269, 270
Mürgenthal, 146
Murray, John, 23, 44, 110

Naples, 56, 58, 59, 61, 62, 78, 80, 82, 83, 84, 86, 87, 89, 91, 100, 103, 107, 193, 228, 249–70, 278
  Chiaja, Riviera di, 249, 252, 257, 269
  Studio, 254, 261, 264, 265
  Teatro S. Carlo, 249, 251, 254, 264
  Villa Reale, 256, 258, 264, 266, 268
Napoleon I, Emperor, 51, 52, 56, 57, 59, 67, 69, 82, 83, 131, 135, 139, 148, 191, 218, 230, 252, 264, 293
Narni, 206, 207
Neefs, Pieter, 277
Nemi, 273
Nepi, 207
Neuchâtel, Lake, 140, 144
Neuchâtel, 153

Index

Newington Green, 36, 37
Nijmegen, 282, 291
Nisida, 268, 269
Normanby, Constantine Henry
    Phipps, Marquis of, 95, 123
Norton, Caroline Elizabeth Sarah,
    the Hon. Mrs., 39
Novara, 90
Nyon, 139

O'Connell, Daniel, 39
Odescalchi [Lady], 227
Ode to Superstition, An, 36, 46
Opie, John, 38
Orbe, 154
Orde, Mrs., 245
Orvieto, 86
Ostade, Adrian, 103, 145, 293
Ostend, 59, 282, 300
Otway, Thomas, 175
Oxford, Lady, 249, 252, 256, 260,
    264, 268, 269

Padua, 82, 106, 169, 170, 171,
    180
Pæstum, 70, 84, 86, 87, 95, 109,
    113–15, 259, 260–4
Palafox y Melzi, José de, 203
Palermo, 84
Palladio, 175, 249
Panini, 94
Paris, 51, 52, 60, 67, 75, 76, 79,
    100, 134–6, 301
Parma, 281
Parmigianino, 199, 281
Passignano, 203, 204
Patch, Thomas, 191
Payerne, 144, 145
Peel, Robert, 50
Pelago, 192, 197
Pelissier, L-G., 122
Pellegrini, Carlo, 122
Pergolesi, 274
Perugia, 86, 204
Petrarch, 98, 101, 102, 104, 174,
    177, 180, 181, 183, 200, 226,
    276
Peyffer, General, 147
Piacenza, 79
Pietra Mala, 79, 186, 278
Piranesi, 65, 215
Pisa, 24, 63, 74, 77, 97, 117
Pius VI, Pope, 206

Pius VII, Pope, 59, 65, 67, 68, 69,
    71, 137, 208, 221, 230, 234,
    236, 252, 274
Pixéricourt, R. C. G., 136
Planta, J., 144
Pleasures of Memory, The, 27, 46,
    48, 52, 68, 104, 120
Pliny, 251
Poggibonsi, 277
Poli, 85
Politian, 190, 193
Polo, Marco, 178
Pompeii, 66, 67, 84, 91, 101, 111,
    211, 253, 256, 259, 260,
    267
Poniatowski, Stanislas, 223, 226,
    232
Ponte d'Arbia, 276
Pope, Alexander, 45, 49, 183
Porson, Richard, 38
Portici, 91, 253, 255, 256, 267
Portsmouth, 74
Posillipo, 254, 266
Poussin, Gaspar, 103, 203, 209,
    211
Poussin, Nicolas, 38, 96, 100, 102,
    138, 211, 276
Power, A. W., 127
Pozzuoli, 250, 251, 254, 257, 258,
    264, 265, 268, 269
Price, Richard, 37
Price, Sir Uvedale, 95
Primaticcio, 136, 137
Prime, Mr., 259
Prothero, R. E., 116, 117, 119
Prout, Samuel, 110
Prunetti, Michelangelo, 231
Pulci, Luigi, 101

Quarterly Review, The, 118
Quixote, Don, 294

Radcliffe, Mrs. Ann, 96, 102, 159
Radford, Mary, 36
Radicofani, 83, 203, 276
Raphael, 27, 52, 73, 93, 103, 124,
    126, 175, 190, 195, 199,
    200, 208, 210, 216, 220,
    221, 222, 223, 228, 231,
    232, 233, 234, 241, 243,
    275, 279, 302
Ravenna, 86
Rawdon, Mrs., 223, 244

Index

Reade, Charles, 235
Reade, John Edmund, 48, 120
Rembrandt, 103, 157, 294
Reni, Guido, 19, 27, 93, 95, 209, 211, 214, 222, 224, 279
Repaille, 143, 155
Resina, 256
Reynolds, Sir Joshua, 27, 230
Richardson, Samuel, 285
Roberts, E. Ellis, 116
Robertson, William, 20, 37
Robinson, Henry Crabb, 24, 31, 32, 42, 116, 117, 119
Rocca di Papa, 273
Rogers, Daniel, 37
Rogers, Henry, 37
Rogers, Sarah, 53, 54, 78, 108, 134, 167, 196, 234, 248, 269
Rogers, Thomas, 36
Rogers, Thomas (junior), 37
Romano, Giulio, 210, 212, 220, 281
Rome, 28, 52, 58, 59, 61, 63, 64, 65, 67, 70, 73, 78, 81, 82, 83, 85, 86, 87, 88, 89, 91, 92, 100, 102, 106, 108, 124, 126, 206, 207–46, 252, 273–6, 278, 282, 301, 302
    Aqueduct of Claudian, 209, 215, 228, 233
    Arch of Constantine, 274
    Janus, 215
    Septimus, 65, 215
    Titus, 65
    Baths of Caracalla, 228
    Livia, 219, 224
    Titus, 209, 211, 212, 224, 302
    Borsa, 218
    Capitol, 66, 73, 93, 207, 209, 214, 217, 219, 224, 229, 232, 233, 274, 301
    Castel S. Angelo, 85, 207, 213, 233
    Circus of Caracalla, 214
    Cloaca Maxima, 215
    Coliseum, 65, 66, 122, 207, 209, 212, 215, 217, 219, 223, 228, 229, 231, 232, 233, 273, 274, 301, 302
    Column, Antonine, 209, 218, 233
    of Phocas, 65
    of Trajan, 125, 211, 229, 233, 274, 302

Corso, 215, 224, 226, 227, 236, 237, 238, 240, 241, 244
Domus Aurea, 219, 228
English College, 228
Forum Romanum, 65, 66, 207, 209, 219, 232, 235, 236, 251, 274
Gardens, Albani, 238
    Borghese, 222, 223, 228, 233, 234, 235, 237, 274
    Corsini, 226
    Medici, 225, 234, 237, 242, 275
    Spada, 228
Gesù, Church of, 228
Grotto of Egeria, 215
Mons Aventinus, 215
Monte Cavallo, 211, 217, 222, 225, 230, 233, 242
Gianicolo, 216
Mario, 217
Orti Farnesiani, 219
Palatine, 217, 219, 227, 229
Palazzo Bolognetti, 225
    Bonaparte, 233
    Borghese, 68
    Braschi, 224
    Chigi, 209
    Colonna, 224, 302
    Corsini, 216, 231, 233
    del Quirinale, 69, 209, 222, 230, 233
    Doria, 209, 302
    Farnese, 209, 211, 231, 233, 302
    Farnesina, 210, 220, 243, 302
    Giustiniani, 209, 224
    Massimi, 230
    Rondinini, 209, 213, 217, 231
    Rospigliosi, 211, 214, 302
    Schiarra, 244
    Spada, 209, 230
Pantheon, 207, 208, 209, 218, 220, 224, 230, 231, 232, 233, 271, 275, 302
Piazza del Popolo, 236, 237, 240
    di Spagna, 58, 61, 87, 88
    di Venezia, 236
Ponte Milvio, 220
Porta del Popolo, 207, 218, 220
S. Andre della Valle, 274, 302
S. Antonio dei Portoghesi, 235
S. Carlo al Corso, 236

Rome (*cont.*)
S. Clemente, 222, 234
S. Egidio, 238
S. Gregorio, 211, 222, 228
St. John Lateran, 99, 221, 229, 231, 233, 234, 243, 246, 273
S. Maria della Concezione (I Cappuccini), 224
S. Maria della Navicella, 232, 233
S. Maria degli Angeli, 302
S. Maria del Popolo, 222, 223, 243, 274, 302
S. Maria Maggiore, 208, 234
S. Maria sopra Minerva, 230
S. Martino, 211
S. Paolo fuori le Mura, 99, 215
St. Peter's, 71, 72, 83, 100, 207, 208, 209, 212, 213, 214, 222, 226, 228, 230, 231, 232, 233, 234, 237, 238, 242, 243, 273, 274, 285, 301
S. Pietro in Montorio, 216, 233, 237, 242
S. Pietro in Vincoli, 211
S. Sebastiano, 214
S. Silvestro, 228
S. Stefano Rotondo, 215, 222, 233
S. Trinita de' Monti, 222, 223, 225, 226, 233
Scala Santa, 112, 219, 235, 302
Sistine Chapel, 71, 124, 208, 212, 241, 274, 301
Teatro Aliberti, 241
Temple of Antoninus and Faustina, 65
  Concord, 65
  Jupiter Stator, 65
  Jupiter Tonans, 65
  Peace, 65, 229
  Vesta, 65, 220, 239
Tomb of Augustus, 221
  Caius Cestius, 215, 228, 233
  Cecilia Metalla, 209, 214, 217, 228, 233, 235, 302
Trevi Fountain, 211
Vatican, 52, 93, 124, 207, 212, 213, 217, 218, 223, 224, 229, 231, 233, 234, 236, 237, 274, 275, 301, 302

Villa Albani, 108, 214, 227
  Borghese, 218
  Doria Pamphily, 216, 228, 236, 243, 275, 302
  Farnese, 230
  Lante, 231, 243, 302
  Ludovisi, 93, 226, 233
  Madama, 217, 220, 232, 302
  Mattei, 222, 232, 233, 236
  Medici, 213, 218, 221, 222, 233
  Mellini, 217, 232, 233, 302
Ronciglione, 276
Rosa, Salvator, 94, 103, 205
Rose, William Stewart, 234
Rossi, Giovanni Gherardo di, 73, 227
Rotterdam, 282, 298
Rouen, 133
Rousseau, Jean-Jacques, 49, 100, 102, 142, 143, 152, 153, 155
Rousses, Les, 138
Roverbella, 282
Rovigo, 182
Rubens, 27, 298, 299
Ruffo, Cardinal, 221, 224, 244
Ruskin, John, 47, 50, 86, 111, 127, 128
Ruspoli, Prince, 225
Russell, Lord John, 59, 116, 122, 227, 246, 267, 278, 279
Russell, Lord William, 223
Rutli, 147, 149
Ruyter, Admiral De, 293

Saardam = Zaadam
Sacchini, Antonio, 133
St. Gingolph, 143, 155
St. Helena, 131
St. James's Place, 26, 35, 38, 50, 108
St. Martin, 142
St. Maurice, 156
St. Paul's, 200
St. Pierre, isle de, 140, 152
Salerno, 260, 263
Sallust, 213
Salorno, 283
Sandrart, Joachim von, 201
San Gimignano, 86
Sansovino, 175, 176, 177, 178
Sarti, Giuseppe, 274

Index

Sarto, Andrea del, 190, 191, 192, 198, 201, 202, 230, 278
Sass, Henry, 86, 123
Scarlicalasino, 186
Schiantarelli, Angel, 166
Schlegel, August Wilhelm von, 139
Schneider's Hotel, 61, 87, 90, 166, 187, 278
Schönberg, 285
Schwyz, 140, 149, 150
Scott, Sir Walter, 31, 44, 45, 48, 50, 117, 127
Sebastiani, Antonio, 122
Sécheron, 140
Selincourt, Ernest de, 128
Sempach, Lake, 147, 151
Semple, Robert, 121
Sens, 137
Sermione, 169
Sessa, 271
Sesto, 79, 163
Severn, Joseph, 66
Shakespeare, William, 49, 174, 183
Sharp, Richard, 38, 39, 41, 102, 107, 117, 140, 250
Sharp, Sutton, 38
Sharp, William, 122
Sharpe, Samuel, 120
Sharpe, William, 54, 122
Shee, Sir Martin Archer, 38
Shelley, Frances, Lady, 40, 57, 118
Shelley, Percy Bysshe, 43
Sheridan, Richard Brinsley, 20, 31, 32, 38
Shücking, L. L., 120
Siddons, Mrs. Sarah, 27
Siena, 85, 97, 276
Simplon Pass, 69, 72, 79, 82, 83, 87, 100, 109, 123, 140, 158, 160–1, 165, 203, 284
Sion, 156, 157, 158
Sismondi, J. G. L. de, 131, 139, 142
Sloan, James, 126
Smith, Adam, 37
Smith, C. E., 118
Smith, John, 185
Smith, Nowell C., 117
Smith, Sydney, 28, 39, 40, 41, 46, 51, 53, 117, 260
Solfatara, The, 250
Sotheby, William, 48, 63, 120

Souchat, Marshal, 134
Southampton, 74
Southey, Robert, 44, 45, 50, 109
Spagnoletto, 260
Spencer, William Robert, 45
Spoleto, 205
Stabia, 256, 259, 260, 267
Staël, Madame de, 96, 131, 139, 155, 229
Stansstad, 147
Starke, Mariana, 56, 76, 81
Stendhal (Marie Henri Beyle), 70, 71, 123
Sterzing, 284
Stewart, A. Francis, 121
Stonehenge, 141
Stothard, Thomas, 26, 38, 110, 287
Strabo, 258
Strathern, 28, 29
Strozzi, Giovanni Battista, 189
Stuttgart, 282, 287
Subiaco, 85
Sumiswald, 151
Sursee, 146, 151
Swift, Jonathan, 49
Symonds, John Addington, 86

Table-Talk, 50, 118, 120
Tacitus, 254
Talleyrand-Périgord, C. M. de, 20
Tarentum, Archbishop of, 106, 252, 256, 258, 262, 264, 266, 269
Tasso, 73, 102, 182, 183, 224, 263
Tassoni, Allessandro, 280
Taylor, Abbé, 230
Taylor, Sir Herbert, 287
Tell, William, 147, 148, 149
Teniers, 96, 145, 294
Tennyson, Alfred, Lord, 20, 27, 34, 41
Terni, 205
Terracina, 248, 272, 274
Thackeray, William Makepeace, 225
Thonon, 143, 155
Thorwaldson, Bertel, 67, 223, 230, 234
Ticknor, George, 117, 122, 252
Tiel, 292
Times, The, 61
Tintern, 262
Tintoretto, 103, 165, 173, 175, 176

323

Index

Titian, 19, 27, 93, 94, 95, 102, 173, 174, 175, 185, 190, 191, 195, 199, 201, 209, 230
Tivoli, 66, 85, 275, 276
Torre del Greco, 84, 253, 256
Torretti, Giovanni, 176
Torricella, 203
Torrigiani, 191
Toussaint-Louverture, 139
Towneley, Charles, 230
Traieti, 271
Trench, Melesina, 41, 118
Trento, 282, 283
Turin, 57, 75, 76, 82
Turner, Joseph Mallord, 110, 111

Udine, Giovanni da, 175, 212
Ulm, 282, 286
Utrecht, 292, 296

Vallombrosa, 102, 112, 202, 250, 302
Vanderveldt, 294
Vandyke, 299
Van Eden, A. C., & Co., 296
Van Huysum, 293
Vasari, Giorgio, 78, 178, 180, 189, 199
Vasi, Marien, 88, 93, 231, 233, 234, 249
Vaudricourt, Mme., 254, 267
Vaudricourt, M., 249
Velletri, 92, 247, 272
Venice, 52, 60, 61, 78, 82, 83, 86, 87, 89, 90, 91, 97, 100, 106, 108, 111, 124, 169, 170, 172–9, 193, 277, 295
    Arsenal, 175, 177
    Bridge of Sighs, 173, 174, 179
    Bucentaur, 174, 178
    Campanile, 172, 177
    Doges' Palace, 97, 172, 173, 174, 178, 179, 180
    Frari, 174
    Ghetto, 173
    Grand Canal, 176, 179
    Lido, 173
    Palazzo Albrizzi, 173
        Barbarigo, 174
        Grimani, 175
        Manfrin, 178
    Piazza di S. Marco, 172, 174, 175, 177, 179

Rialto, 172, 173, 174, 178, 179
S. Cristoforo della Pace, 176
S. Giorgio Maggiore, 178
SS. Giovanni e Paolo, 176, 178
S. Maria della Salute, 178
St. Mark's, 52, 97, 112, 172, 173, 190
S. Martino, 177
S. Sebastiano, 174
Scuola di S. Rocco, 176
Torre, Orologio, 177
Venus de' Medici, 52, 60, 73, 94, 190, 199, 200
Vergil, 169, 226, 249, 254, 255, 257, 271
Vernet, Claude Joseph, 194
Vernon, George Granville, 139
Verona, 66, 78, 82, 86, 87, 106, 169, 170
Veronese, 103, 165, 173, 174, 175
Very (restaurateur), 136
Vesuvius, 84, 248, 249, 250, 252, 253, 255–6, 259, 268
Vevey, 139, 143, 155
Vicenza, 87, 170, 171
Victor, Marshall, 134
Vinci, Leonardo da, 106, 136, 164, 166
Viterbo, 86, 276
Vitruvius, 171, 177
Volpato, 226
Voltaire, F. M. Arouet de, 49, 140
Volterra, Daniel da, 229, 233

Waagen, Gustav F., 26
Waldie, Jane, 79
Walpole, Horace, 159
Walpole, Spencer, 122
Ward, J. W., Lord Dudley, 28, 33
Warens, Mme. de, 143
Waterloo, battle of, 60, 62, 70
Webb, Mr., 134
Weenix, Jan Baptist, 277
Weissbach, 286
Wellington, Arthur Wellesley, 1st Duke of, 20, 59, 60, 289, 299
Westmorland, Lady, 217, 224, 233, 237, 245
Whately, Richard, 39
Willemstad, 298
Williams, H. W., 124, 125
Williams, S. T., 116

Index

Willis, N. P., 252
Windermere, Lake, 54
Woods, Joseph, 91
Wordsworth, William, 24, 27, 32, 41, 44, 47, 48, 50, 67, 109, 110, 119, 128
Wright, Richard Payne, 37
Wyndham, The Hon. Mrs. Hugh, 122

Yosi, A., 123
Yverdon, 154

Zaandam, 295
Zay, Dr., 149, 152
Zofingen, 146
Zuccarelli, 190
Zug, 54, 150